MARTIN MUELLER is a professor of English and comparative literature at Northwestern University.

The essays in this volume deal with the uses of Greek tragedy by European playwrights and aim at isolating the strategies of adaptation and patterns of transformation shared by the different writers as heirs to a common dramatic tradition.

The first essay traces the crucial impulses that European tragedy received from the humanist imitation of ancient drama. This is followed by a study of Racine's *Phèdre* as both an embodiment of and an exception to the characteristic strategies of adaptation used by seventeenth-century playwrights. A turning point in the understanding of Greek tragedy is illustrated by a comparison of Goethe's *Iphigenia auf Tauris* and Kleist's *Penthesilea*. A fourth essay, analysing two characteristic strategies in coping with the problem of knowledge in *Oedipus Rex*, examines the approaches taken by Voltaire, Kleist, Corneille, and Schiller and glances at Ibsen's *Ghosts* as the prototype of modern analytical tragedy. The next essay turns to Buchanan's *Jephtha* and its influence on a handful of scriptural tragedies, including *Samson Agonistes* and *Athalie*, that combine the close observance of the conventions of Greek tragedy with a choice of theologically intractable subjects from the Old Testament. Finally, the volume addresses the interaction of epic and dramatic traditions in two essays showing Milton's use of the conventions of the tragedy of knowledge in *Paradise Lost* and Racine's use of the Dido tragedy as the model for *Bérénice*.

This encompassing survey of an enduring dramatic tradition offers useful background for the student of drama and all those interested in the continuing life of the classical tradition.

MARTIN MUELLER

CHILDREN OF OEDIPUS,
and other essays on the
imitation of Greek tragedy,
1550-1800

UNIVERSITY OF TORONTO PRESS
Toronto Buffalo London

© University of Toronto Press 1980
Toronto Buffalo London
Printed in Canada

FOR RUDOLF SÜHNEL

Library of Congress Cataloging in Publication Data

Mueller, Martin, 1939–
    Children of Oedipus, and other essays on the
    imitation of Greek tragedy, 1550–1800.
    Bibliography: p.
    Includes index.
    1. European drama (Tragedy) – Greek influences –
    Addresses, essays, lectures.   2. Greek drama (Tragedy)
    – History and criticism – Addresses, essays, lectures.
    I. Title.
    PN1899.G74M8   809.2   79-26018
    ISBN 0-8020-5478-1
    ISBN 0-8020-6381-0 pbk.

CONTENTS

INTRODUCTION

My aim in these essays has been to trace patterns of response to Greek tragedy characteristic of Humanist and neoclassical playwrights and to identify the strategies of transformation used by them in adapting the dramatic products of a very different age to their own changing (and not always consciously articulated) purposes. My procedure has been for the most part to look in detail at plays that are versions of extant Greek tragedies. I use the term 'version' in a quite precise sense to refer to a play that is based on the plot pattern, though not necessarily on the story, of a particular model. Thus *Phèdre* is a version of Euripides' *Hippolytus* (and also uses the same story), whereas *Samson Agonistes* is a version of *Prometheus Bound* and *Oedipus at Colonus*, although it does not follow the story of either play. For my purposes, versions have a methodological priority at times disproportionate to their literary merit or historical significance in the evolution of particular dramatic traditions, for they raise with exemplary clarity the difficulties European playwrights faced in coming to terms with the heritage of Greek tragedy. The practices and procedures that collectively make up the institution of Greek tragedy were developed by artists who, working within the moral and intellectual framework of fifth-century Athens, devised structures appropriate to the dramatic treatment of the relatively homogeneous body of heroic legends that form the subject matter of Greek tragedy. Almost two thousand years later, these practices and procedures were adopted by Humanist writers as canonical models for the development of a modern drama that would be the equivalent of Attic tragedy. But this canonical status created problems all the more important for being recognized imperfectly if at all. The two profound shifts in the moral and intellectual framework of Western culture associated with the names of Socrates and

Jesus had far-reaching consequences for the continued validity of the conventions of Attic tragedy. As a consequence of these two shifts, the modern dramatist had come to live in a world in which the problems of Greek tragedy did not always make sense. And the dramatic conventions established by Attic playwrights were not necessarily suitable to the dramatic representation of the situations that were likely to interest the modern dramatist. There was thus a tension between the world of the modern dramatist and the models that imposed themselves with the full authority of antiquity.

In principle, this tension can be observed in any play for which Greek tragedy is a 'precursor.' But versions are test cases because in them the peculiar intentions of the modern writer and the difficulties he encounters can be isolated and measured by means of a detailed comparison with the concrete contours of a specific ancient model. And among versions, certain types of failure have a privileged status, if the failure is not a matter of sheer incompetence but results from the recalcitrance of the model to a particular transforming intention. Rotrou's *Antigone*, Racine's *Iphigénie*, the Oedipus plays of Corneille and Voltaire, and Schiller's *Braut von Messina* belong to this category of instructive failures.

Versions thus have a paradigmatic status in the study of the *Nachleben* of Greek tragedy. What we learn from them is also, if not always so obviously, true of other plays on which Greek tragedy had a shaping influence. Because of this methodological priority, I have limited my inquiry to versions of extant Greek plays, and I have excluded some famous and historically important plays that would figure prominently in any history of the influence of Greek tragedy on the development of modern drama. Trissino's *Sofonisba* and Jodelle's *Cléopatre*, to name only two, are absent. Both plays are landmarks in the Humanist attempt to restore ancient tragedy; both closely observe the conventions of Greek tragedy as their authors understood them; and both allude frequently to scenes and particular passages in Greek tragedy. But neither is a version of an extant Greek tragedy. Both are displaced Dido tragedies, and their structural debt to Greek tragedy is mediated through the fourth book of the *Aeneid*, itself of course a kind of Greek tragedy.

The definition of a 'version' is not quite so simple as I have made it appear so far. 'Version' is a concept with uncertain boundaries, and a few of the plays I discuss are located in that boundary region. One ambiguity arises from the fact that few versions are derived from a single model, a fact that is in part due to the peculiar conditions under which Greek tragedies were transmitted to Renaissance Europe. Some of the most famous ancient tragedies were available in Greek and Senecan doublets (*Hippolytus, Trojan Women*), and Greek tragedies themselves frequently overlap in subject matter (the Electra plays, *Trojan Women, Hecuba*), with the result that ancient tragedies were often less powerfully present to the minds of European writers as specific texts than as images of myths envisaged in dramatic form and made up of memories not only of different plays but also of narrative sources (the *Metamorphoses* for the figure of Hecuba) and mythological dictionaries. Take the cases of *Hamlet* and *Rodogune*. These two plays are strongly indebted to the ancient Orestes plays because the choice of subject is governed by the perception of it as an Orestes equivalent. In both plays there are more than casual echoes of the Orestes legend. But clearly these plays are not versions in the sense that a particular play or set of plays provided the plot pattern, although it may be useful for certain limited purposes to treat them as if they were such versions.

Conflation of several models is unproblematical where the contours of the particular models remain clearly visible in the version. It is easy to see *Prometheus Bound* and *Oedipus at Colonus* in *Samson Agonistes, Ion* and the *Oresteia* in *Athalie, Iphigenia in Tauris* and *Philoctetes* in *Iphigenie auf Tauris*. In the context of my inquiry problems arise where a version depends on Greek and Senecan models – a very common occurrence. My concern has been specifically with Greek tragedy; Seneca and his tremendous influence on European drama lie outside the scope of my work. But the separation of Greek and Senecan tragedy, though familiar to us, is difficult and often meaningless for the sixteenth and much of the seventeenth century. Few readers of that period had a clear notion of the differences between Greek and Senecan tragedy; most of them saw the works of Aeschylus, Sophocles, and Euripides only through the medium of Senecan doublets. The distance between Seneca and his Greek models is small in the case of *The Trojan Women*, but immense in the case of *Oedipus* and *Medea*. My rule has been to stay away from Senecan versions as much as possible and to deal with them only where the Senecan model is a relatively undistorted image of Greek tragedy, as in the case of Garnier's *Les Juifves*, which draws on the immensely influential triplet of Seneca's *Trojan Women* and Euripides' *Trojan Women* and *Hecuba*.

Although my essays are intended as a contribution to the history of the influence of Greek on European tragedy, they are not a history of that influence, however skeletal. Rather, they attempt to derive from the analysis of selected examples, chosen primarily for their methodological significance, answers to such questions as: What generalizations are possible about the uses of Greek tragedy by Humanist and neoclassical playwrights? What understanding of Greek tragedy guided their choice of models and their strategies of transformation? What changes are there in the strategies of transformation and how do these changes reflect corresponding changes in the understanding of Greek tragedy?

Questions of change and evolution dominate the first three essays. The temporal limits I have chosen point to landmarks in the understanding and use of Greek tragedy; prior to the sixteenth century, the imitation of ancient tragedy is a very marginal phenomenon, and the use of Greek myth and tragedy in Romantic and modern drama, while not unrelated to neoclassical strategies of transformation, is very different. On the other hand, within the span of the three centuries that one can call neoclassical by a slight extension of the customary meaning of that term, there is a world of difference between the Humanist ethos of Buchanan or Garnier and the nostalgic Hellenism of the late eighteenth century. To identify the phases of this change has been my concern in these essays. The first two articulate the stages of the process that begins with the Humanist imitation of ancient tragedy and culminates in *Phèdre* as the chief embodiment of neoclassical tragedy. The differences that divide sixteenth- from seventeenth-century versions can be and often have been formulated in evolutionary terms: it is difficult to deny the name of progress to the increase in dramaturgical skills that separate Garnier's *Antigone* from Racine's *Phèdre*. But the two plays also reflect very different ways of understanding Greek tragedy, and the category of progress is quite inappropriate to a shift from a hermeneutical horizon that is collective and political to one that is individual and psychological. In dealing with the differences between Humanist and neoclassical versions, it has been my special concern to correlate changing approaches to practical problems of adaptation with changing responses to the moral vision of Greek tragedy.

The essay on eighteenth-century versions focuses on Goethe's *Iphigenie auf Tauris* and seeks to develop the pivotal position of that play. Like *Phèdre*, Goethe's play is the most successful embodiment of the moral and aesthetic tendencies that shaped contemporary adaptations, and like *Phèdre*, it stands apart from its contemporaries through the depth of its response to the mythical dimensions of its models. In that response, which looks forward to Romantic and modern forms of understanding myth and tragedy, the characteristically eighteenth-century idealization of Greece appears as the precarious victory over a world of bondage and terror. The resurgence of that world and the destruction of the neoclassic vision of Greece are my concern in the discussion of the eccentric counterpart to *Iphigenie*, Kleist's *Penthesilea*.

The following two essays are less concerned with questions of change and address instead two perennial problems in the discussion of ancient and modern tragedy: the emphasis of Greek tragedy on knowledge and the relationship of tragedy to Christianity. The peculiarly cognitive cast of the Greek mind is reflected in the preoccupation of Greek tragedies with the opposition of knowledge and ignorance and their preference for situations involving recognition. *Oedipus Rex* is the fullest and most paradoxical expression of this tendency. For this reason, versions of *Oedipus Rex* have a special methodological interest in that they show typical strategies of coping with a particularly puzzling aspect of Greek tragedy. My essay on versions of *Oedipus Rex* makes this difficulty the point of departure and sketches the two main lines of approach that playwrights have used in order to make sense of the Sophoclean model.

The relationship of tragedy and Christianity is a profound and difficult problem, which for the dramatist, however, poses itself in the simple question whether either damnation or salvation is a suitable subject for a tragedy. A few Humanist playwrights, following the lead of Buchanan's *Jephtha*, thought that neither was suitable and attempted to locate Christian tragedy in an area of doubt and obscurity. I have given the name of 'scriptural tragedy à l'antique' to the handful of scriptural tragedies that are distinguished by a close observance of the conventions of ancient tragedy and a choice of Old Testament subjects that were theologically intractable. Formal austerity and thematic difficulty are the defining features of this genre, of which *Samson Agonistes* and *Athalie* are the belated masterpieces. The genre is based on an implicit theory about reconciling Greek tragedy with Christianity which I have sought to make explicit in my discussion of the plays.

In classical and neoclassical genre theory, the neighbourhood of epic and tragedy gave rise to endless disputes about their differentiating features and respective claims to supremacy. In practice, epic and tragedy were inextricably intertwined, and the importance of this intertwining has led me to include in this volume two previously published essays on Milton and Racine that explore different aspects of it. Vergil's ambition to make the epic an encyclopedic genre led to the decision to include a tragedy in it: the tragedy of Dido, modeled after the passionate heroines of Euripides, had a powerful impact on European tragedy. Racine's *Bérénice*, the finest and most subtly displaced of Dido tragedies, is a splendid example of the mediation of the influence of

Greek tragedy through the epic. In Milton's case, on the other hand, we see a deliberate attempt to solve certain problems involved in a Christian epic by going back to Greek tragedy: the false tragedy of the Fall is structured along the lines of a tragedy of knowledge derived from the *Iliad* and from his intimate knowledge of Greek tragedy. These two essays mirror each other and at the same time round out the rest of the book, which in one place or another includes detailed discussions of most major uses of epic and tragic materials by Milton and Racine, the two poets who rivaled one another and surpassed all others in the brilliance and subtlety with which they made use of Greek tragedy.

While my examples are in the main drawn from French and German literature, with occasional sallies into English, Italian, and neo-Latin drama, my perspective has been European in the sense that I have been interested in shared responses and strategies of transformation and have for the most part neglected those aspects of my examples that are rooted in particular vernacular traditions. My analysis of Humanist tragedy, for instance, seeks to isolate the common features of its contribution to the rise of modern tragedy and systematically ignores the differences between the practices of Italian, French, German, and English writers. Nor have I paid any attention to the divergent ways in which Humanist drama interacted with popular dramatic forms. The relationship of Kyd, Marlowe, and Shakespeare to the university drama of their day is quite different from the relationship of Corneille, Rotrou, and Racine to French Renaissance tragedy. Again matters are different in Spain or in Italy and Germany, where Humanist drama was not followed by a major period of vernacular drama. Drama is an intrinsically popular genre that must speak to the here and now of a contemporary audience. Its development in different countries has from the beginning been much more subject to the pull of vernacular influences than such learned forms as epic and pastoral that were addressed to a literary élite that practised cultural and linguistic conservatism and set a high value on the maintenance of continuity with ancient models. In the face of such diversity, a procedure that purposely neglects the density and particularity of vernacular traditions will sometimes produce readings that are a little abstract and schematic. I acknowledge from the outset the justice of such a criticism but hope that the reader will accept it as the cost of a perspective that seeks to isolate those features of Humanist and neoclassical versions of Greek tragedy that were shared by them regardless of their place in a vernacular context.

Even admitting the irrelevance of distinct national traditions for my particular purposes, the reader may well wonder at the predominance of French, and the lack of Italian, examples. There can be no question that the Humanist revival of ancient tragedy first occurred in Italy, and that similar movements in the rest of Europe followed the Italian lead. At the same time, there is a strong predominance of the Roman and Senecan perspective in Italian Humanist tragedy. Even in Trissino's *Sofonisba*, the most consciously Hellenizing tragedy by an Italian humanist, the subject is Roman and the governing literary model is *Aeneid* IV. Thus while a historian of the Humanist revival of ancient tragedy must give pride of place to Italy, the analyst of the uses of *Greek* tragedy finds his methodologically most interesting examples elsewhere. The greatest Italian contribution to the restoration of ancient tragedy, the invention of opera, lies outside my field of inquiry.

Compared with the dearth of Italian versions, French plays figure so prominently in my essays that the reader may be tempted to think of them as a contribution to the history of classical influences on French drama rather than as a study of plays that happen to be French for the purpose of arriving at generalizations that apply across national boundaries. That would be to misread my intention. My choice of French examples is in part a matter of convenience, in part a reflection of the distinct and distinguished role that versions of Greek tragedy have played in the history of French drama, but most importantly it reflects the cultural hegemony of France during the seventeenth and eighteenth centuries. Between Corneille's *Médée* and Goethe's *Iphigenie* there is little to be learned about the imitation of Greek tragedy anywhere that cannot be learned more quickly and profitably from an analysis of the French versions that provided the strategies of transformation. The *Oedipus* of Dryden and Lee is a good example of the derivative character of non-French versions. The reader who approaches this play in the expectation that it will be a return to Greek tragedy via Shakespeare will be sorely disappointed. The Shakespearean elements of this play are simply the results of the attempt to modify Corneille's version in accordance with the more irregular conventions of the English stage. This is a subject of interest to the student of Restoration drama, but it has nothing to do with the uses of Greek tragedy.

Beyond this historical fact it is tempting to speculate a little about the intrinsically European nature of French versions of ancient tragedy. In England and Spain popular traditions were of overwhelming force in the establishment of a modern theatre. The remarkably similar complaints of Sidney in his *Apology* and of the Canon in *Don Quixote* about what they perceived as a lawless and vulgar stage were impotent: as early as 1590, the academic plays of the Countess of Pembroke and her circle were moribund protests. But French seventeenth-century drama always pretended to the greatest possible conformity with ancient theory and practice, and its peculiar genius may almost be said to consist in the suppression of the local and vernacular. It is surely a telling fact about the art of Corneille and Racine that none of their plays treats a subject from French history or legend. Whereas Elizabethan tragedy proudly measures its distance from ancient models in *King Lear*, French neoclassical tragedy proclaimed its affinity with these models in *Phèdre*. This is not to say that *Phèdre* is in fact closer to Greek tragedy than *King Lear*, but it means that we are indeed on firm ground in giving to French versions a paradigmatic status. This is most evident in the evolution of seventeenth-century drama: the sequence of adaptations that leads from Garnier through Corneille and Rotrou to Racine is a much more clear-cut instance of the merger of tragic and comic conventions from which modern tragedy was born than the history of Elizabethan drama, where a similar process had occurred earlier and in a much more diffuse form.

A summer grant and a senior leave fellowship from the Canada Council enabled me to write this book; it has been published with the assistance of a grant from the Andrew W. Mellon Foundation to the University of Toronto Press and a research grant from Northwestern University. I acknowledge these sources of support with gratitude.

The library staff at Indiana University, the British Library (in particular the North Library), and the University of Toronto made their libraries good places for me to work in. Hans Eichner, Alexander Leggatt, John Margeson, and Sheldon Zitner read various parts of the book in manuscript form and made valuable suggestions. Carol Widrig typed the final manuscript fast and very accurately. Jean L. Wilson copy-edited the manuscript meticulously. My thanks to all of them.

The material in chapter six first appeared as articles in *Comparative Literature Studies* volume 6, number 3 (1969) and *Canadian Review of Comparative Literature* volume 1, number 3 (1974) and is reprinted here by permission.

I dedicate this book to Rudolf Sühnel. When I was a very young student at the Freie Universität Berlin he encouraged me by his example and advice not to choose between ancient and modern literature but to study both.

CHILDREN OF OEDIPUS AND OTHER ESSAYS

1

HUMANIST TRAGEDY

HUMANIST TRAGEDY AS THE MEDIATOR BETWEEN ANCIENT AND MODERN TRAGEDY

The Humanist Revival of Ancient Tragedy

Until the latter part of the sixteenth century, when something like a professional national theatre arose in Elizabethan England, the composition and performance of tragedy all over Europe was largely in the hands of amateurs. The writers were mostly schoolmasters or young noblemen who followed the examples of Julius Caesar and Augustus in trying their wits at tragedy before moving on to war and politics or settling down to the more serious business of estate management.[1] The actors were schoolboys: Montaigne proudly remembers that he played the principal roles in Buchanan's plays when he was enrolled at the Collège de Guyenne in the 1540s.[2] Sometimes they were princes and princesses: Brantôme speaks of Catherine de Medici's delight in dramatic performances and in particular of '*Sofonisba*, composée par M. de Sainct-Gelays et très-bien représentée par mesdames ses filles et autres dames et damoiselles et gentilshommes de sa court, qu'elle fit jouer à Bloys aux nopces de M. de Cipière et du marquis d'Albeuf.'[3] The places of performance were the schools, colleges, academies, and courts; the times were school holidays, the visits of dignitaries, and special court occasions.[4] This 'occasional' character of the genre is important to an understanding of the aims and limitations of 'Humanist' tragedy, which is perhaps the most precise name that can be given to the kind of tragedy that dominated the first three quarters of the sixteenth century.

Humanist tragedy was self-consciously literary and understood itself as a revival of ancient tragedy in an age that had allowed its theatres to be taken over by vulgar and decadent entertainment. Du Bellay, who did not write tragedies himself, admonished the future poet in his *Deffence et Illustration de la langue francoyse*: 'Quand aux comedies & tragedies, si les roys & les republiques les vouloint restituer en leur ancienne dignité, qu'ont usurpée les farces & moralitez, je seroy bien d'opinion que tu t'y employasses, & si tu le veux faire pour l'ornement de ta Langue, tu scais ou tu en doibs trouver les archetypes.'[5] The same tone is still heard over a hundred years later in the preface to *Samson Agonistes*, the single and belated masterpiece of Humanist tragedy: 'they only will best judge who are not unacquainted with Aeschylus, Sophocles, and Euripides, the three Tragic Poets unequal'd yet by any, and the best rule to all who endeavour to write Tragedy.' Buchanan, who translated Euripides' *Medea* and *Alcestis* into Latin and wrote two scriptural tragedies, one of them closely modeled on *Iphigenia in Aulis*, gave the following illuminating account of the origin of his plays, emphasizing by implication the polemical nature of the Humanist revival: 'eas enim [sc. the plays], ut consuetudini scholae satisfaceret, quae per annos singulos singulas poscebat fabulas, conscripserat: ut earum actione juventutem ab Allegoriis, quibus tum Gallia vehementer se oblectabat, ad imitationem veterum, qua posset, retraheret.' ('He had written these plays to meet the school's demand for a play each year, so that by acting in them the students would be turned away from the allegories that were then very popular in France and towards the imitation of the ancients, wherever possible.')[6]

Humanist tragedy of course shared this opposition to popular culture with Humanist drama in general. But in the case of comedy the opposition was counteracted by the perception of comedy as a genre dealing with ordinary people. If comedy was, in Cicero's words, a 'mirror of common life,' then the common people had to appear on the stage in the dress, custom, and language of their day.[7] Thus it was easy in comedy to mediate between the literary conscience of the Humanist and the intrinsically popular demands of dramatic art. *Ralph Roister Doister* and *Gammer Gurton's Needle* are decidedly Humanist in their close adherence to ancient models and conventions, but they are also markedly successful as popular plays in their own right.

It was different with tragedy. Here the Humanist writers inherited from antiquity the concept of the tragic style as the *non plus ultra* of rhetorical dignity. Ovid summed up the consensus of Hellenistic and Roman literary theory in the words 'omne genus scripti gravitate tragoedia vincit.' ('Tragedy exceeds all other discourse in gravity.')[8] The Sophoclean cothurnus appears to have been a Roman cliché, and it was a good weapon to hit Euripides with for being insufficiently tragic, that is to say, insufficiently elevated in diction.[9] Occasionally the charge could be directed against Sophocles himself. Thus the quarrel between Teucer and the Atreidae in the *Ajax* seemed to be ancient scholiast unworthy of the dignity of tragedy.[10]

This heritage of tragic decorum was the cause of both the failure and the achievement of Humanist tragedy. Whether one looks at them from a dramatic or a poetic perspective, Humanist tragedies are for the most part wretched works: even the tragedies of Trissino, Buchanan, de la Taille, and Garnier, however estimable they may be, engage our interest in terms of their unquestionable historical role rather than as works that have weathered the test of time. The failure of practically all Humanist tragedies as works in their own right can be directly attributed to their obsession with tragic decorum and to their inability to remove tragedy from the pedestal on which literary and rhetorical theory had put it. The enslavement of Humanist tragedy to the doctrine of tragic decorum grew worse as the century went on. Tasso, for instance, in his marginalia on Trissino's *Sofonisba*, complained repeatedly of the play's lowly diction.[11] Similarly Hugo Grotius mixed his praise of Buchanan's tragedies with some strictures on his lapses from tragic loftiness.[12] To revive ancient tragedy in such a spirit of defiance to popular drama was a quixotic attempt and all the more ironic for the fact that the models of Attic tragedy had a broader popular base than perhaps any serious theatre has enjoyed since. As Hegel shrewdly observed, the playwright, unlike the scholar or epic poet, must hold the interest of his audience here and now.[13] The play, like Wallace Stevens' modern poem

> has to be living, to learn the speech of the place.
> It has to face the men of the time and to meet
> The women of the time.[14]

The playwright who relies on the enthusiasm of 'fit audience though few,' is doomed, because the few, considered as a dramatic audience, have always had anemic tastes. It is not hard to draw up a list of plays that would have met with the approval of Prince Hamlet, the Canon in *Don Quixote*, and Sir Philip Sidney. The plays of Buchanan and Garnier would rank high on such a list, but *Hamlet* would be unlikely to be on it at all.

But the poverty and inadequacy of most Humanist tragedies should not tempt us to neglect the crucial role the genre played in the emergence of European tragedy. Humanist tragedy is the link between ancient and modern tragedy. A play like Legge's *Richardus Tertius*, which stands half way between Seneca's *Hercules Furens* and Shakespeare's *Richard III*, symbolizes the achievement of its genre, which was broadly speaking the revival and perpetuation of tragedy as a distinct dramatic genre into the modern world.

Repeatedly in the history of drama new movements have defined themselves in terms of a return to ancient tragedy, but none of these returns was so momentous and so universal in its consequences as the ambition of sixteenth-century Humanists to restore the dignity of ancient tragedy. And if we are wearied by the unremitting grandeur and tedious monotony of the plays of Garnier, whom his contemporaries praised for exceeding all others 'en parler haut, grave, et tragiq,'[15] we must remember that the quest for a majestic style, however self-defeating if carried on uncompromisingly, established new norms of tragedy as a form with a special obligation to dignity, austerity, and formal rigour. In his mature tragedies Shakespeare never used the tragic style without contrasting it with a deflationary perspective, usually given to a special character and in *Hamlet* to the protagonist himself. But the Shakespearean juxtaposition of 'high' and 'low' styles is not a survival of a medieval indifference to the distinction. Rather, it is a recognition of the vulnerability of the precious acquisition of the grand style, which is protected aesthetically by this juxtaposition even where, as in *Othello*, the destructiveness and destruction of grand language are the subject matter of the play. Shakespeare's use of the tragic style is unthinkable without the norms of Humanist tragedy; the player's speech in *Hamlet* may be seen as the author's reflection both on his debt to and transcendence of the rhetoric of that genre.

Humanist Tragedy and the Quest for Equivalents

If in its rigid adherence to the ideal of the tragic style Humanist tragedy seems slavishly tied to its models, it was, on the other hand, very enterprising in extending the range of subject matter for tragedy. In their ambition to restore ancient tragedy, sixteenth-century writers realized from the beginning that this goal could not be achieved by simple imitation. Like other Renaissance artists, they faced the problem of the dialectical nature of 'translation' in the literal and broadest sense of the word, and like them they saw the solution to the problem in what I shall call the quest for equivalents.

The problem itself appeared on different levels and most fundamentally on the level of language itself. Should the man of letters write in Latin, the language of his models, or in the vernacular? Renaissance writers recognized that they were confronted with the same dilemma that Roman writers had faced before. Cicero and Vergil had been able to compose their exemplary works only because they had boldly decided to forego writing in Greek, in which they would have been forever condemned to second-class status, and to choose instead their own primitive and crude vernacular, which by their genius and by skilful importation and assimilation of Greek models they raised to a level of equal splendour and dignity. So Du Bellay in the *Deffence et Illustration de la langue francoyse*. And unlike Cicero and Vergil, the Renaissance writer had inherited from the Graeco-Roman tradition not only exemplary models but, equally important, a method for coming to terms with them.

In the theory of translation proper it had long been acknowledged that languages have individual characteristics that defy translation. Thus Jerome speaks of the 'ipsum ... suum et, ut ita dicam, vernaculum linguae genus' ('the distinct and as it were vernacular nature of each language'), and Du Bellay argued that literal translation destroys the 'je ne scay quoy' of a language.[16] Implicit in such arguments, and in their conclusion that one must translate the 'meaning' rather than the words, is the premise that the identity to be preserved in the process of translation is not the identity of the text itself but that of the original relationship between the text and its reader.

It is easy to see how such an understanding of translation will lead to the production of new works whose relationship to their models is considerably more independent than that of translations. The history of Latin literature is the purest example of the self-emancipation of a literature, which begins in translation and culminates in the creation of equivalents that replace and supersede their models. The distance of this journey is measured by the difference between the *Aeneid* and the translation of the *Odyssey* by Livius Andronicus, the first work of Latin literature of which we have any knowledge.

The *Aeneid* may in fact be read as an allegory on the development of Latin literature, beginning entirely on Greek (or rather Trojan) soil and moving away from it in such a way that on the one hand the continuity with the source is never broken, but that on the other hand the hero and his praise become fully autochthonous in the end. When Aeneas is finally compared to the Appenine mountains, Vergil has fully achieved the literary program, outlined in the *Georgics*, of creating an indigenous literature on Italian soil (*Aen.* 12.701–3; *Georg.* 3.1–39).

Itself the most perfect equivalent, the *Aeneid* established a precedent for their creation at other times and in different places. In this regard it differed markedly from Roman drama, and especially from Roman tragedy, which never achieved this emancipation from its Greek models. Attempts to write serious drama on Roman subjects (the so-called *fabula praetextata*) never got off the ground. Among the roughly 100 titles of Roman tragedy that we know of, less than ten are on Roman subjects, and this distribution is echoed in the ten Senecan tragedies, of which nine deal with Greek mythology and one with contemporary Roman history (*Octavia*).[17] But for the Roman, Greek mythology was not what it had been for fifth-century Athenians: a past consecrated by cult and tradition and in which no firm distinctions were made between history, myth, and legend. The subject matter of Senecan tragedy changed paradoxically by not changing; the plays of Seneca are 'mythological' in a way in which Greek tragedy rarely is, and they lack the resonance in the history and experience of the people that Greek tragedy always had.

The poets who aimed at restoring ancient tragedy in the sixteenth century, although they felt constrained by formal conventions of their models, felt free from the beginning to choose 'equivalent subjects.' In this regard they followed the precedent of Vergil rather than of Terence and Seneca, and in so doing they had a large share in staking out the field of possible dramatic subjects from which the great masterpieces of Elizabethan and French neoclassical drama arose.

The ambition of the Humanist playwrights was to write plays that were related to their audience as Medea, Oedipus, or Agamemnon were to fifth-century Athenian audiences. For the Roman poet there was only one answer to this equation: he replaced the mythology and legendary history of Greece with that of his own country. But for the European poets there were several possible answers to the 'x.' It was possible to keep the Greek subjects and maintain that our relationship to them did not differ from that of fifth-century Athens. With such a view the characters of Greek tragedy ceased to be figures from local history and acquired an abstract and timeless status, like the Greek statues whom posterity came to know only after they had lost their colour. The sixteenth century saw itself in the figure of Hecuba, the 'mobled queen,' and it saw in the fratricidal discord of Eteocles and Polynices, and more generally in the fate of Thebes, a paradigm of its own turmoil. But this perspective opened the way for the degeneration of the figures from Greek tragedy into mere names, however sonorous, and laid the ground for the innumerable plays in which the writer, as Voltaire said of Mlle de Scudéry, 'peignait des bourgeois de Paris sous le nom de héros de l'antiquité.' As if Voltaire's own plays had been exempt from this fault![18] On the other hand, this perspective could also reveal the mythical dimension of Greek tragedy, which lends vitality to the best plays of Seneca and to such modern plays as Racine's *Phèdre*, Goethe's *Iphigenie*, or Hofmannsthal's *Elektra*.

It was possible to replace Greek mythology with Roman history. In his *Sofonisba*, the first European tragedy to be modeled consciously on Greek tragedy, Trissino assumed that the Punic Wars were to the Italy of his day what the Trojan War had been to Athens. And Sofonisba, the beautiful sister of Hannibal, was, like Medea or Phaedra, a foreign temptress from a country historically associated with sex and violence. This equation held good for all of Europe: it underlies the Roman plays of Shakespeare as well as of Corneille, however little else they may have in common.

Third, the 'x' could be defined more particularly as a country's local or vernacular history. Thus Rucellai, a contemporary of Trissino, wrote a tragedy (*Rosmunda*) on an incident from the invasion of the Lombards and cast it in the mould of Sophocles' *Antigone*.[19] Local history is the origin and richest source of Shakespearean tragedy, which moves backwards in time from the almost contemporary historical conflicts of *Henry VI* and *Richard III* to the legendary past of *Macbeth* and *King Lear*.[20] Local history could appear in a slightly displaced form. Attic tragedy had dealt by preference with Theban or Argive history: as Mycenae and Thebes are to Athens, so Hamlet's Denmark is to Shakespeare's England and the Seville of the *Cid* to the audience of Corneille.

Inasmuch as ancient tragedy was religious, the 'x' could finally be taken for biblical history, which, like Roman history, was common to all Europe. This was in some ways the closest and most obvious equivalent. There was a long tradition of juxtaposing pagan mythology with scripture. If *Iphigenia in Aulis* was one of the two Euripidean tragedies Erasmus translated, his choice was plainly motivated by the resemblance of the story to the sacrifice of Isaac.[21] Moreover, the contemporary perception of religious discord and error as a great cause of disaster would lead to this equation.[22] *Les Juifves*, Garnier wrote in the preface of his tragedy, represents 'les souspirable calamitez d'un peuple, qui a comme nous abandonné son Dieu.'[23]

On the other hand, the purification of religion, whether through the Reformation or Counter-Reformation, ended up be establishing the theatre firmly as a secular art. If a play like Buchanan's *Jephtha* aimed at replacing the debased form of religious drama with a purer form, the impulse to decontaminate the sacred ended in the rigid separation of the sacred and the profane. In no European country did biblical drama gain a foothold on the public stage. By the end of the seventeenth century it was possible only on an imaginary stage (*Samson Agonistes*) or in a convent school (*Athalie*).[24] But the handful of plays in which a fusion of ancient plot patterns and biblical subject matter was carried out systematically constitute the most successful achievement of Humanist tragedy and are distinguished by their formal rigour and a tragic vision of uncompromising austerity.

In the initial stages of the quest for equivalents, the desire to extend the range of subject matter went together with a desire to stay close to the formal models. But the process of defining and extending the range of equivalent subjects had its own dynamic, and in the establishment of vernacular dramatic traditions, the original goal of restoring ancient tragedy was gradually subsumed in a greater and more independent enterprise. In a play like Trissino's *Sofonisba* or Rucellai's *Rosmunda*, the formal debt to ancient tragedy is overwhelming, both in the observation of general principles and in the adaptation of particular scenes. The same is true of the relationship of *Gammer Gurton's Needle* or *Ralph Roister Doister* to their sources in Roman comedy. In Shakespeare's *Richard III* a different stage has been reached. The fundamental principles of organization are quite different from those of ancient tragedy; nonetheless we recognize that the author wanted to write a tragedy that proclaims its equivalent status by formal devices. The marked use of stichomythy is ancient, and so is the choric use of female figures to lament the tragic events. The Duchess of York, in particular, recalls Hecuba in her general plight as well as in her specific laments. The most striking echo is, of course, the wooing of Anne by Richard, which, through the intermediary of Legge's *Richardus Tertius*, is a transposition of the scene in *Hercules Furens* in which the tyrant Lycus woos the wife of Hercules by blackmail.[25] *Hamlet* goes further in destroying the original balance of formal imitation and substantive innovation. It is very likely that the author of the *Ur-Hamlet* chose this obscure story as the subject of a play because he saw in it an equivalent to the Orestes myth. By its abundant allusions to classical antiquity, Shakespeare's play perhaps acknowledges the fact that it originated from such a transposition. At the same time the play proclaims its emancipation from its origins. The player's speech belongs to the kind of play from which Shakespeare's play derives but which it has now transcended. Finally, if *Macbeth*, and *King Lear* invite, and to a certain extent, demand comparison with the *Oedipus Rex* and *Oedipus at Colonus*, we know that there can be no longer any question of formal or thematic dependence.

Aristotelian Dramaturgy and the Comedies of Terence

The social context of the Humanist revival of ancient tragedy meant that tragedy was seen as a form of rhetoric rather than drama. The dignity of the genre depended on its status as the most elevated exercise of human speech. This rhetorical perception of ancient tragedy was greatly strengthened by the pervasive inability of sixteenth-century readers to distinguish clearly between Greek and Senecan tragedy. The knowledge of Greek was restricted to a small circle of scholars, and the special problems of language and metre presented such grave difficulties even to those privileged readers that Senecan tragedies, which with two exceptions happen to be versions of extant Greek originals, were widely confused with Greek tragedies, and the originals, even if they were read at all, were interpreted in the light of their Latin versions. Senecan tragedy is itself a rhetorical genre, and its almost total indifference to the Aristotelian ideal of a plot constructed in accordance with the demands of probability and necessity suggests that this ideal was not even pursued as a goal. The critical categories of the *Poetics* do not exhaust Greek tragedy – their failure to do justice to Aeschylus is notorious – but Aristotle's crucial premise that plot is the 'soul' of tragedy goes straight to the heart of Greek tragedy. It is therefore a matter of cardinal importance that Renaissance readers approached the plays of Sophocles and Euripides – Aeschylus was virtually ignored – through the distorting medium of Senecan tragedy, which is structured as a sequence of passionate discourses and requires to be judged as a kind of oratorio rather than as a drama in an Aristotelian sense. Inasmuch as differences between Greek and Senecan tragedy were seen at all, they were perceived in stylistic terms. In the preface to his translation of *Hecuba*, Erasmus wrote that he had tried to maintain the plainness of Euripides' idiom since he had little use for tragic fustian, an indirect hit at Seneca.[26] Conversely, Scaliger thought it a matter of praise that in the grandeur of his language Seneca outdid his models (*Poetics*, Bk 6, ch. 6). But although Seneca and his Greek models were known to differ with regard to specific dramatic conventions, such as the handling of the Chorus, no critic saw the role of plot construction as the crucial differentiating factor between

Greek and Senecan tragedy, and no sixteenth-century imitation of an ancient tragedy honoured Aristotle's identification of plot as the soul of tragedy.

The Humanists' persistence in seeing Greek tragedy as a rhetorical genre greatly limited the usefulness of Greek plays as models of dramatic construction. When English, Spanish, and French playwrights developed forms of European tragedy that were broadly, though in very different ways, Aristotelian in their acknowledgement of the primacy of plot, and sometimes demonstrated the mastery of plot construction that had previously been attained by Sophocles, they did not learn their skill from Sophocles. Nor, on the whole, did they learn it from Aristotle, despite the great strides in the understanding of the *Poetics* made about the middle of the sixteenth century, largely as the result of the three great commentaries by Robortello, Maggi, and Vettori, which identified the major problems of the text and provided a firm base for their later discussion by scholars and critics.[27] The crucial ancient influence on the dramatic structure of modern tragedy, although Aristotelian in a roundabout way, was not the *Poetics*, but the comedies of Terence and the body of criticism gathered in the commentary of Donatus and perpetuated in innumerable Renaissance editions. If one sets aside general medieval and specifically vernacular traditions, European tragedy may be defined as a merger between Terentian dramaturgy and the subject matter and elevated diction that traditional rhetorical theory associated with tragedy. Neo-Aristotelian dramaturgy, especially in France, gave the playwright a powerful tool for explaining, defending, and dignifying what he thought he was doing. But the decisive factor in accounting for the dramaturgical difference between Garnier and Racine or *Gorboduc* and *King Lear* is Terence, though his significance was overlooked by contemporary critics, partly because they knew him too well and partly because they were increasingly mesmerized by the *Poetics* and the dramaturgy that went by the name of Aristotle. Their mistake has been repeated by many modern critics to whom the history of the *Poetics* is a more familiar and more interesting territory than the reception of Terence.

The plays of Terence dominated the Latin curriculum of the early grammar school years from the Renaissance well into the eighteenth century and beyond.[28] One of the first books printed by Gutenberg was an edition of the comedies of Terence, and this was only the first of a flood of school editions and commentaries. In order to assess the influence of Terence one must constantly keep in mind that for several centuries educated men all over Europe shared the experience of reading a play of Terence as one of their first literary texts. And Terence was the one dramatist they all knew, whether they had a special interest in literature or not. For moral and linguistic reasons, Plautus was absorbed into the school curriculum with some caution, and Seneca, even at the height of his fame, was never a standard author in the grammar schools.

This dominance of Terence had little to do with an interest in drama as such. His comedies were considered the purest source of conversational Latin, highly prized by an age in which boys (and some girls) who had any pretensions to higher education were taught to read, speak, and write Latin as soon as or even before they learned to read their mother tongue. Terentian comedy was also highly valued by schoolmasters for its celebration of moral and social virtues. The fact that these master-pieces of linguistic purity and social and moral decorum were also plays was a pedagogical asset in teaching them to children. It was the sugar coating on the pill of instruction, and many a boy who played a role in a comedy of Terence had little idea that his master thought of him as imbibing moral lessons and practising his skill in Latin conversation and in the art of public speaking.

If the comedies of Terence were read for reasons that had little to do with their particular excellence as plays, the special circumstance of their transmission ensured that the schools would nonetheless give attention to their dramatic structure. For the Renaissance, as well as the Middle Ages, inherited from late antiquity an extensive commentary on Terence's comedies by the Roman grammarian Donatus. This commentary formed the basis of all Renaissance editions. Among the many grammatical and antiquarian notes to be found in Donatus, there was also a fair number of remarks about dramatic construction. Equally important was the fact that the work of Donatus included a short and very primitive dramaturgical treatise entitled 'de fabula' and attributed to the Roman grammarian Evanthius. Donatus and Evanthius together did not amount to much of a dramatic theory, but it was enough to provide a framework within which at least a rudimentary analysis of the specifically dramatic features of a play could be attempted.

The treatise by Evanthius included a very simple comparative definition of tragedy and comedy in which the two genres were distinguished by the social status of the characters, the level of diction, and the direction of the action, which moved from happiness to disaster in tragedy and from confusion and danger to a happy ending in comedy. There was also a schematic division of dramatic action according to which a comedy consisted of a 'protasis' (exposition), an 'epitasis' (complicating moment), and a 'catastrophe' (dénouement). In his commentary Donatus would praise Terence for turning monologues in his Greek sources into dialogues or for accompanying them with action and gesture 'ut ... agi res magis quam narrari videantur' ('so that the events appear enacted rather than narrated').[29] The most common device of this kind was the 'prosopon protaticon,' a character who appears only in the beginning to enliven the exposition and has no further role in the action. Another useful technical term was 'paraskeue,' the designation of lines that prepared for subsequent developments, in the simplest and most common case the imminent entrance of a new character.

It is evident from this cursory description of the dramaturgy of Donatus and Evanthius that its terms apply to general principles of dramatic construction rather than to comedy in particular. But it is extremely important to remember that during the sixteenth century these general principles were primarily associated with comedy. There was no comprehensive theory of drama which developed a common dramaturgy separately applied to tragedy and comedy. There was on the one hand a comic dramaturgy associated with Terence, and on the other hand a theory of tragedy that was part of a theory of style. The dramaturgy of tragedy developed to a large extent from the adaptation of 'comic' principles and devices.

The dominance of comic dramaturgy is quite apparent in sixteenth-century editions of Greek tragedy. The ancient scholiasts gave the scholar very little guidance in analyzing the dramatic structure of the tragedies. One might have expected some attempt to see Greek tragedies in the light of the *Poetics* and to look for instances of simple and complex plots, peripeteia, hamartia, and the like. But this did not happen until the seventeenth century. The commentators were content with using the terms of comic dramaturgy. Camerarius, for instance, who had previously edited Plautus, faithfully marked the epitases of Sophoclean plays. In the *Trachiniae* he finds the epitasis in the false report of Heracles' captivity by Lichas: 'Haec nunc deinceps argumentum fabulae in difficultates & facinus deducunt. in comoediis epitasin nominant. fit enim res iam varia, periculosa, & progressione sua difficilior atque perturbatior. In hac omnis est fabularum laus, propter casuum et fortunae explicationes' ('These events move the plot towards its complications and crime. In comedy they call it "epitasis." For the plot thickens and increases in complexity and commotion. Such unfolding of the turns of accidents and fortune is the hallmark of a good plot.') (note on *Trach.* 248).[30]

On a longer view the application of comic principles to tragedy is nothing but the return of an originally tragic dramaturgy to its own genre. Comic plots are descended from tragic plots. The art of plot construction developed in fifth-century tragedy. Attic comedy originally had no plot at all, but rather like a musical was a succession of numbers with traditional structures. The comedies of Aristophanes largely preserve this practice intact, but their own minimal plots are already influenced by tragic conventions, and in some cases, as in the *Acharnians*, or the *Thesmophoriazusae*, they are parodies of Euripidean plots.

In the course of its evolution, fifth-century tragedy developed a typology of dramatic structures with a marked preference for situations involving intrigue and recognition. Some plays of Euripides can without much difficulty be reduced to common schemata of plot construction.[31] This typology of dramatic schemata gave rise in the fourth century to two developments, one practical, the other theoretical. From the perspective of dramatic structure, the true successor of fifth-century tragedy was not Hellenistic or Roman tragedy, but the New Comedy of the fourth century. New Comedy carried further the development implicit in the Euripidean *Helen* and *Ion,* which a modern reader usually finds hard to accept as tragedies and would classify as romances or tragicomedies. Taking plays of this type as a point of departure, fourth-century comedy went further in reducing the status of the protagonists from the heroic level to that of ordinary human experience and in constructing plots in which an action full of surprise, complication, and narrowly missed disasters was resolved in a happy ending. In practice, many fourth-century comedies were transpositions of actual tragic plots, mostly Euripidean, to the level of ordinary experience; others followed the abstract schemata developed by tragedy without imitating particular models.

Aristotle's *Poetics*, the first theory of drama to centre on plot construction, must be understood in the light of these developments. Written in the second half of the fourth century – some sixty or seventy years after the last plays of Euripides and Sophocles – its preference for complex over simple plots and its emphasis on recognition and the closely related concepts of hamartia and peripeteia clearly assume the practice of the later fifth century as a norm. Aristotelian dramaturgy, with its indifference to Aeschylus and its limited understanding of the role of the Chorus, is in some ways more relevant to New Comedy than to many aspects of fifth-century tragedy.

After the fourth century, tragic *drama* and Aristotelian dramaturgy disappeared from view for many centuries. Roman tragedy was a rhetorical genre, and just as Roman tragedy neglected plot, so the theory of tragedy came to concern itself exclusively with diction. In Hellenistic and Roman literary theory the defining feature of tragedy is not a mode of structuring an action, but a particular style of elevated diction. Thus it happened that 'plot,' the great discovery of the fifth-century tragic poets (who did, however, freely acknowledge their overwhelming debt to Homer), was transmitted to European literature not in its original genre, but through Roman comedy, the successor of Attic New Comedy, and in particular through the plays of Terence. Camerarius' note on line 1404 of Sophocles' *Electra* charmingly sums up this roundabout history. He comments on the convention of marking off-stage deaths by shouts: 'clamore autem Clytaemnestrae indicatur aggressio facinoris: atque ita res quidem plane indicatur, sed mora nuntii praeciditur. clamat autem intus, quod foeditatem caedis ante oculos spectatorum peragi non oporteret. ut in comoedia intus clamat parturiens, Iuno Lucina fer opem.' ('The scream of Clytaemnestra marks the moment of the crime. Thus the action is clearly marked, and the delay of the messenger report is cut short. She screams indoors because the horror of the deed rules out its representation before the eyes of the spectators. So in comedy a woman at the point of giving birth will shout inside: Help me, Juno Lucina.') Historically, off-stage birth is a comic adaptation of tragic off-stage death. But because Camerarius is familiar only with comic dramaturgy, he unknowingly accounts for the original phenomenon in terms of its derivative.

The practice of the critics is echoed with equal naïveté in that of the playwrights. When Trissino set out to write *Sofonisba*, the first Hellenizing modern tragedy, he had an uncommon awareness of the fact that Greek tragedy was more dramatic than its Senecan counterpart. He wanted to create a more animated and life-like exposition than the Senecan prologue provided. Instead of a monologue by the heroine, we therefore find a scene in which Sofonisba tells her sorrowful history to a friend, whose only function is to listen and to given an air of verisimilitude to the procedure by remarking that although she knows the story well, it will bring relief to Sofonisba to tell it again. In short, Trissino does what Terence, according to Donatus, had done to the prologues of his models, and his resolution of speech into at least a nominal form of dialogue by the introduction of a kind of *prosopon protaticon* leads to a form of exposition for which there is no precedent in fifth-century tragedy.

Wherever Humanist writers of tragedy attempted to introduce features that we would recognize as specifically 'dramatic,' the advice of Donatus seems a great deal closer to their minds than the theory of Aristotle, which had never been applied to a corpus of plays with anything like the wearisome pedantry with which generations of schoolboys were taught to see the epitases, and so on, in the comedies of Terence.* But the dramatic aspects of Humanist tragedy remained largely embryonic. Although in the plays of Buchanan, de la Taille, and Garnier we can identify tentative moves towards a more dramatic structure, even they remain fundamentally examples of a stationary form of drama, more heavily indebted to rhetorical than to dramatic conventions.

THE HISTORICAL VISION OF TRAGEDY: GARNIER'S *ANTIGONE*

The rapidity with which genuine dramatists like Marlowe or Shakespeare passed beyond a rhetorical conception of tragedy is one, and perhaps the most decisive, form of the verdict that history passed on the intrinsic limitations of the genre as conceived by Humanist writers. Yet the formal structure of Humanist tragedy is not entirely a matter of shortcomings. It is in part the correlative of a tragic vision that is as primitive as it is powerful, and this vision accounts for precisely those formal aspects of Humanist tragedy that a modern reader might find most objectionable. Garnier's *Antigone* is a good example of this slightly

---

* Take as an example the question of the *prosopon protaticon*, one of the regular topics that Donatus discusses in the prefatory remarks to each play, and always in the same order. Thus the prefaces to *Adelphoi* and *Eunuchus* note the absence of a special *prosopon protaticon*; in the preface to *Hecyra* he argues that there are two of them. The comment on the first scene of *Phormio* also states the convention of the ignorant listener who is in the situation of the audience: 'quod in omnibus fere comoediis, in quibus perplexa argumenta sunt, fieri solet, id in hac quoque Terentius servat, ut προτατικὸν πρόιωπον id est personam extra argumentum, inducat; cui dum ob hoc ipsum, quo ueluti aliena a tota fabula est, res gesta narratur, discat populus textum et continentiam rerum sitque instructus ad cetera.' ('He does here what he does in nearly all comedies with a complicated plot: he introduces a *prosopon protaticon*, a character outside the action, and this character, who is a stranger to the action, is told what has happened so that the audience is briefed on the background and is prepared for the events of the play.') In view of the insistence on this point in Terentian dramaturgy, it is not surprising that Trissino should have followed the example of Terence and the precepts of Donatus even when he was trying to be 'Greek.' Shakespeare makes savage use of the convention in *Julius Caesar*, where the *prosopa protatica* Murellus and Flavius 'are put to silence,' not because it suits the playwright – as it plainly does – but 'for pulling scarfs off Caesar's images' (1.2.284).

paradoxical situation in which gross dramaturgical deficiencies may appear, from another perspective, as the formal correlative of thematic concerns of unquestionable strength and integrity.[32]

Garnier's *Antigone* is neither his finest nor his most influential play, but for reasons that have to do with the nature of its model it is particularly well suited to illustrating the formal and thematic tendencies of Humanist tragedy. A major argument of this and the next essay concerns a shift from a collective to a private vision of tragedy. This shift involved changes in the relative standing of Greek tragedies and the frequency of their adaptation. It is not an accident that Racine's masterpiece deals with a myth of sexual passion or that such 'city tragedies' as *The Phoenician Women* gradually lose ground after the sixteenth century. In this shift *Antigone* occupies a pivotal position. Whether or not Hegel's interpretation of the tragedy is fully acceptable, he was surely right in seeing this play as a paradigm case of the opposition of the individual and the social collective. In a shift from a collective to a private vision, one would therefore expect interpretations of the *Antigone* to be especially accurate measures of change. And this is in fact the case. Garnier's assimilation of Sophocles' *Antigone* to the dimensions of a city tragedy is just as indicative of the aims of Humanist tragedy, as two generations later the version of Rotrou, discussed briefly in the following essay, reflects the aims of seventeenth-century playwrights.

The action of Garnier's *Antigone* covers the events immediately preceding and following the fatal duel of Eteocles and Polynices. The *Thebaid* of Statius and the fragmentary Thebes play of Seneca are Garnier's chief sources for the events up to and including the brothers' deaths. For the remainder (Acts 4 and 5), the only source is the *Antigone* of Sophocles, to which Garnier had access in the original, but which he probably consulted in the Latin translation by Luigi Alamanni and the French version by Jean de Baïf.[33]

In the first act, a free translation of Seneca's Thebes fragment and a kind of prologue to the play as a whole, we find the blind Oedipus as his daughter implores him not to seek death at his own hands. The act, which includes a detailed exposition of the sufferings of Thebes *ab ovo*, concludes with Oedipus' retirement to a cave, where he hopes a natural death will come to him, while Antigone goes to the city to encourage her mother in her role as conciliator. The second act opens the play proper. A messenger reports on the imminent outbreak of hostilities and urges Jocasta to undertake a last attempt to reconcile the warring brothers. Antigone lends her support to this request, which Jocasta vainly seeks to carry out in the following scene, the heart of which is an impassioned plea by Jocasta to Polynices, in which she describes to him the ravages that civil war has brought to the country and which ends with a vision of Thebes destroyed (704–841). This scene ends abruptly, and after a choral ode we move to Act 3, in which a messenger arrives with the news that the brothers have killed one another. In the remainder of this act the prologue is re-enacted with variations, for now Antigone tries to dissuade her mother from committing suicide but fails in this attempt. Hemon suddenly arrives and Garnier has the doubtful privilege of being the first dramatist to include a love scene between Antigone and Hemon, if we except Euripides' lost play on the subject. The last two acts are a reasonably faithful adaptation of the Sophoclean *Antigone*.

To the reader whose expectations of dramatic conflict are shaped by neoclassical dramaturgy, the action of this play represents a glaring failure to acknowledge even the most rudimentary distinctions between plot and story. In this play, as indeed in Garnier's *Troade*, the ancient sources are strung together with no other apparent purpose than to make use of all of them and to provide as encyclopedic a version of the story as possible. The modern reader will take particular exception to Garnier's failure to splice his sources so as to ensure smooth transitions from one to the other. Thus Act 4 begins with a translation of the opening scene of Sophocles' *Antigone*, and there is no sign of awareness on the author's part that the use of the opening scene of a play in the fourth act of another play is at all problematical.

In his preface to *Porcie* Garnier was very forthright about his premises of dramatic construction. After citing his historical sources, he continues: 'Au reste, je luy ay cousu une pièce de fiction de la mort de la Nourrice, pour l'envelopper d'avantage en choses funèbres et lamentables, et en ensanglanter la catastrophe.'[34] What these 'choses funèbres et lamentables' are we learn from Scaliger's definition of the subject matter of tragedy as '[res] grandes, atroces, iussa Regum, caedes, desperationes, suspendia, exilia, orbitates, parricidia, incestus, incendiae, pugnae, occaecationes, fletus, ululatus, conquestiones, funera, epitaphia, epicedia' ('affairs of state, atrocities, king's orders, slaughter, acts of desperation, hangings, exile, orphans, parricide, incest, arson, fighting, blinding, weeping, howling, complaints, funerals, epitaphs, and dirges').[35] The implication is plainly that a tragedy cannot fail entirely if it has all these things.

The structure of Scaliger's definition bears a striking resemblance to the plot structure of Garnier's *Antigone*: in the definition as well as in the play the complex 'syntax' of Aristotle's *Poetics* has given way to a process of mere agglutination that measures effect by quantity alone. This is only in part a matter of tragic drama degenerating into melodramatic rhetoric; it also reflects a conception of tragic experience in collective terms. For Garnier, as for other sixteenth-century dramatists – the Shakespeare of *Henry VI* is a notable example – the matrix of tragedy is history, which is conceived in terms of the sufferings it has always brought to the many. The tragedy of history, according to this view, does not respect the division between actor and spectator; it stands always ready to engulf both in a holocaust, as Rosenkrantz, though hardly an innocent bystander himself, clearly states in an unwitting anticipation of his own ruin:

> The cess of majesty
> Dies not alone, but like a gulf doth draw
> What's near with it. Or 'tis a massy wheel
> Fix'd on the summit of the highest mount,
> To whose huge spokes ten thousand lesser things
> Are mortis'd and adjoin'd, which when it falls
> Each small annexment, petty consequence,
> Attends the boist'rous ruin. Never alone
> Did the king sigh but with a general groan. (*Hamlet* 3.3. 15–23)

Garnier expresses the same thought when he defines the subject matter of tragedy not simply as the fall of princes but as 'les malheurs lamentables des Princes, avec les saccagemens des peuples.'[36]

From this sense of the public dimension of tragedy – the indiscriminate reverberations that great events have in the lives of the innocent and the uninvolved – arises the quantitative view that tragic effect can be measured by the magnitude of the disaster. 'Für das Trauerspiel des siebzehnten Jahrhunderts wird die Leiche oberstes emblematisches Requisit schlechthin' ('For seventeenth-century tragedy the corpse is the emblematic stage property par excellence'), Walter Benjamin writes, limiting to German baroque tragedy an insight that applies with equal force to European tragedy of an earlier generation and explains the charnel house atmosphere that occurs at the conclusion of such diverse Shakespearean plays as *Titus Andronicus* and *Romeo and Juliet*, not to speak of *Hamlet* and *King Lear*.[37]

The vision of history as indiscriminate disaster is the hermeneutical horizon for Garnier's choice of subject in *Antigone* and for the agglutinative structure of its plot. In both these regards *Antigone*, like its close relative, the *Troade*, resembles the two Greek tragedies to which the sixteenth century responded most immediately and intensely: *Hecuba* and *The Phoenician Women*. The immense prestige of these plays was due to the interpretation of Troy and Thebes as emblems of tragic suffering. Erasmus chose to translate *Hecuba* not for its dramatic excellence but because the fall of Troy was the most tragic subject there was. The widowed Hecuba was a living monument to the 'instability of human affairs,' and it was through her suffering rather than through any action that for the sixteenth century Hecuba became the tragic figure par excellence. But as the very embodiment of tragic suffering – one remembers Polonius' response to the player's 'mobled queen' – she points to the fate of her community. And one may also claim that, until it came irrevocably under the sway of Aristotle's *Poetics*, the sixteenth century saw in Oedipus less the hero in *Oedipus Rex* than a character in *The Phoenician Women*, the unfortunate king of Thebes whose blindness, misery, and exile correspond to the misfortunes of his city.

It is no accident that both the *Hecuba* and *The Phoenician Women* are loosely plotted – at least by Aristotelian criteria – and that *The Phoenician Women* in particular shows some of the agglutinative features that characterize Garnier's *Antigone*. Since the nineteenth century, critics have generally despised *The Phoenician Women* because its indiscriminate piling up of horrors appeared to them the first evidence of the decline of Attic tragedy into melodrama and sensationalist rhetoric that characterized the history of the genre in later antiquity.[38] Sixteenth-century critics thought very differently. Far from despising the play for its loose structure and crudely quantitative conception of tragic suffering, they admired it for precisely the same reasons that later brought it into disrepute. 'Est autem admodum tragica ac plena vehementibus affectibus' ('It is highly tragic and full of vehement passions') Stiblinus commented in his preface, and Hugo Grotius, in the dedication to his translation of the play, singled it out as the masterpiece of Euripides, and indeed of Greek tragedy as a whole.[39]

The Renaissance assimilation of ancient tragedy into primarily historical categories of understanding calls for some comments in the light of the conviction, current since the Romantic period, that ancient tragedy is pre-eminently mythical. Walter Benjamin, for instance, developed a typology of ancient and modern tragedy, in which ancient tragedy dealt with Myth and had as its protagonist the Hero, whereas modern tragedy, which he called *Trauerspiel*, had History for its subject matter and the King for its protagonist.[40] But this perception of Greek tragedy rests on premises virtually unknown before the Romantic period. Romantic and post-Romantic poets have returned to ancient myths for reasons that are wittily set forth in the account of Faust's journey to the 'mothers' in the second part of Goethe's *Faust*. When at the high point of the festivities at the emperor's court Faust is asked to conjure up the shades of Paris and Helena, Mephistopheles tells him how to go about this difficult assignment:

> Ungern entdeck ich höheres Geheimnis. –
> Göttinnen thronen hehr in Einsamkeit,
> Um sie kein Ort, noch weniger eine Zeit;
> Von ihnen sprechen ist Verlegenheit.
> Die Mütter sind es!
> F. *aufgeschreckt* Mütter!
> M.   Schauderts dich?
> F. Die Mütter! Mütter! – 's klingt so wunderlich!
> M. Das ist es auch. Göttinnen, ungekannt
> Euch Sterblichen, von uns nicht gern genannt.
> Nach ihrer Wohnung magst ins Tiefste schürfen;
> Du selbst bist schuld, daß ihrer wir bedürfen;
> F. Wohin der Weg?
> M.   Kein Weg! Ins Unbetretene,
> Nicht zu Betretende! Ein Weg ans Unerbetene,
> Nicht zu Erbittende. (*Faust* 6212–25)

> MEPHISTOPHELES I loathe to touch on more exalted riddles. –
> Goddesses sit enthroned in reverend loneliness,
> Space is naught about them, time is less;
> The very mention of them is distress.
> They are – the Mothers.
> FAUST *starting* Mothers!
> MEPHISTOPHELES Are you awed?
> FAUST The Mothers! Why, it strikes a singular chord.
> MEPHISTOPHELES And so it ought. Goddesses undivined
> By mortals, named with shrinking by our kind.
> Go delve the downmost for their habitat;
> Blame but yourself that it has come to that.
> FAUST Where is the road?
> MEPHISTOPHELES   No road! Into the unacceded,
> The inaccessible; toward the never-pleaded,
> The never pleadable.

In translation, these playfully portentous creatures of Goethe's mytho-poeic imagination lose much of their power, which they owe to a simple pun: the phonetic resemblance between 'Mütter' and 'Mythos.' The mothers are mythical: their realm is the dark and hidden world of the womb, more real and more powerful than the everyday world which it both sustains and threatens. Myths accordingly are stories that deal with the most elemental human desires and conflicts and are placed beyond any social or historical restrictions that might detract from their universal validity. Freud's interpretation of the Oedipus story as a paradigm of a fundamental and universal human conflict exemplifies the Goethean conception of myth: who could deny that Freud, the great poet-explorer of the soul, descended to the 'mothers'? Hofmannsthal, influenced by Bachofen and Rohde rather than by Freud, spoke of his plays on mythical subjects as a 'descent' into the lowest depths of the 'Höhlenkönigreich Ich' where he expected to find the 'nicht-mehr-Ich.'[41] And in his *Oedipus und die Sphinx* he attributed to his protagonist words that epitomize a dominant romantic and modern attitude towards myth. After relating the dream vision in which he foresees his crimes, Hofmannsthal's Oedipus exclaims:

> Was nach diesem Wort blieb denn
> noch übrig als wir drei: der Vater,
> die Mutter und das Kind, mit zuckenden,
> mit ewgen Ketten des Geschicks geschmiedet Leib an Leib.[42]

After that word what remained but the three of us: the
father, the mother, and child, chained to each other
with the twitching and eternal chains of fate.

The perception of Greek tragedy as eminently 'mythical' in this sense gained ground in the course of the nineteenth century and found its classical expression in Nietzsche's *Birth of Tragedy*. For Nietzsche every Greek tragedy was a voyage to the mothers; the hero's particular identity was always a mask for the God Dionysus.

Since Nietzsche, we have come to think of Greek tragedy as the privileged expression of Greek myth, but it is important to remember that most of Greek tragedy was not considered mythical at all in this sense by its original audience and for many centuries to come. Indeed, the absence of a systematic distinction between myth and history is a cardinal point about fifth-century tragedy. The actions of most Greek tragedies do not occur *in illo tempore* but in a distant past bordered on the one side by the supernatural and on the other side by the exclusively human and historical. Plays like *Prometheus Bound*, set almost entirely in a supernatural world, and *The Persians*, which deals with practically contemporary history, are the exceptions that define the limits of this border region inhabited by heroes who live in historical places and circumstances but have a close and direct relationship with the gods whom they count among their fathers and grandfathers, or, in the case of the heroines, among their lovers. Thus the subject matter of Greek tragedy partakes of both history and myth in our sense, and the treatment often inclines towards the 'historical,' especially in the many tragedies taken from the Troy cycle. If Thucydides, among the most skeptical minds of his generation, did not hesitate to accept many events of the *Iliad* as historical, we may assume that for a fifth-century audience the Trojan War provided a firm historical background and that Agamemnon was no less historical to them than Richard ii or King John to a Shakespearean audience, and probably rather more so than King Lear. In *The Trojan Women, Hecuba, Philoctetes*, as well as in the *Heracleidae* and in the suppliant plays of Aeschylus and Euripides, the characters move in a political and historical rather than in a mythical world.

In the Hellenistic period, and a fortiori in Roman and Christian times, the mythical heroes ceased to be ancestors who were, in the broad and undifferentiated sense of the term, 'historical.' They came to be 'mythological,' and were now inhabitants of the realm of general human nature, no longer rooted in a particular space and time. Myths became the property of poets and mythographers; they lived in such artificial collections as Apollodorus' mythological encyclopedia or Ovid's *Metamorphoses*, and they became a metaphor for the psychological and in particular for the irrational. When Vergil's Juno exclaims: 'flectere si nequeo superos, Acheronta movebo' ('If I cannot bend the gods I shall raise hell') (*Aeneid* 7.312), the hell she speaks of is a metaphor of the violent and destructive forces of the human soul. The use of the mythological as a psychological metaphor was common to all genres of Roman poetry, and it played an important role in Senecan tragedy. In *Phaedra*, and more explicitly in *Hercules Furens*, Seneca relies on the ironic coincidence that the hero on his return from a mythical underworld is plunged into a psychological hell of passion and madness. In *Hercules Furens*, Theseus, left behind on the stage as Hercules prepares for the purifying ritual that will see the outbreak of his madness, gives a long account of his voyage to the underworld, his captivity there, and his liberation by Hercules. This mythical world, described in the gloomiest colours of Senecan rhetoric, is plainly a metaphor for the destructive psychic reality that the spectator is about to witness.

The tradition of the mythological as a psychological metaphor survived into the Middle Ages and the Renaissance through allegorical and iconographical forms of exegesis attached above all to those stories of Ovid's *Metamorphoses* in which the transformation of gods and men alike into beasts could be interpreted as the revelation of the destructive and degrading force of passion. We find this tradition in Renaissance epic and lyric poetry, and we find it in such special dramatic genres as the Elizabethan masque and the Spanish mythological drama. But we do not find it in Renaissance tragedy which, following a tradition of long standing, aligns itself with history and politics.[43] This tradition can be traced back to the fourth century BC through the complaints that Polybius makes about the contamination of historical writing with tragic conventions.[44] Polybius sharply attacks a 'tragic historiography' which subordinates factual accuracy and a strict concern with natural causality to rhetorical effects achieved by the exaggerated description of violent or other extraordinary events and by an uncritical fascination with oracles, prodigies, and strange coincidences. The perception of history as tragic in a certain form of historiography points to the perception of tragedy as historical. Once the distinction between myth and history had been made, tragedy followed history, and myth, as it appears in tragedy, was assimilated to the categories of historical understanding. The strength of the association of History and Tragedy is very clearly seen in the quest for equivalents by European playwrights of the sixteenth and seventeenth centuries. Playwrights in search of new plots looked for equivalents to the subjects of Greek tragedy in Roman, scriptural, and vernacular history, but they did not take their plots from vernacular mythology, which could appear in comedy (*Midsummer Night's Dream*) or masques (*Comus*) but not in tragedy. Wagner's *Ring des Nibelungen*, an unthinkable choice of subject for a Renaissance playwright, drastically illustrates the Romantic shift from a historical to a mythical perception of Greek tragedy.

The association of History and Tragedy was not a mere theoretical matter for sixteenth-century critics. In France and England especially, it grew out of an experience of domestic discord and religious wars. The relevance of ancient tragedy to the modern experience is a commonplace in prefaces and dedications of the period. 'Mitto tibi Andromacham Euripideam cum Notatis aliquot, veram nostrorum temporum imaginem' ('I am sending you the Euripidean Andromache with some notes, a faithful mirror of our times.'), Florent Chrestien wrote in the dedication to his translation of the play.[45] A generation earlier Hervetius said of his translation of *Antigone*: 'Tragoediae autem, quae est humanarum calamitatum quoddam veluti spectaculum, eo est tempore iucundior lectio, quod his iam viginti annis tot tumultus sunt excitati, ut perpetua quaedam tragoedia iure videri possit ... sed age, videamus in nostro Sophocle, quam sit iucundius tragoediam legere, quam tragoediae argumentum esse.' ('The reading of tragedy, which is a mirror of human disasters, is more enjoyable in our day because the past twenty years have been so tumultuous as to seem a perpetual tragedy in their own right ... But let us take our Sophocles as proof how much more enjoyable it is to read a tragedy than to be the subject of one.')[46] Matthieu described his *Aman* as a 'Tragedie composee en un siecle tragique' and amplified the definition of a tragic century by speaking of 'la prodigieuse *Tragedie du Schisme, du Discord, de la Desloyauté, de l'Heresie, quatre monstres cruels*, qui ensanglantent la Scene tant esleuee de ceste iadis tant florissante Monarchie.'[47] And Garnier speaks of 'les cris et les horreurs de mes Tragédies (poème à mon regret trop propre aux malheurs de nostre siècle).'[48]

The sense of living in an age torn by civil and religious discord endowed Thebes with a special relevance as an image of tragic suffering. The lessons of Troy were universal: Paris exemplified the folly and wickedness of human desire, Hecuba the instability of human affairs. But in the fratricidal fate of Thebes the sixteenth century discovered a faithful mirror of its own peculiar fate. It comes therefore as no surprise that in Garnier's *Antigone* the contemporary relevance of the subject is a major source of tragic effect. In most of Garnier's tragedies the choice of subject grows out of a political concern. In an occasional poem he speaks of his plays on Greek and Roman subjects as an act of 'pleurant nos propres maux sous feintes etrangeres.'[49] In his earlier plays, he had explored the relevance of events from the collapse of the Roman Republic. In the dedication of *Marc-Antoine* he wrote: 'Mais sur tout, à qui mieux qu'a vous se doivent addresser les représentations tragiques des guerres civiles de Rome, qui avez en telle horreur nos dissentions domestiques et les malheureux troubles de ce Royaume, aujourd'huy despouillé de son ancienne splendeur et de la révérable majesté de nos Rois, prophané par tumultueuses rébellions?'[50] And the title-page of the first edition of *Porcie* (Paris 1568) reads: 'Porcie, Tragédie françoise, représentant la cruelle et sanglante saison des guerres civiles de Rome: propre et convenable pour y voir dépeincte la calamité de ce temps.'[51]

In the laments about the misfortunes of Thebes, the contemporary application of the tragic events on stage finds its most eloquent expression. The third chorus of *Antigone*, for instance, begins with general and rather Senecan reflections on the fickleness of fortune and after dwelling on the fears and ambitions of sovereigns suddenly sees the quarrels of Eteocles and Polynices from the perspective of the suffering people:

> L'un le retient à son pouvoir,
> L'autre s'efforce de l'avoir:
> Ce pendant le peuple en endure,
> C'est luy qui porte tout le faix.
> Car encore qu'il n'en puisse mais,
> Il leur sert tousjours de pasture.
>
> Mars dedans la campagne bruit,
> Nostre beau terroir est destruit:
> Le vigneron quitte la vigne,
> Le courbe laboureur ses bœus,
> Le berger ses pastis herbeus,
> Et le morne pescheur sa ligne. (972–83)

The first ode, an invocation of Bacchus as the 'patron saint' of Thebes, also deviates from its Senecan source in its insistence on the ravages of civil war:

> Escoute pere, ô bon Denys,
> Rassemble les cœurs desunis,
> Des freres plongez en discords,
> Et de nos Beotiques bords
> Toutes calamitez banis.
>
> Garde la Thebaine cité
> De domestique adversité: (443–9)

But nowhere does the contemporary perspective appear with such eloquence as in the magnificent speech in which Iocasta implores Polynices to desist from his fratricidal enterprise. I quote part of the speech to give some sense of how on this occasion the heavy, relentlessly plangent rhetoric of Garnier becomes a fully 'answerable style' to his subject matter:

C'est la ville, mon fils, où Dieu vous a fait naistre,
Et où vous desirez l'unique seigneur estre.
Quelle bouillante rage et quel forcenement
Vous espoind de vouloir destruire en un moment
Vostre propre Royaume, et le voulant conquerre
Le faire saccager par des hommes de guerre?
    Comment? et voudrez-vous jetter pié contre-mont
Ces grands monceaux pierreux, qui sourcillent le front,
Ouvrage d'Amphion? les riches edifices
De tant de beaux palais, decorez d'artifices?
Aurez-vous, Polynice, aurez-vous bien le cœur
D'y prendre du butin, si vous estes vainqueur?
Et aurez-vous, helas! aurez-vous le courage
De les voir ravager, les voir mettre au pillage?
Trainer par les cheveux les vieux peres grisons,
Et leurs femmes de force arracher des maisons?
Les filles violer entres les bras des meres?
Et les jeunes enfans mener comme forçaires,
Le col en un carcan, et les bras encordez
Pour leurs maistres servir en plaisirs desbordez? (810–29)

The hermeneutical horizon, within which Thebes appears as the image of a sixteenth-century commonwealth, naturally affects Garnier's interpretation of Sophocles' *Antigone*, his exclusive model in the final two acts of his play. In the debate of Creon and Antigone, he saw a dramatic enactment of one of the root causes of tragedy in his own age: the conflicting claims of secular and religious authority. This perspective is of course not peculiar to Garnier. It appears, for instance, in the Latin translation of the play by Winshemius, a German Protestant scholar of the mid-century. Winshemius, who published his translation 'ad utilitatem juventutis quae studiosa est Graecae linguae' ('for the benefit of young students of Greek'), prefaced each of his translations with an interpretative essay in which he applied to the particular play his general thesis that the tragedies of Sophocles are 'imagines ... consultationum & rerum politicarum' ('images of deliberations and political actions'), and that each tragedy contains 'aliquas insignes disputationes de rebus magnis & gravibus, quae in gubernatione Rerumpublicarum incidunt' ('famous disputations about serious and grave problems that occur in government').[52] In the *Antigone* this question is 'utrum religioni et pietati obediendum sit, etiamsi id Tyranni vel Magistratus prohibeant' ('whether religion and piety should be obeyed even in defiance of the orders of a tyrant or magistrate').[53] If Antigone was to be justified from such a perspective, then Creon must be a tyrant who had set himself above the law and had therefore forfeited the obedience that is due a lawful sovereign. Winshemius does indeed describe Creon in such terms:

Depingitur etiam ipse Tyrannus, qui quanquam, ut popularis videatur, omnes iubet libere quod sentiant dicere, tamen ita postea impatiens est veritatis, ut ne filium quidem monitorem ferre possit ... Tyrannus vero opponit & religioni & caeteris argumentis, necessitatem tuendae authoritatis in imperio. id enim argumentum speciosissimum est ad excusendam saevitiam.[54]

We see a tyrant who wants to appear popular and tells everybody to speak their mind freely but subsequently is so impatient of the truth that he cannot even bear the advice of his son ... The tyrant counters religion and other arguments with the need for maintaining the authority of his rule. That is the most specious excuse for savagery.

Garnier not only opposes the tyranny of Creon to the *piété* of Antigone but takes care to stamp Creon as a tyrant even before he appears on stage. When Iocasta learns of the death of her sons, she gives as one motive for her suicide the face that she will be powerless to stop the usurpation of the throne by Creon, a strange argument in view of the fact that he is her brother and by law the next in the line of succession (1208–11). And in her dispute with Antigone, Ismene imputes to Creon the tyrant's desire to rid himself of all possible opposition:

Creon est obey, qui, tyran, voudroit bien
Déraciner du tout nostre nom ancien. (1574–5)

The characterization of Creon as tyrant subtly but radically changes the opposition of Creon and Antigone, as may be seen by looking in detail at Antigone's defence of her action. In Sophocles' version the condemnation of Creon's edict occurs only by implication. In the context of the play's world the situation of Antigone has no precedent. Through her act she steps into new moral territory, which perhaps only the emergence of this situation has brought to her consciousness. Her rhetoric therefore has the freshness of discovery.

Garnier's Antigone, on the other hand, defends herself by applying known maxims to a particular situation. She attempts to portray her situation as one in which civil disobedience is legitimate:

> Le grand Dieu, qui le Ciel et la Terre a formé,
> Des hommes a les loix aux siennes conformé,
> Qu'il nous enjoint garder comme loix salutaires,
> Et celles rejetter qui leur seront contraires.
> Nulles loix de Tyrans ne doivent avoir lieu,
> Que lon voit repugner aux preceptes de Dieu.
> Or le Dieu des Enfers qui aux Ombres commande,
> Et celuy qui preside à la celeste bande,
> Recommandent sur tout l'humaine pieté:
> Er vous nous commandez toute inhumanité. (1810–19)

The speech is more negative, polemical, and legalistic than that of the Sophoclean character. The statement of principle yields in importance to the correct identification of a situation in which certain established principles will apply. When Creon argues: 'Dieu ne commande pas qu'aux loix on n'obeïsse,' Antigone retorts: 'Si fait, quand elles sont si pleines d'injustice' (1808–9). This is on a level with her premise: 'Nulles loix de Tyrans doivent avoir lieu,' and neither statement is found in Sophocles, although both are implicit in the position of the Sophoclean Antigone. In Garnier's play the statement of belief appears as the minor premise in a syllogism ('Or le Dieu des Enfers ...'), and his Antigone uses 'la loy de nature et des Dieux' (1876) with the precision of an expert on constitutional theory.

We find the same transformation in the quarrel between Hemon and Creon. When the son mentions that the city is on the side of Antigone, the following exchange ensues in Sophocles' play:

> CR Is the town to tell me how I ought to rule?
> H Now there you speak just like a boy yourself.
> CR Am I to rule by other mind than mine?
> H No city is the property of a single man.
> CR But custom gives possession to the ruler.
> H You'd rule a desert beautifully alone. (734–9)

This appears as follows in Garnier:

> CR Qu'ay-je affaire d'advis? telle est ma volonté.

H   N'estes-vous pas suget aux loix de la cité?
CR Un Prince n'est sujet aux loix de sa province.
H   Vous parlez d'un tyran, et non pas d'un bon Prince.
CR Tu veux que mes sujets me prescrivent des loix.
H   Ils doivent au contraire obeir à leurs Rois,
    A leurs Roix leurs seigneurs, les aimer et les craindre:
    Aussi la loy publique un Roy ne doit enfreindre. (2034–41)

Here again the Sophoclean quarrel is interpreted in the light of sixteenth-century constitutional theory, whose language and distinctions (tyran, bon prince) are freely used, especially by Hemon, who becomes the author's mouthpiece in the emphatic last lines, which are not in Sophocles and which Garnier or his printer considered sufficiently important to mark with quotation marks. (Ismene's parting words similarly confirm the identification of Creon with the tyrant of constitutional theory: 'Je ne crains d'un Tyran les injustes coleres' [1940]).

That Hemon's position is indeed the author's emerges very clearly in the choral ode that follows this scene. In an ode that has no precedent in either the Sophoclean or any other ancient play, the Chorus praise justice and life in a constitutional monarchy. But they also dwell on the difficulty of choosing the way of justice and in particular on the temptation to mistake severity for justice.

Car celuy mainte fois
Qui de cruelles loix
Une cité police,
Par sa rigueur mesfait
Plus que celuy ne fait
Dont il punist le vice. (2135–9)

If Creon is a tyrant, Antigone is a saint who suffers martyrdom for her special virtue of *piété*. The celebration of this virtue is the point of the kommos in which, probably influenced by Buchanan's *Jephtha*, Garnier replaces the Sophoclean chorus of hostile old men with a chorus of admiring maidens who praise Antigone as an exemplar of *piété* to which future ages will pay homage:

Consolez-vous, ô vierge, et ne vous affligez,
D'un magnanime cœur vos tourmens soulagez.
Vous n'irez sans louange en cet antre funebre:

Vostre innocent mort vivra tousjours celebre,
Et celebre le los de vostre pieté.
Chaque an lon vous fera quelque solennité
Comme à une Deesse, et de mille cantiques
Le peuple honorera vos ombres Plutoniques. (2170–7)

The end of Creon, by contrast, is that of the tyrant whom retribution overwhelms with misfortunes. In his verse argument to his translation of *Antigone*, Jean de Baïf had summarized the fifth act as follows:

Ainsi grieues douleurs
Dessus grieues douleurs, malheurs dessus malheurs,
Troublent Creon le Roy de la terre Thebaine.[55]

The lines are also an excellent description of the accumulation of disaster and of the prolonged laments and self-recriminations of the late-repentant king in Garnier's play, which concludes as if it had been not so much a tragedy of Antigone as a tragedy about 'The Troublesome Reign of King Creon.'

2

TOWARDS *PHÈDRE*

DRAMATURGICAL AND THEMATIC ASPECTS OF VERSIONS IN SEVENTEENTH-CENTURY FRANCE

The sixty years that separate the *Antigone* of Garnier from that of Rotrou witnessed a dramaturgical revolution that destroyed the Humanist conception of tragedy as a form of rhetoric existing in the schools, the courts, and the academies, rather than on the public stage. It substituted instead a tragic drama capable of pursuing an action to its outcome through a varied and rapidly shifting sequence of events. This dramaturgical revolution took different forms in different countries, and in each case came about through the convergence and fusion of multiple influences and traditions. But from the perspective of the continuity between ancient and modern tragedy it is not too gross a simplification to describe this revolution, considered as a European phenomenon, in terms of a merger between tragic rhetoric and comic or Terentian dramaturgy. *Romeo and Juliet* is certainly the product of such a merger, and in very different ways *Richard III* and *Hamlet* testify to the importance that the overcoming of rhetorical tragedy had in Shakespeare's development as a writer of tragic drama.

The merger between tragic rhetoric and comic dramaturgy is particularly apparent in the versions of ancient tragedy that play a key role in the development of French neoclassical tragedy. When in the third decade of the seventeenth century Rotrou, Mairet, and Corneille wrote the first 'regular' tragedies, their intention was in some ways comparable to that of Trissino and Buchanan. They wanted to restore the dignity of an art form debased by popular entertainment. What the mysteries had been to Buchanan, early seventeenth-century tragicomedy was to these playwrights. Mairet's *Sofonisbe*, Rotrou's *Hercule Mourant*, and Corneille's *Médée* are the results of a deliberate return to the dignity and austerity of ancient tragedy. Rotrou and Corneille, not content with following ancient rules, even imitated particular ancient models, though these were Senecan rather than Greek. In later years Corneille defended his dramatic practice by invoking Aristotle, but that was an apologetic and ideological exercise, and Corneille nowhere pointed out that Aristotelian precept was far less important to his art than the fact that both he and Rotrou came to tragedy as writers who had learned the craft of plot construction by writing comedies and tragicomedies. Their careers as writers repeat the evolution of European tragedy as a whole, and their early plays are pioneering attempts to fuse the dignity of tragedy with the suspenseful action of comedy on a much larger scale than had hitherto been attempted in continental drama. In these plays – as indeed in *Romeo and Juliet* – tragic and comic conventions are still easily separable, but if they fail as plays, their failure points forward to *Phèdre*, which employs fundamentally the same techniques of adaptation but in which the separate elements are perfectly fused to form a new genre.

The notion of dramatic action that guided Corneille and Rotrou in their adaptations was shaped by comic plots in which a rhythmically structured flow of action overcomes multiple obstacles in its course towards final resolution. The requirement of a flowing action demanded a seamless transition from scene to scene – in practice the liaison de scènes, which especially in Rotrou is not yet fully observed. The requirement of a structured action demanded the articulation of larger units, in practice acts, whose conclusions mark well-defined moments of suspense or complication.

It is not surprising that the chorus should have been dropped from seventeenth-century adaptations, because it both impeded the flow of the action and obscured its articulation. The loss of the Chorus emphasized the skeletal and disjointed nature of the Senecan plots that Corneille and Rotrou adapted in their versions. In the manner of their introduction of new materials the aims of their dramaturgy are particularly apparent. Sixteenth-century playwrights had found ancient tragedies too short for their taste even when the choruses were included. Rhetorical amplification and the addition of related incidents had been the characteristic devices for achieving the desired magnitude. Their combined effect strikes us as singularly undramatic. Garnier's *Troade* and *Antigone* are crammed with incident, but there is hardly a pretense that the separate incidents are woven into a unified and dramatically

structured whole. At the same time, the unremitting grandeur and ex-
pansiveness of the style reduces the pace of these unassimilated events to
a crawl. *La Troade* has 2265 lines, *Antigone* 2741. By comparison, *The
Trojan Women* of Euripides has 1332 lines, *Hecuba* has 1295, and with 1179
lines Seneca's *Troades* is more economical still. In their prolixity and in
their lack of any sense of pace Garnier's plays are representative even of
more dramatically conceived plays such as *Jephtha* or *Saül le Furieux*.

In the adaptations of Rotrou and Corneille new incidents are not
simply added, but they form a sub-plot consisting of a love interest that is
interwoven with the main action. The ultimate reason for this procedure,
which became an essential feature of neoclassical tragedy, must be
sought in a generally European preference for interwoven structures that
were indigenous with the Romance tradition, from where they spread to
drama as well as to other narrative forms. An aesthetic of the sub-plot
would have to account not only for *Phèdre* and *Médée* but for *Hamlet* and
Don Quixote as well. Here it will be sufficient to state that whatever the
ultimate cause of the sub-plot or 'episode,' Terence provided an important and often-cited precedent. Evanthius remarked that it was a laud-
able practice in Terence that 'he made his plots more abundant by
choosing them from two separate events; for with the exception of
Hecyra, which deals only with the love of Pamphilus, all his other comedies have two young men.'[1] Abundance was no doubt one of the aims of
Corneille and Rotrou. But unlike Garnier, they did not aim at encyclopedic completeness. Rather the additional incidents in their versions
serve to give greater speed and variety to the action, to create moments of
suspense at act conclusions, and to articulate the rhythm of the action
more firmly.

This aim was achieved in large part, and from a strictly dramaturgical
perspective the difference between the versions of Garnier and Rotrou –
not to speak of Corneille or Racine – can only be described as progress.
But these dramaturgical advances were accompanied by changes in
thematic response to which the category of progress is quite inapplicable
and which on the contrary testify to loss and uncertainty. As Hegel
argued, the interest of European drama in the themes of love and honour
is a reflection of the specifically modern concern with individual subjectivity.[2] From this perspective, it is not accidental that the dramaturgical
advances of neoclassical over Humanist versions occurred through the
introduction of erotic sub-plots. The new dramaturgy finds its appropriate subject in the psychology of the individual, in what Milton called 'the
wily subtleties and refluxes of man's thoughts from within.'[3]

With the exception of Racine in his *Phèdre*, no seventeenth-century playwright was able to cope successfully with the consequences that the introduction of erotic episodes had for the coherence and integrity of the version as an interpretation of the thematic structure of its model. A successful version will always be, in Harold Bloom's language, a strong (mis)reading, but however far it moves away from its original, it must engage some crucial element of that original to benefit from its allusive relationship with it. The best Humanist versions, whatever their other shortcomings as plays, do engage their models in this way and reveal the depth of their authors' response to those Greek tragedies that answered to their vision of tragedy as collective suffering. Such engagement is rarely found in seventeenth-century versions. In many cases, authors were so busy restructuring their models to satisfy criteria of vraisemblance, bienséance, and poetic justice that they did not stop to consider what the models were about. In other cases, the sub-plot turned out to be the focus of real interest: Corneille's *Œdipe*, for instance, gives the impression of an old tree buried under and choked by a parasitical vine. Such evasions are evidence of an inability to relate the new interest in individual and in particular erotic psychology to the thematic structure of the models.[4] The most interesting evidence, however, of this inability is provided by those plays in which the attempt to refine the psychological motivation of the original undermines the thematic relationship of the version to its model in ways that the authors did not anticipate and which are clearly at odds with their intentions. Rotrou's *Antigone* and Racine's *Iphigénie* are instances of this subversive process.

Rotrou's *Antigone* is for the most part a reworking of Garnier's version, although there is evidence that Rotrou went back to both Sophocles' play and Euripides' *Phoenician Women*.[5] In the preface to *La Thébaide* Racine blamed Rotrou for filling his play with the subject matter of two tragedies. The charge is not entirely just, for it ignores Rotrou's systematic efforts to weld together the ancient sources that Garnier had been content to juxtapose. Whereas Garnier had begun his fourth act with a translation of the opening scene of Sophocles' play, Rotrou put the transition from the Thebes plot to the Antigone plot in the middle of his third act, and he added a new scene to obscure the transition from one model to another. He also shaped the first part with a view to the catastrophe of the second. Garnier's heroine is characterized by her *piété*, which she demonstrates equally in her behaviour towards father, mother, and brother. Rotrou's heroine, on the other hand, is motivated by a special love for her brother, which goes well beyond the ordinary love brother and sister owe one another. Whereas the demonstration of *piété* in scene after scene is a sufficient principle of unity in Garnier's version and accounts for its paratactic structure, Rotrou aims at subordination: the chief function of the first part of his play is the exposition of the special and mutual relationship on which the tragic events of the second part hinge. Parallel to the development of this special relationship is the elaboration of the love of Hémon and Antigone. The crisis of the play thus occurs as the conflict of Antigone's feelings for her brother and her fiancé. Hémon loses out in this conflict, but the last act of the play is given over to Hémon and Antigone as star-crossed lovers. In keeping with a common European practice of replacing messenger reports of ancient models with direct representation, we see him at the end of the play lamenting over Antigone's body and committing suicide in his father's presence.[*,6] Thus the play ends as the tragic spectacle of the ruin of young and innocent love.

Rotrou's changes give to his play a more clearly articulated plot and a more rapid and varied motion than Garnier's dramaturgy was capable of. At the same time, the elaboration of Antigone's sentimental and romantic attachments to brother and fiancé is accompanied by the loss of a social vision of tragedy. Garnier's heroine is an embodiment of the values that civil war threatens to destroy, and her martyrdom contains a lesson that Creon learns – though too late – and which the author hoped the feuding parties of France would take to heart. His Antigone is somewhat wooden and rather too much of an expert in constitutional monarchy to move us as the Sophoclean heroine did, but there is no

---

* The on-stage deaths of Créon and Créuse in Corneille's *Médée* are a good example, but an even more striking illustration is found in the practice of school performances of ancient tragedies in the vernacular by the famous grammar school at Strassburg. The great educator Sturm had made the recitation of ancient plays an important part of rhetorical instruction when he was headmaster of the school. Gradually a practice developed of performing plays for the townspeople. At first the plays were given in Latin with German arguments (Joseph Scaliger's translation of *Ajax* was performed in this manner); later, German translations were performed. A typical feature of these translations was the restoration of events related in messenger reports. Thus in *Hecuba* the sacrifice of Polyxena is represented on stage (and so are the murder of Polydorus, which precedes the play, and the blinding of Polymestor). In the performance of *Ajax* the audience were no doubt delighted at seeing the hero maltreat a real goat! In all these cases the messenger reports were kept in addition to the representation of the events they reported; indeed, the messenger report was considered so integral a feature of tragedy that it was added where it was missing in the models: the adaptation of *Ajax* boasts a full-fledged report on the death of Ajax by Agamemnon.

question that Garnier develops a coherent and moving social vision that clearly derives from the concerns of the Sophoclean model. The terrors and ravages of civil war are kept constantly before our eyes, and in the darkness of the world in which Jocasta's great plea goes unheard, Antigone's saintliness appears all the more noble for being rejected.

The disappearance of such a social vision in Rotrou's play appears most sharply in his version of Jocasta's plea to her sons. Whereas in Garnier's version the horrors of civil war find their most eloquent expression in this plea, Rotrou's Jocaste uses civil war as a subject for rhetorical conceits and concludes her argument with a singularly frigid couplet in which the subordination of a social vision to individual psychology is complete:

> Enfin sans vous, mon fils, je n'aurois pas la guerre;
> Mais sans la guerre aussi je ne vous aurois pas. (2.4)[7]

Although Rotrou does not make significant changes in the encounter of Creon and Antigone, his revisions displace that encounter from the centre of the play and deprive it of much of its significance. What is the point of the debate between Creon and Antigone if her drama turns on a clash of feelings for brother and fiancé and if the ultimate motive of her act is that Polynice is her very favourite brother? Who is Antigone if not the opponent of Creon? To the extent that a version of Antigone undermines the centrality of their opposition, it ceases to be an Antigone drama. Anouilh, who radically transformed the characters and principles of both protagonists, nonetheless made their encounter the centre of his play, as did Garnier in his interpretation of them as tyrant and martyr. Rotrou, trying to make his heroine psychologically more interesting and plausible, inadvertently moved away from the thematic centre of the model, and in his version there is finally no satisfactory answer to the question why it pursues its particular aims by way of a transformation of the Sophoclean Antigone.

Racine's Iphigénie is a much subtler and more distinguished play than anything Rotrou was capable of, but it suffers from an uncertainty of purpose that results, as in Rotrou's Antigone, from the unforeseen and subversive consequences of motivating the events of the model in terms of a specifically modern psychology. This subversion takes a curiously similar form in the two plays: both elaborate a subordinate motif of the models in which the heroine's prospect of marriage is blocked by allegiance to a brother or father. But in both plays the elaboration of the psychological triangle 'fiancé-heroine-brother/father' loses sight of the thematic range of the model, and in both cases the reader finally wonders whether the heroines are Antigone and Iphigenia figures in anything but name.

Iphigenia in Aulis belongs to the group of late Euripidean plays in which the crisis of values experienced in the latter half of the Peloponnesian War is projected into the legendary past. Specifically, the play deals with the disintegration of political leadership and its replacement by mob violence. The ultimate pressure on Agamemnon is neither the will of the gods nor his allegiance to the Greek cause, but the fear of reprisal from a rebellious army:

> O child, a mighty passion seizes
> The Greek soldiers and maddens them to sail
> With utmost speed to that barbarian place
> That they may halt the plunder of marriage beds
> And the rape and seizure of Greek women.
> The army, angered, will come to Argos,
> Slaughter my daughters, murder you and me
> If the divine will of the goddess
> I annul. It is not Menelaus
> Making a slave of me – Nor am I here
> At Menelaus' will, but Greece lays upon me
> This sacrifice of you beyond all will
> Of mine. We are weak and of no account
> Before this fated thing. (1264–72)

Is this 'mighty passion' – *aphroditê tis* – any better than the passion of Paris it seeks to avenge? Does it not unmask its baseness in its readiness to turn upon itself? And does it not reveal the 'will of the gods' and the patriotic cause as mere pretexts? Before this passion, all previous notions of heroism fail: the strength and valour of Achilles are rendered futile by the mob that shouts him down and threatens to stone him – his own Myrmidons being the very first to rebel.

Euripides' play draws its energy from its trenchant critique of this lawless world. The most effective scenes may appear to be the private scenes in which the emotions of father, mother, and daughter find a touching expression. But the pathos, especially of the scenes between father and daughter, derives precisely from their being misplaced in the play's primary context, a corrupt political world in which the values of elementary human bonds cannot flourish.

Racine was unable or unwilling to make use of this source of moral energy in Euripides' play. The political and social sphere of his model remains as foreign to him as it had been to Rotrou. His handling of the *deus ex machina*, the principal stumbling block for a modern imitator, provides the best evidence for the loss of the collective vision of tragedy. In Euripides' play, the fantastic solution achieved by the *deus ex machina* underscores by its very lack of credibility the theme of moral chaos. The demands of poetic justice, vraisemblance, and decorum ruled out such a solution for Racine, who invented a second Iphigenia and derived the complications of the plot from a misunderstanding concerning the identity of the victim. 'Une fille du sang d'Hélène' turns out to be not the daughter of Agamemnon, but a daughter of Theseus and Helena who was likewise called Iphigenia, but unknown to others and to herself grew up under the name of Eriphile. For several reasons her sacrificial death is quite acceptable. First, a daughter of Helen is a more appropriate victim since the war is about Helen. Second, although Eriphile is not strictly speaking a bastard child, the circumstances of her birth are sufficiently dubious to persuade an audience of her dispensability: she is the product of the clandestine marriage that followed the scandalous abduction of Helen by Theseus. Third, and most important, in the course of the play Eriphile thoroughly lives up to her doubtful origins, so that even the most tenderhearted spectator must admit that she gets what she deserves. Moreover, her death turns out to be on one level a plausibly and independently motivated suicide, thus removing the remaining scruples that might still be attached to the notion of human sacrifice in whatever form.

Eriphile enters the play because on one of Achille's raids she was captured by him. She had the misfortune of falling in love with him, and Achille, ignorant of her passion, sent her to Iphigénie as a kind of engagement present, thus compounding her plight by forcing the society of her rival upon her. Overcome by jealousy at Iphigénie, she decides to destroy her. When she learns that Agamemnon is secretly sending Iphigénie home in order to avoid being forced into the sacrifice, she betrays him to Calchas and the army. But her betrayal leads to her own disaster. As the army and Achille are about to come to blows over the fate of Iphigénie, Calchas receives a second illumination and announces the presence of the other Iphigénie. Without being mentioned by name, Eriphile recognizes her fate and anticipates the priest by plunging the sacred knife into her breast, proud perhaps that she can die for the glory of Achille if she cannot live with him, and certainly compensating for her life of jealousy and treason by the courage and resolution of her death, her last words being: 'Le sang de ces héros dont tu me fais descendre/Sans tes profanes mains saura bien se répandre' (5.6).

Granted the probability of this dénouement, or at least its avoidance of the patently miraculous, it must be admitted that in solving the problem of vraisemblance, Racine destroyed all morally significant links between the war and the sacrifice, and indeed destroyed the significance of the sacrifice. The fate of Eriphile is a psychological study of the destructiveness of passion as it lures the self into betrayal and humiliation. Her life and death constitute an independent fate that does not require a fuller context to disclose its moral meaning. Viewed as sacrifice, her death at the most offers the reflection that the gods were very considerate in demanding a victim to whom they could offer in return a face-saving way out of the mess in which it had got itself by its own desires.

The counterpart of Eriphile's convenient wickedness is the justice of the Trojan War, which appears in the play as a glorious and heroic enterprise to which hardly any doubts are attached. In Euripides' play Helen as the *casus belli* is vilified in no uncertain terms, and it is hard to think of this Greek army as engaged in any just war or as not corrupting and perverting in the execution whatever justice its cause may originally have had. Racine softens or omits most passages relating to the folly of the war and suppresses the more contemptible goings-on in the Greek camp. Thus the role of Menelaus, and with it the scandalous interception of Agamemnon's letter, is cut entirely. Also Achille's Myrmidons are not the first to turn against their master but stand valiantly by his side when immediately before the 'happy' dénouement Achille attempts to rescue Iphigénie by force.

As the war assumes the form of a distant, glorious, and unproblematic enterprise, and as the sacrifice exacted by the gods in return for victory turns out to be the just punishment for a life misspent, and even the restoration of some dignity to it, the moral problems of the Euripidean play dissolve – and with it the context in which the self-sacrifice of Iphigenia can be meaningful. This is clearly seen by comparing the situations in which the heroine changes her mind and volunteers for her death.

In Euripides' play Iphigenia makes her decision at a moment when the entire Trojan enterprise threatens to collapse in anarchy. She has only one protector, Achilles, but even he is powerless against the fury of the mob. If she relies on his help for her safety, she will save neither him nor herself, and the Greek cause may be ruined. This situation of imminent chaos is the consequence of the intrigues and machinations that precede it, and it is also the disclosure of their moral reality. In order to understand the open and forthright manner of Iphigenia's decision, one must recognize how every step that has brought her to her impasse has been beset by falsehood. She was lured to the camp through the false promise of marriage – a contrast between promise and reality which is structurally identical with the contrast between Electra's pretended childbirth and her plan to kill Clytaemnestra in the Euripidean *Electra*. In both cases the flagrant abuse of one of the great life-giving occasions of human existence points to the despicable nature of the intrigue. Falsehood is equally present in Agamemnon's futile effort to save Iphigenia. When his intrigue fails, he refuses to save her openly, but his fear of army reprisals is not morally sanctioned by the fact that it is only too well founded. This army and its leaders are responsible for each others' actions and thoroughly deserve one another. Iphigenia's action not only saves the Greek camp from the threat of moral anarchy on this particular occasion; more important, it sets an example for future action and demonstrates moral values that have been conspicuously absent. At the same time, the play leaves little hope that the example will in fact be followed. This is the source of the despairing pathos of the play.

The context for the decision of Racine's Iphigénie is not the Trojan War, but the hostility between her father and the man she loves, a hostility which emancipates itself from its political background and turns into purely personal opposition. Racine's Iphigénie chooses her sacrifice not out of any sense of public virtue, but because death offers her the only way of reconciling her conflicting loyalties to suitor and father. The development of this conflict is a major purpose of Racine's revisions of the Euripidean plot, especially of the motif of the intercepted letter. In Racine's version, Achille and Iphigénie have known each other for a long time and are formally engaged. Agamemnon, looking for a convincing pretext for turning mother and daughter back before they arrive, writes in a letter that Achille has fallen in love with Eriphile and no longer loves Iphigénie. The letter is not received until Iphigénie arrives, and it leads to a hurried departure, which Achille is barely able to reverse. The function of this contretemps becomes clear in the third act when Achille, having learned of Agamemnon's plan to sacrifice Iphigénie, fulminates against him and is surprised when Iphigénie takes her father's side and urges consideration of his plight. Achille thereupon argues that she no longer loves him and elicits from her a passionate denial:

> Ah cruel! cet amour, dont vous vouler douter,
> Ai-je attendu si tard pour le faire éclater?
> Vous voyez de quel œil, et comme indifférente,
> J'ai reçu de ma mort la nouvelle sanglante.
> Je n'en ai point pâli. Que n'avez-vous pu voir
> A quel excès tantôt allait mon désespoir,
> Quand presque en arrivant un récit peu fidèle
> M'a de votre inconstance annoncé la nouvelle!
> Quel trouble! Quel torrent de mots injurieux
> Accusait à la fois les hommes et les Dieux!
> Ah! que vous auriez vu, sans que je vous le die,
> De combien votre amour m'est plus cher que ma vie!
> Qui sait même, qui sait si le ciel irrité
> A pu souffrir l'excès de ma félicité?
> Hélas! il me semblait qu'une flamme si belle
> M'élevait au-dessus du sort d'une mortelle. (3.6)

The fourth act brings the showdown between Agamemnon and Achille, liberally adapted from their quarrel in the *Iliad*, which was also over a young girl. At the end of their quarrel, Agamemnon decides to sacrifice his daughter out of sheer pride, because the thought of yielding to Achille is intolerable to him:

> Et voilà ce qui rend sa perte inévitable.
> Ma fille toute seule était plus redoutable.
> Ton insolent amour, qui croit m'épouvanter,
> Vient de hâter le coup que tu veux arrêter.
> Ne délibérons plus. Bravons sa violence.
> Ma gloire intéressée emporte la balance.
> Achille menaçant détermine mon cœur:
> Ma pitié semblerait un effet de ma peur.
> Holà! gardes, à moi! (4.7)

This fit of spitefulness passes, however, and overcome by remorse Agamemnon decides to save his daughter while at the same time vowing to take her away from Achille forever:

Qu'elle vive. Mais quoi! peu jaloux de ma gloire,
Dois-je au superbe Achille accorder la victoire?
Son téméraire orgeuil, que je vais redoubler,
Croira que je lui cède, et qu'il m'a fait trembler.
De quel frivole soin mon esprit s'embarrasse!
Ne puis-je pas d'Achille humilier l'audace?
Que ma fille à ses yeux soit un sujet d'ennui.
Il l'aime: elle vivra pour un autre que lui. (4.8)

For Iphigénie, this decision, by which Agamemnon feels he has vindicated both his honour and his conscience, makes matters only worse. 'Mon père, en me sauvant, ordonne que j'expire,' she exclaims at the beginning of the fifth act. The choice between death and life without Achille, hypothetically raised in the first encounter with Achille, now has become real, and she confirms her previous opinion that death is the lesser evil:

Ah, sentence! ah, rigueur inouïe!
Dieux plus doux, vous n'avez demandé que ma vie!
Mourons, obéissons. (5.1)

Her decision is hardly a sacrifice, let alone a sacrifice for a public cause. She is willing to die for the Greek cause only inasmuch as it is that of Achille. Her sacrificial death will be a substitute for the life with Achille from which she was excluded:

Je meurs, dans cet espoir, satisfaite et tranquille,
Si je n'ai pas vécu la compagne d'Achille,
J'espère que du moins un heureux avenir
A vos faits immortels joindra mon souvenir;
Et qu'un jour mon trépas, source de votre gloire,
Ouvrira le récit d'une si belle histoire.
Adieu, Prince, vivez, digne race des Dieux. (5.2)

Racine's Iphigénie does not stoop to the passionate and tearful words with which Euripides' heroine begs for her life. If she does beg for it, it is on behalf of her distressed mother and on behalf of Achille to whom she had been promised. She is to that extent 'nobler.' On the other hand, the more closely one analyzes the motives for her change of mind, the more questionable her decision becomes as a voluntary sacrifice in a greater cause. If Iphigénie is driven into her 'choice' by the sense of disappointed love, she is not in fact very different from Eriphile. Both women are driven by passion; if one is led into crime and the other into the appearance of martyrdom, the difference is not due to strength of character, but the luck of circumstances.

A similar point can be made about Achille. The Euripidean Achilles is so impressed by Iphigenia's vow that he really falls in love with her and proposes marriage. When Iphigenia turns him down, he agrees to her sacrifice but promises to fight for her if she should repent of her decision even at the last moment. Is Racine's Achille more gallant or more selfish when he persists in his hatred of Agamemnon and despite Iphigénie's pleas remains determined to wreak havoc at the altar? Neither Achilles nor Iphigénie differs in moral stature from Eriphile: they are noble only as long as their desires are or appear to be reciprocated. To the threatened loss of the object of desire Achille reacts with the same disregard for moral principle that Eriphile showed; Iphigénie, on the other hand, is offered the luxury of stylizing her resentment into a martyr's crown.

In my reading of *Iphigénie*, the play appears as an exercise in unmasking, intent on obliterating the distinction between selfish and unselfish actions and revealing selfish passion as the hidden motive of all actions, whatever their appearance. This is a subtle theme, but what does it gain from being cast in the mould of an Iphigenia drama? And how does it interpret the model of which it is the version? Is *Iphigénie* a 'Euripidean' reading of Euripides, a play that questions even the child's idealism, the last residue of selflessness in a selfish world? Is this critique the link between model and version, a response to a crucial feature of the model, which in the process of being questioned, interpreted, and transformed sheds light on both the model and the version? I doubt it and find greater plausibility in an account that is less flattering to Racine. Through the introduction of Eriphile, Racine created a sexual triangle that is a recognizable variant of the triangles Atalide-Bajazet-Roxane, Andromaque-Pyrrhus-Hermione, and Aricie-Hippolyte-Phèdre. This triangle, which comes to dominate our attention, makes use of rather than interprets the Euripidean model. The link between the model and the version in this case comes about through levelling the specific contours of the model and assimilating them to a very abstract pattern whose presentation through the characters and events of the model is ultimately contingent. Racine's heroine, who prefers death to the prospect of separation from her fiancé, is not really an Iphigenia figure at all, but is more at home in the world of Mlle de Scudéry, whom Voltaire attacked for portraying the bourgeoisie of Paris under the names of heroes of antiquity.

PHÈDRE

Among the multitude of hellenizing dramas in seventeenth-century France *Phèdre* is unique for reasons that allow us to classify the play both as a fulfilment of and exception to the thematic and dramaturgical tendencies governing the adaptation of Greek tragedies.[8] It is an exception because it is the only adaptation – not excluding Racine's own earlier plays – in which the process of modernization neither evades nor erodes but interprets and explores the thematic potential of the models. But in so far as the achievement of *Phèdre* rests on the skilful use of the same strategies of transformation that vitiated the adaptations of Corneille and Rotrou, and indeed Racine's own *Iphigénie*, the success of the play vindicates those strategies, and *Phèdre* may be seen as the unique fulfilment of contemporary tendencies.

The compatibility of psychological and dramaturgical sophistication with the thematic structure of the myth is only one aspect of the uniqueness of *Phèdre* as a seventeenth-century version. Another is the recovery of the mythical dimension of ancient tragedy, which was without precedent and remained without followers until a century later Goethe made the challenge to the mythical world the point of departure in his *Iphigenie auf Tauris*. *Phèdre* shares with other seventeenth-century versions the loss of a historical and political response to tragedy: the world of princes and princesses is merely an elevated stage for the portrayal of individual psychology. But in *Phèdre* alone this loss is compensated by the discovery – new in the context of tragedy – of myth as a metaphor for psychodrama. What appears on the level of plot and character as the heroine's loss of control over her passions appears on the level of image and metaphor as the regression from a world governed by the moral and aesthetic criteria of bienséance and vraisemblance to a world of monsters and mythical terrors. To be more precise: the action of the play can be analyzed as the transformation of myth from metaphor into dramatic reality. It is not an accident that *Phèdre* alone of seventeenth-century adaptations has continued to hold the European imagination. As the most sophisticated and psychologically most persuasive adaptation of an ancient model, it epitomizes the results of a century of dramaturgical endeavour; in its thematization of the play's mythical setting, it established a link between myth and tragedy which, although without parallel in its day, has become fundamental to our understanding of ancient tragedy.

Phèdre as Drama of Disclosure and Complicity

Phèdre moves towards an act of confession that concludes the protagonist's moral career and to some extent restores the dignity she has lost in the course of the action. The speech that breaks her silence of complicity compensates for the silence she was unable to preserve with Hippolyte. In the representation of the psychomachia within Phèdre the act of disclosure is the central and morally ambivalent motif. Disaster occurs because Phèdre speaks where she should be silent and, until the very end, remains silent where she should speak. The plot of *Phèdre* may be called a system of complications to facilitate or prevent disclosures. All the resources of Racine's stagecraft are used to establish a progression of external events that release her inhibitions and arrest her moral impulses in such a manner as to mock her conscious intentions and to disclose to the audience and finally to herself the savage world of her passion. We have seen that the technical achievement of seventeenth-century adaptations consisted in the creation of a more animated dramatic rhythm, but that the twists and turns of surprise, moving towards their final resolution in the dénouement, often amounted to little more than empty bustle. In *Phèdre*, however, the dramatic rhythm is firmly anchored in the données of the models: Phaedra's disclosure of her passion, the accusation of Hippolytus, and the final confession. Between these great moments the play establishes psychological and moral links that elaborate and explore but never evade or contradict the thematic concerns of the models.

In Euripides' *Hippolytus*, Phaedra's nurse wrests from her the secret of her love and reveals it to Hippolytus in defiance of her mistress' explicit orders. This version of the disclosure was Euripides' second attempt to deal with the myth; a previous play in which Phaedra openly declared her passion for Hippolytus had failed some years before because the audience were outraged by such shameless behaviour on the part of a woman. Seneca's play derives from the earlier Greek play. Here the motif of difficult disclosure appears in the scene between Phaedra and Hippolytus. When the play begins, the nurse already knows Phaedra's secret, and like the other counsellors in Senecan plays, she fails in her endeavour to keep her mistress from yielding to passion and confessing her love to Hippolytus. The Senecan Phaedra is resolved to declare herself to Hippolytus even before she meets him. But she does not come straight to the point. Whether a sense of shame still restrains her, whether she seeks for an opportunity to disclose a shocking truth in a gentle and persuasive manner, whether the playwright delights in exploring the ironic effects of prolonged misunderstandings, or whether all three factors are at work, Phaedra delays and contents herself with hints that baffle Hippolytus and make him urge her to speak openly. She confesses that a great passion rages in her. When Hippolytus interjects: 'For Theseus surely,' she has found her cue. She loves the features of Theseus and describes them as they were when he slew the Minotaur. The evocation of the youthful Theseus modulates insensibly into a declaration of love for his son in whom she recognizes the image of the father. She concludes with an open confession:

> en supplex iacet
> adlapsa genibus regiae proles domus.
> respersa nulla labe et intacta, innocens
> tibi mutor uni. certa descendi ad preces;
> finem hic dolori faciet aut vitae dies.
> miserere amantis. (666–71)

> See, a king's daughter lies fallen at thy knees, a suppliant. Without spot or stain, pure, innocent, I am changed for thee alone. With fixed purpose have I humbled myself to prayer; this day shall bring an end either to my misery or my life. Have pity on her who loves –

It goes without saying that Racine could not avoid the challenge of the Senecan scene. The brilliant device of the modulation from father to son was irresistible, quite apart from the fact that a failure to make the antagonists meet would have violated all conventions of neoclassical stagecraft. Racine's adaptation of this Senecan scene is difficult to reconcile with his virtually complete silence about Seneca in his preface, a fact noted with due surprise by Brumoy.[9] To the scene of the encounter must be added another important Senecan debt. In Phèdre's soliloquy in the fourth act (4.6) the projection by her troubled conscience of the threatening presence of mythical judges in heaven and hell owes its substance, if not its function, to the Senecan nurse's warning that she will not escape the watchful eyes of Minos, the Sun, and Jupiter himself (*Phaedra* 149–57). And Phèdre's suicide in the final scene follows Seneca rather than Euripides, in whose play the ending is given over to the scene between the dying Hippolytus and Artemis appearing as *deus ex machina*. From Racine's obligation to Seneca at such crucial moments of his play it may appear that his chief model was Seneca rather than

Euripides and that his preface is a hypocritical exercise designed to cover up his true sources at a time when Senecan tragedy no longer enjoyed its former prestige and was coming under increasing attack for its un-dramatic structure and excessive rhetoric.

There is some truth in this charge, but it simplifies the relationship of Racine's play to its sources. The Euripidean elements of *Phèdre*, although less immediately striking, are equally important to the play's economy. We see this clearly if we ask why Racine used both the Euripidean and the Senecan scenes of disclosure. In Racine's version Oenone wrests Phèdre's secret from her, and in her encounter with Hippolyte, Phèdre, although unlike the Senecan heroine she has not resolved to speak, is unable to conceal the truth of her passion. This doubling does not serve the encyclopedic purpose so frequent in sixteenth-century adaptations; rather, the two scenes become stages in a larger process of Phèdre's increasing loss of control over her passions. And this process is extrapolated from the Euripidean scene between Phaedra and the nurse, which thus provides the governing structure for Racine's play as the drama of difficult disclosure.

In Racine's presentation of the process of disclosure great emphasis is given to the related motifs of complicity and evasion, which are both present in a seminal form in Euripides. The Euripidean Phaedra is torn between criminal desire and the commitment to her reputation. She experiences the conflict as the opposition between her hands, which are pure, and her mind, which is stained. To the outside world her sickness is the only symptom of the conflict. Although Phaedra knows that silence is the only way of protecting her honour, she is tempted into speech, but at the very moment of speaking she shifts the responsibility on someone else. When she replies to the nurse's entreaties: 'I yield. Your suppliant hand compels my reverence' (335), she pretends that she is not yielding to an impulse of her own but is instead fulfilling a social obligation. Similarly when the nurse correctly identifies the 'son of the Amazon' as Hippolytus she refuses to acknowledge responsibility for the statement and replies: 'You have spoken, not I!' (352) – although in the context of the play 'son of Amazon' cannot refer to anyone but Hippolytus.[10] The nurse thus appears to be the initiator of the action, but she is in reality the instrument of Phaedra's desire, for she brings about a goal that is secretly desired by Phaedra, while Phaedra, although the hidden beneficiary of this action, retains the power to disavow both the nurse's means and her ends as alien from her own intentions. Whereas on the surface the mistress suffers the servant to take over, this reversal of roles is in reality the mistress' device for evading the responsibility for an evil act secretly desired.

The same relationship between mistress and servant appears in the following scene, which begins with Phaedra's address to the Chorus. She rehearses the stages of her passion and of her futile endeavours to control it and concludes with her resolution to die. She appears to have regained her strength and integrity as a moral agent. But in the subsequent dialogue she is tempted by the nurse's plausible arguments for a shameful position:

> For God's sake, do not press me any further!
> What you say is true, but terrible!
> My very soul is subdued by my love
> and if you plead the cause of wrong so well
> I shall fall into the abyss
> from which I now am flying. (503–6)

And when the nurse takes the initiative she puts up only a nominal resistance. To the nurse's talk about a love charm her only question is whether it will be a salve or a draught (516). More important is her failure to follow up the nurse's noncommittal response to her order: 'Do not tell Hippolytus of this!' (520). For the nurse only says: 'Don't you worry, child' (*eâson ô pai*) (521). When the nurse's intercession with Hippolytus fails, the wrath of Phaedra predictably falls on her, and in retrospect Phaedra's command appears a great deal more emphatic than it actually was:

> Did I not see your purpose,
> did I not say to you, 'Breathe not a word of this'
> which now overwhelms me with shame? But you,
> you did not hold back. (685–7)

If she foresaw what the nurse was up to, should she have been satisfied with her evasive reply? Did she foresee the nurse's purpose and give her order simply to protect herself?

These hints of the theme of complicity – perhaps overinterpreted in the light of the later play – become the basis of Racine's portrayal of the moral career of Phèdre, which extends from the 'Euripidean'

> Grâces au ciel, mes mains ne sont point criminelles.
> Plût aux Dieux que mon cœur fût innocent comme elles! (1.3)

to her horrified recognition of the moral degradation she has suffered:

> Mes homicides mains, promptes à me venger
> Dans le sang innocent brûlent de se plonger. (4.6)

The first scene between Phèdre and Oenone (1.3), adapted from the two Euripidean scenes, is both the first stage in this descent and an anticipation of Phèdre's entire career, including her eventual 'return.' The scene begins with Phèdre's delirium. The clinical symptom of her sickness, her fear of light, also symbolizes her moral state: it is the fear of the guilty soul to be discovered in its darkness. The scene ends with a reasoned speech by Phèdre in which she analyzes her passion, gives the history of her unsuccessful attempts to come to terms with it, states her sense of guilt and hatred of her crime, and awaits the approach of death. These two appearances of the protagonist in a state of distress and composure frame the action of the scene, which is the revelation of Phèdre's passion. Euripides is on the whole followed closely, but the significance of Phèdre's submission to Oenone is more clearly articulated. Phèdre yields with the words: 'tu le veux.' The transfer to another person of the responsibility for an action secretly desired could not be more emphatically expressed. The three words epitomize the moral tragedy of Phèdre.

If her review of her case gives the appearance of moral recovery, instability enters with the sudden news that Thésée has died (1.4). Oenone grasps the import of this news: 'votre flamme devient une flamme ordinaire' (1.5). And immediately she thinks of reasons why Phèdre should see Hippolyte: his good will is politically important if Phèdre is to secure the succession for her son; in particular she might form an alliance with him against Aricie. Phèdre consents: 'Eh bien! à tes conseils je me laisse entraîner.' She will live if 'l'amour d'un fils' – a studied ambiguity on the poet's if not on her part – is capable of reviving her spirits.

The news of Thésée's death is the catalytic external event without which the tragedy could not occur. It also is one of the many circumstances that on the surface appear to excuse Phèdre's action. Racine's heroine would never act, as Seneca's did, on the mere supposition that Thésée might not return. On the other hand, Phèdre's readiness to believe what turns out to be only a rumour is morally significant. The flat announcement of the king's death is curiously qualified even before it is refuted in the third act. The sceptical Aricie questions it as a 'bruit mal affermé,' a judgement well supported by the arguments with which her confidante attempts to refute it (2.1). Hippolyte accepts it as a fact when he meets Aricie (2.2), but in the scene with Phèdre expresses hope about his father's return (2.5). Thus it is evident that Phèdre's uncritical acceptance of its truth is proof of her proneness to delusion. And it is remarkable that although Oenone announces the transformation of guilty love into a 'flamme ordinaire' she also offers her mistress an opportunity to cloak her true motives for seeing Hippolyte under the guise of political necessity. Phèdre embraces this means of self-deception as eagerly as she had accepted the fact of Thésée's death.

In Phèdre's first appearance we recognize a counterpoint between extreme lability and a conscious moral stance. The precarious ascendancy achieved by the latter is overthrown by an accident, the news of Thésée's death, which is readily interpreted in such a manner as to give the appearance of legitimacy to an action previously held culpable. In the encounter with Hippolyte (2.5) and the events that follow from it, this sequence is repeated with variations. In particular, the motif of an accident incorporated into a culpable design is sounded more explicitly as a malign fate puts Hippolyte's sword in Phèdre's hands and gives her an opportunity for saving her honour by destroying that of another. We may observe that on the surface Racine's queen behaves more morally than her Senecan model in seeking out her stepson. She has 'reasons' for seeing Hippolyte, and it is not her intention to declare her passion to him. Instead of resolution there is hesitation in her mind as she senses the flimsiness of her pretext:

> Le voici: vers mon cœur tout mon sang se retire.
> J'oublie, en le voyant, ce que je viens lui dire. (2.5)

But it is also possible to read the scene as a triple refusal by Phèdre to seize an opportunity for honourable retreat. The first occurs when she allows Oenone to dispel her fear by the briskly hypocritical: 'Souvenez-vous d'un fils qui n'espère qu'en vous.' The other two opportunities result from Racinian changes in the Senecan motif of modulation. To Hippolyte's remark that Thésée may still be alive, Phèdre opposes her certainty of his death but adds her sense that he still lives on:

> Que dis-je? Il n'est point mort, puisqu'il respire en vous.
> Toujours devant mes yeux je crois voir mon époux.
> Je le vois, je lui parle, et mon cœur ...

This goes very far – too far, as Phèdre herself concedes in words that both state her sense of guilt and signal their hidden meaning: 'Je m'égare,/Seigneur; ma folle ardeur malgré moi se déclare.' Hippolyte is obligingly obtuse, whether out of tactfulness or because his mind is too full of Aricie, we cannot tell. But by design or accident, he gives her a cue for retreat by praising the magnitude of her love for Thésée. Phèdre picks up the cue, perhaps in good faith, but soon the modulation begins again, and this time with an openness that cannot be ignored. But Hippolyte is only too willing to allow Phèdre a face-saving retreat when she upbraids him for construing her words in a compromising sense. Nonetheless, he deems it safe to terminate the interview and leave:

> Madame, pardonnez. J'avoue, en rougissant,
> Que j'accusais à tort un discours innocent.
> Ma honte ne peut plus soutenir votre vue;
> Et je vais ...

But Phèdre rejects the offered retreat and with the famous and brutal change to the intimate 'tu' drops all her pretenses. Her confession, however, turns immediately into self-incrimination. Nobody could be more conscious of her crime than herself, Phèdre argues:

> ... Ne pense pas qu'au moment que je t'aime,
> Innocente à mes yeux, je m'approuve moi-même,
> Ni que du fol amour qui trouble ma raison
> Ma lâche complaisance ait nourri le poison.

Phèdre's expressions of guilt and self-accusation are presumably the 'sentiments si nobles et si vertueux' which in the preface Racine declares to be incompatible with the 'bassesse' of the direct calumniation of Hippolytus in Euripides and Seneca. But the preface is no more reliable as a statement of Racine's intention with regard to Phèdre's moral stature than it was an honest acknowledgement of his debt to Seneca. The self-incriminations of Phèdre point to the existence of her conscience, but they are not necessarily evidence of contrition. They may also be read as excuses. As an 'objet infortuné des vengeances célestes' Phèdre is beyond blame and can take comfort in an imagined determinism. 'Cet aveu si honteux, le crois-tu volontaire,' she exclaims almost self-righteously, but the reader may hear an echo of the 'tu le veux' with which she yielded to Oenone. Like Milton's Satan, Phèdre resorts to 'necessity the tyrant's plea.' And evidence of her 'lâche complaisance' will continue to accumulate.

The moral stance Phèdre takes in her declaration of love leads to her desire to become the object of Hippolyte's vengeance. When Hippolyte recoils again, she wants to commit suicide and wrests the sword from his hands. But her action is prevented by the practical Oenone: 'Mais on vient: évitez des témoins odieux.' The expectations aroused by this ending are necessarily conditioned by our knowledge that once before the fine words of Phèdre had proven unfounded. With the news of Thésée's death the necessity for her own death had rapidly dissolved, although death had seemed imminent and ineluctable. Thus we are not surprised to find Phèdre at the beginning of Act 3 regretting the missed chance of death but not intending to make up for it (3.1). And indeed, the encounter with Hippolyte seems to have broken whatever moral strength remained in her. To Oenone's suggestion that she might flee, she replies that it is too late, not forgetting to blame Oenone for preventing her from dying while there still was time:

> Toi-même rappelant ma force défaillante,
> Et mon âme déjà sur mes lèvres errante,
> Par tes conseils flatteurs tu m'a su ranimer. (3.1)

Her sense of guilt soon gives way to new delusions, as she attempts to interpret the encounter in a more favourable light. Perhaps Hippolyte's outrage was the reaction of a man unused to love. From the knowledge of his general hostility to women she even derives the comfort that at least she need not fear a rival. Oenone is dispatched with the order to offer the kingdom to the prince – perhaps this will soften his ambitious heart – but returns almost immediately with the news of Thésée's safe return (3.3).

Phèdre's response to this development drastically changes the degree of her complicity. Her acceptance of the news of Thésée's death had been a deluded act, but in submitting to Oenone's plans on that occasion she had been weak rather than immoral. Now she becomes an accomplice to a clearly criminal act. If fate or accident played into her hands the sword of Hippolyte as the instrument of slander, the sword is an inert object, requiring a wicked intention to fulfil its fatal role. And although the intention is Oenone's, Phèdre consents:

> Fais ce que tu voudras, je m'abandonne à toi.
> Dans le trouble ou je suis, je ne puis rien pour moi. (3.3)

The similarity of phrasing points to the difference between criminal consent and delusion that was still innocent. Phèdre's 'fais ce que tu voudras' states the consequences of the 'tu le veux' by which she had disclaimed responsibility for the first disclosure of her passion.

Phèdre confirms her complicity through her words to Thésée:

Arrêtez, Thésée,
Et ne profanez point des transports si charmants.
Je ne mérite plus ces doux empressements.
Vous êtes offensé. La fortune jalouse
N'a pas en votre absence épargné votre épouse.
Indigne de vous plaire et de vous approcher,
Je ne dois désormais songer qu'à me cacher. (3.4)

The words can be taken as incriminating Hippolyte, but they can also be taken as self-incrimination, which is the way in which Hippolyte understands them. What meaning does Phèdre intend? It might be argued that if she did not intend the sense that incriminates Hippolyte, her share in the crime diminishes. But this is not so. If one takes her words as a veiled confession, their hypocrisy becomes, if anything, even more marked. As in the case of Dimmesdale in *The Scarlet Letter*, the self escapes discovery by appearing to accuse itself.

In the ancient plays Phaedra's accusation of Hippolytus is not problematic; her motives of revenge and self-protection are taken for granted. Whereas both Euripides and Seneca are interested in the psychological process of disclosure, neither pays much attention to motivating the slander. It is the great merit of Racine's version that it establishes a continuity between disclosure and slander through the motifs of complicity and transferred responsibility. The same psychological forces operate behind the separate events. But the slander is not a simple repetition of the disclosure, for it incriminates Phèdre much more seriously. The sequence of events is in fact a progression towards increasingly open criminality.

In the continuation of this progression Racine resorts to the invented sub-plot between Hippolyte and Aricie. The interaction of this plot with the main plot marks the final step in Phèdre's moral degradation. The sub-plot was criticized by contemporary and early eighteenth-century critics as a concession to the audience, which demanded a romantic interest. It is true that in one respect the premises of the sub-plot weaken the myth. If Hippolytus is in love, then the meaning of his death is obscured. In Euripides' play the image of the hero entangled in the reins of his chariot as he vainly tries to escape from the bull is a terrifying image of the futility of repression. We can understand how such an end should follow from the hero's open defiance of Aphrodite and from his narcissistic self-righteousness. In Racine's play the thematic relation between the hero and his death is weakened and the premises of the sub-plot undermine the tragedy of Hippolyte no less than the significance of the heroine's sacrifice is undermined in *Iphigénie*. On the other hand, the fate of Hippolyte is a subordinate aspect of *Phèdre*, and if the sub-plot destroys the significance of his death, this loss is amply compensated by its contribution to the tragedy of Phèdre.[11]

As Racine piously informs the reader in the preface, his Phèdre was too good to invent the slander of Hippolyte herself; she even consented to it only in a temporary 'agitation d'esprit qui la met hors d'elle-même' and almost immediately repented of her action and went to Thésée 'dans le dessein de justifier l'innocence et de déclarer la vérité.' But of course she does not confess: Thésée's accidental disclosure that Hippolyte loves Aricie reduces her to silence (4.5). The scene makes sense only if we assume that given the chance Thésée would be able to revoke his curse and would do so. By withholding that chance Phèdre becomes guilty of Hippolyte's death. In proposing the accusation of Hippolyte, Oenone had made light of its consequences – exile at the most:

> Un père en punissant, Madame, est toujours père:
> Un supplice léger suffit à sa colère. (3.3)

If the anticipation of trivial consequences had helped to persuade her, the recognition of her misjudgement is her motive for seeking out Thésée. She fears for Hippolyte's life:

> S'il en est temps encore, épargnez votre race,
> Respectez votre sang, j'ose vous en prier.
> Sauvez-mois de l'horreur de l'entendre crier;
> Ne me préparez point la douleur éternelle
> De l'avoir fait répandre à la main paternelle. (4.4)

Her silence is therefore an intentional sin of omission, undertaken in the full knowledge of its likely consequences. Through her decision to maintain her complicity with Oenone's action, the guilt of that complicity has been transformed into full responsibility for a crime.[12]

The love of Hippolyte and Aricie is not only a mirror in which the destructive passion of Phèdre appears in its clearest light; without it, that destructiveness could not fully manifest itself. In the reasoning of the Euripidean Phaedra the desire to protect her own reputation dominates over the desire for revenge; in the Senecan play the reasons for the slander are barely mentioned, and never by Phaedra herself. In Racine's play Phèdre is urged by Oenone to act in the interest of her children, and to weigh the small evil that would befall Hippolyte against the total ruin that would befall her children. The recognition of a rival dispels these rationalizations and reveals the desire to destroy what cannot be possessed. And Phèdre is not satisfied with the doom that her silence pronounces on Hippolyte: she wants to destroy Aricie as well. For the first time in the play Phèdre contemplates direct criminal action, but in so doing she tears the veil of complicity and evasion by which she had hidden her moral degradation from herself and from others:

> Que fais-je? Où ma raison se va-t-elle égarer?
> Moi jalouse! Et Thésée est celui que j'implore!
> Mon époux est vivant, et moi je brûle encore!
> Pour qui? Quel est le cœur où prétendent mes vœux?
> Chaque mot sur mon front fait dresser mes cheveux.
> Mes crimes désormais ont comblé la mesure.
> Je respire à la fois l'inceste et l'imposture.
> Mes homicides mains, promptes à me venger,
> Dans le sang innocent brûlent de se plonger.
> Misérable! et je vis? et je soutiens la vue
> De ce sacré Soleil dont je suis descendue? (4.6)

The moral reckoning that begins with this speech is real, and its significance is underscored by a powerful allusion to the conscience-stricken Dido, whose 'return' is marked by a similar question: 'quid loquor? aut ubi sum? quae mentem insania mutat?' ('What do I say? Where am I? What madness changes my mind?') (*Aen.* 4.595). For the first time Phèdre rejects the advice of Oenone, and, not content with suicide as an act of expiation, she insists on clearing the reputation of Hippolytus by an act of confession. But even in this final act of disclosure there is still an echo of the old Phèdre, who minimizes her complicity and seeks refuge in transferred responsibility. While conceding that she desired Hippolyte, she adds immediately:

> Le ciel mit dans mon sein une flamme funeste;
> La détestable Œnone a conduit tout le reste.

The Mythical Dimension of Phèdre

As we have seen in the discussion of Rotrou's *Antigone* and Racine's *Iphigénie*, the growing interest in individual psychology was accompanied by a decline in a socially oriented response to tragic experience. Neoclassical tragedy in France progressively lost its concern with a political and collective vision, perhaps in part as a response to political absolutism. The bond between ruler and people ceased to be a source of emotional power, as it had been in Humanist and Elizabethan tragedy. In Corneille's *Oedipe* the people enter the play only as shadowy entities, and the king's power and central position are no longer, as they were in Shakespeare, a subject of moral and intellectual concern; rather – as the rhyme 'roi-moi' tellingly reveals – they become metaphors of the self and are diminished in their concrete and political reality. Despite the dominance of sophisticated diplomatic activity in the play, Corneille's *Oedipe* is fundamentally a non-political play, both by comparison with *Oedipus Rex* and with Shakespeare's political dramas. In Racine the decline of the historical and political vision of tragedy is complete: in *Phèdre* the throne of Athens has become a pawn in the struggle of individual and utterly non-political desires.

The decline of the historical vision of tragedy is accurately measured by the emptiness of allusions to Troy and Thebes, which to the sixteenth century were the great emblems of tragic suffering. In Corneille's *Rodogune*, for instance, the two brothers who vie for the love of the princess lend a borrowed grandeur to the conflict of love and friendship by pointing to Troy and Thebes as the great exemplars of destructive passion.

> Ces deux sièges fameux de Thèbes et de Troie,
> Qui mirent l'une en sang, l'autre aux flammes en proie,
> N'eurent pour fondements à leurs maux infinis
> Que ceux que contre nous le sort a réunis. (1.3.171–4)

A structurally similar but more extended allusion occurs in Racine's *Andromaque*, where the burning Troy is compulsively present in the minds of the characters as the metaphorical equivalent of the passions that consume them, especially in the famous lines of Pyrrhus:

> Je souffre tous les maux que j'ai faits devant Troie.
> Vaincu, chargé des fers, de regrets consumé,

Brûlé de plus de feux que je n'en allumé,
Tant de soins, tant de pleurs, tant d'ardeurs inquiètes ... (1.4)

But there is more to the burning Troy than a young man's sexual passion expressed in the erotic code language of his day. In *Andromaque*, as in *Rodogune*, the Troy images fail of their intended purpose of adding a special dimension to the action and reveal the poet's limited grasp of the great symbol he had dared to appropriate.

In *Phèdre*, and in *Phèdre* alone, the vacuum created by the loss of a historical vision is filled by the recovery of the mythical setting as the correlative of psychological drama; and *Phèdre* is the first modern version of an ancient tragedy in which the subject matter of the models is interpreted as mythical rather than assimilated to the categories of historical experience. [13]

The mythical dimension appears in *Phèdre* as a shadowy second stage onto which the characters extend through their pasts and which gives them a double identity. Although they appear as princes and princesses moving in the clear light of a contemporary court, from the beginning they cast monstrous shadows into which the sharp outlines of their personalities are slowly dissolved. Racine achieved this double perspective by a deliberate reversal of established procedures for harmonizing mythological subjects with the demands of *vraisemblance* and *bienséance*. [14] A seventeenth-century theatre audience demanded that the characters and actions of mythological heroes should not conflict with its notions of behaviour appropriate to princes and princesses. But princes and princesses did not make expeditions to the underworld, have mothers who slept with bulls, or brothers who were minotaurs. If such incidents formed too prominent and famous a part of the model to be ignored or explained away, it was still possible to soften their impact – as in Racine's handling of the miraculous dénouement of *Iphigenia in Aulis* – or to focus attention elsewhere. When we see Corneille's *Oedipe* playing his intricate game of power politics and dynastic marriages involving the thrones of Thebes, Athens, and Corinth, we have little time to reflect on the brutal outlines of the myth on which the play is supposedly based.

This assimilation of the primitive myth to the conventions of a contemporary court is also present in *Phèdre*. The rivalry between Aricie and Thésée and the struggle for the throne of Athens generated by the false news of the king's death bear a strong family likeness to the sexual diplomacy of Corneille's *Oedipe* and certainly smack of Paris and Versailles rather than of Athens. And Euhemerist explanations easily disposed of the misunderstanding regarding Thésée's alleged trip to the underworld. He had been to Epiros, a region in north-western Greece (just south of modern Albania), then as now a most obscure and inaccessible part of the world, which boasts a real river Acheron, and there he had been imprisoned by a cruel tyrant 'dans des cavernes sombres, / lieux profonds et voisins de l'empire des ombres' (3.6). But although Thésée is established as a properly historical king, mythical attributes surround him in the form of rumours whose poetic and thematic significance in no way suffers from being refuted by the facts:

> On sème de sa mort d'incroyables discours.
> On dit que ravisseur d'une amante nouvelle
> Les flots ont englouti cet époux infidèle.
> On dit même, et ce bruit est partout répandu,
> Qu'avec Pirithoüs aux enfers descendu,
> Il a vu le Cocyte et les rivages sombres,
> Et s'est montré vivant aux infernales ombres;
> Mais qu'il n'a pu sortir de ce triste séjour,
> Et repasser les bords qu'on passe sans retour. (2.1)

Indeed, the mythical attributes are more resonant than the facts, and since they are presented first and positioned more prominently, they are rooted more firmly in the minds of the audience. History yields to myth, as it does in Théramène's account of the search for the lost Thésée, which trailed off at the borders of the known world:

> J'ai demandé Thésée aux peuples de ces bords
> Où l'on voit Achéron se perdre chez les morts;
> J'ai visité l'Elide, et, laissant le Ténare,
> Passé jusqu'à la mer qui vit tomber Icare. (1.1)

Moreover, if in the present myth is tolerated only as rumour, it was real enough in the past, for the precariously 'historical' nature of the present is itself the past achievement of Thésée, who as a new Hercules freed the world from monsters whose reality in the past is untouched by Euhemerist rationalizations. Hippolyte indeed regrets that his father freed the world from mythical terrors and left him nothing to do:

> Tu sais, combien mon âme, attentive à ta voix,
> S'échauffait aux récit de ses nobles exploits,
> Quand tu me dépeignais ce héros intrépide

Consolant les mortels de l'absence d'Alcide,
Les monstres étouffés et les brigands punis,
Procruste, Cercyron, et Scirron, et Sinnis,
Et les os dispersés du géant d'Epidaure,
Et la Crète fumant du sang du Minotaure. (1.1)

Phèdre, who will turn out to be the monster that survived, is even
more insistently surrounded by a mythical aura. She is first referred to as
'la fille de Minos et de Pasiphaé,' and among her first words is an
invocation of the sun as her mythical ancestor:[15]

Noble et brillant auteur d'une triste famille,
Toi, dont ma mère osait se vanter d'être fille,
Qui peut-être rougis du trouble où tu me vois,
Soleil, je te viens voir pour la dernière fois. (1.3)

Neither she nor the audience are committed to the literal truth of
Pasiphaé's daring boast, but as with Thésée's visit to the underworld, the
mythical aura survives the possibility of a factual disclaimer. Similarly,
when Phèdre speaks of being persecuted by Venus, we may take this as
simply mythological periphrasis to which no belief attaches, but in the
context the play has already established the lines increasingly evoke the
threatening presence of a real god:

O haine de Vénus! O fatale colère!
Dans quels égarements l'amour jeta ma mère! (1.3)

Puisque Vénus le veut, de ce sang déplorable
Je péris la dernière et la plus misérable. (1.3)

Je reconnus Vénus et ses feux redoutables,
D'une sang qu'elle poursuit tourments inévitables. (1.3)

Ce n'est plus une ardeur dans mes veines cachée:
C'est Vénus tout entière à sa proie attachée. (1.3)

And we are even further from a mythological façon de parler when
Phèdre's awakened conscience seeks to hide in shame:

Misérable! et je vis? et je soutiens la vue
De ce sacré Soleil dont je suis descendue?

J'ai pour aïeul le père et le maître des Dieux;
Le ciel, tout l'univers est plein de mes aïeux.
Où me cacher? Fuyons dans la nuit infernale.
Mais que dis-je? Mon père y tient l'urne fatale;
Le Sort, dit-on, l'a mise en ses sévères mains:
Minos juge aux enfers tous les pâles humains. (4.6)

In *Iphigénie* the assimilation of the mythical to a historical world had involved drastic changes in the dénouement, which stays narrowly on this side of the openly supernatural. In the report of Ulysse we hear that the common soldiers claimed to have seen Diana descending to the altar in a cloud, but Ulysse is careful not to endorse this inevitable elaboration of the extraordinary by popular superstition. In *Phèdre* Racine makes no attempt to change the supernatural circumstances of Hippolyte's death. Instead he leads the spectator to an acceptance of the final events as real by making him the witness of a gradual regression from the civilized world to a world of mythical terrors. No longer past or rumour, the mythical has become present fact.

The keyword in Racine's manipulation of the audience's suspension of disbelief is the word 'monstre.' Its systematic repetition holds together the psychological theme of Phèdre's monstrous passion and the mythical realm of real monsters that are barely kept off the stage. If in the end we are not sure whether 'la fille de Minos et de Pasiphaé,' the sister of Ariane and the Minotaur, and the wife of the monster-slaying Theseus, is a real or metaphorical monster, that is precisely Racine's intention and the triumph of a strategy of ambiguity in which the safe distance of mythological metaphor is transformed into the ominous threat of a mythical present.

Racine's procedure has 'Ovidian' affinities. The transformation of Phèdre may for instance be compared to the literal transformation of Satan in *Paradise Lost*, but it is essential to remember that Phèdre's metamorphosis has nothing to do with the use of openly Ovidian traditions in mythological drama, a genre in which the supernatural was frankly accepted and afforded ample scope for the ingenious use of stage machinery. The point of Racine's use of myth is precisely that it eschews the mythological. In the story of Phaedra the heroic or historical action is unusually close to the monstrous and mythical. Racine made this borderline quality of the ancient story the pivot of his tragedy: a world relapses into the mythical terrors from which it had believed itself free.*

* Racine's strategy received an important impulse from Plutarch's *Lives*. The life of Theseus being the first in Plutarch's work, he prefaces his account with some general

It is uncertain to what extent Racine was aware of the breakthrough he achieved in correlating the evocation of the setting as mythical with the psychological interests he shared with other playwrights of his time. He says nothing about it in his preface, which is, however, a notoriously disingenuous document and the last place to look for a statement of his intentions. It is certain that Racine's audience, at least in its conscious response, did not recognize the uniqueness of *Phèdre*. After its initial failure, the play quickly established itself as the most famous and most frequently acted Racinian tragedy, but nothing in the seventeenth- or eighteenth-century criticism points to an understanding of the special role of the mythical in this play. In its response to its model as myth, *Phèdre* must therefore be considered as an isolated forerunner of an approach to Greek tragedy that became dominant only towards the end of the eighteenth and beginning of the nineteenth centuries when Goethe with his *Iphigenie auf Tauris* and Kleist with his *Penthesilea* wrote the first versions in which the mythical content of the model is consciously thematized by the modern writer as his point of departure.

remarks about the difficulty of separating history from myth in the case of a legendary ruler (I quote from North's translation): 'Like as historiographers describing the world (frende Sossius Senecio) doe of purpose referre to the uttermost partes of their mappes the farre distant regions whereof they be ignoraunt, with this note: these contries are by meanes of sandes and drowthes unnavigable, rude, full of venimous beastes, Scythian ise, and frosen seas. Even so may I (which in comparinge noble mens lives have already gone so farre into antiquitie, as the true and certaine historie could lead me) of the rest, being thinges past all proofe or chalenge, very well say: that beyonde this time all is full of suspicion and dout, being delivered us by Poets and Tragedy makers, sometimes without trueth and likelihoode, and always without certainty.'

Clearly this splendid opening passage left its traces in the first scene of *Phèdre*, where the exploits of Theseus at the margins of the known world are reviewed by the admiring Hippolytus. But the comparison of the subject matter of tragedy with areas beyond the mapmaker's knowledge may have shaped the play more pervasively and profoundly and one is tempted to think of Conrad's fascination with the early maps of Africa (the centre left white) and their influence on *Heart of Darkness*.

3

THE NEOCLASSICAL VISION
OF GREECE:
Iphigenie auf Tauris and Penthesilea

Iphigenie auf Tauris, the only eighteenth-century version of a Greek tragedy to have weathered the test of time, resembles *Phèdre* in being both the fulfilment of, and exception to, contemporary trends in the adaptation of Greek tragedies. It is a fulfilment because it embodies most eloquently the nostalgic ideal of Greece that inspired the phil-Hellenism characteristic of later eighteenth-century neoclassicism. Certain practices of eighteenth-century adaptators, notably the tendencies to mitigate the thematic harshness of the models and to observe the 'simplicity' of their structure, reveal their full significance in this play, where they cease to be authorial strategies, sometimes mechanically applied, but are motivated in terms of the characters' actions and desires. In particular the resolution of the conflict by the heroine is an embodiment of aesthetic and moral tendencies that had guided earlier writers in their adaptations.

As with *Phèdre*, the exceptional quality of the play lies in the intensity of its response to the mythical dimension of its model and in its dramatization of the mythical world as a metaphor of human passion. When in *Dichtung und Wahrheit* Goethe looked back on this play, he drew attention to the significance of the mythical past in it as 'Glieder einer ungeheuren Opposition im Hintergrund meiner Iphigenie' ('links of a tremendous opposition in the background of my Iphigenia').[1] *Iphigenie* is a journey to the 'mothers' in the course of which the terrors of a mythical world are dramatized with a ferocity for which *Phèdre* provides the only precedent. But whereas in *Phèdre* a civilized world relapses into chaos, in *Iphigenie* a world of 'sweetness and light' is wrested from chaos: the action celebrates the release from the bondage of mythical terror. The celebration of this release established the play as a chief monument of the neoclassical vision of Greece. When fifteen years after its final composition Schiller arranged the play for a public performance in Weimar, Goethe sent him a copy and in the covering letter remarked with studied off-handedness: 'Hiebei kommt die Abschrift des gräzisierenden Schauspiels. ... Ich habe hie und da hineingesehen, es ist ganz verteufelt human' ('herewith the copy of my hellenizing drama. I've looked into it here and there; it is devilishly humane').[2] Goethe's self-deprecating irony on this occasion may hide some reservation about the finality of exorcising the demons which in his later statement he acknowledged as powerful sources of the play's effect. The ambivalence of Goethe's statements points to the janus-faced nature of the play itself. In its systematic and self-conscious evocation of the world of Greek tragedy as a mythical world it looks forward to the linking of myth and tragedy that has become axiomatic in the twentieth century; its belief in the possibility of human reconciliation, presided over by Artemis and Apollo, marks it as a product of its age.

The course of this essay thus moves away from and returns to the type of understanding of Greek tragedy implicit in Racine's *Phèdre*. It traces the growing tendencies of eighteenth-century versions to civilize the brutal, and to value reconciliation over conflict, simplicity over complexity. But the versions that result from these tendencies, while polished, are bland and trivial. Goethe's insistence that simplicity and reconciliation are the fruits of a barely won struggle returns us to the threat of the mythical world dramatized in *Phèdre*. Finally, the essay moves to the massive attack made by Kleist on the precarious triumph of Goethe's play. In his *Penthesilea*, the first version of the *Bacchae*, the most openly Dionysiac of Greek tragedies, the harmonious union of Artemis and Apollo yields to the violent destruction of the Apollinian ideal in a moment of Dionysiac frenzy. Taken together, these two plays fully establish the Romantic and modern interpretation of Greek tragedy as the conflict of Apollo and Dionysus, an interpretation foreshadowed in Racine's *Phèdre* and finally named as such by Nietzsche in his *Birth of Tragedy*.

MORAL AND AESTHETIC TENDENCIES IN EIGHTEENTH-CENTURY ADAPTATIONS OF GREEK TRAGEDY

The Mitigation of Matricide in Eighteenth-Century Versions

The difficulty that the terror and violence of ancient tragedy presented to an eighteenth-century audience was very clearly put by Voltaire in his preface to *Brutus*, where he compares the sensationalism of English (ie,

Elizabethan) and Greek tragedy with the more squeamish standards of French drama and gives a catalogue of 'situations dégoutantes et horribles aux Français' that could please only if they were 'bien ménagées, representées avec art, et surtout adoucie par la charme des beaux vers':

Hippolyte, brisé par sa chute, vient compter ses blessures et pousser des cris douloureux. Philoctète tombe dans ses accès de souffrance; un sang noir coule de sa plaie. Oedipe, couvert du sang qui dégoutte encore des restes de ses yeux qu'il vient d'arracher, se plaint des dieux et des hommes. On entend les cris de Clytemnestre que son propre fils égorge; et Electre crie sur le théâtre: 'Frappez, ne l'épargnez pas, elle n'a pas épargné notre père.' Prométhée est attaché sur un rocher avec des clous qu'on lui enfonce dans l'estomac et dans les bras. Les furies répondent à l'ombre sanglante de Clytemnestre par des hurlements sans aucune articulation. Beaucoup de tragédies grecques, en un mot, sont remplies de cette terreur porté à l'excès.[3]

Matricide is the most shocking and the most challenging of these horrors not only for psychological reasons, but also because as a dramatic subject it both involved a taboo and invited imitation as the subject of one of the most famous Greek tragedies. It may be useful to glance briefly at the history of its treatment in earlier dramatic literature before dealing with the specifically eighteenth-century strategy of mitigation developed by Voltaire.

The range of tragic deeds in Greek tragedy is limited by the extreme cases of Orestes and Oedipus, the man who deliberately slays his mother, and the man who unwittingly marries her.[4] Even within the life span of the three great dramatists, tragic subjects gravitated towards the type of action exemplified by *Oedipus*: the deliberately committed deed of horror gave way to the action that was committed in ignorance and turned on recognition. The Electra plays of Euripides and Sophocles are evidence that Aeschylus' stark portrayal of the son's dilemma as he is confronted by his pleading mother was no longer possible. In Euripides' play the matricide is an event too horrible to be justified by any cause, and least of all by a divine command. Orestes and Electra plan and execute their crime in a state of progressive delusion from which they awaken to grief and despair as soon as the deed is done. In Sophocles' play an open answer to the problem of matricide is evaded because Orestes' deed is only the framework for the drama of Electra, but if we see that drama as a study in the pathology of revenge, Sophocles' play comes close to Euripides in denying the justifiability of Orestes' deed.

These two plays, then, are some evidence that by the last quarter of the fifth century matricide had become taboo, or, in Aristotle's words, *miaron*, and that its deliberate execution could not be reconciled with the concept of a tragic hero who was to engage our sympathies as someone 'like us or rather better than we are.'

If the fifth-century playwrights had difficulties with matricide, those of sixteenth- and seventeenth-century playwrights were even greater. They had inherited from Seneca and from medieval drama the role of the villain and tyrant for whom no crime was great enough. It was only fitting that a Nero should sooner or later murder his mother. But by the same token there was a narrowing in the range of what was possible for a protagonist who had justice and the audience's sympathies on his side. And since the justice of individual revenge was a questionable matter at the best of times, the idea of an avenger purposely taking his mother's life with his own hands was clearly outside the range of tragic drama.[5] Corneille with customary force and lucidity expressed the modern playwright's difficulty in reconciling the challenge of a famous ancient subject with the scruples of a modern sensibility.

Je ne saurais dissimuler une délicatesse que j'ai sur la mort de Clytemnestre, qu'Aristote nous propose pour exemple des actions qui ne doivent point être changées. Je veux bien avec lui qu'elle ne meure que de la main de son fils Oreste, mais je ne puis souffrir chez Sophocle que ce fils la poignarde de dessein formé, cependant qu'elle est à genoux devant lui et le conjure de lui laisser la vie. Je ne puis même pardonner à Electre, qui passe pour une vertueuse opprimée dans le reste de la pièce, l'inhumanité dont elle encourage son frère à ce parricide. C'est un fils qui venge son père, mais c'est sur sa mère qu'il le venge.[6]

Corneille first dealt with this challenge in *Rodogune*, where matricide is introduced as a possibility only to be rejected indignantly by virtuous sons. The play dramatizes an obscure incident from Appian's *Syrian Wars*. That in constructing a tragedy from this obscure and unpromising material Corneille had the Electra plays in mind is proved not only by numerous plot parallels but also by the fact that in his criticism of Sophocles' *Electra* he praised *Rodogune* for avoiding the faults of the ancient tragedy.

The plot of the play thoroughly observes Corneille's maxim stated in the preface to *Héraclius* that 'le sujet d'une belle tragédie doit n'être pas vraisemblable.' Demetrius, the king of Syria, having been captured by the king of Parthia, his wife Cléopatre, believing him dead, marries again, whereupon Demetrius proposes marriage to his captor's daughter, Rodogune, and sets out to conquer his former kingdom. Cléopatre, whose second husband has conveniently died in another Parthian campaign, ambushes and kills Demetrius. Rodogune is taken prisoner and treated with scrupulous but deceptive courtesy. These events precede the action proper, which begins on the day when Cléopatre will reveal to her twin sons Antiochus and Seleucus which of them is the elder and therefore the heir to the throne. It goes without saying that the sons have fallen in love with Rodogune and that each offers the other the crown in exchange for the princess. But they realize that only a king is worthy of Rodogune and that therefore crown and princess are indivisible. They are thrown into the utmost confusion when Cléopatre tells them that she will declare the murderer of Rodogune her heir: 'La mort de Rodogune en nommera l'aîné' (2.3.645). Their confusion is compounded when they take their troubles to Rodogune and are told by her that as the former fiancée of their father she is duty-bound to pursue his revenge and that, regardless of her feelings, her hand will belong to the son who has the courage to avenge his father: 'Appelez ce devoir haine, rigueur, colère; / Pour gagner Rodogune, il faut venger un père' (3.4. 1043–4).

The princes of course do not for a moment consider Rodogune's proposal. In choosing between their love and their obligation to a mother, even so wicked a mother, there can only be one path of honour. Their steadfastness becomes a source of new dangers. Revolted at her sons' disloyalty, Cléopatre now turns against them. She murders Seleucus and plans to poison Antiochus at the wedding ceremony with Rodogune. Antiochus is about to drink the poison offered to him in the wedding cup when a messenger arrives with the news that Seleucus had died, in his own ambiguous words by 'une main qui nous fut bien chère' (5.4.1643). Cléopatre accuses Rodogune of the murder, and Rodogune warns Antiochus against drinking from the wedding cup. Antiochus remains in a state of honourable irresolution that is almost fatal to him. For Cléopatre, seeing that her game is up, would rather die than not avenge herself on her son. She drinks the poison in the hope that it will not take effect until he too has drunk. A slight delay frustrates this last plan and saves the life of Antiochus. This suicide of Cléopatre is a marked departure from Appian's account, where Cléopatre is forced by Antiochus to drink the poison she had prepared for him.

Orestes parallels govern much of the action in *Rodogune*, and the possibility of exploring them and entering into a literary competition with illustrious predecessors was a major reason for Corneille's choice of his subject. The concluding tableau of the play articulates this challenge most clearly: it may be seen as a transformation of the barbarous brutality of Orestes into civilized behaviour. Antiochus has overwhelming proof – if he chooses to look at the evidence – of his mother's guilt; moreover, he has ample reason to fear for his immediate safety. To do nothing in such a situation ceases to be filial obedience and becomes a kind of heroic folly. Nonetheless, Antiochus does nothing. This modern Orestes buries his head in the sand because even to suspect his mother's actions strikes him as an act of criminal disobedience. Such loyalty is rewarded by chance (or destiny) as Cléopatre overreaches herself, and the poison takes effect in time. Her death agony is undeniable evidence of her guilt: she is dying from the poison designed for him. Finally relieved from the necessity of undertaking anything against her, Antiochus rushes to his mother's help: 'N'importe, elle est ma mère, il faut la secourir' (5.4.1810). And he remains incapable of hostile sentiments even in the face of her dying curse on him, exclaiming helplessly: 'Ah! vivez pour changer cette haine en amour' (5.4.1825).

In his criticism of Sophocles' *Electra*, Corneille proposed a different solution to the problem of matricide, which followed the Aristotelian division of actions into voluntary and involuntary and according to which Orestes kills his mother by mistake as she tries to protect Aegisthus from death. Crébillon made use of this scenario, and like Corneille, Crébillon objected not only to Orestes' action but also to the cruelty with which the Sophoclean Electra in her notorious 'strike again' encouraged her brother in the act of revenge.[7] In Crébillon's play, which owes a good deal to *Andromaque* as well as to Corneille, Electra has been pressured by Aegisthus to marry his son Itys, whom she loves but whom her honour forbids her to treat with anything but the utmost scorn. When Orestes' mentor urges her, however, to pretend to accept Itys so that the wedding ceremony will afford an opportunity to kill both father and son at the altar, she bursts out:

L'entraîner aux autels! Ah! projet qui m'accable!
Itys y périrait; Itys n'est point coupable.[8] (4.3)

This Electra is so far from being the hardened and hateful creature of Sophocles that she is unable to carry out her part in the plot and tries to keep Itys away from the altar by refusing at the last minute to marry him. The revenge succeeds without her, since Aegisthus conveniently suspects a plot and forces Orestes into premature but successful action.

Orestes has no intention of killing his mother and has even appointed a special security guard for her, but she succeeds in eluding her guard and rushes to the defence of her husband. Only after the event does Orestes learn to his horror that in the confusion of the crisis he accidentally killed her. In dealing with the relationship of son and mother, Crébillon follows Corneille's practice in *Rodogune* of sharply contrasting the son's filial virtues with the mother's hardened criminality. Orestes and even Electra are moved to pity as they see their mortally wounded mother, who alone remains unrepentant, and it is to her that Crébillon transfers Electra's harsh 'strike again':

> Je ne te revois donc, fils digne des Atrides,
> Que pour trouver la mort dans tes mains parricides?
> Jouis de tes fureurs, vois couler tout ce sang
> Dont le ciel irrité t'a formé dans mon flanc.
> Monstre que bien plutôt forma quelque Furie,
> Puisse un destin pareil payer ta barbarie!
> Frappe encor, je respire, et j'ai trop à souffrir
> De voir qui je fis naître, et qui me fait mourir.
> Achève, épargne moi ce tourment qui m'accable. (5.8)

Corneille had praised his own solution because it followed the donnée of the ancient plot 'sans que la barbarie d'Oreste nous fît horreur, comme dans Sophocle, ni que son action méritât des Furies vengeresses pour le tormenter, puisqu'il demeurerait innocent.'[9] But Crébillon tries to have it both ways. His Orestes is innocent, but so morally sensitive that he is hounded by invisible furies anyhow. He ends in madness, like the Orestes of *Andromaque*, and neatly inverts a famous line from *Phèdre* to indicate his plight:

> Du crime de ma main mon cœur n'est point complice;
> J'éprouve cependant des tourments infinis. (5.9)

Unlike Corneille and Crébillon, Voltaire in his two Electra plays, *Sémiramis* (1748) and *Oreste* (1750), aims at mitigating the opposition between mother and son.[10] Instead of turning the mother into a monster of iniquity, as Corneille had done with Cléopatre, Voltaire takes his cue from the weariness and anxiety of the Euripidean and Sophoclean Clytaemnestra figures, which he turns into outright repentance. He shifts the burden of wickedness to the Aegisthus figure, with the result that the mother's sins appear pardonable. Voltaire even uses the motif of hostility between Orestes and Aegisthus as a means of morally rehabilitating the mother, for in their struggle, in which Aegisthus appears to have the upper hand until the very end, she comes to take the side of her son in both plays.

The character of Voltaire's Sémiramis is a peculiar mixture of elements adapted from *Athalie* and the ancient Clytaemnestras.[11] Like the latter, she murdered her husband, though she never married her Aegisthus, named Assur, lest he should gain the ascendancy over her. In her resoluteness and power she resembles Athalie, and like her she has successfully ruled her country for a considerable period. The play shows her in an unusual state of weakness and vacillation, the cause of which is not, as in *Athalie*, the divinely induced dissolution of her personality but a growing spirit of repentance. The play's Orestes, Arzace, also owes something to *Athalie*: like Joas, he does not know his own identity, which is revealed to him by a High Priest who invests him with the royal insignia. Arzace's ignorance of his true identity allows Voltaire to conflate Orestes with Oedipus and to dangle incest before the eyes and ears of the audience, for Sémiramis proposes to marry Arzace. When his identity is revealed she is doubly struck with repentance and asks him to punish her for her crimes, but Arzace declares himself her loving and obedient son and argues that time and repentance have appeased the gods. It is worth quoting the climax of this scene in full to get a sense of the way in which the cruelty of the ancient story has given way to a softer view of human nature:

SEMIRAMIS:
Eh bien! ne tarde plus; remplis ta destinée;
Punis cette coupable et cette infortunée;
Etouffe dans mon sang mes détestables feux.
La nature trompée est horrible à tous deux.
Venge tous mes forfaits; venge la mort d'un père;
Reconnais-moi, mon fils, frappe, et punis ta mère.
ARZACE:
Que ce glaive plutôt épuise ici mon flanc
De ce sang malheureux formé de votre sang!
Qu'il perce de vos mains ce cœur qui vous révère,
Et qui porte d'un fils le sacré caractère!
SEMIRAMIS: *se jetant à genoux*
Ah! je fus sans pitié; sois barbare à ton tour;

Sois le fils de Ninus en m'arrachant le jour:
Frappe. Mais quoi! tes pleures se mêlent à mes larmes!
O Ninias! ô jour plein d'horreur et de charmes!...
Avant de me donner la mort que tu me dois,
De la nature encor laisse parler la voix:
Souffre au moins que les pleurs de ta coupable mère
Arrosent une main se fatale et si chère.

ARZACE:

Ah! je suis votre fils; et ce n'est pas à vous,
Quoi que vous ayez fait, d'embrasser mes genoux.
Ninias vous implore, il vous aime, il vous jure
Les plus profonds respects, et l'amour la plus pure.
C'est un nouveau suject, plus cher et plus soumis.
Le ciel est apaisé, puisqu'il vous rend un fils:
Livrez l'infâme Assur au dieu qui vous pardonne. (4.4)

The tragic dénouement arises from a coincidence of errors through which, as in *Athalie*, providence fulfils its design. Fearful that Arzace may be killed by Assur, Sémiramis seeks to protect her son, but in the father's tomb, where the final events take place, Arzace mistakes her for Assur and stabs her to death. As in Crébillon's *Electre*, the son is not immediately disabused of his error. Recognition comes to him when the dying Sémiramis appears and asks her son's revenge on the unknown 'monstre sanguinaire' that assassinated her. He recoils in horror as he realizes his error but his mother forgives him: 'J'ai reçu de tes mains la mort qui m'était due.' She dies with the sentimental words:

Songe à Sémiramis,
Ne hais point sa mémoire: ô mon fils! mon cher fils...
C'en est fait. (5.8)

In Voltaire's *Oreste*, as in Crébillon's *Electre*, Clytaemnestra is killed as she seeks to prevent Orestes from killing Aegisthus. [12] Here the accidental matricide is all the more horrible since the possibility of killing his mother had been rejected vehemently by Orestes, and since in the context of the play there are no causes that could justify or even extenuate matricide as a deliberate action. The configuration of characters in the play substantially repeats that of *Sémiramis*. Clytaemnestra is full of repentance for her crime, and in the course of the action she is driven into opposition to Aegisthus, who appears as the true criminal. In her first encounter with the disguised Orestes she believes him to be the assassin of her son, and unlike Aegisthus or the Sophoclean Clytaemnestra, she can find neither pleasure nor relief in the news of her son's death:

> Il naquit pour verser le sang qui le fit naître.
> Tel fut le sort d'Oreste, et son dessein peut-être.
> De sa mort cependant mes sens sont pénétrés. (3.6)

But Orestes, who throughout this scene has the greatest difficulty in controlling himself, nearly falls out of his role in rejecting the imputation of a matricidal intention:

> Qui? lui, madame? un fils armé contre sa mère!
> Ah! qui peut effacer ce sacré caractère?
> Il respectait son sang … peut-être il eût voulu… (3.6)

In the course of the action Orestes and Pylades are imprisoned by Aegisthus, who suspects their identity. As certainty grows, Clytaemnestra champions her son's cause. As in *Sémiramis*, the accidental death of the mother overturns the prospect of reconciliation between mother and son.

The continuity of Voltaire's treatment of matricide with seventeenth-century practice is apparent from the very fact that his versions use Corneille's scenario as a point of departure. But the motif of the mother's accidental death is put to a very different use in his plays. Corneille's objection to the ancient plays had been based on the principle of decorum, and his introduction of Clytaemnestra's accidental death had the limited purpose of removing from the ancient source what he considered to be offensively barbarous. Voltaire's Orestes plays, however, presuppose a sentimental view of human nature. The mother's accidental death does not simply make matricide 'acceptable,' but acquires a special poignancy by being the event that prevents the happy reunion and reconciliation of mother and son.

The changing uses of the motif of the mother's accidental death measure a marked shift in moral sensibility, which is corroborated by the popularity of eighteenth-century versions of ancient plays that end happily.* The eighteenth century stayed clear of *Iphigenia in Aulis* – partly no

---

* An example of thematic mitigation on the English stage is Charles Johnson's *Medaea* (1731), in which a gentle Creusa recognizes in her death a punishment for adultery and Medea kills herself rather than her children, who are adopted by the childless Aegeus. Of much greater interest and value is the *Agamemnon* by James Thomson, the author of *The Seasons* (1738). This play is perhaps the first modern version of the murder of

doubt because Racine's versions had dampened the competitive spirit of would-be imitators – but the story of Iphigenia in Tauris was enormously popular, and the version by Guymond de la Touche (1757) was one of the most frequently performed tragedies on ancient subjects at the Comédie française. Another popular play was Lemierre's *Hypermnestre* (1758), which dramatizes the fate of the one daughter of Danaus in whom love for her husband overcame the obligation of revenge. But most important in this context is Voltaire's *Mérope* – like the *Hypermnestre* a new 'version' of a lost ancient tragedy. This drama is in fact an Orestes drama in reverse, and had been so since the days of Euripides, whose lost play on

Agamemnon that is more than a translation of the Senecan and Aeschylean plays. It was not very successful, but it is a thoughtful play worthy of some attention. Thomson goes as far as he can in removing Clytaemnestra's direct responsibility for the deed. The plan for the murder arises only when Agamemnon is about to return, and it originates with Aegisthus, who does not make his intention explicit to Clytaemnestra until the fourth act. Even then Clytaemnestra is tempted to warn her husband, but, like Phèdre on a similar occasion, chooses silence at the sight of Cassandra, whom, owing to Aegisthus' slanders, she believes to be her husband's mistress. In fact Clytaemnestra had come close to a reconciliation with Agamemnon, for he succeeded in persuading her that the sacrifice of Iphigenia was demanded for the public weal. In this retrospective justification he is enthusiastically supported by Electra, who wishes that the lot of Iphigenia could have been hers. Thomson's emphasis in this scene is less on the distant deed than on the kindness and sincerity of Agamemnon as a generous monarch and a decent man. And the play's thematic centre is the opposition between Agamemnon's concept of a humane constitutional government and Aegisthus' tyrannical ambition, a conflict that involves the further opposition of trust and openness to intrigue and fraud. Thomson's major addition to the plot consists in the elaboration of Orestes' tutor into a wise counselor (Melisander), who was Clytaemnestra's good conscience and was violently transported by Aegisthus to a desert island where he lived the life of Philoctetes until Agamemnon accidentally discovered him on his return voyage, as Aeneas discovered the abandoned companion of Ulysses. His cruel exile has confirmed Melisander in his kindly vision of man as a social animal realizing himself fully in trustful co-operation with others. And indeed his sociable nature went so far that unlike Philoctetes he lived a vegetarian life, considering the birds his fellow creatures and shooting them with the greatest reluctance and only in the winter when forced by the absence of any herbs (cf. Lessing's entertaining demonstration – in the fourth chapter of *Laokoon*, of the origin of Melisander in a common mistranslation of a difficult line in *Philoctetes*).

In the play the attempt of Melisander and Agamemnon to dislodge Aegisthus from his usurped throne fails: Aegisthus' counter plot is executed more swiftly, although Melisander succeeds in rescuing young Orestes. But one senses that the defeat of the good proceeds less from conviction than from the necessity of keeping the dénouement in harmony with the tradition. In Thomson's other tragedy, *Edward and Eleanore*, a transposition of the *Alcestis* into an orientalizing setting of the crusades, the happy ending – brought about by an enlightened Sultan not unlike Mozart's Bassa Selim – is thematized as the triumph of humanity.

the subject was summarized in Hyginus (fabula 137). As in an Orestes drama, a son returns incognito to avenge his father's death. But the mother is entirely innocent, and all crime lies with the usurper who has forced her to marry him. The son's plan nearly miscarries when the mother wants to avenge herself on the man whom she believes to be her son's assassin. At the last moment an old servant recognizes the son and averts disaster, and mother and son join in the execution of the revenge. If we consider Voltaire's *Mérope* – written before *Sémiramis* and *Oreste* – as a contribution to the problems of matricide, we recognize that it fully embodies the tendencies that differentiate *Sémiramis* and *Oreste* from seventeenth-century Oresteias: the innocence of the mother and the wickedness of the usurper are absolute, and the deed of violence between mother and son is avoided. The horrors of the *Oresteia* are invoked from a safe distance, but do not come to pass.

The Return of the Simple Plot

From a formal perspective, the most important influence on eighteenth-century versions was the growing cult of simplicity as the hallmark of Greek art. Simplicity as a concept of dramatic criticism did not derive from some comprehensive aesthetic intuition, but from Aristotle's discussion of unity and from his strictures on episodic plots. From the beginning of Renaissance criticism, the lack of unity had been the chief objection of the ancients to modern literary forms, but equally the preference for double and multiple plots was one of the most deeply ingrained tendencies of modern literature. Such ancient critics as Prince Hamlet or the Canon in *Don Quixote* have the misfortune of existing in texts whose lack of unity they would have deplored.

In seventeenth-century versions of ancient plays, the episode or sub-plot filled the gap left by the disappearance of the chorus and helped to smooth the angular and indeed skeletal structure of the ancient plots deprived of their choruses. Despite consistent disapproval by the 'ancients,' the practice of introducing sub-plots was universal. The most elaborate of these were the sub-plots of Corneille, and it is not surprising that the 'ancient' Racine should have launched his disguised attack on his great rival in the preface to *Bérénice* in the name of 'cette simplicité d'action qui a été si fort du goût des Anciens.' He had long wanted to write a tragedy in this manner, he argued, and had found the opportunity in the story of Bérénice and Titus, which was 'extrêmement simple.' Horace had counseled simplicity and unity, and hardly anything happened in such great plays as *Ajax* or *Philoctetes*. 'L'*Oedipe* même, quoique tout plein de reconnaissances, est moins chargé de matière que la plus simple tragédie de nos jours.' If Plautus is to be preferred to Terence, it is because of the 'simplicité merveilleuse' of his plots, and 'combien Ménandre était-il encore plus simple, puisque Térence est obligé de prendre deux comédies de ce poète pour en faire une des siennes!' Those who think that simplicity points to lack of invention forget that 'au contraire toute l'invention consiste à faire quelque chose de rien' and that 'tout ce grand nombre d'incidents a toujours été le refuge de poètes qui ne sentaient dans leur génie ni assez d'abondance, ni assez de force pour attacher durant cinque actes leurs spectateurs par une action simple, soutenue de la violence des passions, de la beauté des sentiments et de l'élégance de l'expression.'

It should be added that, despite Racine's almost obsessive insistence on simplicity in this preface, *Bérénice* is, technically speaking, not a simple play since the fortunes of Antiochus form an erotic episode of the traditional kind, however subdued and exiguous. Racine was not to achieve 'cette simplicité d'action qui a été si fort du goût des Anciens' until *Athalie*, which was not written for the public stage. His adaptations of *Iphigénie* and *Phèdre* have very prominent sub-plots indeed, and it is entertaining to watch Louis Racine, whose loyalty to the ancients is exceeded only by his loyalty to his famous father, in the valiant attempt to reconcile the ancient doctrine of simplicity with his father's very different procedure in his two famous adaptations. In his comparison of *Iphigénie* and *Phèdre* with their Euripidean models, Louis Racine cannot bring himself to endorse the objections 'ancient' critics had raised to the episodes in his father's plays. But neither does he want to refute them, and in reporting them with studied impartiality he lends his silent approval to them.[13]

The most important champion of the simplicity of ancient drama in the early eighteenth century was the Jesuit priest Brumoy, to whose anthology *Le Théâtre des Grecs* the literary world of France (and not only of France) owed most of its familiarity with Greek tragedy.[14] Simplicity is one of the general headings under which Brumoy conducts his comparison of ancient and modern tragedy:

Rien de plus simple que les actions des Tragédies Grecques. Nul Episode, nul personnage etranger, nul ressort pour ménager ce qu'on appelle aujourd'hui des situations: non qu'il n'y en ait, & des plus interessantes. Mais le progrès tout uni de l'action les amene sans machine, & sans recherche affectée. Ce sont des fleurs qui naissent sous les pas. On ne les verse point à pleines corbeilles. Nos grands maîtres ont crû devoir prendre un tout autre procedé pour piquer leurs spectateurs, ou trop lents à se passioner, ou trop amateurs d'une grande multiplicité d'événemens. Ils ont fait ce que Terence fit des Comédies de Menandre, dont deux lui suffisoient à peine pour en faire une. Chaque personnage a souvent chés-nous son interêt & son action à part; & nous avons vû des piéces où il a été difficile de démêler l'action principale d'avec les actions subalternes, dont elle étoit composée, pour ne pas dire, accablée. Du moins n'y en a-t-il presqu' aucune, & même des plus brillantes, ou il n'y ait tourbillon dans tourbillon, événement sur événement, complication d'interêts, c'est-à dire, ce qu'on est convenu de nommer *Episodes*. Athalie est la seule qu je sçache où il n'y en ait point, non plus que de Confidens. Mais pour y suppléer l'Autheur a sous-divisé son événement, & l'a multiplié avec tant d'art qu'il a joint en quelque sort la simplicité Grecque avec toute la vivacité Françoise.[15]

If *Athalie* provokes Brumoy's special praise for its simplicity, some ancient tragedies do not escape his censure for their double actions, and it is an interesting reflection of shifting tastes that these should be the same plays that previous ages had admired for their wealth of tragic incident. Brumoy complains of the lack of unity in *Hecuba*, but concedes that this flaw does not detract from its tragic stature. He is more severe with the *Phoenissae*, where the Menoecus episode leads him into some general reflections on sub-plots:

C'est là une espece d'Episode ou d'action subordonnée à l'action Théatrale; ces Episodes sont rares chés les Grecs. Ils les croïoient contraires à l'effet de la principale action; & veritablement, quoiqu' on fasse, ils détournent l'attention du Spectateur; ils la partagent du moins; & ils ôtent à la Tragédie les charmes de cette belle simplicité, qui sçait si bien plaire par elle même. Après tout celui d'Euripide quoiqu'un peu tiré, justifieroit ceux de nos jours, si on ne les poussoit pas plus loin qu'il ne l'a fait, & si l'on ne les faisoit rouler presque toujours sur l'amour.[16]

Despite the doctrine of simplicity, erotic sub-plots continued to be fashionable throughout the eighteenth century. Chateaubrun's *Philoctète*, in which a daughter of Philoctetes shares his desert solitude and becomes the object of Neoptolemus' passion, is a particularly fatuous example and attracted the deserved scorn of Lessing in the fourth chapter of *Laokoon*. But in the important eighteenth-century versions a marked preference for simplicity is discernible. Voltaire embraced the idea of the simple action almost from the beginning. In his first play, *Oedipe*, he introduced a very perfunctory sub-plot, which he later disavowed and explained as a mere concession to what he thought was still the prevailing taste. In the preface to *Brutus* he recalls the advice that the action should above all be simple.[17] He was proud to have created in *Mérope* a tragedy without love, and the play's claim to simplicity was endorsed by Père Tournemin, who recommended it to Brumoy for its simplicity.[18] The success of *Mérope* may have influenced Guymond de La Touche who banished from his version of *Iphigenia in Tauris* the Scythian Princess Thomyris, who had complicated the action of several late seventeenth- and early eighteenth-century Iphigenias.[19] Similarly, Lemierre's *Hypermnestre*, although an eventful play, dispenses with a sub-plot.

The slightly polemical relationship of Voltaire's *Oreste* to Crébillon's *Electre* is a good illustration of the growing preference for simplicity. Crébillon's play demonstrates the tyranny of the sub-plot at its luxuriant worst. His Aegisthus has both a son, Itys, and a daughter, Iphianassa. The former loves Electra; the latter is in love with the handsome and unknown stranger who reciprocates her passion and for her sake comes to the rescue of the beleaguered Aegisthus. When he learns his true identity, his passion is of course extinguished, but Iphianassa, not knowing of his identity until the very last, is about to enlist his help in the revenge for her father's death when she learns who he is:

> Dieux! qu'est-ce que je voi?
> Sort cruel! c'en est fait; tout est perdu pour moi;
> Celui que j'implorais est Oreste. (5.6)

The action of Voltaire's *Oreste* is simple in the sense that there is no erotic sub-plot. In his version Aegisthus raises the possibility of his son's marrying Electra, but this son, whom he had sent to Epidaurus with the task of assassinating Orestes, has been killed by Orestes and his ashes are contained in the urn that is alleged to contain the ashes of Orestes. His death before we ever have a chance of seeing him on the stage is a punishment for his wickedness, but it also seems to be an implicit rebuke to Crébillon. Instead of introducing additional material Voltaire restores the intrigue of the Sophoclean *Electra* and elaborates it by assimilating it to the action of his own *Mérope*. Orestes introduces himself as his own murderer, and the recognition between brother and sister occurs at the moment when Electra attempts vainly to kill the man whom she believes to have killed her brother. Whether the plot of Voltaire's *Oreste* is really simpler than Crébillon's may be doubted, but it is evident that Voltaire thought it was, and his elaboration of the ancient intrigue is at least remarkable for its sensitivity to the Sophoclean exploration of the unforeseen suffering that Orestes' plan causes to Electra.

Towards the end of the eighteenth century, the cult of simplicity was so firmly established that it challenged even the traditional supremacy of *Oedipus Rex*. In the preface to his version of *Philoctetes*, La Harpe argued that this play rather than *Oedipus Rex* deserved to be considered the masterpiece of Greek tragedy:

Il y a dans un, il est vrai, un plus grand intérêt de curiosité; il y a dans l'autre un pathétique plus touchant. L'intrigue de l'un des deux sujets se développe et se dénoue avec beaucoup d'art: c'est peut-être un art encore plus admirable d'avoir pu soutenir la simplicité de l'autre; peut-être est-il encore plus difficile de parler toujours au cœur par l'expression des sentimens vrais, que d'attacher l'attention, et de la suspendre, pour ainsi dire, au fil des évènements. [20]

Indeed, with La Harpe the principle of simplicity has become so dominant that he even dropped from his version the scene in which the soldier-merchant comes to urge Neoptolemos' departure, for he felt that this scene was unnecessary, though not quite so superfluous as 'la querelle d'Oedipe avec Créon, qui occupe une grande place, et qui est à-la-fois sans intérêt et sans motif.' [21]

THE INTERNALIZATION OF EIGHTEENTH-CENTURY PATTERNS OF TRANSFORMATION IN *IPHIGENIE AUF TAURIS*

In *Iphigenie auf Tauris* simplicity of design and the mitigation of tragic horrors are not merely principles that guide the playwright in the act of composition: they have been transformed into moral ideals that the characters seek to realize through their actions. [22] Goethe was the first European playwright to accept without change the donnée of intentional matricide for the brutal fact it is, but he sought to dramatize the process by which a world in which such deeds are inevitable is freed from the curse of that necessity. This process is the equivalent of the strategies of displacement and mitigation by which earlier dramatists had made Orestes' matricide conform with their notions of bienséance. Similarly, the simple action of the play is not merely the result of the playwright's decision to resist the temptation of the double plot; it also results from the protagonist's explicit rejection of a course of duplicity and intrigue. Even the absence of love is thematized in the stylization of Iphigenie into the image of the Sister.

Iphigenie differs from other eighteenth-century versions of Greek tragedy not only in the internalization of their moral and aesthetic tendencies; even more important is the fact that, unlike earlier versions, the action of Goethe's play constitutes a severe test of the values it asserts. There is a well-known criticism of *Iphigenie auf Tauris* by Erich Heller, who in his essay 'Goethe and the Avoidance of Tragedy' argued that the curse on the house of Tantalus as well as the deed of Orestes are not dramatically true but are merely 'mythological names for a less spectacular kind of guilt':

The reality of evil asserts itself poetically on only three occasions, which are scattered about the play like three erratic blocks in the gentle groves of human kindness: Iphigenie's story of the horrible deeds perpetrated in her family, Orestes' account of the murder of his mother with the rage of madness that follows, and the *Parzenlied* (the song of the goddesses of Fate). For the rest – and it is all but the whole play – the inexorable hardness of the Greek myth is dissolved into the softer substance of the goodness of human nature.[23]

Heller's criticism was written not long after World War II, when, as he quotes approvingly from Karl Jaspers, 'we came face to face with experiences in which we had no inclination to read Goethe, but took up Shakespeare, or the Bible, or Aeschylus, if it was possible to read at all.'[24] From the perspective of earlier eighteenth-century drama, however, one is not likely to be struck by the dissolution of a harsh mythical world into 'the softer substance of the goodness of human nature.' On the contrary, we may feel that we have come across a play in which the mythical dimension has been evoked with unparalleled ferocity.

Goethe's *Iphigenie auf Tauris* is unique in that it explores the question that Euripides did not choose to ask in his play: How can Orestes be freed from the Furies that persecute him for the death of his mother? In his *Electra* and *Orestes*, Euripides had vehemently denied the possibility of justifying matricide or of resolving the impasse to which it led. But in *Iphigenie in Tauris* he took for granted that the fulfilment of Apollo's command to steal the statue of Artemis would absolve Orestes from persecution by the Furies. The fate of Orestes thus became the unproblematic background for the colourful sequence of events that Euripides sought to dramatize in as suspenseful a manner as possible. And eighteenth-century playwrights, while they elaborated the plot of Euripides beyond all recognition, stayed faithful to the spirit of his play in avoiding an exploration of the moral problems raised by the action. In the many eighteenth-century versions of Iphigenia's return, the crimes of Agamemnon, Clytaemnestra, and Orestes are safely buried in the past.

In Goethe's play, however, the matricide is no longer a mere donnée but is the central event in the unfinished past that threatens to engulf the present. And the first three acts of his play are less part of a traditional Iphigenia in Tauris play than a re-enactment of the events of an Electra drama. This inclusion of an Electra drama in the framework of an Iphigenia in Tauris drama is the systematic exploration of a casual association in Voltaire's *Oreste* between the two types of play.[25] The end of that play looks forward to Orestes' release from the Furies in Tauris. The mad Orestes tries to imagine a place that in barbarity will be equal to his cruel deed and seems to hear a voice that pronounces 'Tauris' to him:

> Dieux, tyrans éternels, puissance impitoyable,
> Dieux qui me punissez, qui m'avez fait coupable!
> Eh bien! quel est l'exil que vous me destinez?
> Quel est le nouveau crime où vous me condamnez?
> Parlez ... Vous prononcez le nom de la Tauride:
> J'y cours, j'y vais trouver la prêtresse homicide,
> Qui n'offre que du sang à des dieux en courroux,
> A des dieux moins cruels, moins barbares que vous. (5.9)

There is a comparable instance of mythological irony in Voltaire's play when Electra, fearing that Orestes and Pylades may be executed by Aegisthus, and trying to intercede with her mother in their behalf, asks sarcastically:

> Sommes-nous dans Argos, ou bien dans la Tauride,
> Où de meurtres sacrés une prêtresse avide
> Du sang des étrangers fait fumer son autel? (4.8)

In both statements the audience discerns a glimmer of hope since it knows the happy outcome that awaits Orestes in Tauris. There is also an interesting moment in Voltaire's play when Aegisthus announces that he will execute the man believed to be Orestes and is surprised when Clytaemnestra, far from rejoicing at this prospect, expresses her weariness at the history of violence that has been the fate of her family:

Assez de sang a coulé dans ces lieux.
Je prétends mettre un terme au cours des homicides,
A la fatalité du sang des Pélopides. (5.3)

But there is no indication that Voltaire's forward allusion to Tauris implies a dénouement in which a sense of renewal would accompany the release of Orestes and be the thematic counterpart to the weariness of Clytaemnestra. In keeping with the conventional treatment of the Iphigenie in Tauris myth, Voltaire looks forward only to the fact of liberation.

The allusion is, however, some evidence that eighteenth-century readers thought of the Iphigenia in Tauris story rather than of the trial in Athens as the counterpart of the Electra tragedy. This is not surprising in view of the low esteem in which the *Eumenides* was held. Brumoy, who had no clear concept of the thematic unity of Aeschylean trilogies, thought it a play too crude and bizarre to lose many words about.[26] But Goethe had a grasp of this unity, and it allowed him to see the thematic potential in the opposition of the plots of *Electra* and *Iphigenia in Tauris*. Although the outward events of his play follow the Euripidean source, its functional model is the final play in Aeschylus' trilogy. The events at Tauris have the significance of the trial scene in the *Eumenides*: an era of conflict and violence is brought to an end in an action that gives rise to a new order of peace and reconciliation. But as the final play in a 'trilogy,' *Iphigenie auf Tauris* must somehow include and imply the plays that precede it. The re-enactment of the Electra plot in the play's gigantic exposition, which fills most of the first three acts, is a formal feature that points to the 'trilogic' ambitions of the play. Its subject is the Orestes myth as a whole, its scope no less than that of the *Oresteia*.

The re-enactment of the events in the minds of the protagonists stays more closely to the 'inexorable hardness of the ancient myth' than any previous version had done. Goethe makes no effort to diminish either the guilt of Clytaemnestra or the responsibility of Orestes for the deliberate killing of his mother. On the contrary, Goethe emphasizes the horror of these events by integrating them into a wider cycle of crime and punishment that extends from the remotest past to the present as a gigantic emblem of unredeemed history. When Iphigenia reveals her identity to Thoas, she goes back to the ultimate ancestor of her race: 'Vernimn, ich bin aus Tantalus' Geschlecht' ('You must know that I am from the House of Tartarus.'). Tantalus is seen as a pagan equivalent to Adam and Lucifer.[27] He once inhabited a world in which gods and men lived together, but he fell like Lucifer:

Uebermut
und Untreu stürzten ihn von Jovis Tisch
Zur Schmach des alten Tartarus hinab. (323–5)

And treachery expelled him from Jove's table
To lasting shame in ancient Tartarus.

Like Adam, he bequeathed original sin to his descendants:

Zwar die gewaltge Brust und der Titanen
Kraftvolles Mark war seiner Söhn und Enkel
Gewisses Erbteil; doch es schmiedete
Der Gott um ihre Stirn ein ehern Band.
Rat, Mäßigung und Weisheit und Geduld
Verbarg er ihrem scheuen, düstern Blick:
Zur Wut ward ihnen jegliche Begier,
Und grenzenlos drang ihre Wut umher. (328–35)

Some power of that prodigious soul, some marrow
of his Titanic bones was surely passed
To sons and grandsons, but the God himself
Had forged a ring of iron about their brows.
Good counsel, moderation, wisdom, patience
Jupiter kept concealed from their dim eyes!
Their every appetite he turned to madness,
A madness without frontier or restraint!

Iphigenia's review of family history provides ample evidence for the assertion. It proves a catalogue of horrors more coherent but no less barbarous than Voltaire's catalogue of excessive horrors in Greek tragedy. Pelops won his wife by fraud and murder. His sons Atreus and Thyestes started their careers of crime by jointly murdering a half-brother from an earlier marriage of their father. Later discord set them against each other and led to the crimes that culminate in the revenge of Atreus on the sons of Thyestes, recalled in Senecan detail:

Er scheint gelassen,
Gleichgültig und versöhnt, und lockt den Bruder
Mit seinen beiden Söhnen in das Reich
Zurück, ergreift die Knaben, schlachtet sie
Und setzt die ekle, schaudervolle Speise
Dem Vater bei dem ersten Mahle vor.

Und da Thyest an seinem Fleische sich
Gesättigt, eine Wehmut ihn ergreift,
Er nach den Kindern fragt, den Tritt, die Stimme
Der Knaben an des Saales Türe schon
Zu hören glaubt, wirft Atreus grinsend
Ihm Haupt und Füße der Erschlagnen hin. (377–88)

Feigning peace,
Indifference, composure, he entices
His brother and his brother's sons together
Back to the kingdom: lays hold of the boys,
Butchers them and sets that nauseous dish
Before the father where he comes to table.
And when Thyestes has been glutted full
With his own flesh, a torpor falls upon him.
He asks to see his children, seems to hear
The footsteps and the voices of his sons
Approach the hall. Then Atreus, leering, tosses
The slaughtered feet and heads towards their father.

The historical review is continued when Pylades, pretending in the best Odyssean manner to be a Cretan adventurer, tells Iphigenia about the fall of Troy and the death of Agamemnon. Pylades stresses the active participation of Clytaemnestra in the crime, thus reversing the tendency to make her a weak woman seduced by Aegisthus:

Am Tage seiner Ankunft, da der König,
Vom Bad erquickt und ruhig, sein Gewand
Aus der Gemahlin Hand verlangend, stieg,
Warf die Verderbliche ein faltenreich
Und künstlich sich verwirrendes Gewebe
Ihm auf die Schultern, um das edle Haupt;
Und da er wie von einem Netze sich
Vergebens zu entwickeln strebte, schlug
Aegisth ihn, der Verräter, und verhüllt
Ging zu den Toten dieser große Fürst. (891–900)

The day that he returned to Greece, the king
Rose from his bath refreshed and unsuspecting.
He begged his wife to bring his robe herself.
Then she, insurged with quickening infamy,

Threw the pernicious tangles of a net
About his shoulders, round his royal head.
And as he sought in vain to free himself
Like some trapped animal, Aegisthus struck!
The traitor struck! And mighty Agamemnon
Was sent ingloriously to join the dead.

The re-enactment of the matricide is reserved for the encounter between
Orestes and Iphigenia. In a previous scene he had described himself as
an accursed man, chosen by the gods to be his mother's 'butcher.' His
vision is one of determinism and despair, returning again and again to
the trauma of the past. His account of it to Iphigenia stays close to the
classical sources. Electra is restored in her role as the spirit of revenge
who urges him on to his deed:

Mit ihrer Feuerzunge schilderte
Sie jeden Umstand der verruchten Tat,
Ihr knechtisch elend durchgebrachtes Leben.
Den Uebermut der glücklichen Verräter
Und die Gefahren, die nun der Geschwister
Von einer stiefgewordnen Mutter warteten. –
Hier drang sie jenen alten Dolch ihm auf,
Der schon in Tantals Hause grimmig wütete,
Und Klytämnestra fiel durch Sohnes Hand. (1030–8)

She painted for him with a tongue of fire
Each circumstance of their atrocious act –
The wretched servile life that had been hers,
The arrogance which victory had sired
Within the traitors! All the threats of danger
The unnatural mother raised about her young!
She pressed into his hand the ancient dagger
Already cursed with their ancestral blood!
Orestes slew his mother, Clytemnestra.

In the fit of madness precipitated by his confession, Orestes returns once
again, and more explicitly to the crime:

Du siehst mich mit Erbarmen an? Laß ab!
Mit solchen Blicken suchte Klytämnestra
Sich einen Weg nach ihres Sohnes Herzen;

Doch sein geschwungner Arm traf ihre Brust.
Die Mutter fiel! (1239–43)

Why turn such piteous eyes on me? Do not!
For Clytemnestra sought to find a way
That breached her own son's heart with such a look!
Yet still he raised his arm and smote her breast.
He slew his mother!

Voltaire's Orestes had responded enthusiastically to the voice that prompted him to seek 'la prêtresse homicide' in Tauris. Goethe explores this external connection between Argos and Tauris. His Orestes sees his crimes as part of a cycle that cannot be broken and will come to an end only if there is nothing left to destroy. Consequently he interprets the fate that awaits him as the fitting conclusion to the house of Tantalus:

Im Kreis geschlossen tretet an, ihr Furien,
Und wohnet dem willkommnen Schauspiel bei,
Dem letzten, gräßlichsten, das ihr bereitet!
Nicht Haß und Rache schärfen ihren Dolch;
Die liebevolle Schwester wird zur Tat
Gezwungen. Weine nicht! Du hast nicht Schuld.
Seit meinen ersten Jahren hab ich nichts
Geliebt, wie ich dich lieben könnte, Schwester.
Ja, schwinge diesen Stahl, verschone nicht,
Zerreiße diesen Busen und eröffne
Den Strömen, die hier sieden, einen Weg! (1244–54)

You Furies enter! Gather close around us!
And be spectators of a welcome show!
It is the last, most hideous, you shall see!
For neither Hate nor Vengeance whet their knives.
No! A sister, filled with love, is driven
To enact the deed. No tears! No guilt is yours!
Even in childhood I have never loved
As I, perhaps, might come to love you, sister.
Yes! Raise your sword! Let pity have no quarter!
Rip up my bosom! Open up the streams
Of seething torment! Let them flow at last!

In Euripides and in the eighteenth-century versions, the release of Orestes from the Furies is a function of his rescue, which hinges on the recognition that is brought about by chance. In Goethe's play Orestes' release from madness is the central theme of the first half, and it results not from the coincidence of recognition, but from an ethically significant action. The gentle voice of Iphigenia has other words for the suffering stranger than Elektra 'mit ihrer Feuerzunge.' Confronted with Iphigenia's compassion, Orestes abandons the disguise that Pylades had prudently designed for him:

Ich kann nicht leiden, daß du große Seele
Mit einem falschen Wort betrogen werdest.
Ein lügenhaft Gewebe knüpf ein Fremder
Dem Fremden, sinnreich und der List gewohnt,
Zur Falle vor die Füße; zwischen uns
Sei Wahrheit! (1076–81)

I cannot let so pure a soul as yours
Endure the hollow cunning of evasion.
Let strangers weave a web of lies between them,
Let them ensnare each other's feet with tricks
And wonted treachery. Between us two
Let there be Truth!

Orestes' release from the world of mythical bondage follows ultimately from this decision. It is a demonstration of the healing power of radical openness in human relations. Not the goddess, but the human sympathy of the sister, breaks the iron chains of the curse:

Es löset sich der Fluch, mir sagt's das Herz.
Die Eumeniden ziehn, ich höre sie,
Zum Tartarus, und schlagen hinter sich
Die ehrnen Tore fernabdonnernd zu.
Die Erde dampft erquickenden Geruch
Und ladet mich auf ihren Flächen ein,
Nach Lebensfreud und großer Tat zu jagen. (1358–64)

　　　　　　　　Now my heart
Assures me that the curse has spent itself.
The Eumenides draw back. I hear them go,
And Tartarus has closed its brazen gates
Behind them with a roar of distant thunder.
The earth gives out the odours of new life,
Inviting me to walk upon her plains
In search of happiness and living glory.

Orestes' release from madness occurs prior to and quite independently of his rescue, but the rescue is affected by the manner of the release. For the divine command to steal the image of the goddess and the need to escape in secrecy involve Iphigenia in a moral dilemma. She had preserved herself in the saintly purity of her office, hoping that she could keep' [her] hand unstained, [her] heart/Immaculate, and thus redeem the house/So deeply steeped in evil' (1701–2). This hope was partly fulfilled in the encounter with the brother, and in his sudden and complete release from madness the healing power of her values had received a striking confirmation. Yet Pylades' escape plan – the Euripidean intrigue – would compromise those values, since it is based on deception and secrecy rather than openness and truthfulness. This dilemma could not arise in the Euripidean play, which is premised on the opposition of Greeks and barbarians. The use of fraud to protect oneself and one's friends from barbarous enemies was not problematical at all. But in Goethe's play the opposition of Greeks and barbarians is suspended. Iphigenia herself brought to the formerly barbarian country a humanitarian gospel that was gratefully received because it appealed to fundamental values of human nature. And as the fulfilment of her most ardent wish seems close at hand, Iphigenia recognizes that the Greece of her imagination is more of a moral ideal than a real place, and that she cannot return to the place without destroying the ideal if she leaves Tauris by fraud.

The scruples of Iphigenia are given expression in the scene with Pylades, who accuses her of trying to apply in the real world an uncompromising morality that can flourish only in the purity of the temple. But Iphigenia does not trust the pragmatism that he has learned from Odysseus, his great model, and the ultimate ground of this distrust appears when Pylades, ignorant of the wider implications of the phrase, speaks of the 'ehrne Hand der Not.' For the iron hand of necessity – Milton's 'necessity, the tyrant's plea' – was precisely the curse that had condemned the house of Tantalus to its violent existence. If they were still subject to it, was not the release of Orestes an illusion? Iphigenia sees through the pragmatism of Pylades to the 'original sin,' which it disguises. And in the soliloquy that follows the scene with Pylades, she conjures up once more the nightmare vision of the mythical underworld. The crisis of Orestes had involved a descent to the underworld, but his exhausted vision was curiously peaceful and did indeed foreshadow his release. Orestes was also spared the sight of the ultimate cause of evil: he did not see Tantalus and remarked on this fact. But Iphigenia's evocation

of the mythical underworld in the *Parzenlied* concludes with the vision of
Tantalus-Adam, unredeemed man, despairing of his progeny:

> So sangen die Parzen;
> Es horcht der Verbannte
> In nächtlichen Höhlen,
> Der Alte, die Lieder,
> Denkt Kinder und Enkel
> Und schüttelt das Haupt. (1761–6)

> Thus sang the dread sisters:
> Below them the exile,
> The gnarled and benighted,
> Takes heed of their singing.
> He thinks of his children
> And shakes his sad locks.

Ipigenia's resolution of her dilemma is to tell the truth. In the speech
with which she prefaces her disclosure of the plot against Thoas, she calls
her decision 'ein kühnes Unternehmen,' and she contrasts it with the
actions to which traditional morality has given heroic stature. Her one
example of such an action, a secret nocturnal attack on the enemies'
camp, recalls the adventure of Diomedes and Odysseus in *Iliad* 10 and
serves further to define and expose the pragmatism of Pylades. For if
Pylades chose Odysseus as the model of prudent conduct and a heroic
image of *fortitudo et sapientia*, Iphigenia sees fraud and violence as the
basis of his actions. To those she opposes trust, non-violence, and
truthfulness. Her decision is bold because it involves the application of
values that have only been privately tested to the world of public affairs.
Orestes had been truthful with Iphigenia, but his action had involved no
risk. The mutual loyalty of fellow Greeks had created a climate in which
prudent disguise was an obstacle to a fully human relationship. Thus
Orestes' oppenness occurs in response to a relationship which it
confirms. Iphigenia, on the other hand, acts in the expectation that her
truthfulness will transform a relationship of hostility into one of
friendship.

Because Iphigenia's action involves a rejection of the Euripidean intrigue, it is 'simple' in a double sense. The plot of Goethe's play satisfies
the aesthetic requirement of simplicity by making an act of childlike
truthfulness the cause of the dénouement. The playwright's rejection of
intrigue and sub-plot as aesthetic devices is achieved through the re-

presentation of an action whose moral significance is the triumph of an ethics of simplicity over a world of deception. This rejection of the Euripidean intrigue involves a return to another classical model, which is significantly enough Sophocles' *Philoctetes*, the play admired by eighteenth-century critics precisely for its coincidence of moral and aesthetic simplicity.[28] The *Philoctetes* provided Goethe with a model for both the impasse towards which the action moves and for its resolution. In that play Neoptolemos is persuaded by the unscrupulous Odysseus to obtain the bow of Philoctetes by fraud, and Odysseus justifies his course of action by reference to the benefits that will accrue to the Greeks and indeed to Philoctetes himself. Confronted with the suffering humanity of Philoctetes and with the trust that the latter immediately put in him as the son of Achilles, Neoptolemos cannot maintain a part that goes against his own nature. He tells Philoctetes the truth. Like Neoptolemos, Iphigenia is persuaded by an Odysseus figure to practise deception for a just cause, and like him, she consents only as long as she is not faced with the concrete human consequences of her action, but she cannot maintain her deception in the face of the human reality she is asked to betray. In Goethe's play it is in fact the apparent necessity for such a betrayal which impresses upon Iphigenia the reality of the human ties that she had developed in Tauris and had long overlooked in her nostalgic desire for Greece:

> Und wie den Klippen einer wüsten Insel
> Der Schiffer gern den Rücken wendet: so
> Lag Tauris hinter mir. Nun hat die Stimme
> Des treuen Manns mich wieder aufgeweckt,
> Daß ich auch Menschen hier verlasse, mich
> Erinnert. Doppelt wird mir der Betrug
> Verhaßt. (1520–6)

> And as a sailor gladly turns his back
> Upon the cliffs of a deserted island,
> I turned my back on Tauris. Now the voice
> Of faithful Arkas rouses me again
> To see that I forsake humanity
> Not emptiness. Deception doubles then
> Its hideous impact!

In the Sophoclean play Neoptolemos' honesty fails to change Philoctetes' mind. The divine intervention of Heracles is needed to break the deadlock. But the gods so often invoked in Goethe's play are only images of human perfection. Thus the *deus ex machina* of the *Philoctetes* is internalized into the voice of humanity that speaks to Thoas through Iphigenia and brings about the final reconciliation.

It is tempting to derive Iphigenia's moment of truth not only from the truthfulness of Neoptolemos but also from the disavowals of Phèdre, for the moral crisis of Goethe's play offers a curiously precise counterpoint to that of Racine's.[29] Phèdre becomes a full accessory to the schemes of Oenone when she does not carry out her resolution to tell Thésée the truth. Shortly after this scene, her repentance leads to the vision of Minos judging the dead. Iphigenia's revulsion at the prospect of becoming the accomplice of Pylades leads to a vision of the damned Tantalus, from which follows the decision to tell the truth. Thus Phèdre's silence before Thésée and Iphigenia's speech before Thoas are structurally equivalent moments, and the reversal of significance is mirrored in the fact that one leads to, whereas the other proceeds from, a vision of ultimate doom. These visions are displaced forms respectively of the last judgement and the harrowing of hell. Like Adam in the Garden, or Marlowe's Faustus in his last moments, Phèdre is the sinful soul vainly seeking to hide itself from the call of judgement. Iphigenia's vision of Tantalus on the other hand is unmistakeably modeled on the typological contrast of Christ and Adam as it appears in Romans 5:12–21, and it identifies her mission as a secular version of Christ's redemption.

Phèdre may or may not have influenced *Iphigenie auf Tauris*, but the comparison gives us at least another perspective on the very different directions in which the two plays pursue a very similar response to the mythical dimension of Greek tragedy. And in so doing, it allows us to get a clearer sense of the unease with which readers have often responded to the ending of Goethe's play. To see Iphigenia as a secular redeemer protects the play from misinterpretation as the embodiment of a passive humanitarianism. Iphigenia's achievement appears on the contrary as an act of great daring born from suffering. Yet the comparison with the redemptive sufferings of Christ forces us to ask in what sense Iphigenia's act could be called sacrificial. What is the price she pays to make 'redemption' possible? And if she does not pay a price, is such redemption credible?

The story of Iphigenia is, like that of Abraham and Isaac, the story of the replacement of one form of sacrifice by another. Because the hind and the ram replace the human victim, sacrifice becomes a ritual that no longer involves suffering and loss. The formal survival of the 'sacrifice' points to its substantive disappearance. The Christian interpretation of the myth re-establishes the correlation between reconciliation and suffering by seeing in the ram a foreshadowing of Christ. Abraham and his race are freed from the necessity of sacrifice only because the 'price' of redemption is paid by someone else. In the crucifixion the violent conjunction of redemption and sacrifice appears in its most horrifying form. Goethe's play reinterprets that interpretation. By once more denying the necessity of the 'price' of the sacrifice it restores the original significance of the myth. The fact of this return to the original structure and significance of the myth of the 'replaced' sacrifice points to the conclusion that disagreements about the credibility of Iphigenia's act are in principle irreconcilable. The myths of Iphigenia and Isaac in their simplest form assert the possibility of reconciliation without loss, of redemption without a price. The age and universality of the myths establish this assertion as a permanent possiblity. It is in the very nature of such an assertion that it will not be endorsed by all people, let alone at all times. The story of Hippolytus, sacrificed to the passion of Phaedra and the anger of a capricious deity, may speak to us with greater force. But a reflection on Goethe's return to his story in its simplest form should persuade us that the problematic nature of credibility in this play is not due to some deeply-rooted failure in the poet's sensibility, but to the nature of the assertion itself, in whatever form it may appear.

THE FALL OF AN IDEAL: KLEIST'S *PENTHESILEA*

Eighteenth-century critics associated ancient simplicity so closely with the absence of love that in practice the ideal of the simple tragedy was indistinguishable from that of the *tragédie sans l'amour*. In this regard, too, *Iphigenie auf Tauris* thematizes the dramaturgical practices of its day, and it does so through the significance it attaches to the status of Iphigenia as Sister. The dénouement of Goethe's play turns on the removal of a misunderstanding. Orestes had come to Tauris because Apollo had promised release from his suffering if he obtained the 'image of his sister.' At first Orestes takes Apollo's promise to mean – as it does in Euripides' play – that he should by fraud or violence get possession of the cult statute of Artemis. But he learns that the phrase refers to his own sister and that her 'image' is the world of values embodied in and realized through her actions. The incarnation of the values of truthfulness, gentleness, and charity in a woman is a subject of reflection for the play's protagonist. In her deliberative monologue in Act v, Iphigenia

meditates on her status as a female hero and asks: 'Hat denn zur un-
erhörten Tat der Mann allein das Recht?' ('Has man alone the right to
unimagined valour?') But the protagonist's reflection is not sufficiently
specific: Iphigenia embodies the values of the play not simply as woman,
but more specifically as sister, and the play's paradigmatic human relationship becomes that of brother and sister. The absence of an erotic
interest becomes itself a theme of the play, which in the relationship of
brother and sister offers an alternative to sexually based relationships:
Orestes is released from the Furies and restored to human freedom and
dignity when he experiences woman as Sister.

This thematization of the formal ideal of the *tragédie sans l'amour*
appears to have been rooted deeply in Goethe's personality. Richard
Friedenthal has drawn attention to Goethe's 'abbesses,' the sexless
women with spiritual leanings who haunted his life and works and for
whom his own sister Cornelia may have been the biographical prototype.[30] Though biographically rooted, the theme of the Sister and Saint
was important in the official history of the play as a chief monument to
the neoclassical vision. *Iphigenie auf Tauris* was the play chosen for the
opening of the new Schauspielhaus in Berlin in 1821; in 1825 a lavish
edition was published to commemorate Goethe's fiftieth anniversary in
the service of the Duke of Weimar, and it was in a copy of this edition,
presented to an actor who had distinguished himself in the part of
Orestes, that Goethe, forgetting both his ironic misgivings and his sense
of the 'tremendous opposition,' enclosed the little poem with the fatal
lines that were to govern the interpretation of the play in the theatres and
schools of the German bourgeoisie: 'Alle irdischen Gebrechen / sühnet
reine Menschlichkeit.' ('Pure humanity expiates all mortal failings.')[31]
The canonization of Iphigenie as the patron saint of 'reine Menschlichkeit' even produced an appropriate icon: copies of Feuerbach's
picture of Iphigenia at the shore, 'das Land der Griechen mit der Seele
suchend' ('her soul longing for Greece'), hung on countless nine-
teenth-century walls.

Interpreted in the pale light of pure humanity, *Iphigenie* had some
singularly feeble literary offspring, but the play was far more productive
as a challenge to writers who, perhaps irritated by its canonization,
questioned its premises and solutions.[32] Hofmannsthal's challenge in
his *Elektra* is particularly well documented. Inspired by Max Reinhardt's
dissatisfaction with the 'plaster cast' character of existing versions of
Greek tragedy, he tried his own hand at a version, and in choosing the
tragedy of Electra he had Goethe's play especially in mind: 'Mein Aus-

gangspunkt war der Elektra-charakter, das erinnere ich mich ganz genau. Ich las die sophokleische einmal im Garten und im Wald, im Herbst 1901. Die Zeile aus der "Iphigenie" fiel mir ein, wo es heisst: "Elektra mit ihrer Feuerzunge," und im Spazierengehen phantasierte ich über die Figur Elektra, nicht ohne eine gewisse Lust im Gegensatz zu der "verteufelt humanen" Atmosphäre der Iphigenie.'[33] (My point of departure was the character of Electra; I remember it very well. I was reading the Sophoclean play in the garden and in the forest, in the autumn of 1901. I remembered the line from *Iphigenia*, where it says: 'Electra with her fiery tongue,' and as I was walking I phantasized about the figure of Electra, not without a certain pleasure in the contrast to the 'devilishly humane' atmosphere of *Iphigenia*.) Hofmannsthal's challenge responds specifically to the association of humanity with sexlessness: the Mycenaean palace of his setting, conceived in exotic and orientalizing terms, is metaphorically associated with a gigantic cave that is Clytaemnestra's womb, and on this stage the 'bed-less' heroine acts out her frustrated sexuality in manifold ways that include even a lesbian attack on her sister.[34]

In writing an 'anti-Iphigenie' that dramatizes the dissolution of the personality as a sexual tragedy, Hofmannsthal had been anticipated by Heinrich von Kleist, in whose *Penthesilea* the tremendous opposition that is morally and aesthetically controlled in Goethe's play wins the upper hand. *Penthesilea* is the first modern version of the *Bacchae* – a play treated previously with indifference or contempt; it is also the first play in which the Dionysiac substratum of Greek tragedy is identified as such and shown in its full destructive force.[35] As a critical and indeed despairing answer to *Iphigenie auf Tauris*, *Penthesilea* draws our attention to that aspect of Goethe's play which was ignored in its canonization.

Penthesilea is not as explicitly linked to *Iphigenie auf Tauris* by external evidence as is Hofmannsthal's *Elektra*, but there is some biographical connection. Early in 1808 Kleist sent Goethe a copy of the initial issue of *Phoebus*, a literary magazine of which he was co-editor. The issue included substantial excerpts from *Penthesilea*, linked by explanatory summaries, and Kleist drew Goethe's attention to the play, arguing that despite its extremeity it had an inner logic and adding that it was not written for the popular stage. Goethe replied laconically and unsympathetically: 'Mit der Penthesilea kann ich mich noch nicht befreunden' ('With your Penthesilea I cannot make friends yet'), and he proceeded to lecture the young dramatist on the folly of ignoring the conditions of the contemporary stage.[36] There is enough in *Penthesilea* to make one look forward to Kleist's suicide three years later, and Goethe's coolness towards the play may well derive from the fact that he saw in it a terrifying response to the hidden centre of vitality in his own play. He may have remembered the psychological terrors that had been objectified in the madness of Orest; he may also have remembered that the control over the mythical world was a much more precarious achievement than the form of the play's final version suggests.[37] This is, of course, pure speculation, but the biographical links between Kleist and Goethe assume some interest in view of the remarkably systematic network of correspondences by which Kleist's play answers to, and destroys, the vision of Greece embodied in *Iphigenie auf Tauris*. To the Apollinian vision of Goethe's play Kleist opposed a tragedy that was based on the most openly Dionysiac of ancient tragedies, revealing in his response to the *Bacchae* the same intuitive grasp of the thematic centre of his model that had distinguished his interpretation of *Oedipus Rex* in *Der zerbrochene Krug*. And just as in his comedy Kleist anticipated the derivation of modern analytical drama from *Oedipus Rex*, so his identification of Goethe's tremendous opposition as the Dionysiac force anticipated the revaluation of ancient myth and tragedy that twentieth-century writers, following Nietzsche's lead in *The Birth of Tragedy*, have claimed as peculiarly their own.

The action of Kleist's tragedy is derived from a short passage in Ovid's *Metamorphoses*, where the narrator interrupts his account of the death of Achilles to express his indignation at the triumph of the cowardly Paris and states that Achilles would have died more gloriously at the hands of Penthesilea (12.610–11). The inspiration for modeling a Penthesilea-Achilles drama on the *Bacchae* may well be due to the quite prosaic circumstance that in the popular mythological dictionary by Hederich, which Kleist is known to have used, Pentheus and Penthesilea are adjacent entries.[38] A more important cause is the fact that both figures are by their names 'sufferers.' Kleist's play, however, differs in fundamental respects from the traditions regarding both Pentheus and Penthesilea. The story is briefly summarized: Penthesilea has led her Amazons to Troy on one of their annual campaigns in which they take prisoners to serve them as temporary husbands. In her first skirmish she encounters Achilles and falls in love with him. But the code of her tribe, fully internalized in her immense pride, forbids any relationship with a man she has not conquered in battle. When Achilles defeats her, despair and rage drive her into madness. But Achilles, who loves her in his own more light-hearted way and reckons that the reality of a sexual conquest is worth the semblance of a military defeat, challenges her to a second duel in which he intends to lose, believing Penthesilea incapable of harming him. But the mad Penthesilea attacks him with all her forces, including dogs and elephants, and after fatally wounding him with an arrow, she joins her dogs in tearing his body apart. She returns to her camp in the grim parody of a triumphal procession, and having regained her senses, dies.

The action of the play unfolds in a virtually unbroken sequence of scenes and does not take more time than its representation. It opens with a vivid account by Odysseus of the confusion caused by the Amazons' indiscriminate attacks on Greeks and Trojans alike. He describes how the first sight of Achilles put Penthesilea into a state of ecstasy from which she awoke to pursue him with increased ferocity. Through messengers and eyewitnesses we then follow her wild pursuit of Achilles, from which he escapes almost miraculously, arriving finally on stage only to prepare immediately for a return to battle, aroused by the vision of a sexual and military triumph. As the Greeks leave, the Amazons occupy the site. Penthesilea is acclaimed by her followers and is urged to call off the campaign, since its objective, the requisite number of prisoners, has been obtained. But, like Achilles, she is determined to see her opponent humiliated at her feet, and scornfully rejects such advice. As they prepare for battle again, a messenger arrives with the news of Achilles' approach. A lyrical scene follows, in which the High Priestess of the Amazons supervises young girls who are gathering roses for the feast of roses, the traditional wedding celebration of the Amazons with their prisoner husbands. Their peaceful activity is rudely interrupted by reports of the nearby battle in which Penthesilea is decisively defeated but rescued by her followers, who bring her on stage in a state of utter distraction. Alternating uncontrollably between states of tenderness and violence, she lapses into a state of madness, in which she thinks of herself as piling up mountains and ascending to the sun, who merges with Achilles in her diseased imagination. Then she falls unconscious. A surprise attack by the Greeks puts Penthesilea and her immediate entourage temporarily into the hands of Achilles. Fearing for Penthesilea's reason, her friend Prothoe, following a sudden impulse, succeeds in persuading Achilles to pretend he is her prisoner in a military as well as in a sexual sense. Penthesilea thus awakes to find herself in a false setting that allows her to discard as a dream the memory of her defeat. On the basis of this delusion alone the love of Achilles and Penthesilea is allowed to blossom for a short while. But the peaceful interlude is soon brought to an end by the Amazons, who, although decisively routed only a few minutes before, attack again and liberate their queen. Under the pressure of events Achilles reveals the truth to Penthesilea and offers to make her his queen, but refuses her repeated request that he follow her to her capital. As the victorious Amazons swarm across the stage, Achilles is forced to flee.

For Penthesilea, the awakening from delusion brings grief, shame, desire for revenge, and renewed madness which is precipitated by the arrival of Achilles' messenger with his mock challenge. She summons her cavalry, sickle chariots, elephants, and dogs to accompany her in her final battle. Against this orientalizing background of madness and violence, the Achilles who in the following scene expresses his light-hearted belief that Penthesilea will not hurt him, appears in an ironic and pathetic light. The dénouement of the tragedy closely follows the *Bacchae*. Achilles' death is told by a messenger who reports how Achilles, realizing his error too late, like Pentheus hid in a pine tree and was shot in the neck with an arrow by Penthesilea, who, like Agave, no longer aware of her or of his identity, joined her hounds in tearing him to pieces. Agave is also the model for Penthesilea's mad triumph and slow awakening, but the manner of her death – possibly a variation on Othello's suicide – is Kleist's own invention.

The plot of *Penthesilea* has manifest weaknesses. The see-sawing of the battle, however appropriate it may be as a metaphor for this war of the sexes, follows no other logic than the convenience of the playwright, whose arbitrary manipulation of events is particularly apparent in the two turns that bring about and abruptly conclude the crucial interval of delusion during which Achilles and Penthesilea meet peacefully as lovers. But *Penthesilea* is not a play in which, as in *Phèdre*, the understanding of the full meaning requires or is even much helped by an analysis of events in their sequence. *Penthesilea* follows its Greek model in dramatizing the extreme fluctuations of a force that defies reason and causality. Therefore both plays rely for their coherence less on the temporal structure of a plot than on a pattern of metaphors designed to express extreme opposition and unmediated transitions.

Like the *Hippolytus*, the *Bacchae* dramatizes the revenge of a god on a mortal. In both plays the god is an irresistible natural force that crushes individual opposition to it; both plays are, in modern terms, studies in the futility of repression. But there is a marked difference between the two plays in the relationship of plot to thematic pattern. In the *Hippolytus*, as in practically all other Greek tragedies, the primacy of the concrete action is unchallenged; the spectator witnesses the unfolding of a particular chain of tragic events. In the *Bacchae*, on the other hand, the individual fate of Pentheus is only an example, if an important one, of the strange power of Dionysus. What the spectator witnesses in the *Bacchae* is less the fate of Pentheus than the terrifying ambivalence of the God Dionysus, manifested in a number of related incidents. The thematic pattern takes precedence over the plot.

The ambivalence of Dionysus is the point of the two messenger reports in the play. The messenger who reports the celebration of the maenads describes their peaceful rites in which they appear to achieve a complete and oblivious fellowship with the forces of nature. But as soon as they notice the intruding spy, their behaviour suddenly changes to the utmost ferocity, and in their pursuit of the intruder they kill with apparently supernatural force whatever crosses their path. The same oblivion that blesses their peace curses their violence: when they are disturbed a second time, the ill-fated intruder is Pentheus, whom his mother, far from recognizing, is the first to attack and tear to pieces.

The abrupt changes in the mood of the maenads are triggered both times by the discovery of a spy, but it is hardly the play's intention to set forth a harsh if intelligible system of retributive justice. The destructive violence of the maenads transcends its specific causes and occasions; it is an essential attribute of this irrational god and reflects the ambivalence of his nature. Although Euripides admirably succeeded in tracing the causes of Pentheus' tragedy and the steps that lead to this ruin, his greater objective in the play was to represent the pattern of unpredictable and abrupt alternations in the manifestations of Dionysus.

Kleist's construction of an equivalent pattern proceeds from an initially narrower definition of the Dionysiac force as sexual passion. If the blueprint for his design is derived from the *Bacchae*, much of the building material is furnished by traditional paradoxes of love poetry. Chief of these is the metaphorical identification of love with war, familiar from Ovidian poetry and from the mythographical tradition of Venus and Mars. Kleist's habitual way with established metaphors is to squeeze surprising results from them by taking them literally. Thus the plot of *Penthesilea* is premised on a real war between the sexes, and the history which Kleist invented for his Amazones by using elements from the myth of the Danaids reveals that the events of the plot are only one battle in a permanent war.

Sexual relations appear in the play primarily as acts of violent conflict and humiliation. Achilles seems incapable of distinguishing between military and sexual conquests when he vows not to cease fighting

Als bis ich sie zu meiner Braut gemacht,
Und sie, die Stirn bekränzt mit Todeswunden,
Kann durch die Straßen häuptlings mit mir schleifen. (613–15)

Until I first have had my sport with her,
And then, her brow adorned with bleeding gashes,
Shall drag her by the feet behind my car.

When after Penthesilea's capture Prothoe asks him what he intends to do with her, he replies that he will do to her what he did to Hector, and when Prothoe is struck with horror, he suddenly changes his tack and claims that he loves her and wants to make her his queen. On both occasions, gentleness and violence co-exist, and the point of the lack of any connection seems to be that the speaker is incapable of distinguishing between them.

In Penthesilea's response to what she calls 'meiner Seele Donnersturz' violence and tenderness co-exist in a similarly unstable union. Her first impulse is to humiliate the opponent who has threatened her sense of self:

Ich will zu meiner Füße Staub ihn sehen,
den Uebermütigen, der mir an diesem
Glorwürdgen Schlachtentag, wie keiner noch,
Das kriegerische Hochgefühl verwirrt. (638–41)

I long to see him grov'lling at my feet,
This haughty man, who in this glorious
And gentle field of arms, as no man yet,
Sows strange confusion in my warlike heart.

But her confusion forces violence into the service of tenderness in an ironically mistaken vision of the outcome of her passion:

Ich nur, ich weiß den Göttersohn zu fällen.
Hier dieses Eisen soll, Gefährtinnen,
Soll mit der sanftesten Umarmung ihn
(Weil ich mit Eisen ihn umarmen muß!)
An meinen Busen schmerzlos niederziehn. (856–60)

'Tis I alone know how to fell this man.
These mailèd arms, dear friends, shall draw him down
(Since thus in suits of mail it must be done!)

Into the tenderest of love's embraces
And press him all unscath'd against my breast.

In portraying the gentle aspect of love Kleist transformed another traditional metaphor into literal truth. The memories and anticipations of the feast of roses – for which there is no precedent in the Penthesilea myth – are the structural equivalent of the chorus' celebrations of the peaceful Dionysus in the *Bacchae*. War and the feast of roses mark the opposite poles of love, but their opposition differs substantially from the ambivalence of Dionysus. The two faces of Dionysus are equally real manifestations of the same natural force, but the two faces of love are related to one another as false semblance and underlying reality. The rose metaphor itself points to that relationship, for roses have thorns, and their colour is that of blood, as Kleist reminds us repeatedly and most insistently in a dubiously tasteful reminiscence of Christian inconography when Penthesilea contemplates the body of the dead Achilles:

> Ach, diese blutgen Rosen!
> Ach, dieser Kranz von Wunden um sein Haupt!
> Ach, wie die Knospen, frischen Grabduft streuend,
> Zum Fest für die Gewürme, niedergehn! (2907–10)

> Ah, all these bleeding roses!
> Ah, this red wreath of gashes round his head
> Whose buds, scattering scent – fresh scent of graves –
> Go down to make a festival for worms!

The horror of the tragic action of the *Bacchae* arises from the unpredictable nature of the god. He will certainly revenge himself if opposed, but he will not necessarily remain peaceful if propitiated. In *Penthesilea*, however, the tragedy arises from the disclosure of the true nature of love. Peace and harmony appear unambiguously as the result of delusion, which hides the reality of chaos and violence. Kleist's metaphor for the disclosure of this process is falling. One of the rose-gathering maidens experiences a benign version of 'falling' when she stumbles into a field of roses growing in an abyss:

> Auf eines Felsens Vorsprung wagt ich mich,
> Um eine einzge Rose dir zu pflücken.
> Und blaß nur, durch des Kelches Dunkelgrün,
> Erschimmerte sie noch, ein Knösplein nur,

Für volle Liebe noch nicht aufgeblüht.
Doch greif ich sie, und strauchl' und sinke plötzlich
In einen Abgrund him, der Nacht des Todes
Glaubt ich, Verlorne, in den Schoß zu sinken.
Mein Glück doch wars, denn eine Rosenpracht
Stand hier im Flor, daß wir zehn Siege noch
Der Amazonen hätten feiern können. (908–18)

I ventured on a sharply jutting rock
To pick thee one rose, lovelier than all:
Pale still through the embracing, dark green cup,
A scarcely opened bud its beauty gleamed,
Not yet expanded to the kiss of love.
But still I grasp it – then slip, reel, and fall
Down into the abyss and think myself
Lost to the world of day in death's dark womb.
And yet it brought me luck, for there I found
Such myriad splendour of wanton-blooming roses
As would deck out ten feasts of victory.

But for Penthesilea as well as for Achilles the fall is deadly. In the beginning of the play both escape unharmed from spectacular physical falls, described with all the breathless energy that Kleist's style can muster. In her pursuit of Achilles Penthesilea had driven him to the edge of an abyss, from which his horses shied and caused his chariot to crash. But he escaped unharmed and Penthesilea, seeking to cut off his way, climbed up a sheer rock face

                              und da sie jetzt auf einem
Granitblock steht, von nicht mehr Flächenraum
Als eine Gemse sich zu halten braucht;
Von ragendem Geklüfte rings geschreckt,
Den Schritt nicht vorwärts mehr, nicht rückwärts wagt;
Der Weiber Angstgeschrei durchkreischt die Luft:
Stürzt sie urplötzlich, Roß und Reuterin,
Von los sich lösendem Gestein umprasselt,
Als ob sie in den Orkus führe, schmetternd
Bis an des Felsens tiefsten Fuß zurück,
Und bricht den Hals sich nicht und lernt auch nichts:
Sie rafft sich bloß zu neuem Klimmen auf. (319–30)

And as she perches there
Upon a jutting block of granite, where
No room would be ev'n for the chamois' hoof,
O'ertower'd on every hand by fearful cliffs,
Not forward and not back daring to move
While with shrill cries her maidens cleave the air,
Sudden to earth she tumbles, rider and steed,
With loosened boulders thund'ring down around,
As though to deepest Tartarus she were bent.
Right to the foot of that sheer cliff again
– And neither breaks her neck nor nothing learns,
But only girds herself again to climb.

At the end of this 'fall' stands the utter dissolution of the personality. Here again Kleist resorts to a metaphorical tradition. The dissolution of Penthesilea's self appears when she faces Achilles no longer as a heroic individual, but as one among a pack of dogs which she joins in mutilating the body of Achilles. The names of her dogs are Ovidian, and they point to the story of Actaeon, who, transformed into a stag and torn to pieces by his own hounds, was a Renaissance textbook example of man turned into beast and destroyed by his own passions.

The 'metamorphosis' of Penthesilea is not only a sexual drama. As in *Phèdre* – or in *Othello* – the chaos caused by sexual passion is interpreted as an exemplary case of the self battling in vain against forces that seek its destruction, and Penthesilea's dogs are, like the monsters that haunt Racine's play, an image of the chaos into which the disintegrating self dissolves. The interpretation of the play in this wider sense opens the way to a perception of the systematic network of contrapuntal correspondences that relate Kleist's tragedy to *Iphigenie auf Tauris*. For Kleist's portrayal of the dissolution of the self into the Dionysiac chaos of sexual passion is his answer to Goethe's portrayal of the integration of the mad Orestes into an Apollinian society through the 'image of the sister.'

In different ways both Goethe and Kleist heeded the advice of Voltaire, who had deplored the contemporary practice of interweaving tragic plots with trivial erotic intrigues and had argued that love should either occupy the first place in a tragedy – as in *Phèdre* – or be banished from it altogether: 'L'amour furieux, criminel, malheureux, suivi de remords, arrache de nobles larmes. Point de milieu: il faut, ou que l'amour domine en tyran, ou qu'il ne paraisse pas; il n'est point fait pour la seconde place.'[39] If the subject of Kleist's play had been announced to an eighteenth-century reader, he would no doubt have expected a play about the love of Penthesilea and Achilles, which, like Poinsinet de Sivry's *Briseis, ou la colère d'Achilles*, approached the austere world of the *Iliad* in the light of a more delicate sensibility. It was, after all, a long-established claim of modern playwrights that in their refined attitude towards love they had the advantage over the crudeness of their ancient predecessors. But *Penthesilea* is a far cry from the embroidery of the *Iliad* in the spirit of chivalric romance. Kleist exploded the pretensions of 'modern' sensibility and turned the warlike virgin of romantic legend into a worthy sister of Phaedra, Medea, and Dido, the great sex-ridden heroines of antiquity. And in so doing he created the character and fate of Penthesilea as the negation of the achievement of Iphigenie.

Kleist's tragedy is firmly focused on the heroine, but the catastrophe of the play is the death of Achilles, the noblest and most brilliant of ancient heroes, and it is as the 'Death of Achilles,' that *Penthesilea* reveals its opposition to *Iphigenie auf Tauris* most fully. Goethe's psychological drama, in which the restoration of an integrated personality is asserted through the negation of sexuality, has wider cultural implications. The action results in the establishment of a classical world of individual freedom and social harmony, of which Iphigenie is the individual, Greece the collective, and Artemis and Apollo the divine symbol. The efficacy of Iphigenie's 'cultural revolution' is measured by the test case of Orestes, who in the literary tradition appears as the most unstable and least classical of Greek heroes.[40] Conversely, the magnitude of destruction in Kleist's tragedy is measured by the test case of Achilles, because for Kleist's contemporaries Achilles was the most radiant embodiment of Apollinian Greece. Renaissance critics had often had difficulties with the Homeric Achilles because he fell so manifestly short of the ideal of the Epic Hero, who combined the virtues of soldier, governor, and counselor in one person. But eighteenth-century German phil-Hellenists responded to Achilles almost exclusively in aesthetic terms, as is vividly apparent from Friedrich Schlegel's extraordinary attempt to dissolve the brutality of the famous scene in which Achilles refuses to extend mercy to Lykaon:

Nur der Grieche konnte diese brennbare Reizbarkeit, diese furchtbare Schnellkraft wie eines jungen Löwen mit so viel Geist, Sitten, Gemüt vereinigen und verschmelzen. Selbst in der Schlacht, in dem Augenblicke, wo ihn der Zorn so sehr fortreißt, daß er, ungerührt durch das Flehen des Jünglings, dem überwundenen Feinde die Brust durchbohrt, bleibt er menschlich, ja sogar liebenswürdig und versöhnt uns durch eine entzückend rührende Betrachtung.[41]

Only a Greek could unite and combine this furious temper, this young lion's tensile terror, with so much reflection and ethos. Even in battle, at the point when, carried away by anger and unmoved by the youth's supplications, he stabs the breast of the conquered enemy, he remains humane, even gracious, and reconciles us with a delightful and moving contemplation.

Kleist's Achilles is not a well-realized dramatic character, but he need not be so since his significance in the play derives from his symbolic function as an image of Hellenic perfection. Whereas Orestes first appears in a state of psychological disintegration, Achilles is seen as the embodiment of the beauty and dignity of human individuality. Penthesilea above all recognizes him for his Apollinian splendour, and in her recognition of him proves herself his equal. Thus the union of Achilles and Penthesilea appears as a worthy counterpart to the union of Iphigenie and Orestes or Artemis and Apollo, but it turns out to be a mirage, collapses under the onslaught of Dionysiac fury, and ends with the literal dismembering of the idol of Greece.

Through the emphatically sexual drama of Penthesilea and Achilles, Kleist expressed the triumph of Dionysus and reversed the triumph of Apollo figured forth in the curiously asexual drama of Iphigenie. Kleist's choice of the *Bacchae* as the instrument of his challenge to Goethe's classicism no doubt anticipates Nietzsche's explicit formulation of the opposition of Apollo and Dionysus. But in his valuation of the opposition Kleist is closer to Schopenhauer (and Goethe) than he is to Nietzsche. Kleist's portrayal of the precarious security of the individual looks forward to a memorable passage from Schopenhauer, which Nietzsche quoted:

Wie auf dem tobenden Meere, das, nach allen Seiten unbegrenzt, heulend Wellenberge erhebt und senkt, auf einem Kahn ein Schiffer sitzt, dem schwachen Fahrzeug vertrauend; so sitzt, mitten in einer Welt von Qualen, ruhig der einzelne Mensch, gestützt und vertrauend auf das *principium individuationis*.[42]

Just as in a stormy sea that, unbounded in all directions, raises and drops mountainous waves, howling, a sailor sits in a boat and trusts in his frail bark: so in the midst of a world of torments the individual human being sits quietly, supported by and trusting in the *principium individuationis*.

Penthesilea's 'fall' into Dionysiac frenzy is a striking instance of the collapse of the *principium individuationis*; it bears out the truth of her name by delivering her to the reality of a 'world of torments' that bears no trace of the joy and enthusiasm that Nietzsche found at the heart of the Dionysiac experience.

4

CHILDREN OF OEDIPUS

Since the Renaissance, *Oedipus Rex* has enjoyed a virtually unchallenged reputation as the Greek tragedy par excellence. When in 1585 the Teatro Olimpico was opened with a gala performance of an ancient tragedy, there was no doubt in the minds of the planners that *Oedipus Rex* was the appropriate choice for so prestigious an occasion. [1] This reputation, however, originated less in a recognition of the play's excellence than in the prominence given to the play in Aristotle's *Poetics*. It is apparent from Aristotle's frequent references to *Oedipus Rex* that he considered it an outstanding example of a well-made play, but he also referred to a number of other plays no longer extant, and their loss has given to the references to *Oedipus Rex* a singularity that rests to some extent on an optical illusion and encouraged the notion that Aristotle had derived the rules of the genre from the play he considered the 'vera idea della perfettione della Tragedia.' [2] Whether Aristotle had in fact done so is open to some question, but Renaissance writers believed it and conferred on the work the same canonical status that they had given to the work in which it received such prominent notice: as Aristotle ruled in the field of literary theory, so did *Oedipus Rex* in the field of tragedy. But it is significant that this paradigmatic status was a matter of prestige rather than of a thematically oriented response to the subject matter of the play, as in the case of *Hecuba* or *The Phoenician Women*. These plays spoke more immediately to Renaissance writers and were much more frequently translated and adapted. [3]

With the evolution of neoclassical dramaturgy and the fading of a subject-centred response to ancient tragedy, the prestige of *Oedipus Rex* increased even further, but the enshrinement of the play as the paradigm of Aristotle's rules blocked rather than aided a fruitful understanding. The attempts by French playwrights, including Corneille and Voltaire, to correct those aspects of the paradigm that did not quite follow the rules are remarkable chiefly for their perversity.

Schiller was the first modern critic to break the crippling association of Sophocles' play with the *Poetics*. In the famous letter to Goethe (2 October 1797) in which he expresses both his desire of finding a modern equivalent to the Sophoclean play and his sense of despair at the impossibility of such a task, he summarized his new approach to the play in two short sentences: 'Der Oedipus ist gleichsam nur eine tragische Analysis. Alles ist schon da, und es wird nur herausgewickelt.'[4] ('Oedipus is a tragic analysis. Everything is there and ready to be unravelled.') This definition of the play as tragic analysis is the first conscious articulation of that structural aspect of the play which posed the greatest difficulty to modern imitators of *Oedipus Rex*. To be more precise, the difficulty resides less in the concept of analysis than in the concept of resistance, which Schiller did not articulate, but which his definition implies as its hidden correlative. Resistance is that aspect of the Sophoclean drama which transforms analysis from logical demonstration into dramatically effective action. And it is the specific nature of this resistance which constitutes the play's source of tragic emotion. Schiller's remarks point to a definition of the Sophoclean plot that they do not fully articulate: *Oedipus Rex* is a tragic analysis that overcomes resistance. This expanded definition will serve here as the conceptual framework for the comparison of works that on the surface seem to share little more than their descent from a common model. As in the previous essays, I have made no attempt to be comprehensive; instead, I have focused on five 'versions' of *Oedipus Rex* – not counting the incidental mention of some others – to sketch the history of the *Nachleben* of *Oedipus Rex* as the misunderstanding, evasion, and transformation of the peculiar form that the theme of resistance takes in Sophocles' play.

In defining resistance as it appears in *Oedipus Rex* we may begin with a peculiarity of the play that Aristotle singled out as requiring some defence. Oedipus rules in Thebes for twenty years before the truth is discovered. Aristotle thought that Oedipus' failure to investigate the murder of Laius was an improbability excused only by the fact that Sophocles had put it 'outside the action.'[5] Later critics and playwrights were less friendly; a recurrent feature of seventeenth- and eighteenth-century adaptations is the attempt to correct the Sophoclean 'error.'[6] But these attempts only prove that the lapse of twenty years and Oedipus' failure to investigate the past are in fact crucial to the thematic structure of the play.

Until Jocasta casually mentions the fact that Laius died at the cross-roads, Oedipus is free from fears about his personal future. This absence of subjective foreshadowing, which is especially remarkable if we remember the 'horrible imaginings' of the Senecan Oedipus, has its counterpart in the univocity of the oracle. Something is clearly wrong with Dacier's famous argument to the effect that a man who had been foretold such a terrible future should have sufficient prudence not to kill men (or marry women) old enough to be his parents.[7] This prudential argument pales before the absolute certainty of the oracle that does not use the mode of 'either-or' – as in the *Trachiniae* – or of 'if-then' – as in *Ajax* – but flatly predicts what will happen. Oedipus' lack of fear is a sign of his forgetfulness, which is paralleled by the short memory of Thebes. To Oedipus' astonished question why the murder of Laius had never been investigated, Creon replies:

> The riddling Sphinx induced us to neglect
> mysterious crimes and rather seek solution
> of troubles at our feet. (130–1)[8]

Note that Creon provides the excuse in generic form. In abandoning *taphanê* (invisible matters) for *to pros posi* (troubles at our feet), the Thebans acted as human beings always do and as Oedipus did too: the twenty years of uninterrupted peace are a metaphor as well as a measure of their forgetfulness. This forgetfulness is the opposite of *alêtheia*, the Greek word for truth, which is derived from a root signifying concealment and oblivion (*lêthê*); the literal meaning of *alêtheia* is 'unconcealing' or 'unforgetting.'[9]

Truth is a process: it is born from the struggle with the force that resists memory and disclosure, and that resistance is itself part of the truth. The difficulty of inquiring into the truth is sounded very early in the play in one of its most memorable lines:

> Where shall we find
> the hard-to-decipher tracks of this old guilt? (108–9)

Oedipus Rex is the drama of the process of truth. Paul Ricoeur has advanced a most plausible interpretation of the resistance that is both part of and obstacle to that process by relating it to Freud's theory of the Oedipus complex: 'Sophocles' creation does not aim at reviving the Oedipus complex in the minds of the spectators; on the basis of a first

drama, the drama of incest and parricide, Sophocles has created a second, the tragedy of self-consciousness, of self-recognition.'[10] The drama
of truth grows out of the oedipal situation but it cannot be reduced to it,
although it neither evades nor conceals it. And 'the oedipal situation
contains all the "spiritual" overtones developed by the process of truth:
curiosity, resistance, pride, distress, wisdom.'[11]

In the Tiresias scene Sophocles establishes most firmly his interpretation of the myth as the drama of truth. In the quarrel of Tiresias and
Oedipus, the resistance inherent in truth, first sounded in the haunting
question about the barely decipherable tracks of an old guilt, finds its
most spectacular dramatic expression. And in the Tiresias scene the
connection between the substratum of the oedipal situation and its
interpretation as drama of truth is especially close, as Ricoeur saw in
arguing that 'the king's anger toward the seer derives its energy from the
resistance stemming from the oedipal situation.'[12] The knowledge of the
prophet frustrates the curiosity of the king as the power of the father
frustrates that of the son. The anger of Oedipus, which far transcends the
conventional impatience of the stage tyrant, feeds on the truth that resists
it. Underneath Oedipus' denunciation of the prophet there is a suspicion
that he might speak the truth, and at one brief moment in the quarrel that
suspicion breaks out in the anguished question: 'who begot me?' only to
be drowned in the riddling answers of the prophet.

In view of the programmatic nature of the Tiresias scene, the neglect
and distortion it suffered at the hands of later playwrights is a good
illustration of the difficulty posed by the theme of resistance. Seneca, for
instance, may have seen in the confrontation of the blind old seer and the
powerful king a meaningless duplication of the quarrel between the king
and his imagined rival; he did, in any event, delete the Tiresias scene and
transferred elements of it to the Creon-Oedipus scene. In the *Oedipus* of
Dryden and Lee, parts of the Sophoclean scene are translated almost
literally, but the words lose their meaning in their new context. In this
play, an apparition of Laius clearly reveals the guilt of Oedipus but
disappears on sensing his arrival because 'his murd'rous breath/Venoms
my aiery substance!' (3.1.372–3)[13] The Tiresias of this version is full of
compassion for his unfortunate sovereign, and he is understandably
fearful and reluctant to disclose a horrid truth from whose impact he has
not yet recovered himself. Whereas the Sophoclean Tiresias utters his
truths as counteraccusations that create a context of angry disbelief for
their reception, this prophet is desperately anxious to insure his credibility and becomes indeed a martyr to the truth when he is slandered by

Creon, here a real conspirator and modelled in part on Richard III. In other versions, such as the adaptations of Corneille, Voltaire, and other eighteenth-century Oedipus plays, the Tiresias scene plays a marginal role and becomes at the most a vehicle for the expression of ideas about the Church.

From the perspective of the Sophoclean theme of resistance, the history of *Oedipus Rex*, as reflected in later versions of it, may be described as the development and eventual convergence of two quite distinct approaches to the play. On the one hand, there are those plays which are most fruitfully approached by analyzing them as responses to the problem of resistance. With such a view, Voltaire's *Oedipe* emerges as the utter failure to grasp the theme of resistance, whereas Kleist's comedy *Der zerbrochene Krug* emerges as a brilliant and pioneering attempt to substitute a modern equivalent to the peculiar form that resistance takes in Sophocles. On the other hand, there are a number of versions that evade the problem of resistance altogether by seeing *Oedipus Rex* as a tragedy that hinges on the concept of fate. Corneille's *Oedipe* and Schiller's *Braut von Messina* are the most prominent examples in a group of versions in which the response to the model takes the form of denying or reconfirming the fatalism that is perceived as its thematic center. These two lines of response converge to some extent in the *Braut von Messina*, but much more definitely in Ibsen's *Ghosts*, which is of course not a version at all in any narrow sense, but which, whatever Ibsen's intentions may have been, was from the very beginning recognized as a kind of Oedipus tragedy. This play, while outside the temporal limits of these essays, is a fitting epilogue to a discussion of the 'children of Oedipus' in that it makes visible the structural continuity, if not the genetic link, between *Oedipus Rex* and its versions on the one hand, and on the other hand the genre of analytical tragedy, which has been of great importance in the drama of the last hundred years.

OEDIPUS REX AS TRAGEDY OF KNOWLEDGE:
VOLTAIRE'S OEDIPE AND KLEIST'S DER ZERBROCHENE KRUG

Voltaire's 'Oedipe'

The dramaturgical aspect of the theme of resistance is the delay it causes in the revelation of truth. The failure to relate this delay to its thematic base leads to the conclusion that it is merely a device for the purpose of generating suspense. This is the mistake of Voltaire, who in his critical remarks on the Sophoclean play came so close to grasping its essential point that his failure to do so strikingly proves how alien the Sophoclean dialectic of truth as resistance and disclosure had become to succeeding ages.[14]

Voltaire cannot understand why the process of discovery takes so much time. How, in the first place, was it possible for the murder of Laius to remain uninvestigated? Why does Oedipus repeatedly fail to put two and two together? The accusations of Tiresias hardly resemble 'l'ambiguïté ordinaire des oracles; il était difficile de s'expliquer moins obscurément; et si vous joignez aux paroles de Tirésie le reproche qu'un ivrogne a fait autrefois à Oedipe qu'il n'était pas fils de Polybe, et l'oracle d'Apollon qui lui prédit qu'il tuerait son père et qu'il épouserait sa mère, vous trouverez que la pièce est entièrement finie au commencement de ce second acte' (Moland 2: 21). In the face of such evidence, can Oedipus think of nothing better than to suspect Creon 'sans aucune raison, sans aucun fondement, sans que le moindre jour puisse autoriser ses soupçons?' (2: 22). Again it is unbelievable that the resemblance between Oedipus' life story and Jocasta's account of her lost son should escape the attention of both. Even the news that Polybus is not his father does not fill Oedipus with suspicion but only arouses speculations about his birth in which he is supported by the Chorus, who, although allegedly 'une assemblée de gens éclairées,' show 'aussi peu de pénétration qu'Oedipe' (2: 24). No wonder that Voltaire exclaims with exasperation: 'Cet Oedipe, qui expliquait les énigmes, n'entend pas les choses les plus claires' (2: 24). He objects to Dacier, who, following Plutarch, had seen curiosity as one of the faults that brought ruin to Oedipus.[15] Far from blaming Oedipus' curiosity in the cross-examination of the shepherd, Voltaire argues that it was 'la seule chose raisonnable qu'Oedipe eût faite dans toute la pièce, si cette juste envie de se connaître n'était pas accompagnée d'une ignorance ridicule de lui-même' (2: 25).

Instead of being led by such perceptions towards an appreciation of the play's peculiar theme, Voltaire interprets Oedipus' failure to put two and two together as an 'artifice grossier du poëte, qui, pour donner à sa pièce une juste étendue, fait filer jusqu'au cinquième acte une reconnaissance déjà manifestée au second' (2: 24). He fails to see that his criticism of Oedipus' obtuseness is identical with Sophocles' criticism and that he indeed echoes the Sophoclean Tiresias when he exclaims: 'Cet Oedipe, qui expliquait les énigmes, n'entend pas les choses les plus claires.'

Since Voltaire could see in Sophocles' strategy only a sequence of lapses in verisimilitude for the sake of theatrical effect, he tried to patch up some of his predecessor's more glaring errors. Voltaire is not at all satisfied with the manner in which Sophocles interweaves what one might call the clerical and secular lines of his inquiry. In the Sophoclean play Oedipus learns very early about the surviving shepherd, but the consultation of Tiresias takes precedence over summoning him, and as a result of the quarrel with Tiresias and Creon the shepherd is forgotten until Jocasta's narrative arouses Oedipus' fear that he himself might be the murderer. Voltaire has three objections to this procedure: (1) Oedipus should have summoned the shepherd immediately. (2) There is no reason why the shepherd should have spread the story of the robbers, and it is unlikely that this false information should have delayed the truth for so long. (3) It is unlikely that Oedipus, having summoned the shepherd, should never bother to find out the truth about the murder of Laius. In his version of the play, Voltaire corrects these mistakes in the following manner. The information about the unpunished murder of Laius comes not from Delphi, but from the ghost of Laius who appeared to the High Priest (a fusion of the priest of the Sophoclean *prologus* with Tiresias). Immediately upon receiving the High Priest's report, Oedipus begins his criminal investigation, learns from Jocasta that Phorbas – the equivalent of the shepherd – is still alive, and asks that he be summoned. Thereupon he dismisses the priest with the request: 'Vous, retournez au temple; allez que votre voix/Interroge ces dieux une seconde fois' (1.3, Moland 2: 69). While the priest is gone, the sub-plot develops. Philoctetes, a former suitor of Jocasta, is accused by the people of being the criminal, and Oedipus, although unwilling to accept the view of the multitude, does not fully accept Philoctetes' categorical denial either. With explicit impatience he awaits the arrival of Phorbas:

> Mais que Phorbas est lent pour mon impatience!
> C'est sur lui seul enfin que j'ai quelque espérance;
> Car les dieux irrités ne nous répondent plus:
> Ils ont par leur silence expliqué leur refus. (2.5)

In a lengthy reply, his confidant Araspe argues that the gods often speak through corruptible voices. Oedipus, however, is unwilling to endorse such scepticism. He will once more implore the gods, at the same time urging Araspe to speed the coming of Phorbas:

> Dans l'état déplorable où tu vois que nous sommes,
> Je veux interroger et les dieux et les hommes. (2.5)

When the priest returns from his second consultation of the oracles he knows the truth. As in Sophocles, he is reluctant to speak, but his reluctance has a simple psychological cause in the fact that he is shocked and terrified by what he has just learned:

> Fatal présent du ciel! science malheureuse!
> Qu'aux mortels curieux vous êtes dangereuse!
> Plût aux cruels destins qui pour moi sont ouverts,
> Que d'une voile éternel mes yeux fussent couverts. (3.4)

Despite the importunate requests of Oedipus, Philoctetes, and the Chorus, the priest refuses to yield his knowledge, but continues to lament Oedipus. The scene, while seemingly derived from the Tiresias scene, has its true parallel in the forced confessions of French drama. It is an unambiguous power struggle in which the king's power prevails over the priest:

> OEDIPE
> Obéissez.
> PHILOCTETE
> Parlez.
> OEDIPE
> C'est trop de résistance.
> LE GRAND-PRETRE, à Oedipe
> C'est vous qui me forcez à rompre ce silence.
> OEDIPE
> Que ces retardements allument mon courroux!
> LE GRAND-PRETRE
> Vous le voulez ... eh bien! ... c'est ...
> OEDIPE
> Achève: qui?
> LE GRAND-PRETRE
> Vous. (3.4)

Araspe's reflections on the venality of priests in the previous scene now reveal their dramatic function. Jocasta challenges the priest's truthfulness, and her attempts to persuade Oedipus of the priest's fraudulence are joined successfully by Philoctetes. Oedipus turns in anger on the priest, who after a heated exchange leaves with a lengthy indictment based on that of the Sophoclean Tiresias, but couched in considerably more ambiguous language.

> Vous apprendrez trop tôt votre funeste sort;
> Ce jour va vous donner la naissance et la mort.
> Vos destins sont comblés, vous allez vous connaître.
> Malheureux! savez-vous quel sang vous donna l'être?
> Entouré de forfaits à vous seul réservés,
> Savez-vous seulement avec qui vous vivez?
> O Corinthe! ô Phocide! exécrable hyménée!
> Je vois naître une race impie, infortunée,
> Digne de sa naissance, et de qui la fureur
> Remplira l'univers d'épouvante et d'horreur. (3.4)

But Voltaire's Oedipus, unlike his 'obtuse' original, senses the threat in these words and feels that they contain some truth:

> Ces derniers mots me rendent immobile:
> Je ne sais où je suis; ma fureur est tranquille:
> Il me semble qu'un dieu descendu parmi nous,
> Maître de mes transports, enchaîne mon courroux,
> Et, prêtant au pontife une force divine,
> Par sa terrible voix m'annonce ma ruine. (3.5)

Neither Philoctetes nor Jocasta can distract him from the fears aroused by the priest's words. To the former he speaks of an unspecified foreboding; replying to Jocasta, he is more specific and refers in veiled terms to the suspicion aroused by the priest's mention of Phocis:

> Suivez mes pas, rentrons; il faut que j'éclaircisse
> Un soupçon que je forme avec trop de justice. (3.5)

The fourth act opens with Oedipus' questioning Jocasta about the circumstances of Laius' death, whereas in Sophocles these circumstances are mentioned only incidentally in the course of Jocasta's effort to discredit oracles. The questioning confirms Oedipus in his opinion that his suspicions are only too well founded:

> Je crains que par les dieux le pontife inspiré
> Sur mes destins affreux ne soit trop éclairé. (4.1)

Voltaire here clearly aims at giving us the portrait of a chief magistrate who is rational and conscientious in the examination of evidence and the assessment of probabilities, whatever his state of mind. When Jocasta tries to soothe his fears and attempts to discredit the oracles by telling the story of her lost son, he recognizes immediately the corroborative nature of this evidence and anticipates that Jocasta will find in his own account reasons for fear:

> Lorsque vous aurez su, par ce triste entretien,
> Le rapport effrayant de votre sort au mien,
> Peut-être, ainsi que moi, frémirez-vous de crainte. (4.1)

Which indeed she does:

> Où suis-je? Quel démon en unissant nos cœurs,
> Cher prince, a pu dans nous rassembler tant d'horreurs? (4.1)

Voltaire does not make use of the ambiguity concerning the number of murderers, and Phorbas, who enters immediately following the scene between Oedipus and Jocasta, can only confirm that Oedipus is indeed the murderer of Laius. The act concludes with Oedipus' resolution to leave Thebes forever.

By making Oedipus formally conclude his investigation of the murder of Laius, Voltaire may have achieved vraisemblance in the portrayal of a thorough and energetic chief magistrate. But he has lost the effect of the specifically Sophoclean irony by which the investigation of the parricide is overtaken by the disclosure of Oedipus' identity as constituted both by the murder of the father and the marriage with the mother. Voltaire's fifth act with its revelation of Oedipus' identity therefore appears as a mere appendix to a successfully concluded investigation and is distinctly anticlimactic.

In his criticism Voltaire had deplored the absence of what I have called 'resistance' in the play and had charged Sophocles with adding incidents and intrigues merely for the sake of padding out the plot to its required length. But it is Voltaire's play that is much more liable to this charge, for his solution consists in introducing resistance of a wholly contingent type. His Oedipus proceeds rationally and speedily; what delays the discovery is merely the inability to procure Phorbas on the spot. Oedipus' investigation may be an example of good judicial procedure, but it is no longer a drama of truth. We may repeat this point by returning to one striking detail. Voltaire sought to remedy the improbability of the twenty-year lapse by reducing the interval between the death of Laius and the discovery to four years. Moreover, his Oedipus did not arrive in

Thebes until two years after Laius' death, so that only a two-year lapse has to be accounted for. This interval Voltaire justified by making Oedipus reluctant to disturb his wife's feelings by an investigation into a still recent grief:

> Pour moi qui, de vos mains recevant sa couronne,
> Deux ans après sa mort ai monté sur son trône,
> Madame, jusqu'ici, respectant vos douleurs,
> Je n'ai point rappellé le sujet de vos pleurs;
> Et, de vos seuls périls chaque jour alarmée,
> Mon âme à d'autres soins semblait être fermée. (1.3)

Later on, not even Voltaire thought very much of this device.[16] But whether or not a four-year lapse is more probable than a twenty-year lapse, it certainly destroys the theme of truth emerging at last. Can one ask in Voltaire's play: 'Where shall be found the hard-to-decipher tracks of this old guilt?'

Der zerbrochene Krug

Voltaire responded to *Oedipus Rex* only at the level of dramatic technique. Concerned with patching what he considered deficiencies in the process of Oedipus' enquiry, he lost sight altogether of the *raison d'être* for the play's analytical structure. His adaptation is like an idling engine that nowhere engages the thematic structure of the original. The cause of this failure is deeply rooted in whole development of European tragedy, which from its beginning preferred the moment of choice to the moment of discovery. In Trissino's *Sofonisba*, the first 'modern' tragedy, the dilemmas of Massinissa and Sofonisba look forward to the dominance, and indeed the tyranny, of the dilemma situation in neoclassical drama. In *Macbeth*, the strangely Oedipal drama of a parricide destroyed by oracles, the author traces the growth of a resolution and the psychological effects of a crime committed in full consciousness. This study has its own ironies and 'discoveries,' but nothing could be further from the process of discovery that leads to the recognition in *Oedipus Rex*.[17]

The blindness of European playwrights to the thematic implications of ancient recognition plots is well demonstrated by Corneille, who sensed the incompatibility of such plots with his own thematic concerns and met the problem head-on with his usual combination of candour and casuistry. In his second *Discours*, he criticized Aristotle's preference for plays that hinge on recognition. That preference is based on a classification of tragic actions according to the agent's knowledge of the victim's identity. If an agent knows the identity of his victim, action or non-action hinges on a decision of the will. If he is in ignorance of the victim's identity, recognition, if it occurs in time, will prevent the action. If the deed is done in ignorance, recognition will reveal its significance. We may thus attribute to Aristotle a broad distinction between tragedies of the will and tragedies of knowledge.

Because the reputation of some of his most famous plays is at stake, Corneille is concerned with rehabilitating the class of plays – despised by Aristotle – in which an action is planned in full knowledge of relevant circumstances but is not executed. Corneille argues that such plays can be very effective provided the failure to act is well motivated. Thus in *Cinna* the clemency of Augustus deprives the conspirators of the ground of their rebellion, 'et [il] faudrait qu'ils n'eussent aucune teinture d'humanité si une clémence si peu attendue ne dissipait toute leur haine' (p. 40).[18] Had Aristotle known this play, Corneille implies, he would have appreciated the fact that conversion is a highly dramatic cause of willing non-action.

Corneille goes further and raises questions about the alleged virtues of recognition: 'Je sais que l'agnition est un grand ornement dans les tragédies: Aristote le dit; mais il est certain qu'elle a ses incommodités' (p. 42). This 'inconvenience' consists of the incompatibility of recognition with dilemma situations. Corneille believes that by restricting the opportunities for dilemmas, the ignorance required by recognition plots robs tragedy of its finest source of pity:

Quand elle [sc. l'agnition] ne se fait qu'après la mort de l'inconnu, la compassion qu'excitent les déplaisirs de celui qui le fait périr ne peut avoir grande étendue, puisqu'elle est reculée et renfermée dans la catastrophe. Mais lorsqu'on agit à visage découvert, et qu'on sait à qui on en veut, le combat des passions contre la nature, ou du devoir contre l'amour, occupe la meilleure partie du poème, et de là naissent les grandes et fortes émotions qui renouvellent à tous moments et redoublent la commisération. (p. 41)

To this Corneille adds a historical speculation. Perhaps recognition was the most suitable criterion of excellence in Aristotle's time, 'mais aussi je ne me puis empêcher de dire que le goût de notre siècle n'est point celui du sien sur cette préférence d'une espèce à l'autre, ou du moins que ce qui plaisait au dernier point à ses Athéniens ne plaît pas également à nos

Français' (p. 43). In this discussion Corneille stumbles unwittingly on the decisive insight that the distinction between tragedies of the will and tragedies of knowledge broadly overlaps with the distinction between ancient and modern tragedy, and by his reversal of the Aristotelian preference he confirms the fact that the modern dramatist had little use for the pure tragedy of recognition.

From the perspectives of Voltaire's blindness to the drama of recognition and Corneille's embryonic formulation of a typology of ancient and modern drama, the brilliance of Kleist's response to *Oedipus Rex* stands out clearly. *Der zerbrochene Krug* reconciles the recognition plot with the drama of the will by making the will actively oppose the discovery of the truth. The resistance that in Sophocles was part of the truth as *alêtheia* appears in his play as deliberate repression. Kleist's comedy is the first modern 'analytical' drama in Schiller's sense, and it gives a new meaning to the Sophoclean procedure of tragic analysis by transforming the source of resistance in a manner that should have pleased Corneille: here recognition results from the prolonged struggle of the will for concealment with those forces that ultimately compel discovery. [19]

In the preface to his comedy, Kleist acknowledged as its source an engraving that portrays a trial scene in an eighteenth-century Dutch village. [20] His dramatization of the picture follows a pattern familiar from Roman and European comedy. Adam, an old and ugly village judge, attempts to win the favours of young Eve by means of blackmail. He pretends that Ruprecht, her fiancé, who is about to be conscripted, will be sent to Indonesia, where mortality rates are very high, and he promises that it would be in his power to get the young man off the hook by a forged medical certificate. Under various false pretenses he procures himself entrance to her room, but Eve is spared the fateful choice between her chastity and her fiancé's life by the arrival of Ruprecht himself, who happened to see them in the garden and suspected her of being unfaithful. The judge is beaten up severely, but manages to make his escape unrecognized, though he loses his wig in the dark. A jar is broken and remains behind as evidence of the scuffle. When the mother arrives on the scene, she finds Eve and Ruprecht in the room and naturally accuses Ruprecht of breaking the jar. He disputes the charge violently and instead accuses Eve of being unfaithful, but she agrees with her mother, because to reveal the intruder's identity would be to endanger Ruprecht's life. Thus she decides to save him, but at the apparent cost of losing him, since he is convinced of her unfaithfulness and will no longer have anything to do with her.

The action proper of the play begins on the following morning when the mother, irate at the loss of her precious jug, sues Ruprecht. Adam is the judge, but he is prevented from covering up his own guilt because on this very day a government official with the revealing name 'Inspector Lord' visits the village for the purpose of inspecting the execution of local justice.[21] Despite Adam's Herculean endeavours to obfuscate the situation, the truth is finally discovered as the inspector insists on a properly conducted inquiry, which leads step by step to Adam himself.

There is a good deal of Shakespeare in this comedy. The motif of slandered innocence comes from *Much Ado about Nothing*, to which Kleist alludes in a strategic line.[22] *Measure for Measure* is a source both for the problem of the sacrifice of chastity and for the ironic situation of the judge who is forced to convict himself. And, of course, the farcical aspects of village justice are a recurrent Shakespearean motif. The framework, however, that supports and unifies these different motifs is the representation of the trial as a parody of Oedipus' enquiry. In his preface, Kleist himself drew attention to the resemblance when in his description of the picture on which the play is based he says: 'und der Gerichtsschreiber sah jetzt den Richter mißtrauisch zur Seite an, wie Kreon, bei einer ähnlichen Gelegenheit, den Ödip' ('and the clerk of the court, looking askance at the judge, is full of suspicion, like Creon on a similar occasion with Oedipus'). The identity of Adam and Oedipus is established in the very first scene when attention is drawn to the judge's club-foot (21–6). But above all, the procedure of the play is Sophoclean, especially in the dénouement. In *Oedipus Rex* one messenger performs two functions: the old shepherd summoned by Oedipus to testify about the circumstances of Laius' death turns out to be the same man who handed the infant Oedipus to the Corinthian messenger. In Kleist's play Frau Brigitte is summoned to testify about the identity of a man she saw in the garden with Eve. Both Adam and Frau Marthe eagerly await her testimony, since for different reasons they expect her to identity the man as Ruprecht. But when Frau Brigitte arrives, she carries with her a wig found under Eve's window, and she reports the terrifying vision of a monster that disappeared into the night and whose man-horse tracks led to the judge's house where they stopped. She believes, or pretends to believe, that the apparition was the very devil himself, and Adam eagerly seizes on this theory but finds no favour with the Inspector for his proposal to adjourn the trial and consult the High Court in The Hague on the question of whether the devil can be sued. Convicted by the evidence of the tracks and the wig, he makes his escape and in the last scene of the play is seen wandering about in the hills, like the exiled Oedipus. And just as in *Oedipus Rex* the case against the murderer of Laius is forgotten in the sensational discovery of Oedipus' identity, a fact that annoyed Voltaire, so the case of the jug is forgotten by everybody in the play except Frau Marthe, who in the concluding lines asks the inspector where she can find the government building in Utrecht, for she intends to carry on her suit for damages.

The function of the Sophoclean allusions does not consist in underlining the rivalry of an older and younger man for the same woman as a comic version of the Oedipus myth. From that perspective some Plautine comedies are a good deal more 'oedipal' than either *Der zerbrochene Krug* or *Oedipus Rex*. Kleist used Sophocles because like him he was interested in the obstacles to truth. Truth is the perspective from which the situations of Judge Adam and Oedipus are related in a significant counterpoint. Whereas the latter is engaged in a relentless search for truth that he does not know, the former is bent with equal determination on concealing a truth that he knows only too well. In both plays a web of falsehood obscures the truth. But in *Oedipus Rex* this web is woven by the delusions of which Oedipus becomes a victim through the very strength of his desire for the truth. In *Der zerbrochene Krug* it is created by Adam's prodigious capacity for lying, which he indulges beyond all bounds of prudence.

Adam's genius for lying flowers in the stories he tells about the disappearance of his wig, the appropriate symbol of the judicial authority on which he wants to rely for the concealment of his own sins. The wig is first mentioned when Adam orders a maid to look for it on the book shelf. The maid cannot find it there and points out that her master must have lost it outside the house since on the previous night he returned without it and with a bloody head. Adam violently disputes her statement since it contradicts his allegation to Licht, his clerk, that he had taken a bad fall early in the morning. But he quickly goes on to send the maid to a neighbour from whom she might borrow a wig, giving the fantastic pretext that his own wig was spoiled by a cat who gave birth to a litter of kittens in it:

> Geh, Margarete!
> Gevatter Küster soll mir seine borgen;
> In meine hätt die Katze heute morgen
> Gejungt, das Schwein! Sie läge eingesäuet
> Mir unterm Bette da, ich weiß nun schon. (240–4)

Go. Marguerite!
Our friend, the sacristan, must lend me his
Tell him the cat, the dirty pig, has had
Her litter in mine this very day. And it
Now lies befouled beneath my bed. Now I know!

The rational Licht is dumbfounded: 'Die Katze? Was? Seid Ihr – ?'' But Adam is unperturbed. He elaborates the pretext with great detail, and as the subjunctive gives way to the indicative mood, he seems to believe in his story himself:

So wahr ich lebe.
Fünf Junge, gelb und schwarz, und eins ist weiß.
Die schwarzen will ich in der Vecht ersäufen!
Was soll man machen? Wollt ihr eine haben? (245–8)

As true as I live
Five kittens, yellow and black, and one is white
The black ones I will drown in the Vecht
What shall I do? Do you want one of them?

To the Inspector he gives a very different account. When asked why just on this day he should be without the wig that might cover his wounds he replies that he lost it when his wig caught fire as he was reading up on a case. Here his desire to portray himself as a victim of his sense of duty, reinforced by hypocritical references to his own sinfulness, contrasts wonderfully with the ironic images of doom:

Ja, seht. Ich sitz und lese gestern abend
Ein Aktenstück, und weil ich mir die Brille
Verlegt, duck ich so tief mich in den Streit,
Daß bei der Kerze Flamme lichterloh
Mir die Perücke angeht. Ich, ich denke,
Feu'r fällt vom Himmel auf mein sündig Haupt,
Und greife sie, und will sie von mir werfen;
Doch eh ich noch das Nackenband gelöst,
Brennt sie wie Sodom und Gomorrha schon.
Kaum daß ich die drei Haare mir noch rette. (1489–98)

ADAM
You see, last evening I sat down to read
A document, and since I had mislaid

My glasses, I bent down so low to read
The case, that by the candle-flame's bright glow
My periwig caught fire. I, I think:
Fire falls from Heaven upon my sinful head,
And seize the wig to cast it far from me:
But ere I have unloosed the ribbon-ties
The wig flames up like Sodom and Gomorrah
So that I barely save my last three hairs.

Adam's hour seems to have come when Brigitta comes with the missing wig. But no, he turns on Ruprecht, and remembering that a week ago he gave Ruprecht his other wig to take to the wig maker for repairs, he accuses him of having kept the wig and of having used it to visit Eve in disguise. But he forgets this lie when in a final challenge to the truth he declares:

Hier auf dem Richterstuhl von Huisum sitz ich,
Und lege die Perücke auf den Tisch:
Den, der behauptet, daß sie mein gehört,
Fordr' ich vors Oberlandgericht in Utrecht. (1855–8)

I sit here on the Judge's bench in Huisum
And lay this wig before me on the bench,
And him who says that it belongs to me
I'll hail before the highest court in Utrecht.

And when Licht puts the wig on his head with the remark that it fits perfectly, he exclaims in defiance of the visible truth:

Als Mantel um die Schultern
Mir noch zu weit, wie viel mehr um den Kopf. (1861–2)

It's far too large
To cloak my shoulders, let alone my head.

Kleist's drama of truth is patterned on *Oedipus Rex*, but equally important to the play is the myth of the fall.[23] The visit of the Inspector 'Lord' is the visit of the Lord who draws the guilty Adam from his place of hiding in the Garden of Eden. The identity of the judge as Adam is of course implicit in his name, but is also commented on by Licht and becomes the source of dramatic irony in the reference to the judge's fall. Thus Licht remarks in the opening scene:

Ihr stammt von einem lockern Aeltervater,
Der so beim Anbeginn der Dinge fiel,
Und wegen seines Falls berühmt geworden. (9–11)

Your family-tree sprouts from a fallen forebear,
Who at the very start of all things fell,
And through his fall has made himself quite famous.

And he mockingly reacts to Adam's statement that he had hurt himself while falling out of bed, implying that this Adam had a way of 'falling' into beds. Again to the Inspector's inquiries about his wounds he replies: 'Ich fiel,' and to the question what he fell over, he replies with unconscious irony:

Ueber, – gnädger Herr Gerichtsrat,
Die Wahrheit Euch zu sagen, über mich. (1462–3)

               Over-Gracious District Judge,
To tell the truth, I stumbled o'er myself.

The association of Adam with Oedipus is based on the perception of the central role that knowledge plays in both myths. Both deal with the 'fall' from a state of happiness and innocence into a state of guilt, misery, and exile, and this fall is linked to knowledge. In the Greek myth the fall is brought about by a change from ignorance to knowledge. Oedipus' fall into knowledge is the most spectacular example of the crisis of recognition, which is a central situation of Greek tragedy and which Greek playwrights explored by stressing the radical discontinuity of ignorance and knowledge and the abruptness of the transition from one to the other. Adam's fall, however, is a fall from knowledge. Caused by the deluded hope for a divine knowledge, it involves in fact the loss of the immediate intuition of the good and creates a world in which good and evil, being and seeming, are radically intermingled and can no longer be told apart without great difficulty. The fall brings to the self only a knowledge of its own evil, a knowledge that the despairing self seeks to hide from itself and from others.

The drama of knowledge based on the Judaeo-Christian tradition of the fall therefore distinguishes two phases. The first is the phase of evasion and concealment; as Macbeth puts it: ''twere best not know myself.' The second phase is the recognition of the sinfulness of the human heart. In both phases, the loss or gain of self-knowledge is dependent on the activity of the will. Kleist's transformation of the Sophoclean resistance in truth into the wilful repression of truth is clearly an interpretation of the Oedipus myth in terms of the first phase of the tragedy of Adam. This fusion of the most famous Greek and Christian paradigms of tragic knowledge is more than an exercise of literary virtuosity, for to the extent that the transformation of resistance into repression is seen as a replacement of Oedipus by Adam, *Der zerbrochene Krug* is a brilliantly witty acknowledgement of the roots of modernity in the Christian tradition.[24]

Judge Adam is a comic hero in that his predicament is seen only from the outside and exposed to ridicule rather than sympathetic understanding. The brilliance with which he is made to reenact the careers of his mythical paradigms rests on a simple psychological basis. There is nothing subtle about his desire to escape punishment and evade the truth. His unregenerate ethos remains unshaken by any touch of doubt or self-knowledge. His final words of excuse are not an acknowledgement of guilt, but a phrase to ensure his way past the crowd that blocks his escape.[25] But the Oedipus and Adam parallels do not exhaust themselves in illuminating the conviction of the judge and in creating the effect of comic discrepancy between myth and farce. *Der zerbrochene Krug* contains a very serious and nearly tragic drama of truth, which centres on Ruprecht and Eve as Adam and Eve and has for its theme the loss of innocence as the self-evidence of truth and the coincidence of seeming and being. In this drama Judge Adam is Satan, with whom he is also pervasively identified, especially towards the end of the play.

In approaching this drama it is best to start with a consideration of the role of the jug, which, like Adam's wig, is far more than a stage property.[26] The breaking of the jug is considered by its owner an almost apocalyptic event, and at the beginning of the trial she receives permission to describe the jug and does so in a manner that is clearly a parody of an epic description. It is evident that Kleist has some fun at the expense of Frau Marthe, who makes much ado about nothing, but it is also clear that in his own way he takes the jug as seriously as his character does. The jug and its destruction are symbolic of the action of the play as a whole, and by means of the characters' attitude towards the jug, Kleist epitomizes the conception of a reality from which the complications of the action arise.

That attitude is characterized by a naïve inability to conceive of reality in any other than physical terms. The unbroken jug is the emblem of truth in a radically undifferentiated world. The breaking of the jug is the fall that divides reality as it shatters the jug into separate parts, but this new, divided reality remains incomprehensible to the characters. Ruprecht and Eve's mother cannot distinguish between damage to the jug and to Eve's virginity. Kleist uses the jug as a symbol of virginity, but for Ruprecht and Frau Marthe the two are the same, or at any rate, exist on the same level of reality. The breaking of the jug, which is alternately described as shattered to pieces and as having a hole (666–9), is the loss of Eve's virginity, and Ruprecht remarks with unmistakable clarity: 'Die Hochzeit ist es, die ein Loch bekommen' ('It is the wedding that has got a hole.') (441).

Frau Marthe tells us in her description of the jug that it was decorated with scenes from Dutch history. But just as she cannot distinguish between damage to the jug and the loss of her daughter's honour, so she cannot distinguish between the jug as a material object and the imitated reality of the scenes that decorate it. The habit of animating painted realities in the act of description ceases to be the author's use of an epic convention and serves to describe a mind utterly incapable of making distinctions between categories of reality:

> Hier in der Mitte, mit der heiligen Mütze,
> Sah man den Erzbischof von Arras stehn;
> Den hat der Teufel ganz und gar geholt,
> Sein Schatten nur fällt lang noch übers Pflaster.
> Hier standen rings, im Grunde, Leibtrabanten,
> Mit Hellebarden, dicht gedrängt, und Spießen,
> Hier Häuser, seht, vom großen Markt zu Brüssel,
> Hier guckt noch ein Neugierer aus dem Fenster:
> Doch was er jetzo sieht, das weiß ich nicht. (666–74)

> Here in the middle, in his sacred mitre,
> The Archbishop of Arras formerly stood.
> But him the devil has taken hide and hair.
> His lengthy shadow alone falls o'er the pavement,
> Here in the background stood the body-guard
> With hallebards and spears in close array;
> Here houses on the market-place in Brussels.
> Here peeps a prying soul from out his window.
> But what he now can see I do not know.

The fall of the jug is very appropriately caused by the judge's wig.[27] The jug, as a self-contained and perfect object, embodies the Homerically concrete and innocent world of the village. On it the judge hangs his wig, the deceiving object that conceals the truth and lends to it a false appearance. The wig, hastily seized as the judge makes his escape, tears the jug from its place and dashes it to the ground, where its shattered pieces cease to be self-evident and are transformed into 'evidence' of a truth that is suddenly in dispute.

The jug has always stood in an ironic relationship to the fortunes of its owners. When the French occupied the house of the tailor Zachaeus, he threw it out of the window and jumped after it. He broke his neck, but the jug remained intact. Similarly, it survived a great fire:

> Ganz blieb der Krug, ganz in der Flammen Mitte,
> Und aus des Hauses Asche zog ich ihn
> Hervor, glasiert, am andern Morgen, glänzend,
> Als käm er eben aus dem Töpferofen. (726–9)

> The jug remained quite whole among the flames
> And from the ashes of the house I pulled it,
> Both glazed and shining on the morning after,
> As if it came straight from the potter's oven.

This ironic relationship, which of course escapes the characters, is reversed in the present. For the truth is that the broken jug is evidence of Eve's innocence and integrity; its destruction results from an action that she undertook out of loyalty to Ruprecht. And the same loyalty enforces her complicity with the judge. Since she believes in the authenticity of the forged letter that orders Ruprecht to do military service in Batavia, she cannot expose the judge, and she can only save Ruprecht by seeming to accuse him.

The discovery of this truth is the task that Ruprecht must solve and for which he is singularly ill prepared, since he is very much an inhabitant of the world of the jug, in which things are what they seem. His account of his falling in love with Eve is proof of his innocent literalism:

> Ein rüstig Mädel ists, ich habs beim Ernten
> Gesehn, wo alles von der Faust ihr ging,
> Und ihr das Heu man flog, als wie gemaust. (876–8)

> A sturdy gal she is. I noticed how
> At harvest time she handled work with ease.
> The hay flew fast, just like a frightened mouse.

These lines do not mean that with a peasant's pragmatism Ruprecht chooses a wife for her likely usefulness as a worker, but that in the strength and skill of Eve her personal integrity and moral excellence are fully apparent.

Ruprecht's failure is on one level simply due to his physical inability to see in the dark. He cannot make out the stranger to whom Eve is talking in the garden, and when later he pursues the stranger through the window, the latter throws a handful of sand in his eyes and escapes unrecognized (998–1007). But if it is true that Ruprecht cannot see the identity of the stranger, the same is not true of Eve's innocence, which he will not see. While he remains naïve in his attitude towards evidence, he is by no means innocent in his imputation of motives, and the combination of credulity and suspicion creates his specific moral blindness, which is metaphorically expressed in the physical blinding he suffers at the hands of Adam. 'To throw sand in someone's eyes' is a German idiom meaning 'to deceive,' and Kleist makes use of this idiom through his characteristic strategy of taking metaphors literally.[28] The sand recurs twice in the play. Ruprecht, remembering the painful moment, answers the judge's malicious reproach that he did not keep his eyes open:

> Die Augen auf! Ich hatt sie aufgesperrt.
> Der Satan warf sie mir voll Sand. (1552–3)

> My eyes unbarred! I had them open wide.
> The devil filled them full of sand.

And when Ruprecht finally learns the truth he exclaims: 'Heut streust du keinen Sand mir in die Augen!' ('Today you'll throw no sand into my eyes!') (1871) The sand that is thrown in Ruprecht's eyes by the devil is his own spiritual unfaithfulness, which prevents him from seeing the truth beyond the evidence. For the truth about Eve is finally a matter of trust inaccessible to evidence, and the evidence that 'Satan' puts in Ruprecht's way is a temptation to which he yields. Like Othello, or the Red Crosse Knight, to whom Archimago shows the false image of Una's unfaithfulness, Ruprecht forsakes his faith for 'ocular proof' and is blinded in the process. The failure of all three is neatly epitomized in the Spenserian line: 'The eye of reason was with rage yblent' (Faerie Queene 1.2.5). Eve puts the case against Ruprecht in unanswerable terms when she turns on him at the trial and accuses him of not seeking the truth beyond the evidence:

Pfui, Ruprecht, pfui, o schäme dich, daß du
Mir Nicht in meiner Tat vertrauen kannst.
Gab ich die Hand dir nicht und sagte, ja,
Als du mich fragtest, Eve, willst du mich?
Meinst du, daß du den Flickschuster nicht wert bist?
Und hättest du durchs Schlüsselloch mich mit
Dem Lebrecht aus dem Kruge trinken sehen,
Du hättest denken sollen: Ev ist brav,
Es wird sich alles ihr zum Ruhme lösen,
Und ists im Leben nicht, so ist es jenseits,
Und wenn wir auferstehn ist auch ein Tag. (1164–74)

Fie! Ruprecht, fie! Oh shame on you that you
Can't simply trust me in this whole affair.
Did I not give my hand and answer: Yes,
When you entreated: 'Eva, will you have me?'
And do you think the cobbler is more worthy?
E'en had you peeped in through the key-hole then
And seen me drinking from the jug with Lebrecht
You should have thought: My Eva, she is too good,
This whole affair will clear up to her credit,
If not in this life, in the Great Beyond,
For the last Judgment Day will be her chance.

In the ancient drama of recognition truth is a final value; its discovery
either spells irreversible doom or, as in the story of Merope, completely
dispels the possibility of a tragic dénouement. This is not so in Ruprecht's drama of recognition, because his ignorance is culpable in origin.
As it proceeds from unfaithfulness so it must be followed by repentance
and forgiveness to set matters right. Adam's final and desperate attempt
at evading his guilt is to declare Ruprecht guilty of the crime and to
sentence him:

Den Hals erkenn ich
Ins Eisen ihm, und weil er ungebührlich
Sich gegen seinen Richter hat betragen,
Schmeiß ich ihn ins vergitterte Gefängnis.
Wie lange, werd ich noch bestimmen. (1876–80)

His neck I do condemn
To wear the irons, and since he has made bold,

With conduct unbecoming to his judge,
I'll throw him into jail behind the bars.
How long I shall determine later.

While the Inspector takes a philosophical view of this sentence and encourages Ruprecht to appeal it to a higher court, Eve intervenes indignantly, and in a triple accusation of the judge she reveals the truth and urges Ruprecht to take the law into his own hands. But at the same time she acknowledges the iron as the just punishment for Ruprecht's real crime:

Das Eisen ist verdient, geh, Ruprecht!
Geh, schmeiß ihn von dem Tribunal herunter. (1898–9)

You've earned your irons. Go, Ruprecht!
Go, knock him down from his high tribune there.

Through the metaphor of the iron collar Kleist establishes an explicit link between the Adam dramas of Ruprecht and that of the judge. For the image had previously occurred in a prophetic dream in which Judge Adam, like a tragic hero, had forecast his own doom:

Mir träumt', es hätt ein Kläger mich ergriffen,
Und schleppte vor den Richtstuhl mich; und ich,
Ich säße gleichwohl auf dem Richtstuhl dort,
Und schält' und hunzt' und schlingelte mich herunter,
Und judiziert den Hals ins Eisen mir. (269–73)

I dreamt a plaintiff had laid hold of me
And dragged me here before the seat of justice,
And yet, 'twas I who sat upon the bench
And scolded, sauced, browbeat my very self,
And finally put the shackles' round my neck.

In establishing a link between the two Adam figures, the image allows us to distinguish between the brilliant but static farce of the judge's evasions, and the psychological drama of Ruprecht, which despite its sketchiness, does, like the drama of Milton's Adam or Spenser's Red Crosse Knight, go through the phases of temptation, fall, repentance, and regeneration.

OEDIPUS REX AS TRAGEDY OF FATE: CORNEILLE'S OEDIPE AND SCHILLER'S DIE BRAUT VON MESSINA

The discussion of Corneille's critique of Aristotle's preference for recognition-centred tragedies revealed the prejudices that prevented the perception of *Oedipus Rex* as a tragedy of knowledge. But in addition to blocking such a perception, the modern preoccupation with the will also shaped the interpretation of the play as the most extreme paradigm of the allegedly pagan doctrine of a fate that persecutes innocent victims. The interpretation of *Oedipus Rex* in terms of a dialectically conceived opposition of fate and free will grew in importance during the seventeenth and eighteenth centuries, until during the nineteenth century it became a part of conventional wisdom that *Oedipus Rex* was the tragedy of fate par excellence.[29]

This interpretation involves a crucial distortion of the role that fate plays in Greek tragedy. Fate, as predicted in the oracles and prophecies of Greek tragedy, is in the widest sense that which lies beyond human control. The assertion of the power of fate is simply a metaphorical transformation of human limitations into a counterforce actively resisting or oppressing human aspirations. Oracles are metaphors that emphasize the solidity of the walls against which human heads are apt to run. The pervasive language of fate in Greek tragedy is part of a poetic vocabulary that is rooted in common usage and popular religion but makes no claim to systematic coherence and does not imply the existence of a comprehensive providence, benign or otherwise, that guides human actions. Least of all does it imply a dialectical opposition of fate and free will, but it is precisely this opposition that is stressed in the language of fate we associate with the rise of European tragedy in the sixteenth century. The century that saw the emergence of modern tragedy also produced Reformation theology and neo-Stoicism, both of which have much to say about fate. The latter emphasized the concept of Fortuna as the blind force of the world against which the constancy and patience of the sage and martyr were the only weapons. The former wrestled with the great themes of predestination and free will, the enslavement of the human soul by sin and the impossibility of meriting redemption and grace. Both traditions were part of the mental furniture of educated men even if they were not professional philosophers, capable, like Milton's devils, of arguing endlessly about 'Providence, Foreknowledge, Will, and Fate, / Fixt Fate, free will, foreknowledge absolute' (*Paradise Lost*

2.559-60). Both traditions enriched the language of fate in modern tragedy and affected the problematic of fate as it appeared in it. If one were to make a broad distinction between fate as it appears in ancient Greek and modern European tragedy, one could point to the fact that the inquiry of Oedipus, in keeping with the strongly cognitive cast of the fifth-century mind, establishes his identity and the cause of his misery rather than the responsibility for his deeds. But in European tragedy a concern with fate is most likely to develop in the context of the search for responsibility. When Cassius argues that 'the fault, dear Brutus, is not in our stars, but in ourselves that we are underlings,' he states an alternative that is central to European, but only peripheral to Greek tragedy.[30] In Garnier's *Marc-Antoine*, a play which in the 'ancient manner' begins after the fall of the protagonists has already taken place, the plot consists in a most unancient manner of the efforts of Antony and Cleopatra to establish the responsibility for their suffering. Both are urged by their confidantes to console themselves with the thought that fortune was against them, but both reject such comfort and seek the cause of their disaster in their own folly. In *Macbeth* the impossibility of deciding clearly about the priority of the witches and the hero's inner promptings is part of Shakespeare's elaborate strategy of portraying the blurred dividing line between individual responsibility and 'metaphysical fate.' In Calderón's *Life is a Dream*, a play with strong, if obscure, links to the Oedipus myth, the challenge to fatalism is the point on which the main action turns. During his experimental release into the world Sigismund almost fulfils the oracle that had predicted the son's violence against the father, but his reflection on his 'dream' teaches him the lesson of the frailty of human affairs, and when reality offers him a second chance, he refuses, despite the injustices he suffered, to revenge himself on his father. Prudence and piety cancel the threat of the oracle and lead to the triumph over fate. In Milton's tragedy of Satan, finally, 'necessity, the tyrant's plea' appears as a delusion that becomes real and enchains the guilty soul once it has turned away from God.

The sixteenth century had seen in the tragedy of Oedipus an eminent example of the fall of princes. But if Oedipus was a good example of the vicissitudes of fortune, his story strongly resisted the attribution of responsibility, and its apparent denial of man's responsibility for his wrongdoing was indeed a scandal crying out for correction. The attempt to attribute to Oedipus' actions some moral failing that might justify or at least explain his 'punishment' runs like a red thread through seventeenth- and eighteenth-century debates about Oedipus' responsibility. The eighteenth-century Jesuit Père Folard, for instance, wrote an Oedipus drama in which he set out to prove that, far from being an innocent victim of fate, Oedipus had repeatedly ignored the clear warnings of the divinity.[31]

'Oedipe'

Corneille did not differ from his contemporaries in considering fatalism the point of the ancient play and its major difficulty for a modern playwright. But he refused to play the game of endowing Oedipus with an appropriate fault, at least not in regard to those actions attributed to Oedipus by the myth.[32] In his discussion of Aristotle's concept of harmartia he expressed his bewilderment at Aristotle's choice of Oedipus as an example and declared that for his part he could not discover any moral failure in Oedipus:

Il reste donc à trouver un milieu entre ces deux extrémités, par le choix d'un homme qui ne soit ni tout à fait bon, ni tout à fait méchant, et qui, par une faute, ou faiblesse humaine, tombe dans un malheur qu'il ne mérite pas. Aristote en donne pour exemples Oedipe et Thyeste, en quoi véritablement je ne comprends point sa pensée. Le premier me semble ne faire aucune faute, bien qu'il tue son père, parce qu'il ne le connaît pas, et qu'il ne fait que disputer le chemin en homme de cœur contre un inconnu qui l'attaque avec avantage. Néanmoins, comme la signification du mot grec ἁμάρτημα peut s'étendre à une simple erreur de méconnaissance, telle qu'était la sienne, admettons-le avec ce philosophe, bien que je ne puisse voir quelle passion il nous donne à purger, ni de quoi nous pouvons nous corriger sur son exemple.[33]

This splendidly honest passage, although published after the appearance of *Oedipe*, is sufficiently close to it in time to attribute to Corneille the intention not to base his solution to the problem of fatalism on the attribution of a 'fault' to the protagonist. What Corneille did in the end was both to challenge and evade the scandal of fatalism, with the result that his version is admittedly unsatisfactory but interesting precisely for its contradictions.

Since the recognition-centred plot of *Oedipus Rex* offered few opportunities for those dilemma situations that Corneille considered the glory of modern tragedy, he invented a sub-plot to remedy the shortcomings of the ancient play in this respect. His Oedipus has a sister, Dirce, who appears in the play as his step-daughter and who as the daughter of Laius

is a constant reminder of the doubtful circumstances of his own acces-
sion. She is wooed by Theseus, the king of Athens, Thebes' traditional
rival. From this situation flows a sequence of events designed primarily
to exhibit the characters' ability to rise above all threatening circumstances by the strength of their will. This is already apparent in the
use of the plague motif in the opening scene. In Sophocles, the suffering
of the people is the motive for the king's dispatch of Creon to Delphi.
Such concern for the well-being of the commonwealth is not a theme of
neoclassical tragedy. The plague functions only as a threat to the safety of
Theseus, whom Dirce nobly wishes to send away lest his great career
should be cut short. But with equal nobility Theseus refuses to listen to
advice that tells him to let danger separate him from his love.

The events that set the play in motion are not the plague but Oedipus'
expectation of the death of Polybus and Theseus' request for the hand of
Dirce. Oedipus had planned to marry Dirce to Haemon, thereby neu-
tralizing her claim to the throne, and to strengthen his own line by
marrying either Antigone or Ismene to Theseus. But the latter's request
for Dirce sparks off a crisis, which is heightened by Oedipus' fear that if
he should have to travel to Corinth to be crowned as the successor of
Polybus, Theseus and Dirce might make use of his absence and stage a
coup d'état.

The motif of the threat to the usurper's legitimacy is adopted from the
suspicion of the Sophoclean Oedipus that Creon is conspiring against
him. Whereas in *Oedipus Rex* this motif is subordinate and serves to
underscore Oedipus' progressive entanglement in delusions, the threat
to the throne is a dominant theme in Corneille's play. Dirce replaces
Creon, and although she is unwilling to engage in open rebellion, there
is nothing imaginary about the reality of her challenge to Oedipus'
authority. She feels cheated by the people of Thebes, who disregarded
her claim to the throne and chose Oedipus instead. And although she
acknowledges his de facto authority in Thebes, she defies his authority
over her person. She will not marry Haemon for the simple reason that 'il
n'est pas roi' (2.1.404), and she insists on her own choice:

Seigneur, quoi qu'il en soit, j'ai fait choix de Thésée;
Je me suis à ce choix moi-même autorisée. (2.1.425–6)

The battle of wills ends in a deadlock. The king can prevent her marriage
to Theseus, for she is too proud to listen to the latter's proposals for a
secret elopement, but he cannot enforce his will upon her. And Dirce is

left in a limbo of impotent defiance. At this juncture the ghost of Laius, conjured up by Tiresias, reveals that the 'blood of Laius' must expiate the crime of his murder. In the context of the action up to this point this oracle seems to refer to Dirce, and she seizes enthusiastically on it as a means of demonstrating her magnanimity. If she cannot have Theseus, her sacrificial death gives her at least an opportunity of demonstrating that she is worthy of him by emulating his benefits to his people. Moreover, she can express her contempt for her own people by proving the greatness of the queen they rejected and did not deserve.

The thematic significance of these additions to the plot emerges most glaringly in Theseus' attempt to match Dirce's magnanimity. He starts a rumour to the effect that he is the lost son of Laius, thus qualifying as a victim. Jocasta is sceptical of this claim and argues that in that case he must have killed Laius because 'c'était là de mon fils la noire destinée' (3.5.1133). But Theseus objects violently to this conclusion, and protesting his utter innocence of so heinous a deed, he launches into a lengthy and vigorous defence of free will that seems to reflect the author's as well as his own opinion (3.5.1149–70). This defence supplies the philosophical basis for the entire Theseus-Dirce sub-plot, which is in a double sense an evasion of the problem posed by the main action. From a formal perspective, the crescendo of dilemmas shifts the focus of attention away from the central recognition scene of the main action. From a thematic perspective, the tragedy of human limitations is not only evaded by flatly contradicted by a series of events celebrating the power and autonomy of the human will. And Corneille does his best to transform even the recognition of Oedipus into a celebration of the will. Oedipus convicts himself of the murder of Laius when in the confrontation with Phorbas he recognizes him as one of the robbers who according to common report killed Laius and whom he was proud to have punished when they attacked him on the road to Delphi:

> Seize ans, à ton avis, m'on fait les oublier!
> Ne le présume pas: une action si belle
> En laisse au fond de l'âme une idée immortelle. (4.4.1444–6)

But the discovery of the truth, which of course follows immediately from this proud boast, becomes merely another occasion for a demonstration of the will, as Theseus, still clinging to his pretended role as son of Laius, and seeking to avenge his 'father,' issues a ringing challenge that Oedipus eagerly accepts.

Corneille's handling of the revelation of Oedipus' identity aims at a complete negation of its impact and differs sharply from the handling of recognition both in Sophocles and in Seneca. In *Oedipus Rex*, the moment of truth is preceded by an outburst of wild hopes and presumptuous speculation on Oedipus' part (1076–85). Oedipus misinterprets the final words of Jocasta, who has recognized her son in the foundling of Mt Cithaeron. He thinks that she is ashamed of his anonymous birth, but he draws comfort from it and speculates that a god might be his father. But such hopes, supported also by the Chorus, are soon ended by the recognition scene, which crushes previous speculations and forces Oedipus to submit to human reality. Seneca, like later writers, was blind to the Sophoclean tragedy as a drama of truth and wrote his own version as a drama of fear. Suspense in his play is generated by the progressive approximation of reality with Oedipus' fears. The Senecan king has never forgotten the oracle. Nor is the plague an extraordinary event that suddenly threatens to destroy a peace of long duration. It is rather an emblem of the suffering that inevitably befalls the sovereign when after the satisfaction of his highest ambition he discovers that in the future he will be cursed with the task of maintaining the position he achieved. Therefore the king is introduced as an almost paralyzed creature awaiting with fear the onslaught of new disasters. Day for him does not bring relief from the terrors of the night, but merely shows them in a clearer light: 'Stragemque quam nox fecit ostendet dies' ('and day will reveal the havoc that night has wrought') (5). Oedipus is obsessed by fear because he is a king. The happy exile who considered himself safe from the threat of fulfilling the oracles that had made him flee his home becomes a king by mischance and must henceforth live in anticipation of nameless evils from which he wants to escape 'vel ad parentes' ('even to his parents') (81), where fear at least has a determinate object. Repeatedly he stresses his helplessness in the hands of fate, and he conceives of the future as a repository of terrors: 'cuncta expavesco meque non credo mihi' ('I fear everything and do not believe myself') (27). When the messenger from Corinth arrives with the news of Polybus' death, he utters a cry that epitomizes the course of the entire action: 'ut undique in me saeva Fortuna irruit' ('how heartless Fortune assails me on every hand') (786). One is tempted to say that revelation comes to this Oedipus almost as a relief, since it creates at least certainty and permits him to do something, even if his actions are necessarily directed against himself.

To the Sophoclean portrait of a man trapped in delusions, and to the Senecan portrait of a king paralyzed with fear, Corneille opposes his

Oedipus as a man always in control. As in Seneca, the final revelation comes as the last in a succession of waves of bad news. Hard on the heels of the revelation that Oedipus himself killed Laius, the messenger from Corinth arrives, but instead of the expected news of Oedipus' succession, he reports that on his deathbed Polybus repented of his fraud and confessed that Oedipus was not his son. Thus Oedipus in one day seems to lose both his kingdom and his status of royal birth. Coming on top of other misfortunes on this 'grand jour des malheurs' one might expect this blow to shatter even a hardy soul. But Oedipus remains unshaken:

> Ce revers serait dur pour quelque âme commune;
> Mais je me fis toujours maître de ma fortune. (5.2.1717–18)

The Sophoclean Oedipus had called himself 'child of fortune' and was cruelly disabused of his fond hope. But the claim of Corneille's hero to be 'master of his fortune' is not denied by and even gains from the final revelation of his identity, whose impact he cancels by his reaction: 'Hélas! je le vois trop!' (5.4.1758)

The facts of the case, even in Corneille's version, vindicate the oracle and seem to give the lie to Theseus' assertion of free will. And Oedipus, although he is conscious of nothing but 'exploits généreux' must concede the power of fate:

> Aux crimes malgré moi l'ordre du ciel m'attache;
> Pour m'y faire tomber à moi-même il me cache:
> Il offre, en m'aveuglant sur ce qu'il a prédit,
> Mon père à mon épée, et ma mère à mon lit.
> Hélas! qu'il est bien vrai qu'en vain on s'imagine
> Dérober notre vie à ce qu'il nous destine!
> Les soins de l'éviter font courir au-devant,
> Et l'adresse à le fuir y plonge plus avant. (5.5.1825–32)

But the concession is made with reluctance, on the author's as well as on the protagonist's part. Both seem intent, if they cannot refute the facts, at least to deny their significance. The apparent triumph of fate gives rise to one last occasion for the display of free will, as Oedipus and Dirce vie with each other for the privilege of being the blood of Laius that must be sacrificed. And when Oedipus' claim wins out, Dirce and Theseus join in their admiration for the equanimity with which Oedipus rises above his fate and shows the neo-Stoic constancy that is the birthright of his majesty:

Parmi de tels malheurs que sa constance est rare!
Il ne s'emporte point contre un sort si barbare;
La suprenante horreur de cet accablement
Ne coûte à sa grande âme aucun égarement. (5.7.1881–4)

Critics since Dacier and Voltaire have pointed out that the Theseus-Dirce sub-plot merely evades and obscures the problem of the main plot. But in the treatment of the main action Corneille shows an equal inability to reconcile the donnée of the play with the intended denial of fatalism. Oedipus' contemptuous indifference to his fate is neither humanly credible nor dramatically effective. Neo-Stoic constancy is one thing in a martyr who rises above the torments inflicted by his persecutors, but it does not seem an appropriate response for a man to shrug off all concern for parricide and incest on the grounds that he did not intend them and is only aware of his 'exploits généreux' (5.5.1820). To Voltaire's incomprehension of the myth, and to Kleist's fruitful transformation, we may add, as Corneille's response, a spirit of aggressive and not entirely conscious opposition that approaches the myth with categories of interpretation to which it remains resolutely closed.[34]

Die Braut von Messina

The plot of Die Braut von Messina is freely invented in the sense that the names of the characters are not taken from history, myth, or legend. But the plot itself is easily recognized as a conflation of elements taken from Oedipus Rex and The Phoenician Women. To the extent that the central event is fratricide – a fact underlined by the subtitle Die feindlichen Brüder – it could be argued that the play would be most appropriately discussed in the context of modern plays about Eteocles and Polynices, such as Racine's Thébaide or the Antigone plays of Garnier and Rotrou. But although by its content Schiller's plot recalls The Phoenician Women more strongly than it does Oedipus Rex, the play's dramaturgical procedure and thematic intention make it clear that in the composition of an 'ancient' tragedy Schiller had Oedipus Rex in mind as his chief paradigm. To view Die Braut von Messina not only as a version of Oedipus Rex but to discuss it in the context of other such versions is to recognize the symptomatic nature of the play's shortcomings and contradictions, which have often been recognized.[35]

Schiller's intention in Die Braut von Messina differed markedly from earlier attempts to restore ancient tragedy. Unlike Corneille or Racine,

Schiller approached his task from the perspective of a theory that distinguished sharply between ancient and modern tragedy as the expressions of fundamentally opposed mentalities. The theory was part of the rage for theorizing about ancient, modern, and future literature that was characteristic of Germany at the turn of the nineteenth century. All these theories were elaborations of the basic opposition of 'objective' and 'subjective,' or as Schiller himself called it, 'naïve' and 'sentimental.' Despite the sophistication and complexity with which this dichotomy was treated by professional philosophers, it had its greatest literary influence as a crude and unanalyzed opposition that became a fashionable cliché.

The theory of tragedy was necessarily affected by this all-embracing opposition. Objective and subjective were lined up with two oppositions considered specific to tragedy: fate and free will, and action and character. The nature of ancient tragedy could thus be summarized under the headings of 'objective,' 'action,' and 'fate' whereas the headings for modern tragedy were 'subjective,' 'character,' and 'free will.'

The admittedly crude parallelism of these dichotomies is essential to an understanding of Schiller's intention in *Die Braut von Messina*. In *Wallenstein* he had aimed at a rebirth of ancient tragedy. The austerity of classical form was to be the formal model, but the substance of the tragedy, the relationship of the hero's destiny and fall to his character, and the emphasis on the portrayal of an individual in all his complexity, were self-consciously 'modern.' But precisely because Schiller was so self-consciously modern, he had from an early date been fascinated by the task of denying his temperament and of writing a tragedy that would be ancient both in form and substance. Not rebirth, but restoration, was the goal that was finally realized – or so Schiller thought – in *Die Braut von Messina*. This effort at restoration was very consciously guided by three interlocking criteria derived from the conventional wisdom about ancient tragedy. The most important of these was the governing role of fate. Two criteria of dramatic form followed from this predominance of fate. First, action had to dominate over character. Second, the subjugation of the individual by fate and the dominance of action over character were most forcefully conveyed by an 'analytical' procedure because the facticity of what had already happened and only needed to be disclosed was the strongest confirmation of 'action' and 'fate.' As it turns out, the play does not fully observe any of these criteria. Fate stops short of being a sufficient cause of the catastrophe and appears on closer examination as the consequence of morally culpable actions. Nor is the play's procedure genuinely analytical, for the action that corresponds to Oedipus' crimes is represented before the eyes of the spectator as a passionate but clearly conscious act.

The play opens with an address by Isabella, the widow of the Duke of Messina, to the elders of the city. She rehearses to them the events since her husband's death three months ago. Her sons, locked in enmity since their childhood, had been restrained from open hostility by their father's repressive power, but since his death they had plunged Messina into civil war. Like the Jocasta of *The Phoenician Women*, Isabella undertakes one last attempt to reconcile the brothers and unexpectedly succeeds, for they discover each other's magnanimity and decide that only ignorance and the flattery of false friends led them into hostility (294 ff.). The real cause of their reconciliation, however, is the fact that they have both fallen in love and have lost their stomach for war. As Don Cesar leaves on a mysterious errand, Don Manuel relates to the Chorus how his hatred had evaporated months ago when on a hunt he had come to a secluded convent where he met a beautiful woman whom he loved instantly and who returned his love (592 ff.). Fearful of satisfying a curiosity that might endanger his happiness, he had never tried to wrest the secret of her identity from an old servant who occasionally visited her. But having heard from his love that the old servant had spoken of an imminent change in her fortune he had decided to abduct and hide her in a convent near Messina, which he did on the previous night. To the Chorus the report of this rash deed recalls the memory of how Isabella was abducted by her husband because his father – shades of *Don Carlos* – had intended her for himself. From this time and from the grandfather's ghastly curses (964–5) the Chorus date the misfortunes of the house, which they do not believe to have ended yet.

The scene now changes to the convent near Messina, where Manuel's love, who is ignorant of her identity, expresses her anxiety and in particular recalls the Duke's funeral to which she went, drawn by an invincible impulse (981 ff.). There she was spotted by a young man whose ardent glances terrified her innermost heart and filled her with a guilt she cannot confess to Don Manuel. Someone approaches, and instead of the expected Don Manuel, he turns out to be that young man, no other than Don Cesar (1109 ff.). He tells her how he had vainly sought her since the funeral and had only discovered her hideout on this morning – she had been seen by one of his spies in a little church to which she had gone, led once again by an invincible impulse. He will not inquire who she is, but declaring his own identity, he claims her as his wife and without waiting for an answer, he leaves, entrusting her in the meantime to his servants.

The scene changes back to Messina, where an elated Isabella seeks to crown the joy of her sons' reconciliation with the news that their sister, whom they believed to have died in infancy, is still alive (1260 ff.). She tells them how during her pregnancy her husband had a dream which an Arab interpreted to the effect that a daughter would bring ruin to her brothers. The daughter was born and condemned to die, but Isabella secretly prevented the execution, driven both by maternal love and another oracle, given by a pious monk which stated that her daughter would unite her brothers in ardent love. Trusting in the 'god of truth' (1353) more than in the god of lies, she had the child brought up secretly and would have revealed her to the brothers at an earlier time but for the violence that erupted between them after their father's death. As they wait for the arrival of the daughter, both brothers tell their mother that they will soon introduce their brides to her. She is overjoyed, but when she asks Manuel who his bride is he puts off an answer, and she does not press him, recognizing in his denial the father's secret nature (1450). Don Cesar, however, claiming that secrecy is not his way, openly declares that he does not know the identity of his bride and does not care since fate brought them together (1458–60, 1477–8).

Diego, the old servant, now returns with the news that Beatrice has disappeared and seems to have been kidnapped by pirates (1562 ff.). The brothers' reaction to this news determines the tragic outcome of the play. Isabella urges them to pursue the pirates, and Don Cesar rushes off the stage without even asking where the kidnapping took place. Don Manuel remains behind, like Oedipus troubled by the resemblance of his own story to what he has just heard (1628 ff.). But his anxious question about the place where this other Beatrice was hidden is not answered because Diego interrupts him and confesses that he had concealed from Isabella the fact that he had yielded to Beatrice's entreaties to let her attend the Duke's funeral. Suspecting that she was seen by a pirate there, he accuses himself of negligence. His interruption, triggered by his acute distress, relieves Don Manuel, just as Oedipus is relieved by the plural of the 'robbers' that killed Laius. For Diego's confession confirms him in his belief that the abducted woman cannot be his Beatrice, who would not have done such a thing or would have told him about it.

In order to dispel his fears entirely Manuel decides to question Beatrice immediately and leaves in haste just as Don Cesar returns to inquire about the place of the daughter's retreat (1669 ff.). Thus the play's tragic dénouement turns on two hasty exits: had Don Cesar not left so quickly, he would have recognized from Diego's confession that the beautiful stranger at the funeral was his own sister; had Don Manuel stayed for another minute, he would have recognized from Isabella's answer to Don Cesar's questions about the place of the kidnapping that there was only one Beatrice.

The scene changes again to Beatrice's convent (1706 ff.). Don Manuel arrives and after revealing his identity to Beatrice learns from her that she was indeed at the funeral. But he has no time to reveal to her the significance of his confession, for Don Cesar also arrives in haste, and seeing Beatrice in Don Manuel's arms, is instantly convinced of his brother's falsehood and without giving him a chance to defend or explain himself stabs him to death. The audience, who are by now fully enlightened about the tragedy, if they were ever in the dark, must wait through several misunderstandings until Beatrice, Don Cesar, and finally Isabella herself learn the truth and acknowledge the veracity of the previously much maligned oracle. Don Cesar resolves to commit suicide in order to expiate the curse on the family by a voluntary deed, and despite the entreaties of his mother and sister he carried out his resolution.

In his letter to Goethe, Schiller had praised *Oedipus Rex* as a play in which 'everything is there and ready to be unravelled.' And he had singled out as a special source of terror in such a play the fact that 'das Geschehene, als unabänderlich, seiner Natur nach viel fürchterlicher ist, und die Furcht, daß etwas geschehen sein möchte, das Gemüt ganz anders affiziert, als die Furcht, daß etwas geschehen möchte' (What has happened, because it is beyond change, is by nature much more terrifying, and the fear that something has happened affects the emotions more powerfully than the fear that something might happen.) Given the prominence of exposition and recognition in *Die Braut von Messina*, there can be no doubt that Schiller did aim at an analytical procedure, but it is equally apparent that his procedure is not in fact analytical at all. The crucial events of Schiller's play are not past horrors discovered through a process of inquiry; rather, past events, having remained latent, realize their full destructive potential as they interact with present circumstances to bring about the catastrophe. Consequently the play differs radically from *Oedipus Rex* in its causes of suspense and in the relationship of fate to truth and revelation. In Sophocles' play, the moment of disclosure is delayed by the resistance inherent in truth, which co-exists with and indeed is generated by the protagonist's earnest inquiry into it.

But in Schiller's play suspense grows from the fact that the characters, who are singularly lacking in curiosity, repeatedly stumble on the truth that would prevent the catastrophe, only to miss it narrowly and by the most extraordinary circumstances. And whereas in *Oedipus Rex* fate and the oracles are aspects of the drama of truth, in *Die Braut von Messina* the motif of narrowly missed discovery is a confirmation of the power of fate.

But that fate, for all its alleged omnipotence, fails to appear as a sufficient cause of the murder of Don Manuel on which the tragic dénouement hinges. Like *Oedipus Rex, Die Braut von Messina* involves a sexual and a violent crime: fratricide and incest with a sister correspond to parricide and incest with the mother. But whereas in *Oedipus Rex* the 'crimes' are just actions in terms of the agent's knowledge and intentions at the time, Schiller, for all his evocation of a daemonic fate, could not concede the possibility of crimes committed innocently or in ignorance.*

---

* In this regard *Die Braut von Messina* bears a striking resemblance to Tasso's conflation of the Oedipus myth with elements of the Tristan story in his tragedy *Il re Torrismondo*. In this play Rosmonda, daughter of the King of the Goths, is fated to cause her brother's death. She is therefore sent to Dacia upon her birth, and the nurse's child is substituted for her. But Norwegian pirates kidnap the baby, who is brought up as Alvida by the childless king of Norway. The tragedy develops when Torrismondo, the fated son, undertakes to woo Alvida on behalf of Germondo, the king of Sweden. Because Norway and Sweden are at war, Torrismondo pretends that he is wooing Alvida for himself. The plan miscarries when on their voyage from Norway Torrismondo and Alvida are shipwrecked on an island and Alvida, after seducing the man whom she considers her future husband, considers herself his wife. The complications of the plot arise from the attempts to find a way out of Torrismondo's dilemma. He plans to placate Germondo by offering him his sister Rosmonda. Germondo consents, but Rosmonda, who finds the burden of royalty too heavy and, like a good philosopher, yearns for the quiet life, realizes her reverse ambitions by revealing the secret of her low birth. Now the search for the real sister begins; at the moment at which her fortunes have been traced to the pirates, a Norwegian messenger arrives with the news of Norway's death and offers the crown to Torrismondo. He provides the information that the kidnapped baby acquired a royal father.

The dénouement is simple and told by a messenger. Alvida, knowing that her 'father' is dead and believing that her husband has rejected her, commits suicide. Torrismondo finds her mortally wounded, tells her the truth, and upon her death likewise kills himself. The evasion of the Oedipus situation is all but complete. As in *Die Braut von Messina*, the maternal incest taboo is replaced with a taboo that can be romantically exploited. But the more important resemblances concern the similar distortion of analytical procedure as the result of the author's reluctance to pivot the tragedy on a crime committed in ignorance. As in Corneille's *Oedipe*, the motif of recognition is overshadowed by the 'combats d'âme' that arise in the course of the play and require exertions of the will. Torrismondo must choose between his love for Alvida and his friendship for Germondo; Rosmonda renounces royalty, and Alvida, life. Recognition,

The critical deed in *Die Braut von Messina* is a crime by any standard: having claimed possession of a woman without even asking for her consent, Don Cesar kills a man whom in his jealousy he perceives as a rival without even considering whether that man has claims on the woman that might be stronger than his own. That the rival is his brother and the woman turns out to be his sister no doubt increases the horror of his deed, but the criminal case against Don Cesar is not substantially affected by the play's relevations, a crucial difference from *Oedipus Rex*. Conversely, the crime of incest is not in fact committed at all, and we may suspect that it was not sexual prudishness but the revulsion at the thought of a crime committed in ignorance that kept Schiller from inventing a plot in which Don Manuel not only abducts Beatrice, but like Romeo consummates his marriage after being married to her by some discreet friar.

The reluctance to attribute the responsibility for criminal actions to a fate that is nonetheless invoked as a malign and daemonic power is a weakness in Schiller's play that has often been recognized. And the contradictory answers that the play gives to the question of responsibility cannot be explained away by crediting Schiller with an interest either in the 'duck-rabbit' problem of external and internal motivation or in the unmasking of fate as a false excuse. The sketchiness of characterization, the unreflective nature of the protagonists, and the deliberate refusal to centre the action on any one of the four main characters all show that Schiller, unlike Shakespeare in *Macbeth* or Dostojevski in the account of Raskolnikoff's crime, was not interested in exploring the double determination of an action that appears both fated and subjectively intended. Similarly, fate is not exposed as 'necessity, the tyrant's plea,' the delusion by which Milton's Adam and Satan convince themselves of the inevitability of their actions. Schiller was clearly concerned in this play with constructing a fate that would have its origin outside any individual consciousness and would overrule individual plans and purposes for the achievement of its own destructive ends. So much is clear from the explosive concatenation of trivial and individually harmless coinci-

in fact, although seemingly the climax of the work, has little causal value. Alvida commits suicide because she believes herself abandoned, and Torrismondo's suicide is less the response of knowledge to Destiny than the reaction of the distraught lover, who like Romeo cannot survive his beloved. And as in Schiller's play, there are no crimes committed in ignorance, but there are morally culpable acts to which the identity of the agents adds a special horror: Torrismondo betrays his friend Germondo, and he is guiltier than Tristan in that he deceives Alvida as well by wooing her on false pretenses.

dences and errors of judgement, as well as from the commonplaces about fate and destiny that Schiller liberally scattered through his play as the kind of thing that the Chorus and characters in an ancient tragedy were supposed to say. Yet at the crucial moment, fate explains very little: jealousy motivates Don Cesar to commit an act the culpability of which is fully apparent in its immediate context.

The contradictions in Schiller's handling of fate are a mirror image of Corneille's failure in *Oedipe*, and in both cases failure derives from the inability to reconcile the myth with the dialectic of fate and free will that was assumed to be its content. If Corneille's ringing assertion of free will was unable to override the donnée of the myth, Schiller, on the other hand, could not carry out his avowed intention of writing a play in the ancient manner, in which, according to his understanding of *Oedipus Rex* as the paradigm of the genre, fate prevailed over free will. Both the attack on determinism and the half-hearted attempt to give it dramatic expression reveal finally the futility of interpreting the Oedipus myth in terms of fate and free will.

A somewhat different approach to *Die Braut von Messina* discloses an interesting link with Kleist's transformation of the motif of resistance. The failure of the truth to emerge in time is a major aspect of Schiller's play, especially in the crucial scene between Isabella and the brothers, where only an extraordinary combination of coincidences prevents the disclosure of an almost ridiculously obvious situation. What is the nature of the 'resistance' of truth at this point? According to an anonymous critic, who reported Schiller's reply to criticisms about the accumulation of coincidences, Schiller equated this resistance with fate: 'Schiller wunderte sich, wie man seine Intention so wenig habe fassen können, da ja eben in diesem Verschliessen des Mundes in so kritischen Augenblicken, wo ein rettendes Wort das eherne Netz des Schicksals hätte zerreissen können, die unabwendbare Gewalt, ja das Dämonische des Verderben brütenden Verhängnisses sich recht deutlich offenbare und alle Zuschauer mit geheimem Grauen durchschauere.' ('Schiller was surprised at this failure to grasp his intention since this silence at a critical moment, when a saving word would break the iron net of fate, demonstrated the demonic power and destructiveness of fate and filled the spectators with secret horror.')[36]

On a closer look, it is not fate that causes silence, but silence that causes fate, and the play is open to an interpretation in which fate, far from being a metaphysical entity, is simply the consequence of the characters' pervasive secrecy and lack of truthfulness. All the characters in the play yearn for a world of love, peace, and reconciliation. The values of this new world are embodied by Beatrice, whose role as healing sister and female Messiah establishes her as a cousin of Iphigenie, not to speak of the associations that the name evokes for a reader of Dante. But Beatrice falls far short of Iphigenie, and her moral passivity finds an echo in the other characters, none of whom has Iphigenie's courage to risk the values of the new world in the very act of bringing it about. Iphigenie's special virtue is openness, and the general failing of the characters in *Die Braut von Messina* is secrecy. It is 'the father's way,' as Isabella comments in an important passage (1450–1), and Don Cesar's first reaction to the news that Beatrice is his sister includes a curse on his mother's 'Heimlichkeit, die all dies Grässliche verschuldet!' ('that secrecy of yours/ Which has occasioned all this horror!') (2472–3).[37] Secrecy, ranging from the prudence of Isabella to the ingrained fears and suspicions of Don Manuel, is the common cause that underlies the fatal coincidences of the play. But whatever the motives for particular actions, secrecy as the modus operandi of an old world governed by fraud and violence, is incompatible with the new world of love. The collective tragedy of the society in Schiller's play is that it fails to disavow the means of the past in time and thus compromises the goals of the future. 'Fate' is the destiny of those who lack the courage of Iphigenie: the cause of the dominance of 'action' in this play is that the characters collectively lack 'character.'

If the failure of the truth to emerge in time is the consequence of a lack of truthfulness, Schiller's play joins Kleist's comedy in transforming the Sophoclean resistance of truth into a form of culpable ignorance. The secretiveness of the characters in *Die Braut von Messina* is the equivalent of Judge Adam's wilful concealment or Ruprecht's lack of faith; in both plays the drama of knowledge is transformed into a drama of the will or, more appropriately in Schiller's case, the lack of will. Such a reading removes some of the contradictions the play exhibits as a tragedy of fate. The demystified fate of the play appears as an appropriate social and psychological background to Don Cesar's act of rash violence: it becomes the metaphor for the environment that gives rise to without compelling crimes such as Don Cesar's, which are the 'necessary' consequences of a complicity of silence and deception. Does this resolution of the problem rescue *Die Braut von Messina* from the charges of incoherence and a thematically misdirected response to its model? I doubt it for two reasons. First, although Schiller touches on the model's theme of knowledge and resistance as the key to a successful transformation, his version seems to stumble on rather than explore this discovery. Whereas Kleist went straight to the heart of the Sophoclean difficulty in making the will to conceal his protagonist's chief motive, it seems that in Schiller's play secrecy is primarily a theatrical necessity to support the semblance of analytic procedure. The thematic motivation of the device looks more like an import from the world of Goethe's *Iphigenie* – Messina is a Tauris without Iphigenie – than a response to the difficulty of resistance in *Oedipus Rex*.

Second, such a reading would attribute the demystification of fate to the play itself rather than make it the work of the reader's consciousness, performed in defiance of the text's explicit intention. The rhetoric of the play runs counter to this view, and so does Schiller's uncritical assimilation of the 'fate' of Greek tragedy to characteristic preoccupations of the late eighteenth century. The fate of Sophoclean tragedy is an expression of the way things are. The fulfilment of the oracle teaches Oedipus the full meaning of the riddle of the Sphinx, for, as Dio Chrysostom ingeniously argued (10.30), the Oedipus who answered 'man' to the Sphinx did not really know the meaning of the word and was very stupid for being so proud of his cleverness. Schiller's fate, on the other hand, is a metaphor – and not a consciously controlled one – of the oppressive power that the past is seen as holding over present and future. As the power that resists deliverance from the past, fate is the counter-revolutionary force par excellence.

The hypostatization of an aspect of time as a daemonic fate may be seen as an instance of the renaissance of the theme of the generational curse in works of Gothic fiction and drama. The generational curse represents an archaic attempt to make moral sense of the universe, and it had very early come under attack from enlightened thinkers, as for instance in Ezekiel's refutation of the proverb: 'The fathers have eaten sour grapes, and the children's teeth are set on edge.' In Greek tragedy, the *Oresteia* and *Seven against Thebes* notwithstanding, the generational curse is a distinctly marginal motif, and sometimes, as in *Antigone*, it seems to be an awkwardly integrated relic of an archaic morality (594–603). In sixteenth- and seventeenth-century tragedy, despite its rich language of fate and fortune, the role of the generational curse is also very minor; even where it seems to be a prominent motif – as in Shakespeare's Histories – its explanatory force is kept at a low level, and in Racine's *Phèdre* and *Athalie* it is generalized into a metaphor of original sin. But in the second half of the eighteenth century, the generational curse – including the haunted house and the walking spectre where conditions of vraisemblance were sufficiently relaxed – became a *sine qua non* of Gothic fate. The specifically modern dimension in this renaissance of a very archaic motif is the theme of time and of generational conflict.

The generational curse of Gothic fate always involves the oppression of youth by age, a theme unknown to Greek tragedy. The origin of the curse is usually an abuse of paternal authority in the widest sense. The victims of Gothic fate are by preference young and innocent. And its peculiar irony consists in the coincidence that it invariably strikes its young and innocent victims at the very moment that promises release from the dark world of their elders.

None of this is in *Oedipus Rex*, but all of it can be found in *Die Braut von Messina*. We may well wonder how Schiller or his audience could fail to notice that whether one regarded the triangle of Beatrice and her brothers as a version of the quarrel between Eteocles and Polynices or as a replacement of the mother-son incest, in either case a banal problem of sexual jealousy was substituted for the moral agony of the ancient characters and given a specious significance by the pretentious agency of a daemonic fate, whose origin was an equally banal case of sexual rivalry. But despite the theoretical halo that surrounds it, *Die Braut von Messina* is a curiously uncritical performance, perhaps as a consequence of the fact that when it came to details Schiller did not have a very intimate knowledge of Greek tragedy. The thematic concerns of Schiller's play are very close to the versions of Goethe and Kleist. One could take *Iphigenie auf Tauris*, *Die natürliche Tochter* (a kind of modern *Oresteia*), *Die Braut von Messina*, and *Penthesilea* and show all of them as turning on a similar conception of the mythical as a vision of disorder seen both in psychosexual and sociopolitical terms. But Schiller lacked Kleist's or Goethe's instinct for relating this thematic interest to a specific mythical configuration. As a productive misreading of a Greek tragedy, *Die Braut von Messina* cannot compare with *Iphigenie auf Tauris* or *Penthesilea*; it is a somewhat diffuse response to Ancient Tragedy considered in the abstract. And for all its self-consciousness as an exercise in restoration, it is most modern where it tries hardest to be most ancient: its thematization of fate, perceived by the original audience as specifically 'Aeschylean' is likely to strike us as a Gothic monstrosity corresponding to the revolutionary anxiety of the age and its changing perception of the relationship between past, present, and future.

OEDIPUS REX AND MODERN ANALYTICAL DRAMA: IBSEN'S GHOSTS

Ghosts differs from the Oedipus plays discussed so far in that it cannot be proved to stand in an intentional relationship to the Sophoclean play at all. There is no evidence for Robert Brustein's argument that 'after careful study of the Greeks' Ibsen 'junked the techniques of the well-made play in favor of the more integrated structure of Sophoclean tragedy.'[38] Ibsen had a spotty education, and throughout his life his reading tastes were not particularly literary. It is certain and needs no special proof that he was familiar with the conventional wisdom about 'Greek tragedy,' but his biographer Michael Meyer writes that when in his mid-thirties Ibsen wrote *Vikings at Helgoland*, his protoanalytical drama on the Siegfried-Brünhilde myth, he had 'very possibly never read a Greek play, even in bad translation.'[39] And Ibsen's few later remarks about Greek tragedy are so pious and vacuous that it is impossible to infer from them a firsthand knowledge of the plays of the three Greek tragedians.[40]

Nonetheless, critics were from the very beginning struck by the resemblance of *Ghosts* to Greek tragedy. In 1883 a Norwegian professor of classics wrote: 'of all the modern dramatic literature we have read, *Ghosts* comes closest to the drama of antiquity. ... Classical drama is called a drama of family and fate because of the tragic destiny inherited by the family. Here we also have a family tragedy, but a social drama as well – classical tragedy reborn on modern soil.'[41] About the same time Georg Brandes wrote: 'His technical mastery has increased in later years from work to work. In *A Doll's House* he surpassed the technique of the most famous French dramatists, and in *Ghosts* ... he displayed a dramatic certainty, simplicity, and delicacy which recalled antique tragedy in the hands of Sophocles (*Oedipus Rex*).'[42] The comparison between *Ghosts* and *Oedipus Rex* has been considered useful ever since: among modern critics Francis Ferguson and Robert Brustein have made Oedipus' quest for the truth their point of departure for the discussion of Mrs Alving's situation.[43]

The usefulness of the comparison rests on the fact that although *Ghosts* is not a version of *Oedipus Rex*, nonetheless as the prototype of modern analytical drama it shares in the links of that genre with *Oedipus Rex* and its history of interpretation. Modern analytical drama is located precisely at the point of convergence between the two main lines of approach to the Sophoclean play. A reading of *Ghosts* as a version of *Oedipus Rex* demonstrates this point very clearly and establishes the nature of the link between ancient tragedy and modern analytical drama. Through its title, *Ghosts* declares its continuity with the 'tragedy of fate,' but, like *Der zerbrochene Krug*, it dramatizes the emergence of truth as the outcome of a struggle between repression and inquiry. Time is the central theme that unites the drama of truth with the tragedy of fate in a manner that made

Ghosts and its successors come closer than Schiller had thought possible – and certainly a good deal closer than *Die Braut von Messina* – to being a modern equivalent to *Oedipus Rex*.

The determinism that contemporary critics of *Ghosts* considered as a transplant of Greek fate on modern soil is easily recognizable as the Gothic fate of *Die Braut von Messina*. When Mrs Alving hears Oswald and Regine in the next room, her exclamation 'Ghosts' interprets the event as the re-enactment of the scene between Captain Alving and Regine's mother, or as the periodic apparition of a family ghost.[44] And like the fate of Schiller's play – or Grillparzer's *Ahnfrau* – Ibsen's fate threatens to bring about incest between brother and sister. Gothic too are the implications of the scientific guise in which fate manifests itself as hereditary syphilis – a generational curse indeed! Oswald is struck down in his youth and innocence, but the ultimate cause of his ruin is the cause that drove his father from Mrs Alving's bed: society's perversion of the institution of marriage, which forced Mrs Alving to marry Alving for his money and taught her to think of marriage as a form of duty. The abuse of 'paternal' authority in a broad sense is thus the origin of Ibsen's fate, which begins with a crime against youth and ends with its destruction.

As in Schiller's play, the fate of *Ghosts* is a metaphor for the oppressive past. Indeed, Ibsen says so explicitly in the famous passage in which Mrs Alving identifies the dead ideas of the past as 'Ghosts':

It's not just what we inherit from our mothers and fathers that haunts us. It's all kinds of old defunct theories, all sorts of old defunct beliefs, and things like that. It's not that they actually *live* on in us; they are simply lodged there, and we cannot get rid of them. I've only to pick up a newspaper and I seem to see ghosts gliding between the lines. Over the whole country there must be ghosts, as numerous as the sands of the sea. And here we are, all of us, abysmally afraid of the light.[45]

But whereas in *Die Braut von Messina* the past appears as an openly violent society, in *Ghosts* it is represented as a hypocritical society that conspires with itself to maintain a semblance of tranquility and in which mutual deception goes hand in hand with self-deception. Moreover, this process has gone on for so long that the web of falsehood enjoys the status of a long-established truth.

It is this conception of society as the deliberate perpetuation of falsehood which makes possible a genuine response to the Sophoclean motif of long oblivion, epitomized in Oedipus' question 'Where shall we find the barely decipherable tracks of an ancient guilt?' Voltaire and Corneille had tried makeshift arrangements to dispose of what they perceived as the awkwardly long interval between the crimes of Oedipus and their discovery. In Kleist's play the question of Oedipus is answered literally by tracks that lead to the judge's door. But the tracks are neither hard to decipher nor ancient. On the contrary: Adam is almost caught in flagranti, and the comic effect of his stubborn attempts to conceal and deny the truth derives to a considerable extent from the very obviousness of his offense. Thus the problem of the twenty-year interval was solved very elegantly: its transformation into instantaneous conviction is an aspect of the contrapuntal relationship in which Judge Adam stands to Oedipus. But Kleist's solution, although brilliantly successful in his comic context, is only the removal of a difficulty; unlike his transformation of the resistance of *aletheia* into the suppression of truth, it is not the discovery of a modern equivalent to the theme of long oblivion. And in Schiller's plan, for all its millennial opposition of past and future, there was no room for the theme of oblivion, because here secrecy derives from the necessity of self-defence in a violent society rather than from repression.

In *Ghosts*, however, as in Ibsen's subsequent analytical dramas, the Sophoclean stretch of long oblivion gives way to a deceptive calm arising from the seemingly successful subjugation of the truth. Time measures the deadening effect that is the cost of such repression, but time also measures the growth of a counterforce in the desire for confession, and if the precarious equilibrium of the hypocritical society is disturbed beyond a critical point, a process of analysis is set in motion that does not stop until the web of the false past is torn to shreds, and the stark truth is known as fully as in *Oedipus Rex*.

In the exploration of this theme Ibsen demonstrates the 'subjectivity' that German Romantic critics had posited as the defining feature of modern literature. The 'objective' nature of *Oedipus Rex* is apparent in the radical separation of the crime from the intention of Oedipus as well as in the concrete nature of the truth that is discovered. In Kleist's comedy, the transformation of the resistance of *aletheia* into the wilful suppression of truth is of course a subjective interpretation of the Sophoclean drama of truth. But through the distancing vision of comedy much of the objective vision of the model is retained. The truth concealed is a concrete situation, and the struggle for repression is externalized in the conflict between Adam and Walter. In *Ghosts*, on the other hand, the focus of dramatic interest is on the struggle of repression and disclosure as it occurs in the individual consciousness. And what is discovered in the end is not a set of facts, but an attitude or disposition, the destructiveness of which is demonstrated by the course of events it set in motion once it had been allowed to govern a single action.

The books that shock Pastor Manders are evidence that Mrs Alving's quest for the truth has been a matter of long standing. But she has not yet acknowledged to herself the full extent of her share in Alving's dissolution; and of course, to society at large she has revealed nothing that would damage the reputation of her family. On the contrary, as the play opens, she is engaged in a desperate undertaking that is intended to wipe out the past forever. On the one hand, the public memory of Alving as a social benefactor, enshrined in the name of the orphanage, is to wipe out the private memory of the dissolute rake. On the other hand, the endowment for the orphanage, which is exactly equal to the capital for which she married Alving, is to protect her son from his father in that he will inherit nothing from him. There is a mistake in this arithmetic, for what right does Mrs Alving have to the amount by which her present fortune exceeds the amount of the original capital, even if that balance is due to her prudent management? Her attempt to dispose of the capital once it has done its work points to more serious errors in her calculation regarding the past. Mrs Alving is plainly a divided creature. Long years of solitude have taught her to think for herself and to question the conventional wisdom of society. But she shrinks from the consequences of such thought. Her enlightenment is of a theoretical nature and contrasts strangely with the preposterous plan by which she proposes to bury the past and obliterate the truth.

The catalyst that translates her theoretical and evasive liberalism into a radical confrontation with her own predicament is the encounter with Pastor Manders. If Mrs Alving is the Oedipus of *Ghosts*, Paster Manders is the play's Tiresias – and the analogy is sufficiently preposterous to be illuminating. That Manders has eyes but cannot (or rather will not) see is made very clear in the play by the ease with which he allows himself to be taken in by Engstrand. What Tiresias is accused of – ignorance, venality, and blindness – Manders possesses in abundance. The bland complacency that hides them all contrasts with the obstinate and harsh nature of the prophet in whom 'truth is strong.' This counterpoint between the two priests extends to their effects on the protagonists. The true but riddling accusations of Tiresias goad Oedipus into delusions. It is different with Manders' accusations. They are not based on knowledge, but on philistine conceptions of the role of women in society. To Manders, Mrs Alving has failed as wife and mother, and his sense of truth and duty makes it incumbent upon him to tell her so.

Stung by Manders' accusations, Mrs Alving sets out to disabuse him of her life with her late husband and in thus uncovering the past thwarts her own purpose of concealment. In the end she is ready to acknowledge Regine's paternity in public: even before the orphanage goes up in flames, it has been spiritually abandoned by Mrs Alving. Her defence to Pastor Manders is a doubled-edged sword. Like Oedipus, she is endowed with extraordinary intelligence and resolution, and because, unlike Manders, she is no longer protected, if she ever was, by the complacency that shrouds morally troublesome connections in convenient darkness, she cannot ignore the evidence where it points at her own guilt. When Manders expresses his indignation at Engstrand's marrying Regine's mother for $300.00, she shocks him even more by turning his indignation against herself and pointing to the similarity between Engstrand's action and her own marriage with Alving for the sake of a fortune.

In the encounter between Mrs Alving and Manders one sees with particular clarity the dependence of the modern tragedy of knowledge on the 'will to see things as they are not.' One year after her marriage Mrs Alving had run away and had sought refuge with Manders whom she loved and who liked her well enough. He lacked the courage to accept her: in retrospect he argues that he had won a victory over himself in ordering her to return to her husband. She calls it a lamentable defeat and calls it a crime to obey the forces of 'law and order.'[46] When Manders protests that they do not understand each other and Mrs Alving corrects him by saying: 'Not any more, at least,' he emphatically states: 'Never once ... not in my most secret thoughts have I ever regarded you as anything other than another man's wife.' To which Mrs Alving dryly replies: 'It's so easy to forget one's own past,' and she changes the topic of conversation when Manders asserts that he is the same man he always was – a statement that she clearly understands in the ironic sense not perceived by Manders.[47]

The plight of Oswald goes much further than Manders' provocative obtuseness in guiding Mrs Alving towards the recognition of the truth. Whereas in the scenes with Manders she was not free from the vanity of martyrdom in dwelling on the sacrifice of personal fulfilment, in the encounter with her son she convicts herself of the responsibility for the dissolution of the father: she herself emerges as the culprit to the extent to which she conformed to the demands of a hypocritical society.

The error of her financial calculation about Oswald's inheritance from his father is brutally demonstrated by the revelation of Oswald's other 'inheritance.' Mrs Alving's error extends not only to the concealment of the past but more importantly to the effort to contain it. Her behaviour after her return to her husband was in one way in keeping with the moral premises of the society she had come to condemn. She sought to protect the reputation of her family, and because she was a woman of unusual energy and competence, she succeeded remarkably well. But fear of scandal had not been her primary motive, at least in later years. She tried to protect her son and hoped to save the future by sacrificing the present to the past.

The news of Oswald's disease brings home to her the failure of her policy of containment and makes irrelevant the strategy of concealment epitomized in the plan for the orphanage. But worse than that she recognizes that her policy not only failed to protect Oswald but had indeed contributed to his ruin. Oswald's yearning for the joy of life, naïvely symbolized in the bohemian life of Parisian artists, recalls to her mind the gaiety and exuberance of his father, and she recognizes that her contribution to their marriage had only tightened the restrictions that a provincial society had imposed upon him. Her success in the ways of the town was built on the wreck of their marriage, which by breaking the father ruined the son.

There is no satisfaction to be gained from the recognition of such truths. The orphanage and Oswald both 'burn up,' leaving behind a despairing Mrs Alving, whose plan to obliterate the past was impotent before its destructive nature. Critics have been strangely silent about the nature of the poison that Mrs Alving holds in her hands as the curtain falls, to administer to Oswald, or perhaps, for all we know, to herself as well. It is morphine, the symbol of forgetfulness even more so than of death, and a powerful antidote to truth. The poison throws an ironic light on Mrs Alving's earlier statement: 'I'm not putting up with it any longer, all these ties and restrictions. I can't stand it! I must work myself free.'[48] Only death or oblivion are 'remedies' to the corrosive disease of truth. Thus the end of Ghosts looks forward to The Wild Duck with its tragicomic doctrine of the life lie.

SCRIPTURAL TRAGEDY
A L'ANTIQUE

The incompatibility of Christianity with tragedy has often been asserted; of equal frequency have been attempts to achieve some reconciliation between them. From the playwright's perspective, this incompatibility arises from the generic rules concerning suitable heroes and endings. Post-Aristotelian genre theory had made an unhappy ending a constitutive feature of tragedy. That is why Dante called his great work *Commedia*: no story, however full of suffering and horror, deserves the name of tragedy if it ends with a vision of salvation. Damnation thus offered itself as the appropriate subject for a Christian tragedy. This view appears in Chaucer's *Monk's Tale*, where the fall of Lucifer heads the list of examples that follow the monk's definition of tragedy. But the tragedy of damnation violates the Aristotelian rule that the hero of a tragedy should not be wicked because the just punishment of a wicked man does not arouse the sympathetic pity that is a necessary feature of tragic response.

How is Christian tragedy possible if both the representation of salvation and of damnation violate fundamental conventions of tragedy? The practice of European playwrights suggests two answers. One approach has been to focus on the process rather than the outcome of damnation and to see the progressive loss of good as a subject to which the responses of pity and fear are eminently suitable. This is the route taken by Marlowe, Shakespeare, Milton, and Racine in their portrayals of Faustus, Macbeth, Satan, and Phèdre. The other approach dwells on the distance that separates the sufferings of the here and now from the eventual achievement of salvation. One common form of this second approach polarizes our tragic response to the opposing figures of tyrant and martyr: our fear at the tyrant's excesses and pity at the martyr's sufferings are not extinguished by the reflection on the eventual reversal of their fortunes.

A more stringent form of this approach increases the distance between salvation and the here and now to the point at which salvation, without being denied, is beset with doubt and obscurity and the contradictions and agonies of the here and now must be endured without the solace of a 'promised end.' This is the vision that Walter Benjamin posited as constitutive of Trauerspiel, the baroque – and more generally modern – equivalent of ancient tragedy. Trauerspiel systematically withholds any vision of transcendence or salvation: 'Kennt es eine Erlösung, so liegt sie mehr in der Tiefe dieser Verhängnisse selbst als im Vollzug eines göttlichen Heilsplans.' ('Salvation, if there is any, resides in the very depth of events rather than in the execution of a divine scheme.')[1]

The deferral of salvation to the point of its disappearance is the common feature of a handful of Christian tragedies by Humanist writers who saw scripture as the modern equivalent of the subject matter of Greek tragedy and practised a rigorous and austere allegiance to both scripture and Greek tragedy without any concessions to the public stage or popular tastes. Buchanan's *Jephtha* is the prototype of this sub-genre and directly or indirectly influenced all the other members of the class, whether the plays of de La Taille and Garnier, or, over a century later, Milton's *Samson Agonistes* and Racine's *Athalie*.

Scriptural tragedy à l'antique, as I call this sub-genre, differs sharply from the religious drama that flourished in the schools and colleges of sixteenth-century Europe. That drama reflects the hegemony of Terence in the school curricula and has many points of continuity with medieval drama. It does not fall easily into the ancient categories of tragedy and comedy, and the self-styled tragedies in particular are not always easy to recognize as such. The German Protestant writer Kirchmeyer, for instance, produced a faithful, lucid, and eloquent Latin verse translation of Sophocles, but the reader would be sorely disappointed if he looked in Kirchmeyer's biblical plays of the same period for any trace of the architectural principles of Sophoclean tragedy.[2] This aspect of Sophocles, which meant so much to Milton and Racine, was completely lost on Kirchmeyer, however much he hellenized his name into Naogeorgus. And in this regard his plays are typical of their genre, as may be seen from the most cursory analysis of the two famous anthologies of neo-Latin religious drama published in Basel in 1540 and 1547.[3]

The mixed character of most sixteenth-century religious drama is well illustrated by Theodore de Bèze's *Abraham sacrifiant*, a self-styled tragedy by a Humanist writer and shaped in part by the imitation of ancient models, but addressed to a popular audience, relaxed in its sense of decorum, and strongly related to the *Vieil Testament* cycle and the Christian Terence tradition. Pastoral elements and a 'vice' devil recall the former, whereas the dramatization of the scenes between Abraham and Isaac echoes the Abraham play by Hieronymus Ziegler. But the most important element of continuity lies in the choice of subject. The story of Abraham and Isaac had been a popular subject in medieval drama not only for its intrinsic dramatic properties, but because the promise to Abraham constituted one of the chief links between the Old and the New Testaments: in some English versions, for instance, the substituted ram of Genesis becomes a lamb to make the foreshadowing of the Incarnation more apparent.

Scriptural tragedy à l'antique measures its distance from the religious drama of its day in the studious avoidance of the story of Abraham and Isaac. De La Taille, Buchanan's most radical follower, openly criticized the choice of the story as a tragic subject – evidently a disparaging comment on de Bèze's play.[4] The criticism is implicit in Buchanan's play, for its subject is chosen precisely for its remoteness from the divine promise given to Abraham and fulfilled in Christ, a remoteness all the more starkly apparent through the resemblance of the story to the sacrifice of Isaac:

And Jephthah vowed a vow unto the Lord, and said, If thou shalt without fail deliver the children of Ammon into mine hands,

Then it shall be, that whatsoever cometh forth of the doors of my house to meet me, when I return in peace from the children of Ammon, shall surely be the Lord's, and I will offer it up for a burnt offering.

So Jephthah passed over unto the children of Ammon to fight against them; and the Lord delivered them into his hands. ... And Jephthah came to Mizpeh unto his house, and, behold, his daughter came out to meet him with timbrels and with dances: and she was his only child; beside her he had neither son nor daughter.

And it came to pass, when he saw her, that he rent his clothes, and said, Alas, my daughter! thou hast brought me very low, and thou art one of them that trouble me: for I have opened my mouth unto the Lord, and I cannot go back. (Judges 11:30–5)

Buchanan's choice of the story of Jephtha's vow implies a recognition of the problem of Christian tragedy and set a precedent for dealing with it:

if tragedy is incompatible with the outright promise of salvation, then Christian tragedy must draw on those phases of Christian experience in which the promise of salvation is attenuated and deferred to such an extent as to raise doubts about its very existence. The promised end need not be denied and may indeed be foreshadowed, but Christian tragedy requires a narrowing of perspective and a focusing on situations of suffering and despair in which a full vision of transcendence is systematically withheld.

In scriptural tragedy à l'antique this retreat from the prospect of salvation takes the form of a twofold return. There is a return to the subject matter of the Old Testament – and more specifically to those parts of it that seem in conflict with the New Testament – and there is the return to the form of Greek tragedy. Because of their uncompromising execution of this double return, scriptural tragedies à l'antique are exceptionally interesting versions of Greek tragedy. They are also exclusive and somewhat disdainful performances. Buchanan wanted to lure his students from the vulgarities of medieval drama; Milton's preface to *Samson Agonistes* speaks contemptuously of the public stage for which his work was not intended, and Racine's *Athalie* – not in every respect a full member of this class – turns away from the tyranny of the erotic sub-plot and realizes at last the ideal of the tragédie sans l'amour that had been impossible on the public stage.[5] There is a price to be paid for such preoccupation with 'fit audience, though few,' and the works in this class pay it. At the same time, in no other group of Humanist plays is the deliberately anti-popular stance so fully motivated in terms of thematic purpose, and no other group of Humanist tragedies comes so close to transcending the intrinsic limitations of the form.

BUCHANAN'S *JEPHTHA*

Quo fortiore nata tulit animo necem
Hoc angit animum tristior meum dolor.

The more of dauntless fortitude displayed
In face of such a death of violence,
The greater and more poignant is the grief
Shall pierce my heart till this heart too is cold.

Buchanan's *Jephtha*, the first scriptural tragedy to be composed strictly according to the rules and conventions of ancient tragedy, is a version of *Iphigenia in Aulis*, but it also borrows important elements from *Hecuba*, and one of its scenes is adapted from Plautus' *Amphitryo* – evidence of the hold of Roman comedy even over this most austere and self-conscious of tragedies. Although it was one of the most frequently reprinted and translated of neo-Latin tragedies, it had few followers.[6] The rareness of its discipline was acknowledged by Ascham, who argued in the *Schoolmaster* that together with Thomas Watson's *Absalom* it was the only tragedy that correctly imitated the ancients.[7]

Jephtha opens with a prologue spoken by an angel who interprets the story of Jephtha against the background of the history of Israel. The sins of Israel have compelled God over and over to mete out punishment in the form of plagues, famines, and military defeats, but the repentance of Israel has again and again moved him to mercy. So on this occasion he has chosen a deliverer to free Israel from the yoke of the Ammonites. But lest Israel should attribute to its own power what was the work of God's mercy he has chosen this latest deliverer 'non e potentum quempiam numero, gravem turba clientum, liberisve turgidum' ('High placed in the proud roll of powerful chiefs'). Instead he has chosen an exile, spurned by his own family, and he will destroy this deliverer as soon as he has raised him:

> Porro ne Jephthes quoque
> Se metiatur exitu hujus praelii,
> Et intumescat insolens rebus bonis,
> Damno obruetur protinus domestico,
> Cedentque fracti contumaces spiritus. (51–5)

> Further, lest Jephthah, he too, should aspire
> To measure his own prowess by the event
> Of battle, and presume on his success,
> Full soon domestic sorrow shall bedim
> His shining victory. Triumph and woe shall meet,
> and woe shall triumph.

The angel briefly summarizes the events about to take place and leaves after announcing the entrance of Jephtha's wife and daughter.

The prologue stands in the Euripidean rather than Senecan or comic tradition. The speaker does not address the audience, as happens in Plautus or Terence; nor, despite its undeniable grimness, does the prologue have the atmospheric function of Senecan ghost prologues. Looking forward and backward in time, it provides information and establishes the moral and historical context within which the action will unfold. As a divine speaker, the angel is closest to the prologue gods of Euripides, such as Venus in *Hippolytus* or Hermes in *Ion*. But towards the end of his speech the angel recalls the ghost of Polydorus in *Hecuba* and, like him, he describes the entrance of a mother terrified by a dream that forecasts the death of her child.

In the first scene Jephtha's wife, Storge, whose name is the Greek word for 'loving care,' relates to her daughter a dream, adapted from the opening scene of the *Hecuba*, in which a lamb was torn from her breast. Storge is characterized as the worried wife: like Andromache, she has lost her father and brother in war, and her life, like that of Deianeira, has been an unending succession of suffering. It is a nice touch of dramatic irony that Iphis, in her desire to comfort her mother, urges her to prepare for the reception of the victorious father and in her eagerness contributes to the disaster dimly foreseen by the mother. The scene ends with an expression of trust in God: 'idem bella qui suasit Deus, / salvum reducet laude cumulatum nova.' ('The Power that moved him to those warlike toils, / Will safe restore him, crowned with honours new.')

In their first ode the chorus of young women lament the servitude of Israel, recognize it as the consequence of their sinfulness, but pray for forgiveness and express the hope that their enemies will be defeated. These hopes are confirmed in the following scene when a messenger arrives with the news of Jephtha's victory. He relates first how Jephtha vainly attempted to arrive at a peaceful settlement with the Ammonites, and how, after the offer to negotiate was haughtily turned down, the Ammonites were decisively defeated. In the account of the battle, of which the Bible gives no detailed account, Buchanan followed the report of Amphitryo's victory in Platus' comedy, but he added a divine omen (304–10), probably adapted from Samuel's victory over the Philistines (1 Sam. 7:10), which tilts the battle in favour of Israel after a long period of indecisive fighting.

The emphasis that Buchanan gives to the negotiations is worth noting. In this, of course, he may be said merely to follow the Bible, and since the negotiations are one of the few incidents from Jephtha's career mentioned in the Bible, Buchanan could hardly afford to neglect them. But it appears that both in the Bible, and even more in Buchanan's play, the motif of negotiations stands in a disturbing relationship to the story of the vow. In the exegetical literature from Ambrose and Jerome on, the story of Jephtha is cited as the exemplum of a misguided vow, and it is argued that Jephtha was punished by God for making a rash and foolish promise.[8] The shadowy portrait of Jephtha that emerges from the Bible is, however, that of a prudent man. In Buchanan's account this impression is even heightened. Whereas the Bible merely reports Jephtha's rejection of the territorial claims of the Ammonites (Judges 11:14–27), Buchanan attributes motives of prudence and justice to Jephtha:

> Ibi noster inter imperator agmina
> Praecone misso, tentat absque sanguine
> Finire bellum jure & aequis legibus:
> Uterque populus ut vetusti finibus
> Contentus agri, ab alteris injuriam
> Vimque abstineret, rapta dominis redderet,
> Pacemque bello & certa dubiis praeferat. (251–7)

> It was then
> Our general between the advancing lines
> Sent forth a herald, if perchance the war
> Might end all bloodless, and the antagonists
> Strike hands on just and equitable terms.
> This was his overture: – That with the bounds
> Of ancient times fixed to their territories
> Each people should content them, and refrain
> From acts of injury and violence
> Done to the other; and whate'er had been
> By rapine taken should restore – preferring
> Peace to grim war, things certain to unknown
> And doubtful issues.

And in Jephtha's recognition of the battle omen we see evidence of his piety (311–13).

Our impression, derived from the messenger report, that Jephtha is pious and prudent in addition to being valiant is amply confirmed by his first entrance. His opening words are a long address in which he expresses his gratitude to God for his victory. Jephtha's praise dwells on the justice of God as it appears in his two aspects as *severus ultor* and *clemens pater*. But it is naturally the second aspect on which Jephtha dwells more. Like the chorus before him, he acknowledges the sins of Israel and praises God for his mercy:

> At tu benignus atque misericors Deus
> Justi furoris frena compescis tui:
> Iram remittis, & oddi oblivisceris:

Et abdicatos filios culpa sua,
Restituis iterum misericordia tua. (455–9)

              but still
Thou art a God benign and merciful,
And thy just rage thou reinest in; thy wrath
Ebbs from thy pitying bosom; guilty deeds
Which thou perforce must hate thou yet dost cease
To call to thy remembrance; and thy children,
Renounced for their deep crimes and held as sons
Forth banished from thy favour, yet again,
Relenting, in thy mercy infinite
Thou to thy love restorest.

The movement of Jephtha's speech follows that of the choral ode which had preceded it. There the women had celebrated the justice of God and had concluded with a vision of festivities and animal sacrifices in honor of God, in which Jephtha's daughter was to be the cult leader:

Et tu progenies ducis,
Magni spes generis, cape
Cultus, filia, splendidos,
Et patrem reducem piis
Laeta amplectere brachiis. (421–5)

And thou, child of our leader bold,
Hope of a name henceforth enrolled
With heroes – in thy bright array
Deck thee, maiden, and away!
Thy sire returned from war's alarms
Embrace with joy in loving arms.

Similarly Jephtha's thoughts turn from the justice of God to ways in which he can express his people's gratitude, however inadequately. He remembers his vow and concludes his speech with another praise of the justice, clemency, and power of God:

At tu benigne memoris animi munera
Interpretaris: ut fideliter tua
Promissa solvis, vota sic reddi tibi
Fideliter gaudes, potentiam exserens

Erga rebelles, exserens clementiam
Erga timentes. Vis nec ulla est altera,
Cui terra, coelum, pareant, & tartara. (488–94)

              But thou interpretest
Kindly and generously the offerings
Laid on thine altar by a grateful heart;
And as thou ever faithfully dost keep
Thy promises, so art thou pleased when we
Do faithfully to thee perform our vows.
And thou dost deal with men as are their deeds –
Stern to revolters, making them to feel
The curbing and the stroke of thy strong hand;
But ever gentle, ever merciful
To all who meekly venerate thy name:
Nor is there other Power whom heaven and earth
And the dark shadowy realm of death obey.

The build-up of happy expectations which began with the comforting words of Iphis in the first scene, continued through the choral odes and the messenger's report, and culminated in Jephtha's praise of God, is an eminent example of what Donatus calls *parektasis tragica*, the deliberate raising of false hopes before the catastrophe. It shows on Buchanan's part a remarkable grasp of dramatic irony as a structural principle. And it greatly increases the effect of the fatal encounter between Jephtha and his daughter, which follows immediately on Jephtha's prayer. All his expectations are suddenly dashed as his daughter comes out of the house to embrace him, and, checked in her joy by his change of expression, asks in bewilderment: 'Cur, genitor, a me torva vertis lumina?' ('Why do you turn your cruel eyes from me?') (501). The question is adapted from *Iphigenia in Aulis*, where the daughter, similarly rebuffed by her father, exclaims: 'You say you are glad to see me, / But your eyes have no quiet in them.' But as Raymond Lebègue points out, Buchanan increases the dramatic effectiveness of the question.[9] Whereas Agamemnon is embarrassed in the extreme to see his daughter, their encounter is not in itself an event that has consequences. But Jephtha's first glimpse of Iphis constitutes the play's tragic reversal; he averts his eyes in horror, attempting, as it were, to undo the event retroactively. Hence the skilful variation in the question.

In the remainder of the scene Buchanan is equally skilful in adapting the structure of the Euripidean scene to his own needs. The relationship between father and daughter is substantially different. The Euripidean daughter is clearly characterized as a child. She cares for Agamemnon only as her father, does not know where Troy is, and conceives of the war as an incomprehensible nuisance that keeps her away from her Daddy. Iphis is rather more heroic, as the Protestant Humanist Sturm pointed out in his preface to the 1567 Strassburg edition of the play: 'Iphis ejus ita ad mortem accedit ut Iphigeniam graecam animi magnitudine superet.' ('By her manner of meeting death Iphis exceeds the Greek Iphigenia in magnanimity of mind.') This comment may refer specifically to the ending, but her greater heroism is already apparent in this earlier scene. Iphis wonders whether her father's grief is due to the losses of the army, showing a social awareness which at that point is alien to the Euripidean child. When she is reassured about the victory, she assumes that she must in some measure have sinned against her father, but Jephtha denies this and indeed accuses himself of having sinned against her, where-upon Iphis gravely and somewhat sententiously argues that even if he had done her wrong he should not worry: 'nam parentum injurias / Aequo necesse est liberi ut animo ferant' ('for children should bear injustice at the hand of their parents with equanimity'). (512–3). There is poignant irony in the exemplary behaviour of Iphis, for it is she who turns the dialogue to prayers and to the observation of vows, arguing that the pious man who does not beseech God in distress and forget him in times of good fortune can count on his help in a crisis:

> Facilem quisquis incolumis Deum
> Sibi demereri studuit, ubi res ingruit
> Adversa, nixus conscientiae bonae
> Fructu, rogare numen audet propitium
> Jam sponte, vota nuncupat securius,
> Et certiore spe futura concipit. (535–40)

> And he who in his clear and sunny days,
> When all is well, has striven to be approved
> Of God – he, when the adverse storm assails,
> Is buttressed by his sense of rectitude,
> And unpresumptuous but confident
> Kneels known to seek the aid vouchsafed of Heaven,
> The aid already in Heaven's self-moved grace
> Descending to his side. Serene in heart

He utters forth the vows devotion claims,
And firm in hope forecasts the coming years.

The irony is apparent. It is adapted from Euripides' play, which is echoed more specifically in Jephtha's ambiguous remark: 'adesse oportet te sacrificio statim' ('there is a sacrifice that calls thee soon') (599). But the irony extends beyond the immediate scenic effect to the theological substance of the play. The reasonableness of Iphis' arguments as well as of the hopes of Jephtha and the Chorus is confuted by the grim and inexplicable nature of God's justice.

Buchanan's skilful use of irony throughout the opening scenes sets the stage for the play's intellectual centre, a discussion between Jephtha and an unnamed priest about the validity of the vow. This scene presents considerable difficulties of interpretation, which are compounded by ambiguous biographical evidence about Buchanan's position on the status of Jephtha's vow. The priest takes up the eminently reasonable position that Jephtha's vow is invalid because Nature, piety, and the explicit commandments of God forbid human sacrifices. He points to the universal bond between parents and offspring in the animal kingdom (880–5). Would God delight in a sacrifice that is not even pleasing to the idols of Egypt and Assyria (888–91)? And he cites Psalm 51 to the effect that God delights in the contrite heart rather than in the slaughter of bulls (895–9). Jephtha replies that vows must be fulfilled, but the priest argues that this applies only to just vows (904–5). Jephtha concedes that it would have been better not to make a vow that was unlawful, but that once made, it had to be kept. Jephtha refers to the precedent of Abraham and Isaac, which he interprets as enjoining obedience, whereas for the priest it proves that God forbids human sacrifice (920–1).

The priest then shifts the argument to a different level. The truth of God is simple, univocal, and laid down in his law, which should be observed. It is impious to vow new rites, and more impious to add to the crime of an illegitimate vow the further crime of its execution (938–61). This argument is very close to Calvin's discussion of vows in his *Institutes* (4.13.1–3), where he attacks the vanity and superstition of those who want to worship God by their own rather than God's laws. Jephtha does not really reply to this argument but instead launches an attack on the sophisticated clergy who do not care for vows whereas the people in their simple faith stick to what they once promise. He concludes with a general attack on education:

Nam litterarum quo quis est peritior,
Huic est sacrorum cura negligentior. (980–1)

> The better skilled
> In that vain lore, the less of reverence
> For all that men hold sacred.

The priest characterizes Jephtha's position as one of ignorance and obstinacy. The simplicity of God's truth cannot be bent either by a tyrant's will or by the ignorance of the people. It is not enough, he argues, to hold a position blindly; one must inquire 'mala/An recta quae pertinaciter tenet' ('Whether the things he holds/So stubbornly be right or wrong') (1002–3). He returns to the point about the vanity of deciding for oneself how God should be worshipped:

Religio vera est, veraque pietas, Deum
Non instituto colere quod commentus es
Tibi ipsi, sacris victimas non quaslibet
Mactare, sed quas missa legum coelitus
Decreta poscunt, & patrum mores probant (1014–18)

'Tis true religion and true piety
To worship God, not by such ordinances
As thine own erring fantasy may frame:
Nor yet by offering in sacrifice
Such victim as caprice may bid thee burn;
But by such only as his high behests,
From heaven delivered, in his law prescribe,
And our ancestral customs ratify.

When Jephtha replies the God accepts gratefully 'quodcumque gestum est mente sincera' ('whatever is done sincerely') (1019) the priest accuses him roundly of self induced blindness. But Jephtha remains unimpressed and leaves with a contemptuous attack on hypocritical prudence:

Ego veritatem malo stultam & simplicem,
Quam splendidam fuco impiam sapientiam. (1054–55)

> More to me
> Simple and foolish truth than the false glare
> Of godless learning tricked with sophistries.

In the exceptionally diffuse ode that follows this debate the Chorus seem to endorse the priest's position when they seek the cause of human disaster in blindness and ignorance rather than in the whims of fortune:

> Nempe erroris nebula, & tetris
> Ignorantia septa tenebris
> Sic humanas sepelit mentes.
> Nec perspicuis animi quisquam
> Oculis radios cernere potis est
> Veri simplicis, aut virtutis
> Nudae rectum insistere callem. (1075–81)

> Doubtless, it is the enfolding cloud
> Of error, as a dark-spun shroud,
> And ignorance, wrapt in loathly gloom,
> That thus the human mind entomb.
> There lives not 'neath this azure sky
> A man whose clear-discerning eye
> Can mark the pure unsullied ray
> Of Truth; not one to tread the way
> Where forthright Virtue onward leads
> With open mien and open deeds.

Since Buchanan was a prominent reformer who on more than one occasion had difficulties with Catholic authorities, it is tempting to see in the debate a quarrel between Catholic and Protestant positions.[10] Vows were a bone of contention in the religious quarrels of the sixteenth century. Protestants objected not only to the monastic vows and their abuses, but also to the practice of invoking the aid of the Trinity, the Virgin Mary, and the saints by all manner of vows. In a well-known contemporary debate the Strassburg reformer Bucerus took the position that foolish and criminal vows were not binding, whereas his Catholic opponent Latomus argued that all vows were binding but that God was grateful only for legitimate vows and not for criminal vows, as the punishment of Jephtha demonstrates. In 1550 Buchanan was detained by the Inquisition and composed a defence in which he touched on the question of vows and cited *Jephtha* in support of his position: 'de votis scripto (sic) in tragoedia de voto Jephthe meam sententiam ostendi cujus disputationis haec summa est: vota quae licite fiunt omnia servanda, ac multi etiam sciunt Conimbricae me orationem B. Latomi super hac re contra Bucerum et legere libenter solitum, et semper laudare' ('With regard to vows, my tragedy about the vow of Jephtha summarizes my position, which is that legitimate vows must be kept, and it is well known that at Combray I often read and always praised the oration by Latomus against Bucerus on this subject.')[11] Buchanan's own testimony is not helpful. What he gives as the 'gist' of the debate in his play, namely that legitimate vows should be kept, is not a point on which Jephtha and the priest or anyone else would quarrel. But if Buchanan argues that he had always taken the side of Latomus, which is roughly that of Jephtha in the debate, then the priest's position becomes by implication a Protestant one, which is a hard thing to accept in a play written by a prominent reformer, and clearly in contrast to the perception of the priest by Jephtha. For he comes to see in him one of those sophisticated prelates who use their theological acumen to wriggle out of their moral and religious commitments. By contrast Jephtha sees himself as the simple man of the people and a champion of pure faith undiluted by the doubts and evasions that are the result of higher education. But the arguments advanced by the priest hardly answer to Jephtha's description, and in his most telling argument he takes his cue directly from Calvin's attack on vows as an arrogation by man of the right to determine the form of worship.

If we thus try to line up the opposition between Jephtha and the priest with that of Catholics and Protestants, we are left with Jephtha arguing a Catholic position in the manner of a Protestant against a fat prelate who takes his cues from Calvin's *Institutes*. This is not very promising, nor is it attractive to accept Lebègue's position that *Jephtha* was originally a propaganda play against vows and that it was subsequently revised under the influence of the Bucerus-Latomus controversy in order to escape censorship.[12]

These contradictions disappear at once if we credit Buchanan with having dramatized the opposition between a tragic and a problem-solving world. The relationship of Jephtha and the priest is not unlike that of Michael Henchard and Donald Fairfrae in *The Mayor of Casterbridge* – a comparison that will appear less far-fetched if we remember that Hardy modelled his opposition on that of the tragic Saul and the non-tragic David. The world of the priest is that of the reasonable expectations so persuasively raised in the opening scenes of the play. The priest is the spokesman of values that the audience is plainly meant to embrace, but the play centres on a situation that is mysteriously impervious to reason and problem-solving. Conversely, the tragic world of

Jephtha is not held up for disapproval. Although Buchanan put in Jephtha's mouth some outbursts against learning which he cannot have approved of himself, the portrayal of Jephtha, as we have seen, is that of a valiant, pious, and even prudent man. The purpose of the debate therefore is not to reach a conclusion but to present an irreconcilable opposition. The tragic world, though apparently superseded by the more modern and more reasonable age of the priest, remains a threat to order and sanity, and in the tempestuous history of Israel, which is so firmly established as the background for this play, its recurrence is an all too frequent phenomenon.

In the final scenes of the play Buchanan moves away from the intractable dilemma of Jephtha and focuses instead on the spirit of pious submission in which Iphis accepts her ordeal. In the scene that follows the debate between Jephtha and the priest, Buchanan adapts the scene between father, mother, and daughter in the *Iphigenia in Aulis*. As in Euripides, the unsuccessful plea by the mother for the daughter's life is followed by the first plea of the daughter, who subsequently changes her mind and submits voluntarily to her father's will. But the details differ considerably. In Clytaemnestra's plea her revenge is foreshadowed; the audience cannot but read her words against the future. Storge is a dramatic character without past or future; she can only resort to general arguments about parental love and about a mother's right to codetermine her children's fate. Iphis' plea for life is greatly shortened. The Euripidean character begs for her life in a supplication that recalls at length the happiness of family life, and after Agamemnon has left the stage, proclaiming himself the helpless puppet of fate, Iphigenia bewails her lot in a kommos. Her change of mind occurs in a subsequent scene. The plea of Iphis is much more concise:

> Miserere, genitor, te per hanc rogo manum
> Voti potentem, compotem victoriae:
> Per si quid umquam merita sum de te bene:
> Si quando parvis comprimens te brachiis,
> Onus pependi dulce de collo tuo:
> Per si quid ex me tibi voluptatis fuit,
> Depone mentem liberos erga trucem,
> Et diritatis hujus obliviscere. (1215–22)

> Have pity, O my father! By this hand
> That crowned thy vow and won thee victory,
> I pray thy pity. If in infant days

I pleased thee well, and drew thy heart to me:
If e'er, with little arms enclasped around,
I hung upon thy neck, and thou wast glad
To feel the pendent burden; if I gave thee
Solace and joy in good and evil days,
Endearing all thy home – O cast away,
Cast far from thee, this purposed cruelty;
And let the horror which now chills our hearts
Pass from thy thoughts for ever?

And even this plea is modified by her willingness to concede some fault that might justify her punishment:

Aut si quid in te ex parte peccatum est mea,
Profer, quod instat cumque levius perferam,
Si luere poenas jure me cognovero. (1223–5)

       but if aught
Of wrong-doing toward thee be found in me,
O hide it not! It will be lightlier borne,
Whatever now awaits me, when I know
My doom is just. –

Iphis' speech for the first time moves Jephtha to an emotional outburst in which he accuses himself of the rashness of his vow and wishes that he had either never made the vow or else had lost the battle. His daughter thereupon immediately changes her position. The motivation for her change of mind derives from Ambrose rather than from Euripides, who stresses Iphigenia's desire to achieve glory in a pan-Hellenic crusade against barbarians. Ambrose, whose discussion of Jephtha's vow shows embarrassment at the theological intractability of the story, turns with relief to the daughter, whose action can be seen as an exemplum of making a virtue of necessity. She demonstrates piety and obedience: 'rediit ad patrem, quasi ad votum rediret, et voluntate propria cunctantem impulit, fecitque arbitratu spontaneo, ut quod erat impietatis fortuitum, fierat pietatis sacrificium' ('She returned to her father as if returning to the vow, and by her own will persuaded him in his indecision, and through an exercise of her free will converted the impiety of chance into a sacrifice of piety.')[13] This transformation of imposed necessity into voluntary submission is precisely the point of Iphis' change of heart:

Quod non volentem dura te necessitas
Isthuc coëgit, multa mihi faciunt fidem:
Moestitia praesens, pristina indulgentia;
Et nullius mens criminis mihi conscia,
Cur commereri debeam morten a patre.
Quapropter istud quicquid est, necessitas
Quod cogit, ultro non recuso perpeti:
Et quam parenti patriaeque debeo
Animam, libenter reddo: (1261–9)

        That thou art
Unwilling, by strong compulsion, driven
To do this deed is seen from many things –
Thy present deep dejectedness; the love,
The too-indulgent love, of former days;
And, on my part, a mind which blames me not
With crime that merits death, and least of all
Death by thy hand. Wherefore, be what it may
This hard necessity compels thee to,
I now resist no more. The life I owe
To thee, my father, and to this dear land
That gave me birth, I willingly restore.

Her resolution produces another violent outburst of self-recrimination
on the part of Jephtha, who now wants to substitute himself, but Iphis,
who has reached almost a state of serenity, refuses to accept this offer and
leaves with a last farewell to the light:

O fata, fata, & morte defuncti patres,
Accipite placide destinatos patriae
Manes saluti; tuque lux novissima
Hodierna nostris haurienda oculis, vale. (1327–30)

Ye Powers above, that fix the fates of men!
And ye, my dead forefathers? grant, I pray,
To her who died for the deliverance
Of her dear native land, her land and yours,
Gentle and kindly welcome to her shade!
And thou, light of this sun, the last mine eyes
Shall ever look upon, farewell! farewell!

In the biblical account the daughter asks her father for a delay of two months during which she bewails her virginity. In a dramatic representation this delay would destroy not only the unity of time, but more importantly the continuity of action at a crucial stage. There is no precedent in Greek tragedy for a disruption of temporal continuity at so late a point in the action. Buchanan omits it therefore and reaps the additional benefit of increasing the heroic status of Iphis. The biblical account is also silent about the sacrifice itself; so much so that some later theologians felt encouraged to deny that the sacrifice took place at all. The dramatist could not hide his dénouement in such a discreet silence; it is reported by a messenger to Storge in a speech that draws both on Seneca and Euripides. In particular the contrast between the weeping bystanders and the unmoved victim is taken from the death of Astyanax, of whom Seneca says: 'non flet e turba omnium / qui fletur' ('The crowd weeps / for him who alone does not weep') (*Troades*, 1099–1100). This appears in Buchanan as:

> Sed se per ora cum pudore fuderat
> Perspicua certae juncta vis fiduciae,
> Interque flentes sola fletibus carens,
> Vultu remisso constitit firma, ac sui
> Secura fati: quas tenebat lacrymas
> Propinqua morti virgo, populus non tenet. (1378–87)

> But o'er her countenance, mingling with that blush
> And visible to every eyes, there shone
> A fixed unfaltering purpose, and, alone
> Tearless amid the weeping, meek she stood,
> Serenely calm, and to her fate resigned.
> The maiden, death so nigh, wept not a tear;
> Beholders wept for pity – all that crown,
> Swayed by one strong emotion.

Iphis dies as a saint and martyr imploring God in her dying words to accept death as a punishment for the sins of her people. Her interpretation of her death as an expiatory offering overshadows the grief of her father, who, like Agamemnon, shrouds his head in shame and horror. Buchanan follows the Bible rather than his classical sources in passing over the moment of death as quickly as possible:

Fletu sacredos obrutus vix solvere
Animae meatus potuit, & moesto diu
Taciturna turba torpuit silentio. (1432–4)

      All unnerved, unmanned, the priest
Could scarce unstop the outlets of the soul;
And long the silent crowd looked on aghast,
In speechless pity.

In the concluding lines of his speech the messenger attempts to mitigate the sense of tragedy in a manner that distinctly looks forward to *Samson Agonistes*. The people's response to the events, he reports, was not 'ille gemitus, esse nec qualis solet / Fremitus doloris atque lamentatio' ('a sound / Of moaning and lamenting such as comes / Of hearts surcharged with grief'), but admiration for Iphis and praise of Storge as the mother of such a daughter. But this attempt at consolation is not the play's last word. No writer of scriptural tragedy went further than Buchanan in blocking any vision of transcendence that might mitigate the catastrophe by placing it in a wider context. The harshness of his tragic vision finds its last expression in the response of the mother who – unlike the surviving father of Samson – does not even see a 'magni doloris magnum ... solatium' in the heroic manner of her daughter's death. The play concludes with the disconsolate lines of Storge:

Solamen ipso luctuosius malo,
Quod leniendo exasperat malum vetus,
Luctusque acerbi memoriam semper novans,
Reducta cogit vulnera recrudescere.
Quo fortiore nata tulit animo necem,
Hoc angit animum tristior meum dolor. (1445–50)

      Solace, is it not,
More sad and mournful than the grief it soothes?
One that by mitigating aggravates,
And, by recalling ever and again
The memory of my anguish, needs must cause
My closing wounds to rend and bleed anew?
The more of dauntless fortitude displayed
In face of such a death of violence,
The greater and more poignant is the grief
Shall pierce my soul till this heart too is cold.

'Saül le Furieux' and 'Les Gabéonites'

O Roy plus malheureux que la misere mesme

Saül le Furieux, composed about 1562 but not published until 1572, is the chief claim to fame of Jean de La Taille, a French nobleman (1533–1608) whose poetic ambitions were spurred and cut off by the religious wars of his day.[14] He abandoned literature for a military career and after ten years of active service returned briefly to poetry – he supervised the edition of his works – before retiring into the peace and obscurity of private life. *Saül le Furieux* is only marginally a version of an ancient tragedy in my strict use of the term. Its title acknowledges *Hercules Furens* as a model, and the opening scenes are patterned on the mad scenes in Seneca's play. But the use of the model is rather clumsy, and de La Taille abandons it early in his play, which proceeds as a structuring of the scriptural events according to the plot conventions of Greek tragedy and as an interpretation of their significance from a rigorously tragic perspective. Indeed, in his effort to dwell on the obscurity of divine justice, de La Taille deliberately ignores parts of the Old Testament narrative that incriminate Saul and would tend to resolve some of the difficulties in interpreting God's behaviour towards him. In the biblical account, God turns against Saul when the latter fails to carry out an explicit order to destroy the Amalekites and all their possessions: 'And he took Agag the king of the Amalekites alive, and utterly destroyed all the people with the edge of the sword. But Saul and the people spared Agag, and the best of the sheep, and of the oxen, and of the fatlings, and the lambs, and all that was good, and would not utterly destroy them: but everything that was vile and refuse, that they destroyed utterly' (1 Samuel 15:8–9). When Samuel informs Saul that God is angered at his disobedience by permitting Samuel to execute Agag: 'So Samuel turned again after Saul; and Saul worshipped the Lord. Then said Samuel, Bring ye hither to me Agag the king of the Amalekites. And Agag came unto him delicately. And Agag said, Surely the bitterness of death is past. And Samuel said, As thy sword hath made women childless, so shall thy mother be childless among women. And Samuel hewed Agag in pieces before the Lord in Gilgal' (1 Samuel 15: 31–3). Saul's motives in sparing Agag's life appear to be economic rather than humanitarian, and while the Old Testament narrative raises questions about divine cruelty, it does not oppose that cruelty to human clemency. But that is precisely the point on which de La Taille's tragedy turns. De La Taille's Saul did not act out of greed when he spared Agag's life but displayed a humane ruler's moderation in victory, and his anguish at the contradiction of a just God exacting acts of barbarism becomes the focus of the tragedy:

> O que sa Providence est cachee aux humains!
> Pour estre donc humain j'esprouve sa cholere,
> Et pour estre cruel il m'est donc debonnaire!
> Hé Sire, Sire làs! fault-il donc qu'un vainqueur
> Plustost que de pitié use fier de rigueur,
> Et que sans regarder qu'une telle fortune
> Est aussi bien à luy qu'à ses vaincus commune,
> Egorge tant de gents? vault-il pas mieux avoir
> Esgard à quelque honneur, qu'à nostre grand pouvoir? (312–20)

If in much of the tragedy Saul acts like a sinner who has forsaken his God we are never allowed to forget that his sinful despair is the consequence of God's anger at what he considered an act of clemency and justice.

In Saul's response to the ruin predicted by the ghost of Samuel, de La Taille's tragic vision finds its fullest expression. In the prologue to *Jephtha*, the Angel had developed the grim logic by which God elevates men from lowly positions only to plunge them into utter disaster later on. In an impassioned speech, unmatched in the Humanist theatre for its rhetorical and dramatic force, Saul searches for the justice of this logic, which he, as the first divinely elected king, has suffered in such pre-eminent degree:

> O grandeur malheureuse, en quel gouffre de mal
> M'abismes-tu helas, ô faulx degré Royal!
> Mais qu'avois-je offensé quand de mon toict champestre,
> Tu me tiras, ô DIEU, envieux de mon estre,
> Où je vivois content sans malediction,
> Sans rancueur, sans envie, et sans ambition,
> Mais pour me faire choir d'un sault plus miserable,
> D'entree tu me fis ton mignon favorable.
> (O la belle façon d'aller ainsi chercher
> Les hommes, pour apres les faire trebuscher!)
> Tu m'allechas d'honneurs, tu m'eslevas en gloire,

Tu me fis triomphant, tu me donnas victoire,
Tu me fis plaire à toy, et comme tu voulus
Tu transformas mom cueur, toy-mesme tu m'esleus,
Tu me fis sur le peuple aussi hault de corsage
Que sont ces beaux grands pins sur tout un païsage,
Tu me fis sacrer Roy, tu me haulsas expres
A fin de m'enfondrer en mil malheurs apres!
Veux-tu donc (inconstant) piteusement destruire
Le premier Roy qu'au monde il pleut à toy d'eslire! (793–812)

The subsidiary episodes of the play further stress the obscurity of divine justice. In the opening scenes of the play, Saul's sons barely escape their father's efforts to kill them – a conflation of Saul's attack on David with Hercules' murder of his children. But the sons escape their father only to become the victims of God's anger. De La Taille gives us a sympathetic and heroic portrait of Jonathan, who urges his brothers to seize the initiative in the defense of their country while their father is ill. He cites the examples of David and Samson, who overcame their enemies by faith alone, and he cannot believe that God would suffer the victory of Dagon:

N'est-ce pas Dieu qui peut en souflant seulement
Mil et mil esquadrons deffaire en un moment?
Voudroit-il bien qu'on vist son Arche venerable
Honorer de Dagon le temple abominable?
Nous irons en battaille avec l'aide de DIEU,
Plus seure que le fer, la lance, et que l'epieu:
Fussent-ils cent fois plus, s'il prend nostre defense
Contre eux ses ennemis feront-ils resistance? (61–8)

But the answer to such fervent expressions of faith is an omen that clearly forecasts their deaths, without however diminishing their resolution as they leave for their final battle.

If the imminent destruction of three heroic and faithful sons raises questions about the discrepancy between God's anger and Saul's transgression, the catastrophe of the play pursues a similar aim by dwelling on Saul's nobility and suffering rather than on his crimes. In the lengthy report of his death, the messenger stresses his courage and his love of his sons. The listener is David, who, far from rejoicing in the death of the man who persecuted him, breaks out in grievous laments for the deaths of Saul and Jonathan and promises to both the glory of eternal memory. The condemnation of Saul by God, then, contrasts sharply with the celebration of his memory by David. His career is seen less in terms of individual sin and retribution than in terms of the generic miseries of kingship – a perspective apparent in Saul's own reflections and in the wonderfully pithy expression of sympathy by the witch of Endor: 'O Roy plus malheureux que la misere mesme' (788) .

This perspective governs a short but crucial addition by de La Taille to the biblical narrative, which includes two unharmonized reports about the death of Saul. According to one account, the wounded Saul kills himself after his armour-bearer has refused to kill him. According to the other version, an Amalechite soldier did carry out Saul's request, but when he took the crown to David in hope of a reward, David had him executed. In de La Taille's version the Amalechite soldier claims responsibility for the death of Saul to ingratiate himself with the new king, but when this manoeuver fails, he recants and gives the true account, which is later confirmed by the second armour-bearer, the first having killed himself as in the Bible. Despite the soldier's recantation David does not retract the sentence, and the soldier curses David as he is led off to execution:

Je pry que DIEU, qui voit tout de son œil,
Le Foudre sien darde sur ton orgueil,
Et s'il advient par le Destin celeste
Que tu sois Roy, que la Faim, que la Peste,
Et que la Guerre infectent tes païs,
Que contre toy s'arment tes propres Fils. (1291–6)

By dwelling most emphatically on the tragic revolt of Absalom, the soldier's curse establishes the career of Saul as paradigmatic of kingship: the second king inherits from the first his sufferings together with his crown.

Like *Saül le Furieux, Les Gabéonites* turns on a conflict between human clemency and divine cruelty. David learns that the plague that has been decimating Israel is due to Saul's unjust persecution of the Gibeonites. In retribution, he is forced to hand over the remaining children to the Gibeonites, who execute them. In the Old Testament narrative, one of Saul's wives keeps a watch over the bodies, protecting them against rain and vultures until David buries both Saul and his descendants in one place. The figure of the female mourner suggested to de La Taille the possibility of modelling her on Andromache in Seneca's play, *Troades*, whose innocent son was similarly sacrificed to placate the enemy's anger. Seneca's *Oedipus* provided an obvious model for the account of the plague.

The most interesting part of the play consists of the scenes modelled on the *Troades*. In the third act, the king of Gibeon arrives and demands victims. The ensuing debate is modelled on the debate in *Troades*, in which Pyrrhus demands the sacrifice of Polyxena from a reluctant Agamemnon. After vainly pleading humanitarian arguments, David yields, and Joab, like Ulysses, goes to fetch the victims. The scene between Joab and Saul's wife Rezefe closely follows the scene between Andromache and Ulysses, and as in Seneca's play, the threat to tear down the father's tomb determines the outcome. In the fourth act Rezefe calls forth her sons from the tomb as Andromache called forth Astyanax. The sons of Saul oppose to their mother's tears a Stoic constance and *contemptus mundi* that they have learned from the young victims of Senecan tragedy. The messenger report, which fills most of the fifth act, likewise portrays the innocent victims as fearless and defiant martyrs.

If the premises of the new plot were simply indifferent to those of the sources, one might silently pass by this awkward collage. But the fact is that the moral premises of the *Troades* openly conflict with the concept of divine justice, and it seems that this contradiction was not one that de La Taille stumbled into unwittingly but one which he sought out and could not cope with successfully in his attempt to locate the sense of the tragic in the darker reaches of the Old Testament justice. In Seneca's play, as well as in *Hecuba* and *The Trojan Women* of Euripides, the audience is meant to sympathize with the victims, whose plight is an indictment of the arrogance, injustice, and brutality of the victors. The sacrifice of Polyxena is a cruel and unnatural act. Agamemnon is right in resisting it on the grounds of human justice and wrong in yielding to the priest's barbarous superstition. Similarly, the argument that Astyanax should die for reasons of state is preposterous and is exposed in its absurdity when Andromache finally reveals her son to Ulysses with the heart-rending words: 'hic est, hic est terror, Ulixe, mille carinis' ('here is Odysseus, here is the terror to a thousand ships') (*Troades* 707–8). In the ancient Troy plays the innocence of the victims implies the injustice of the victors. This implication survives the transposition into the biblical story, where it clashes with the premise that God is just and that his justice is apparent even in his persecution of the innocent descendants of those who sinned against him. In the play the mothers and their children are portrayed as innocent, and the children even acquire the status of martyrs in the equanimity with which they face death. From the perspective of the victims David and Joab appear therefore as the inhuman tyrant and his ruthless henchman. Armon, one of Saul's sons, even attributes their execution to dynastic considerations on David's part:

Parquoy David fait bien de nous esteindre,
A celle fin qu'il n'aye plus que craindre:
Car il sçait bien qu'en vivant d'avantage,
Nous r'eussions eu nostre droit heritage:
Et que le regne envahy par le traitre
Fut revenu dessus son juste maistre. (943-8)

But David is also portrayed as a humane king who pleads with the Gibeonite king on behalf of Saul's children and is reprimanded by Joab for always showing a 'pitié niaise,' 'douceur cruelle,' and 'bonté si mauvaise' (619–20). And if Joab and the Gibeonite king seem more than eager to sacrifice Saul's children, it is hard to blame them for a desire that agrees with God's intention, for there is no indication in this play that they are divine 'scourges' whose wicked deeds are used by God as instruments of justice but later punished. Thus de La Taille's decision to model the victims of God's anger on Astyanax implies, at least from the perspective of the model, a condemnation of divine justice. That is plainly not intended. But the confusion that results from casting a story of divine retribution into a mould designed to show the sufferings of innocent victims at the hands of barbarous conquerors points to the seriousness of de La Taille's effort to dramatize the difficulties of the notion of divine justice.

There is some evidence that de La Taille thought of his two tragedies as parts of a larger design.[15] Whereas in the Bible Samuel's prediction extends only to the death of Saul and his sons in battle, in *Saül le Furieux* it includes his other descendants as well:

Encor apres ta mort toute ta race entiere
Rendra compte au Seigneur de ta vie meurtriere,
Car tes Fils, test Nepveux, et ton genre total,
Avec mille malheurs verront leur jour fatal.
Par trahison les uns recevront mort piteuse,
Et le reste mourra en une croix honteuse:
Et le tout pourautant qu'à la divine voix

> Obeï tu n'a point ainsi que tu devois,
> Qu'executé tu n'a sa vengeance dépite,
> (Comme je t'avois dit) contre l'Amalechite. (767–76)

Taken together, de La Taille's two tragedies portray a complete cycle of retribution. It is a cycle set in motion by an act of clemency on Saul's part, and it comes to rest on an act of barbarism into which David is forced by divine decree. The tragic world appears as one in which humanist values are powerless in situations governed by a grim and inscrutable justice. Despite imperfections in the execution, the power of design in de La Taille's diptych is unmistakeable.

Garnier's 'Les Juifves'

> Hà qu'il souffre un angoisseux martyre!

Whereas de La Taille's bleak portrayal of the tragic fate of the house of Saul goes almost beyond Buchanan in its questioning of divine justice and returns incessantly to the paradox of humane rulers coerced into barbarous acts by divine command, Garnier retreats somewhat from the harshness and obscurity of Buchanan's vision. *Les Juifves* focuses on the fall of Judah and the beginning of the Babylonian captivity as the point of deepest suffering and humiliation in the history of Israel. But while the play stresses the distance of the promise of salvation, it does not obscure it. On the contrary, the action is framed by a prologue and epilogue that integrate the events into a soteriological perspective for the audience, if not for the characters, and the play concludes with an explicit prophecy about Christ:

> Quelques siecles apres le Seigneur envoyra
> Son Christ, qui les pechez des peuples netoyra,
> Destruisant les Enfers, et desiré Messie
> Viendra pour metter fin à toute Prophetie. (2169–72)[16]

The action of *Les Juifves* is very simple. The defeated Jewish king Sedecie, his mother Amital, and his young children await the sentence of the victorious King Nabuchodonosor. Nabuchodonosor's wife, Amital, and Sedecie in succession ask the king for mercy, but in vain: he has the children of Sedecie slaughtered before his eyes and then blinds him. This action unfolds as a skilful conflation of the Senecan *Thyestes* with the

Troy plays of Euripides and Seneca. The large-scale parallel between the fall of Troy and the fall of Jerusalem is obvious and is supported by more particular correspondences that give to it a coherence and resonance absent from the somewhat arbitrary construction of the tragedy of Rezefe and her children on that of Andromache and Astyanax. In the Troy plays, the surviving women are about to be led into captivity, a situation that corresponds closely to the fate of the Jews awaiting the Babylonian exile. In *Hecuba*, the Thracian king Polymestor is punished for his greed by being blinded after seeing his sons killed before his eyes. Although the context is different, the facts recall the fate of the rebellious Jewish king. And in the biblical account, there is a mother who, although little more than a name, could be given the stature and experience of Hecuba and say of herself:

> Je suis le malheur mesme, et ne puis las! ne puis
> Suffrir plus que je souffre en mon ame d'ennuis. (369–70)

The tyrannical Atreus of Seneca's *Thyestes* provided the model for Nabuchodonosor, and his punishment of Sedecie conflates the Polymestor plot of *Hecuba* with Atreus' revenge on Thyestes.

The events of *Les Juifves* are given their moral significance by the stylization of Nabuchodonosor and Sedecie into the polar opposites of godless tyrant and repentant sinner-saint. It is through this opposition that the play provides answers to questions about the relationship of human suffering to divine justice. Nabuchodonosor's characterization as tyrant begins with his first entrance in which he introduces himself in words that clearly recall the lines spoken by Atreus at the moment of triumph:

> Pareil au Dieux je marche, et depuis le réveil
> Du Soleil blondissant jusques à son sommeil,
> Nul ne se parangonne à ma grandeur Royale.
> En puissance et en biens Jupiter seul m'egale:
> Et encores n'estoit qu'il commande immortel,
> Qu'il tient un foudre en main dont le coup est mortel,
> Que son thrône est plus haut, et qu'on ne le peut joindre,
> Quelque grand Dieu qu'il soit, je ne serois pas moindre. (181–8)[17]

His wickedness is emphasized by two flanking characters that establish the limits of prudent and humane behaviour that he will exceed in his tyrannical licence. His counselor urges restraint in the punishment of the defeated on prudential grounds, but Nabuchodonosor will have none of it. More significantly, his wife, a character without biblical or classical precedents and strangely reminiscent of Zenocrate in *Tamburlaine*, intercedes with him on behalf of the Jewish king and becomes a spokesman of the virtues of moderation and clemency. We see her first in a scene where she takes pity on Amital, who has fallen on her knees before her. She raises her from the ground and in gentle language states the common liability to fortune that despite appearances links the victor and the vanquished – the same argument that had moved Saul to his fateful clemency towards Agag! She does not succeed in her effort to help the defeated Jews, but her failure does not question the values she embodies, for the disregard of her advice is seen as the event that will in turn lead to the doom of Nabuchodonosor and the future fall of Babylon. Thus the Queen's way of moderation, if followed, holds out the promise of a non-tragic life. At least, such a promise is not deliberately destroyed, as in Buchanan and de La Taille.

Just as Nabuchodonosor is magnified in his wickedness, so Sedecie is stylized into a belated saint. The confrontation of Nabuchodonosor and Sedecie is preceded by a scene between Sedecie and the High Priest in which the king fully repents his former sins. From this confession he derives a moral authority that allows him to confront Nabuchodonosor and that is equally remote from the despairing self-abasement of Jephtha or the stoic grandeur of the dying Saul, neither of whom could have uttered Sedecie's prayer as he awaits the approach of Nabuchodonosor:

> Pere, puis qu'il te plaist faire le chastiment
> De nos impietez par juste jugement,
> Et que ta volonté maintenant ne s'accorde
> De nous fair jouir de ta misericorde,
> Fay nous cette faveur de loger nos espris
> Avec nos peres saints au celeste pourpris:
> Expiant nos forfaits par une mort severe
> Que nous fera souffrir ce Prince sanguinaire. (1353–60)

The scene between the tyrant and the repentant king proceeds along predictable lines. At first Sedecie, like the queen and Amital, attempts to persuade Nabuchodonosor to be merciful and to be mindful of God's power. But when the tyrant remains unmoved Sedecie accuses him openly of cruelty and defies him to do his worst, which Nabuchodonosor indeed promises to do.

The dénouement of the piece is adapted from *Hecuba*, but with important changes. In Euripides' play the man who is blinded is a wicked tyrant who in his suffering is just as barbarous as he was before and who shows no insight into his wickedness. There is no question that he gets what he deserves. But it is equally certain that in her revenge Hecuba has become as inhuman as her victim; her action is that of a creature brutalized by suffering and destroyed in the act of revenge. And Euripides is more interested in the dehumanization of the sufferer turned avenger than in the punishment of the wicked.

In Garnier's play the slaughter of the children and the blinding of Sedecie may be seen in two ways: they are a just punishment of Sedecie, both for his general wickedness and more particularly for his insurrection against his secular overlord, but as cruel and inhuman acts on Nabuchodonosor's part they invite retribution. By emphasizing the previous wickedness of Sedecie, Garnier evades the difficult question of the sufferings of the innocent. The children slaughtered before his eyes are presumably innocent, but they appear in the play primarily as a function of Sedecie's punishment; they have nothing like the structural importance of Iphis or the descendants of Saul in both of de La Taille's tragedies. At the end of Garnier's tragedy, the emphasis is squarely on the blinded king who, like Polymestor or Oedipus, exhibits his sufferings on the stage. Sedecie does not question the wisdom or justice of God in punishing him, but merely asks: 'pourquoy/Me fait-il torturer par un pire que moy?' In response the prophet develops the 'scourge of God' theory in full detail:

> Et ne sçavez-vous pas qu'il le fait tout expres,
> Le souffre en ses horreurs, pour l'en punir apres?
> Il use de sa dextre à venger son colere,
> Comme fait d'une verge une prudente mere
> Envers son cher enfant, quand une mauvaitié
> Qu'il a fait à quelqu'un, veut qu'il soit chatié.
> Car apres cet usage en la flamme on la rue,
> Ou avecques mespris est en pieces rompue.
> Ainsi Dieu vengera les massacres commis
> Par ce Roy carnacier, bien qu'il les ait permis.
> Les maux qu'il nous a faits il luy sçaura bien rendre,
> Et quelquefois sera Babylon mise en cendre. (2113-24)

The sense of consolation implicit in this explanation is heightened in the conclusion when the prophet looks beyond the Babylonian exile and promises the liberation of Israel by the Persian king, the rebuilding of Jerusalem and the temple, and finally the coming of the Messiah.

ATHALIE AS DISPLACED *ORESTEIA* AND SCRIPTURAL TRAGEDY

Comment en un plomb vil l'or pur s'est-il changé?

Athalie is too much the work of a successful public playwright to be called a scriptural tragedy à l'antique in every respect; nonetheless, it is descended from, and in some sense deliberately returns to Buchanan's *Jephtha*, which it explicitly recalls in an important passage. Although the play triumphed on the public stage not long after Racine's death and has kept a firm place in the repertoire of seventeenth-century plays, it was not written for the public stage. Like *Jephtha*, it was a school play, written for the girls at Saint Cyr at the request of Mme de Maintenon, the pious mistress of Louis xiv. The play's distance from the public stage involved a return to ancient tragedy: the chorus is restored and the erotic subplot, the greatest obstacle to the proper imitation of ancient drama, is banished. The play remains of course much closer to *Phèdre* in its scenic structure than to *Jephtha* or *Samson Agonistes*. At the same time, as a 'simple tragedy without love' it clearly aspires to the ideal of the strict imitation of ancient tragedy that motivated Buchanan and Milton, and as we shall see, its plot is an exceptionally interesting version of the Euripidean *Ion* and the Electra plays. Above all, the play, despite its prosperous ending, explores in a systematic manner the difficulties of divine justice and plays a surprising and hidden variation on the theme of deferred salvation. Thus, despite certain reservations about its form, the play may be called a scriptural tragedy à l'antique and to treat it as such provides the generic context within which its intentions emerge most fully.

The story of Athalie is quickly told.[18] The daughter of Ahab, King of Israel, and of his Phoenician wife Jezebel, she was, for dynastic reasons, married to Joram, the King of Judah. After his death and that of her son Ahaziah she ruled in Judah, where she promoted the worship of Baal, the Phoenician god, and, out of loyalty to her own dynasty, sought to exterminate the remaining descendants of the house of Judah, although they were her own grandsons. Only one of them escaped and was brought up in concealment by his aunt, who was married to the High Priest Jehoiadah. After a reign of eight years Athalie fell victim to a conspiracy planned and executed by the High Priest, who then acted as regent for the child king.

This unprepossessing story from the more obscure periods of Jewish history has no immediately apparent tragic potential. In this regard it differs from the dilemma faced by Jephtha, or from the spectacular dénouement of Samson's life, not to speak of the counterpoint of the careers of Saul and David in which the splendour and misery of royalty found paradigmatic expression. In immediate dramatic appeal the fate of Joas and Athalie could not even compare with the equally confused and undistinguished reign of King Zedekiah, which had at least the dramatic advantage of ending in the great event of the Babylonian captivity.

The biblical narrative turned on a conflict between the queen and the priests. The coup of Jehoiada and the Levites was provoked by their resentment at her attempts to establish her own religion and dynasty in Judah. But Racine interpreted the biblical story as a conflict between mother and son. The climax of the play is not the priest's revenge on the impious queen for introducing new gods, but the son's revenge on the mother for murdering the father in his offspring, if not literally. The two classical models of *Athalie* establish the hostility between mother and son as the central opposition of the play. On the surface, Euripides' *Ion* may seem to be the more extensively used source. From it Racine took the portrayal of the young orphan boy growing up in the sanctuary of the temple, which filled an obvious lacuna in the biblical narrative. Like Ion, Joas does not know his identity, and God for him, too, takes the father's role. Both plays explore the psychological interest of the first contact with the world forced upon a child that has grown up in the purity and seclusion of the temple. And, of course, the scene between Athalie and Joas is based on the first encounter of Ion and Creusa. But the relationship of 'mother' and son itself is interpreted in terms of the Orestes paradigm, which governs the outcome of the play and is its dominant thematic model. In particular Athalie is identified as a Clytaemnestra figure through her dream, which in position and function, if not in substance, echoes the dream of Clytaemnestra.

The interpretation of the relationship between Athalie and Joas as that of mother and son is first put forward by Athalie herself when she offers to adopt 'Eliacin' as her son: 'Je prétends vous traiter comme mon propre fils.' Joas is horrified at the prospect and expresses his revulsion in the words: 'Quel père je quitterais! Et pour ... quelle mère!' (2.7) When Athalie learns of the child's true identity, she persists in seeing their relationship in those terms and interprets her imminent death as matricide:

Qu'il règne donc ce fils, ton soin et ton ouvrage;

Et que pour signaler son empire nouveaux,
On lui fasse en mon sein enfoncer le couteau.
Voici ce qu'en mourant lui souhaite sa mère. (5.7)

In these words she recognizes the truth and the significance of the dream in which the beautiful and strangely appealing child suddenly stabbed her to death:

Dans ce désordre à mes yeux se présente
Un jeune enfant couvert d'une robe éclatante,
Tels qu'on voit des Hébreux les prêtres revêtus.
Sa vue a ranimé mes esprits abattus.
Mais lorsque revenant de mon trouble funeste,
J'admirais sa douceur, son air noble et modeste,
J'ai senti tout à coup un homicide acier
Que le traitre en mon sein a plongé tout entire. (2.5)

The substance of the dream, which is functionally that of Clytaemnestra, directly recalls the Orestes motif. If the avenging son is still portrayed as the boy of the *Ion*, his sword is that of Orestes and may be metaphorically identical with the sword of David that is later mentioned as among the insignia of royalty (4.1).

As a version of the Electra plot, *Athalie* had to cope with the problem of representing matricide that I have discussed earlier.[19] Racine's solution is very ingenious and involves both a displacement and a sacralization of the action. The interpretation of Joas as the 'son' of Athalie and the fact that he is the cause of Athalie's death reveal the son's revenge on the mother as the 'deep structure' of the action. But this structure appears on the surface in a doubly displaced form: Athalie is executed by soldiers who follow the orders of Joad, who acts on behalf of the boy-king.

The 'sacralization' of the action is a transformation of the concept of a divinely guided action as it appears in the *Oresteia* and in the *Ion*. In some sense theodicy is the basis of all Greek tragedy: the relationship of man and god and the justice of the gods are themes never far below the surface of any particular play. But where the crisis is closely related to the intervention of a god the theme of divine justice is sounded with special force and urgency. Thus it is in the Electra plays, where the horrible deed of matricide is done at the explicit command of Apollo and where – regardless of the dramatist's evaluation of the justice of the god's command – a concern with divine justice and with the interaction of human and divine motives is a shared theme of major significance.

Whereas Corneille had avoided the scandal of divinely ordered matricide by attributing the mother's death to suicide or accident, both eminently secular causes, Racine returns emphatically to the interpretation of matricide as a divinely guided action, and the theme of divine guidance is a subject of much reflection in the play. The very first scene is concerned with the possibility of God's intervention in history. To the disillusioned Abner, God has retired from the world:

> Dieu même, disent-ils, s'est retiré de nous:
> De l'honneur des Hébreux autrefois si jaloux,
> Il voit sans intérêt leur grandeur terrassée.
> Et sa miséricorde à la fin s'est lassée.
> On ne voit plus pour nous ses redoutables mains
> De merveilles sans nombre effrayer les humains;
> L'arche sainte est muette, et ne rend plus d'oracles. (1.1)

To Joad, on the other hand, the world has never been so full of divine intervention; as evidence he cites the disasters that befell Ahab and Jezebel, as well as the miraculous deeds of Elijah and Elisha and the discomforts of false prophets. Thus the stage is set for a further manifestation of divine power. But if in his interpretation of the death of Athalie as a sacred action Racine returned to classical models, his concept of the interaction of human and divine purpose differs completely from what is found in any Greek tragedy.

The interventions of Greek gods emphasize rather than destroy or supersede human intention and responsibility. The Aeschylean Orestes acts at the god's command; he justifies his action by that command, and Apollo stands by him in his trial. But the god's command and support in no way remove from Orestes the burden or responsibility for his action; nor do they protect him from the persecution of the Furies. In Racine's Christian context, however, divine intervention negates the efficacy of the human will. The will of God manifests its power not only by crushing those who resist or oppose it but also by working through agents who are too weak to achieve anything by themselves. For this reason, the sacralization of the action in *Athalie* involves a polarization of the antagonists into good and bad, helpless and powerful, at one and at odds with the will of God.

Not much need be said about the caracterization of Joas. He is an innocent child and despite his arch precocity barely capable of understanding the events of which in his role as king and avenger he is the cause. The discrepancy between the as yet unwritten book of his character and the role that he has been cast in is the point of the play. The harmony between the will of God and that of the child is therefore empty, since this child has not yet learned the possibility of disobedience. The threat of this possibility in the future will throw a dark shadow on the moral vision of the play.

The violent dissonance between God's will and that of Athalie can be resolved only by destroying the will of Athalie, and the process of this destruction constitutes the play's main psychological interest. Until Racine wrote his play, Athalie had no fame either as a biblical or literary character. Considering her obscurity, it is remarkable with what ease Racine establishes her as a monster of impiety, ambition, and cruelty. The definition of Athalie proceeds through partial identification with more famous prototypes. Just as Bérénice gains definition from being seen as a new and different version of Dido and Cleopatra, so the portrait of Athalie is shaped by successive comparisons.[20] The first periphrastic reference to 'l'audace d'une femme' may well allude to the watchman's description of the Aeschylean Clytaemnestra (although this is not an allusion that many seventeenth-century readers could be expected to catch). The identification with Clytaemnestra is more openly achieved in the dream. Athalie is also defined in terms of her more famous mother: in Abner's first speech 'la superbe Athalie' is seen as Jezebel's true daughter: 'de Jezebel la fille sanguinaire.' This identification, too, is confirmed in the dream, in which the mother's horrible fate clearly anticipates that of her daughter. Finally in her dying words Athalie 'becomes' Corneille's Clytaemnestra figure, the wicked Cléopatre, who had wished upon her son and his wife:

> Et, pour vous souhaiter tous les malheurs ensemble,
> Puisse naître de vous un fils qui me ressemble. (*Rodogune*, 5.4. 1832–4)

So Athalie dies with the grim sense of satisfaction that her own and Ahab's blood with survive in Joas:

> je me flatte, j'espère
> Qu'indocile à ton joug, fatigué de ta loi,
> Fidèle au sang d'Achab, qu'il a reçu de moi,
> Conforme à son aïeul, à son père semblable,
> On verra de David l'héritier détestable
> Abolir tes honneurs, profaner ton autel,
> Et venger Athalie, Achab et Jézabel. (5.6)

Because the models of Athalie were so familiar, Racine was able to rely on the reader's construction of the figure from a few hints and could thus concentrate on what is both a change in the character and a transformation of its literary type. Indeed, the identity of Athalie with Jezebel and Clytaemnestra is something that exists only in the memory of the characters. When she appears on the stage she is in crucial respects 'no longer herself.' If we feel that we know her very well as she once was, this achievement is due to Racine's skilful evocation of the literary prototypes that his new version set out to dismantle.

Racine's procedure may well have received an impulse from the perception of the unsatisfactory relationship between character and situation in the dénouement of *Rodogune*, Corneille's Clytaemnestra tragedy. Were it not for the timely arrival of the news of Seleucus' death and for the almost instantaneous effect of the poison, Antiochus would die and Cléopatre would either triumph completely or at least succeed in her desire for revenge. Does Cléopatre in some sense overreach herself so that the apparent concatenation of accidents conceals an underlying necessity? Or does mere chance stop the progress of her wickedness? There is certainly no effective counterforce to her aggressive wickedness, and yet it is unlikely that Corneille wanted to portray a situation in which mere chance prevented the triumph of evil. The likeliest hypothesis is that Corneille was too enamoured of Cléopatre's brilliance and 'grandeur d'âme' and that he chose a conclusion that was theatrically effective but did not bother about its moral implications as long as it satisfied conventional expectations of poetic justice.

There is nothing accidental about the failure and death of Athalie. Its necessity is apparent both from a natural perspective in which we see her as 'losing her touch,' and from a supernatural perspective in which she is defeated by the counterforce of divine justice. The psychological perspective has its point of departure in the anxiety of the Sophoclean Clytaemnestra. It is presented in a very direct, and indeed, almost heavy-handed manner. Even before she appears, attention is drawn to a change in Athalie's behaviour:

Enfin depuis deux jours la superbe Athalie
Dans un sombre chagrin paraît ensevelie. (1.1)

In her first words she refers to 'mon trouble et ma faiblesse,' and to 'cette paix que je cherche, et qui me fuit toujours' (2.3), and after proudly describing the power and security of her situation she returns to her recent anxiety:

> Je jouissais en paix du fruit de ma sagesse;
> Mais un trouble importun vient, depuis quelque jours,
> De mes prospérités interrompre le cours. (2.5)

She is referring to her repeated dream. Her sense of uncertainty is demonstrated in her behaviour towards the boy Eliacin. The old Athalie would have had him executed without further ado, but she opposes to the cruel and pragmatic advice of Mathan arguments of moderation that are quite out of character, as she herself recognizes in analyzing her reactions to the encounter with 'Eliacin':

> Quel prodige nouveau me trouble, et m'embarrasse?
> La douceur de sa voix, son enfance, sa grâce,
> Font insensiblement à mon inimitié
> Succéder ... Je serais sensible à la pitié? (2.7)

In her anger at the boy's parrotting of the priest's lessons there is a verbal bluster that points to a decisiveness and ruthlessness which she no longer commands. No wonder that Mathan speaks of her as a changed person:

> Ami, depuis deux jours je ne la connais plus.
> Ce n'est plus cette reine éclairée, intrépide,
> Elevée au-dessus de son sexe timide,
> Qui d'abord accablait ses ennemis surpris,
> Et d'un instant perdu connaissait tout le prix.
> La peur d'un vain remords trouble cette grande âme:
> Elle flotte, elle hésite; en un mot, elle est femme. (3.3)

The weakness and uncertainty of Athalie can be accounted for satisfactorily in terms of natural psychology.[21] It is the exhaustion of a will that for too long has ruled by sole reliance on its own strength and ability to suppress resistance. But the natural process is also part of a providential design, as she herself recognizes:

> Impitoyable Dieu, toi seul as tout conduit!
> C'est toi qui, me flattant d'une vengeance aisée,
> M'a vingt fois en un jour à moi-même opposée,
> Tantôt pour un enfant excitant mes remords,
> Tantôt m'éblouissant de tes riches trésors,
> Que j'ai craint de livrer aux flammes, au pillage. (5.6)

Just as the death of Athalie is a displaced re-enactment of the killing of Clytaemnestra, so her psychological disintegration re-enacts the physical dismemberment of Jezebel. And her psychological disintegration, like her death, is forecast and interpreted in her dream. The apparition of Jezebel forms the first part of Athalie's dream, which follows the conventions of epic dreams and in particular recalls Aeneas' dream vision of Hector (*Aen.* 2.268–97). The dream figure bends over the sleeper, who vainly tries to embrace it. This is a classical motif, but brilliantly varied by fusing the biblical substance with the most famous feature of Aeneas' account of Hector's apparition.[22] Hector appears as the corpse mangled by Achilles' brutal maltreatment, and Aeneas exclaims in anguish: 'ei mihi, qualis erat, quantum mutatus ab illo / Hectore qui redit exuvias indutus Achilli' (2.274–5). In Athalie's dream this transformation is enacted. Jezebel appears to her daughter 'comme au jour de sa mort pompeusement parée.' But as the sleeper tries to embrace the figure, she finds nothing but

> un horrible mélange
> D'on et de chair meurtris, et trainés dans la fange,
> Des lambeaux pleins de sang, et de membres affreux,
> Que de chiens dévorants se disputaient entre eux. (2.5)

The transformation of the mother from royal splendour into a shapeless mess of blood, flesh, bones, and dirt prefigures the dissolution of her daughter.

The overthrow of Athalie and the liberation of Joas constitute a vindication of God's purpose in history; the apparently triumphant conclusion of the play also satisfies the demands of poetic justice in which the wicked are punished and the good receive their reward. The appearance of triumph is much greater than in *Rodogune*, where the mother's death throws the son into a state of grief and despair from which the play does not explicitly absolve him:

> Oronte, je ne sais, dans son funeste sort,
> Qui m'afflige le plus, ou sa vie, ou sa mort;
> L'une et l'autre a pour moi des malheurs sans exemple:
> Plaignez mon infortune. (5.4.1836–40)

And there can be no question of Joas being hounded by the Furies for what he did. Thus Racine's portrayal of matricide in a displaced and sacralized context seems to overcome the difficulties that Corneille had seen in the Sophoclean *Electra*. Certainly one could apply to *Athalie* Corneille's praise of his own sketch of an Orestes play:

Ainsi elle mourrait de la main de son fils, comme le veut Aristote, sans que la barbarie d'Oreste nous fît horreur, comme dans Sophocle, ne que son action méritât des Furies vengeresses pour le tormenter, puisqu'il demeurerait innocent.[23]

But one may ask in what sense a solution that dispenses with the Furies can still be called tragic. One might argue that the operation which rendered the matricide acceptable also rendered it trivial. If such misgivings are aroused by comparing the new versions of the son's revenge with its ancient models, another source of misgivings exists in the comparison of *Athalie* with earlier scriptural tragedies. We have seen how Buchanan and de La Taille chose biblical stories in which God's punishment of heroes he had himself elevated appeared so disproportionate to their offenses that the assertion of divine justice taxed the believer's faith to the utmost. Even in *Les Juifves*, where the correlation between sin and retribution does not make the notion of divine justice problematic, the emphasis is on the harshness of the sufferings inflicted on the contrite sinners. By contrast, *Athalie* appears as a triumphant vindication of divine justice as it punishes the oppressors and liberates the oppressed. And it appears that Racine in part defined his work against the vision of the earlier plays. The harsh world of Saul and Jephtha is not unknown to his characters. Thus Joad seeks to assure his anxious wife about the safety of Joas in the hands of God by pointing to God's persecution of the house of Ahab:

Dieu, qui hait les tyrans, et qui dans Jezraël
Jura d'exterminer Achab et Jézabel;
Dieu, qui frappant Joram, le mari de leur fille,
A jusque sur son fils poursuivi leur famille;
Dieu, dont le bras vengeur, pour un temps suspendu,
Sur cette race impie est toujours étendu. (1.2)

But Josabet reads history differently:

Et c'est sur tous ces rois sa justice sévère
Que je crains pour le fils de mon malheureux frère. (1.2)

A more prominent and structurally more important echo of God's 'justice sévère' occurs when Josabet, still fearful of the outcome, dresses Joas in the robes of the king. Joas, not yet aware of his identity, misinterprets her tears and thinks of himself as being prepared for a sacrifice:

> Mais j'entends les sanglots sortir de votre bouche!
> Princesse, vous pleurez! Quelle pitié vous touche?
> Est-ce qu'en holocauste aujourd'hui présenté,
> Je dois, comme autrefois la fille de Jephté,
> Du Seigneur par ma mort apaiser la colère?
> Hélas! un fils n'a rien qui ne soit à son père. (4.1)

It seems that the point of this scene is to distance the moral vision of *Athalie* from the grimness of Buchanan's tragic world, and it may be appropriate to recall the occasion for which the work was written: Mme de Maintenon's expectations for a suitably edifying spectacle would hardly have been satisfied by a story as theologically intractable as Jephtha's or as dubious as Saul's in its implications about royalty.

If we feel nonetheless that despite its apparently triumphant ending *Athalie* embodies a moral vision that can properly be called 'tragic,' that impression is due to Racine's consummate management of the implicit future, which in *Athalie* is profoundly ambivalent. On the one hand, the sense of triumph at the play's end rests almost entirely on the future significance of the events portrayed. For the source of our interest in Joas is the fact that he is the weakest link in the chain between David and the Messiah. In his death mankind itself would perish; in his survival its redemption is safeguarded. On the other hand, as king, Joas did not live up to the great role entrusted to him. After the death of Joad, he forsook the service of God and worshipped idols; when Zachariah remonstrated with the people for their idolatry, he had him stoned to death in the court of the temple. The blood of Ahab and Athalie proved stronger than that of David. And the crime of Joas not only led to his own death at the hands of his servants, but according to Racine in his preface, 'ce meurtre commis dans le temple fut une des principales causes de la colère de Dieu contre les Juifs, et de tous les malheurs qui leur arrivèrent dans la suite' – including the Babylonian captivity.

As in the other scriptural tragedies, prophecy is the chief device for integrating the future into the action. The form it takes underscores the importance and ambivalence of its substance. Joad is seized by prophetic fury when the preparations for the revelation and coronation of Joas have been completed; his prophecy concludes the third act. In veiled language Joad predicts first the defection of Joas and the murder of Zachariah:

> Comment en un plomb vil l'or pur s'est-il changé?
> Quel est dans le lieu saint ce pontife égorgé? (3.7)

The more explicit forecast of the Babylonian captivity and of the destruction of the city and the temple gives rise to laments by the Chorus. The forecast of misery is balanced by a second prophecy in which Joad foresees the Incarnation and the rebuilding of a new Jerusalem (the Church). The choral passage that follows on Joad's prophecy reinforces its ambivalent effect. Salomith, who acts as a kind of coryphaeus, is filled with great anxiety – an effect of dramatic irony since the prophecy involves her brother's death. The Chorus as a whole suppress their anxiety in a contemplation of the contradictions in God's nature:

> O promesse! ô menace! ô ténébreux mystère!
> Que de maux, que de biens sont prédits tour à tour!
> Comment peut-on avec tant de colère
> Accorder tant d'amour? (3.8)

But immediately they divide into two voices which alternately stress despair and hope in a stichomythic exchange that is repeated five times and culminates in an accelerated exchange of half lines:

> Quel triste abaissement!
>   Quelle immortelle gloire!
> Que de cris de douleur!
>   Que de chants de victoire! (3.8)

Each time the voice of despair is answered but not overbalanced by a voice of hope. For the antiphonal chant is resolved only in another call to be quiet before the 'grand mystère' of God's providence, and the scene concludes with a wistful and quietist celebration of the tranquil peace of the heart that loves God.

The quiet resignation which here, as in Milton's poetry, appears as the most appropriate response to things seen in their ultimate perspective, gives way in the final act to a renewed polarization of triumph and despair. The intermediate perspective of human sinfulness comes to balance and undermine the immediate and ultimate triumph. In the last act of *Athalie* the future is evoked primarily through the curse of Athalie, which is brilliantly adapted from *Rodogune*. Cléopatre's curse in which she wishes on Antiochus a son who would resemble herself is a grand but empty gesture (5.4.1811–24). The future it evokes is purely hypothetical; we never learn whether the curse bears any relationship to future reality, and indeed its only function is to point one last time to the spitefulness of the dying queen. Athalie's curse gains weight because it is fulfilled. Our knowledge of its fulfilment casts a deep shadow on the triumphant ending, and the more closely we ponder the curse, the more disturbing its implications become for the moral vision of the play.

The action of the play hinges on the radical opposition of good and evil, weak and strong, religious and secular. The place of goodness is the temple, the place of wickedness the court. With the help of God the good and the weak overcome the wicked and the powerful. But can they establish the rule of the temple in the world? From the perspective of future events the goodness of Joas is called into question: his innocence and purity no longer appear as the moral attributes of a deserving individual, but simply as functions of his status as child and therefore bound to disappear with the passing of time. It is reasonable to assume that the choice of a child protagonist had something to do with the occasion for which *Athalie* was written. The relationship of the obedient and affectionate Joas to the priest and his wife, who are both parents and teachers to him, may have been meant to serve as an example to the convent girls for whom the play was written and who acted in it. The life of Joas in the temple is indeed the paradigm of a Christian education, but as an educator Joad fails no less than Seneca and Burrhus did with Nero. The blood of Ahab will ensure that the Joas of *Athalie* will grow up into the Nero of *Britannicus*. Left to his own devices he will return to the temple only to defile it with the blood of the same person whom as a child he innocently embraced as a friend forever (4.4).

THE TRAGEDY OF DELIVERANCE: *SAMSON AGONISTES*

... and he shall begin to deliver Israel out of the hand of the Philistines.

The place of *Samson Agonistes* in the history of English literature, not to speak of its place in English drama, is odd. Well into this century its reception was beset with puzzles that found their strongest expression in Dr Johnson's famous complaint about its lack of a middle. Many aspects of this play are clarified by seeing it as the belated masterpiece in the tradition of scriptural tragedy established by Buchanan. No other version of a Greek tragedy by a major poet is so firmly committed to the observance of ancient rule and practice, nor does any other version rest on a comparable basis of long-standing and intimate familiarity with 'Aeschylus, Sophocles, and Euripides, the three poets unequalled yet by any, and the best rule to all who endeavor to write tragedy.'[24] Goethe testified to the fruits of that familiarity when he remarked to Eckermann: 'I read Samson not long ago; it is more in the spirit of he ancients than any other play by a modern writer.'[25] In its conception of tragic dignity, its notions about the exemplary status of Greek models, and its stance towards the public stage and the vernacular tradition, it is animated by the same nostalgia that informs the closing lines of Sonnet xi:

> Thy age, like ours, O soul of Sir John Cheke,
> Hated not learning worse than toad or asp,
> When thou taught'st Cambridge and King Edward Greek.

But if Samson Agonistes is, from one perspective, a Humanist tragedy composed in the wrong century, it is also the work of a man who described the subject matter of poetry as 'whatsoever hath passion or admiration in all the changes of that which is call'd fortune from without, or the wily subtleties and refluxes of man's thoughts from within.'[26] Samson Agonistes is virtually a contemporary of Phèdre, and its transformation of the plot patterns and conventions of Greek tragedy reflects the growing preoccupation with the 'wily subtleties and refluxes of man's thoughts from within' no less than does Racine's play.

I begin with some simple parallels between Jephtha and Samson Agonistes that appear to have gone unnoticed. The cult of Samson that Manoa proposes to institute is a clear echo of the cult of Jephtha's daughter. More important is the resemblance that Manoa as a solicitous parent bears to Storge. Both Buchanan and Milton conclude their plays with the laments of a parent whose efforts to avert the tragedy are doomed to futility. Whereas in Jephtha the mother resists all efforts at consolation and the memory of her daughter's heroic death only heightens her grief, in Samson Agonistes the father becomes the consoler and makes the arguments to which Buchanan's Storge had remained deaf:

> Nothing is here for tears, nothing to wail
> Or knock the breast, no weakness, no contempt,

Dispraise, or blame, nothing but well and fair,
. And what may quiet us in a death so noble. (1721–4)

This transformation of the disconsolate into a consoling parent is an instance of Milton's strong preference for closing his major works on a quiet note. Like the *Nativity Ode, Lycidas, Paradise Lost,* and *Paradise Regained, Samson Agonistes* retreats from its point of highest tension: quiet resignation characterizes the close of the play by comparison both with the horror of the protagonist's death and the torpor of his despair. But in *Samson Agonistes* alone of Milton's poems, this quiet closure does not follow a climax of ecstatic revelation. The absence of such a moment is a major structural feature of the play and produces its peculiar form of irony, especially at the beginning and end. A reader of the first two lines, 'A little onward lend thy guiding hand/To these dark steps, a little further on,' is likely to hear these words in a wider context than the immediate setting suggests. The 'guiding hand' becomes that of God, and the 'dark steps' measure the steps that Samson has to travel towards his death 'a little further on.' But the poem nowhere reaches a point at which such a reading receives an open confirmation, least of all at the end. The 'copious legend and sweet lyric song' that will commemorate the heroic life of Samson – how lacking in resonance are they to the listener who has been to a *Solemn Music*, listened to the Lady in *Comus*, the 'unexpressive nuptial songs' of *Lycidas*, or the 'inenarrabile carmen' of the *Epitaphium Damonis*, not to speak of the cosmic harmonies that celebrate the days of the Creation. And yet even in the severely restricted vision of this ending, where the burial of the dead is solely a labour of human love, some words point beyond themselves, although even to underline them is to do violence to the delicacy of their resonance:

Let us go find the body where it lies
Soak't in his enemies' blood, and from the stream
With lavers pure and cleansing herbs wash off
The clotted gore. I with what speed the while
(*Gaza* is not in plight to say us nay)
Will send for all my kindred, all my friends,
To fetch him hence and solemnly attend
With silent obsequy and funeral train
Home to his Father's house: (1725–33)

The pointed reticence of this ending looks back to Buchanan's *Jephtha*, both to acknowledge its debt to the most rigorous of scriptural tragedies and to measure its distance from the unrelieved grimness of its vision. It is a peculiar form, both muted and resonant, of the deferral of salvation that is characteristic of scriptural tragedy à l'antique. In Buchanan and in the Saul tragedies of de La Taille, deferral had virtually become denial: nothing mitigates the appalling vision of a God who for reasons of his own rejects rulers who are pious, prudent, and humane. In Garnier, the discovery of a pattern of retributive justice and the prospect of redemption in the distant future sustain the characters at the lowest point of their fortunes. To this discovery of hope in despair, Racine opposes in *Athalie* a gloomy vision that undermines the present triumph of innocence by foreshadowing the sins of the future. In *Samson Agonistes*, as in *Athalie*, the tragic effect of the play results from the spectator's contemplation of the events in a context that reaches far beyond the temporal confines of the action. But whereas in *Athalie* the future subverts the present, in *Samson* tragic effect derives from the failure of the present to share fully in the resolution of the future to which it points.

Milton's tragic vision in *Samson Agonistes* depends on silence and a rhetoric of the unsaid, which involves delicate manoeuvers on the author's part and poses great problems to the critic who by the nature of his enterprise must explicitly mention elements of the text that are present only by their absence. What is 'absent' is, of course, the prospect of salvation whether considered psychologically as the protagonist's sense of salvation, or typologically as the spectator's knowledge of the Incarnation and Redemption that the exegetical tradition associated with the events of the story. What is it about the story of Samson that suggests such reticence as an appropriate strategy for a tragic treatment of it? At first sight the story of Samson is not a particularly promising subject for a scriptural tragedy, despite its spectacular dénouement. It does not raise puzzling questions about divine justice; it does not portray its protagonist as particularly anguished, and in its rough way, it observes poetic justice: the Philistines and Samson both get what they deserve, but Samson regains his heroic self at the point of death and more than compensates for the follies of his life.

The tragic potential of the story emerges only from a perspective that is not satisfied with the calculus of violence expressed in the body count that serves the biblical narrator as a summary of Samson's life: 'So the dead which he slew at his death were more than they which he slew in his life' (Judges 16:30). The problem of a Samson tragedy lies precisely in the relationship of a cycle of retributive violence to the transcendence of violence foreshadowed in the typological reading of the story. But if a typological reading creates the possibility of a tragic interpretation, the celebration of the transcendence of violence destroys it. To see the Samson story as limited and to see it within the limits that it cannot yet transcend is to see it in both a Christian and a tragic manner.

The Typological Drama

In the biblical story an angel announces the purpose of Samson's life to his mother: 'For, lo, thou shalt conceive, and bear a son; and no razor shall come on his head: for the child shall be a Nazarite unto God from the womb: and he shall begin to deliver Israel out of the hand of the Philistines' (Judges 13:5). For a Christian reader these words powerfully suggest a typological reading. The work begun by Samson is completed by Christ, but in a manner that changes the nature of deliverance itself. When Adam in *Paradise Lost* asks Michael about the time and place of Satan's eventual defeat at the hands of Christ, Michael replies:

> Dream not of their fight,
> As of a Duel, or the local wounds
> Of head or heel: not therefore joins the Son
> Manhood to Godhead, with more strength to foil
> Thy enemy... (12.386–90)

But the story of Samson, which begins with a promise of deliverance, ends in a nightmare of destruction. How then does deliverance 'begin' with Samson, and how does his drama, which remains so resolutely enclosed within a world of heroic violence, look forward to the world of the Christian audience to whom *Samson Agonistes* is addressed? These are the questions that Milton's rhetoric of the unsaid both raises and refuses to answer.

In this rhetoric the manipulation of classic models plays an important role. *Samson Agonistes* makes fairly extensive use of plot elements from *Oedipus at Colonus* and *Prometheus Bound*. The beginning and end of the play cast Samson in the role of Oedipus: the blind beggar in rags sitting down in the grove of the Eumenides is the model for the Samson whom the Chorus find 'carelessly diffused' – as indeed the entire aproach of the Chorus is based on the comparable scene in *Oedipus at Colonus*. The bath and fresh clothes that Samson receives recall the similar transformation of Oedipus, and the handling of Samson's exit and report of his death also follows Sophocles. From *Prometheus Bound* Milton took over and greatly elaborated the Manoa plot.

One is tempted at first sight to dismiss these parallels as fairly unimportant scenic materials used by Milton for contingent reasons: in reviewing ancient plays for materials suitable for a hero who was blind and put in brazen fetters, what plays other than *Oedipus at Colonus* and *Prometheus Bound* would provide any materials at all? Conversely, the quite conspicuous absence of compelling Heracles parallels may simply be due to the fact that the extant Heracles plays do not offer any scenic materials suitable to a Samson drama.

But there is a good deal more to these parallels. *Prometheus Bound* and *Oedipus at Colonus* stand to one another as beginning and end, an image of bondage and an image of release. *Prometheus Bound* is the opening play of a trilogy and focuses on the hostility between God and Man with a ferocity that has no parallel in Greek tragedy: for his just and merciful behaviour towards man, Prometheus is chained to a rock by Force and Violence, the servants of Zeus. *Oedipus at Colonus* portrays the hero's death and reconciliation with the gods – also in a manner that has no parallel: the gods call to Oedipus not in a voice of terror or command but in a tone of gentle chiding:

> Oedipus! Oedipus! Why are we waiting?
> You delay too long; you delay too long. (1627–8)

The contrast between these two plays also exists within each. The Io episode of *Prometheus Bound* looks forward to a time of release. Io is, like Prometheus, the victim of divine persecution, but Prometheus knows that some day this persecution will change to gentleness, and among the descendants of Zeus and Io will be Heracles, the liberator of Prometheus. And as *Prometheus Bound* looks forward to a distant point of liberation, so *Oedipus at Colonus* looks back on a terror and violence that indeed threaten to engulf the hero once more before he is finally released.

The juxtaposition of *Prometheus Bound* and *Oedipus at Colonus* as models for *Samson Agonistes* emphasizes by extrapolation the dialectic of bondage and release that exists within each and establishes that dialectic as the framework for Milton's interpretation of the Samson drama as the tragedy of deliverance. This framework replaces the Heracles model suggested by the tradition. Because Samson and Heracles were closely linked as joint precursors of Christ in the exegetical tradition, a patterning of Samson on Heracles would strongly suggest the foreshadowing of Christ through which they are linked in the first place. The avoidance of Heracles is therefore part of Milton's strategy of reticence.[27] But there is more to it. Samson and Heracles are linked through physical and sexual prowess as well as through the disasters they suffer at the hands of women. This linkage is clearly the point of Milton's comparison of Adam's and Samson's disillusionment:

> So rose the *Danite* strong,
> *Herculean Samson*, from the Harlot-lap
> Of *Philistean Dalilah*, and wak'd
> Shorn of his strength. (9.1059–62)

Force is Heracles' mode of liberation, as in Milton's last sonnet, where he provides a temporary and imperfect reunion of husband and wife:

> Methought I saw my late espoused Saint
> Brought to me like *Alcestis* from the grave,
> Whom *Jove's* great Son to her glad Husband gave,
> Rescued from death by force, though pale and faint.

But force is strongly questioned by Milton's Samson from the beginning:

> O impotence of mind, in body strong!
> But what is strength without a double share
> Of wisdom? Vast, unwieldy, burdensome,
> Proudly secure, yet liable to fall
> By weakest subtleties; not made to rule,
> But to subserve where wisdom bears command. (52–7)

This questioning of strength underlies Milton's choice of models: he avoids Heracles and patterns Samson on heroes prominently associated with knowledge. The shift in the models points to the eventual transcendence of force as the mode of deliverance and invokes a typological reading more obliquely than the Heracles parallels would permit. *Prometheus Bound* opens as a terrifying demonstration of brute force, and yet that force appears as an impotent and temporary regression. In his account of the Titanomachia, Prometheus relates how he took the advice of his mother, who said that 'not by strength nor overmastering force / the fates allowed the conquerors to conquer / but by guile only' (212–13). It was this advice that made him join Zeus, who in the first exuberance of his victory relapsed into violence. But this violence is impotent against the knowledge Prometheus possesses. *Prometheus Bound* is thus a drama in which deliverance is not by force, and Milton uses it as a model to suggest the limits of Samson's mode of deliverance without openly invoking its transcendence in a Christian context. To put it in other words: the shift from the hero of force to the heroes of knowledge as governing models for the drama of deliverance is Milton's way of acknowledging the transcendent element in the scriptural annunciation without transgressing the limits that annunciation sets for the drama of Samson: 'he shall *begin* to deliver Israel out of the hands of the Philistines.'[28]

The Psychological Drama

The shift from paradigms of strength to paradigms of knowledge establishes a goal for the psychological drama of Samson. The story of Samson ends with an action that is spectacular and fitting, but abrupt and 'unmotivated.' The playwright's task is therefore to establish a link between the protagonist's intentions and the final action. The ambiguities surrounding this intention and the protagonist's awareness of it are the field in which Milton's strategy of reticence operates. As with the manipulation of the typological link between Samson and Christ, Milton relies heavily on the transformation of classical models and in particular on the ways in which, from a Christian perspective, his hero goes beyond or falls short of the consciousness of the characters on which Samson is modeled.

Towards the end of the play, the Chorus say to Samson:

This Idol's day hath been to thee no day of rest
Laboring thy mind
More than the working day thy hands. (1297–9)

The working days are the days in the mill, but also the days of his former heroic life. The work of the mind does not come easily to Samson; its difficulty is ironically suggested by the classical models that set a goal for Samson's mental labours. These labours unfold before our eyes as a drama of reminiscence and self-recrimination ending in a form of suicide. In this regard *Samson Agonistes* is not unlike Humanist suicide tragedies, for which Sophocles' *Ajax* and more importantly Vergil's Dido tragedy – itself shaped by *Ajax* – provided the most influential models. The Dido tragedy in particular was often imitated in the Renaissance, sometimes directly, more often in the displaced form of Cleopatra and

Sofonisba dramas. The Humanist tragedies of reminiscence differ greatly from their ancient models by virtue of their exclusive preoccupation with what is only one moment in the model. Jodelle's *Didon se sacrifiant*, for instance, which begins with Aeneas' imminent departure, draws out a bare 300 lines of Vergilian narrative into a series of laments many times the length of the original.

The consequence of such expansion is a transformation of the crisis plot of Greek tragedy into a retrospective analysis of failure and a form of confessional literature. The drama becomes an inquest conducted by the protagonist in which he strives not to discover a set of facts, as in *Oedipus Rex*, but to establish motives and allocate responsibility. In Garnier's *Marc-Antoine*, for instance, the confidants try to comfort their masters by pointing to hostile fate as the origin of disaster. But both protagonists insist on putting the blame on themselves. Cléopatre, on being told that it is the fault of the gods, replies:

> Il ne faut nous en prendre à leurs majestez hautes,
> Mais à nous seulement, qui par nos passions
> Journellement tombons en mille afflictions.

Antoine takes more time to make a very similar point:

> Ce ne fut la Fortune à la face inconstante,
> Ce ne fut du Destin la force violente
> Qui forgea mon malheur. Hé! ne sçait-on pas bien
> Que c'est que l'un et l'autre, et qu'ils ne peuvent rien?
> Fortune que l'on craint, qu'on déteste et adore,
> N'est qu'un événement dont la cause on ignore.
> ...
> Le seule volupté, peste de nostre vie,
> Nostre vie, et encor' de cent pestes suivie
> M'a filé ce désastre, estant d'homme guerrier
> Dès le commencement devenu casanier,
> N'ayant soing de vertu, ny d'aucune louange.[29]

Both from the protagonist's and the author's perspective, suicide is a very satisfactory conclusion to an inquest of this kind. For the protagonist it offers a way of regaining moral dignity; for the playwright, the process of self-recrimination provides an adequate motive for suicide and dispenses with the need for additional external motivation in a play that begins when the 'action' is over. It is worth pointing out that the suicide drama provides a very pure and explicit link between the 'inward' drama of self-recrimination and the 'outward' circumstances of the action: suicide in these plays is always a fully conscious deed in which the protagonist's state of mind finds an objective correlative.

The fondness of Humanist playwrights for this form of confessional drama in which motives rather than acts are the object of inquiry clearly reflects modern psychological interests. At the same time, Humanist playwrights lacked the skills to give adequate dramatic expression to such forms of psychological inquiry; in their plays as the quotations from Garnier suggest, the search for causes is likely to take the form of an exchange of moral commonplaces that stand in a rather contingent relationship to the characters who utter them.

Samson Agonistes, which recalls *Ajax* in the important motif of the protagonist's dissimulation prior to his exit, bears many resemblances to the Humanist suicide tragedies of reminiscence and self-recrimination. But, as I said above, it is also the contemporary of *Phèdre*, and Milton rivals Racine in exploring the paradoxical relationship of the 'wily subtleties and reflexes of man's thoughts *from within*' to 'whatsoever hath passion or admiration in all the changes of ... fortune from *without*.' Whereas in *Phèdre* the heroine, compared to her models, is less manifestly criminal and more inwardly corrupt, a similar discrepancy informs *Samson Agonistes*, in which the protagonist's appearance of utter destitution, weakness, and impurity hides the presence of an inward process of regeneration.

The biblical narrative moves directly from the prison house to the festival. Milton's drama interposes several stages between these terminals: the rest in front of the prison, the descent to an intensified experience of despair, the affirmation of faith in response to the taunts of Harapha, the refusal to attend the festival of Dagon, and the experience of the 'rousing motions' that leads to Samson's change of mind. The scenic contrast that frames these stages and serves as a measure of the hero's progress is adapted from *Oedipus at Colonus*. In both plays we first encounter a weakened and filthy man who gains momentary rest; in both plays the last glimpse we have of him is that of a hero, bathed and dressed and once more in possession of his power.

In both plays, the past intervenes between this beginning and end, but nothing could be further from Oedipus' mind than Samson's compulsive reminiscing. In Sophocles' play the hero desires release from the sufferings of a cruel past. The promise of such a release is held out to him at the beginning when he recognizes the grove of the Eumenides as the predestined scene of his death. With that recognition, he ceases to be a beggar and acts in the consciousness of the gifts he has to bestow, imperiously summoning Theseus to the sacred grove that he refuses to leave. But he has not quite found peace yet: the Chorus badger him with questions, Creon and Polynices arrive with different demands, and once more the turmoil of the past threatens to engulf him. Nothing in the play suggests that this enforced confrontation is beneficial, that it is the cause of Oedipus' changed status at the end, or that he learns from it. On the contrary, the play presents us with a strangely static and limited hero, obstinate and self-indulgent in his love and hate, but possessed of a quasi-divine power to curse and to bless.

In *Samson Agonistes*, on the other hand, the stages of the drama measure the hero's re-enactment of the past, which proceeds from his restlessness and sense of guilt. And the play suggests that this voluntary, if obsessive, inquiry into his self is a necessary, though not a sufficient, condition for the hero's changed status at the end. From the very beginning Samson confronts his past in a questioning mood. The Philistine Festival has brought him some 'ease' to the body but

> none to the mind
> From restless thoughts, that like a deadly swarm
> Of Hornets arm'd, no sooner found alone,
> But rush upon me thronging, and present
> Times past, what once I was, and what am now. (18–22)

Samson's self-analysis produces an increasingly ironic correlation of appearance and reality in past and present. Although he had begun by looking for the cause of his fall from splendour into misery, he comes to suspect the splendour of his heroic life as a semblance that concealed a spiritual misery far deeper than his physical suffering. He moves beyond the immediate motives that caused him to betray his secret to Dalila and finally discovers the origin of his sin in his disposition at the height of his career when

> Fearless of danger, like a petty God
> I walk'd about admir'd of all and dreaded
> On hostile ground, none daring my affront.
> Then swoll'n with pride into the snare I fell
> Of fair fallacious looks, venereal trains,
> Softened with pleasure and voluptuous life. (529–34)

In this interpretation the outward change of fortune becomes a manifestation of the more radical fall from his Nazarite status of intimate communion with God to his present state of despair in which he sees himself as abandoned by God:

> I was his nursling once and choice delight,
> His destin'd from the womb,
> Promis's by heavenly message twice descending.
> Under his special eye
> Abstemious I grew up and thriv'd amain;
> He led me on to mightiest deeds
> Above the nerve of mortal arm
> Against the uncircumcis'd, our enemies.
> But now hath cast me off as never known,
> And to those cruel enemies,
> Whom I by his appointment had provok't,
> Left me all helpless with th'irreparable loss
> Of sight, reserv'd alive to be repeated
> The subject of thir cruelty or scorn.
> Nor am I in the list of them that hope;
> Hopeless are all my evils, all remediless;
> This one prayer yet remains, might I be heard,
> No long petition – speedy death,
> The close of all my miseries, and the balm. (633–51)

I have quoted this monody at such length because it marks not only the point of Samson's greatest despair, but also the point at which his mind is most transparent both to himself and to the audience. If Samson committed suicide at this point, we would think of his action as adequately motivated, and we would not raise questions about the relationship of the inward to the outward events. But he does not commit suicide, and in the following encounters with Dalila and Harapha, anger has an energizing function that causes him to regain his faith and a measure of his former confidence. In this state of mind he once again follows an intuition to commit an act that is ritually unclean: he attends the festival of Dagon, where he seizes the opportunity for his sudden revenge.

It is a reasonable assumption that the stages Milton interposed between the monody and the dénouement are intended to motivate the dénouement. Samson acquires and displays the faith, anger, and energy that enable him to commit his final act. Indeed, the play sets up more precise expectations. Samson's inquiry into his change of fortune concludes by making external circumstances the manifestation of an inward disposition. In so doing, it also sets a standard for what counts as a satisfactory explanation: an event must be traced back to the inward disposition from which it receives its meaning. Thus we look forward to a dénouement in which the consciousness of the protagonist is as clearly linked to the external state of affairs as it was at the lowest point of his despair. But this expectation is systematically frustrated by the play. The link between Samson's consciousness and his actions becomes increasingly opaque to the audience, and the text nowhere compels us to assume that the link is transparent to Samson himself.

This loss of transparence is very noticeable from a comparison of Samson's exit scene with the two Greek scenes it conflates, the protagonist's exit in *Oedipus at Colonus* and Ajax's speech of deception. The divine signal that motivates Samson's exit is adapted from *Oedipus at Colonus*, where similarly a divine call initiates the protagonist's last journey. But how open is the relationship of human consciousness to the divine call in Sophocles' play! Sudden thunder and lightning terrify the Chorus but give strength and assurance to Oedipus, who summons Theseus and gives him advice about his burial and the benefits that the city will receive from it. Then, in a reversal of roles, the blind Oedipus becomes the guide. He refers to the divine prompting that urges him (1541) and departs in search of the tomb that he will find without human aid, guided by Hermes and the goddess of the dead. In the messenger's report, the divine summons appears once more in the explicit form of a voice from the skies chiding Oedipus for his delay. Although the transfiguration of Oedipus is a sacred mystery that only Theseus is allowed to witness, the poet could hardly be more explicit about the interaction of the human and the divine. Oedipus departs as a prophet, and his audience, both on stage and in the audience, share in his clairvoyance. But this scene of imminent transfiguration becomes the model for a scene in which the interaction of the human and the divine finds its laconic expression in Samson's

> Be of good courage; I begin to feel
> Some rousing motions in me which dispose
> To something extraordinary my thoughts. (1381–3)

Much has been written about the 'rousing motions,' but surely the most important point to be made about this phrase is how much it withholds. If we remember with Hegel that *Oedipus at Colonus* comes closer to a

Christian vision of transcendence than any other ancient tragedy, it is surely significant that Milton's version falls far short of its model in suggesting a moment of revelation.[30] It is the Christian tragedy that maintains its silence even at the point where its classical model begins to speak!

A similar emphasis on opaqueness governs Milton's use of the Sophoclean *Ajax*. In that play, the protagonist is urged by the Chorus and Tekmessa not to carry out his intention of killing himself. In a long speech he appears to yield to their entreaties. He leaves, but when he returns we discover that the speech was merely a device to gain solitude. In retrospect, his speech of deception appears shot through with ironies. He announces that he will go to a place where he will cleanse himself from the blood of slaughter and from his madness (654–6). He will bury his sword where no one will see it (658–9). He has learned that masters must be obeyed (667–8) and

> Now I am going where my way must go.
> Do as I bid you, and you may yet hear
> That I, though wretched now, have found my safety. (690-2)

Samson's last conversation with the Chorus clearly goes back to this scene. The ironic submission to the power of masters ('Masters' commands come with a power resistless/To those that owe them absolute subjection') is an open allusion, and in both plays there is a very similar tension between violence and purification. But whereas the riddles of Ajax's speech are resolved in his final soliloquy, Samson's words remain ambiguous to the end. Does he envisage his revenge but wish to keep it from the Chorus? Is some knowledge of the end his motive for dissuading his friends from coming along on his final journey? Or is the irony the author's, and his character knows no more than he says?

From Milton's particular models, and indeed from virtually all death scenes in Greek tragedy, we expect that the hero will at the point of death attain complete self-knowledge and will share that knowledge with the audience. Not so Milton's Samson, and in this regard he differs not only from his Greek models but from his Old Testament prototype. The biblical Samson is quite straightforward in the statement of his intentions:

> And Samson called unto the Lord, and said, O Lord God, remember me, I pray thee, and strengthen me, I pray thee, only this once, O God that I may be at

once avenged of the Philistines for my two eyes. And Samson took hold of the two middle pillars upon which the house stood, and on which it was borne up, of the one with his right hand, and of the other with his left.

And Samson said, Let me die with the Philistines.

The ensuing act fully realizes the protagonist's stated intention and testifies to the efficacy of his prayer.

Milton's Samson, by contrast, does not utter a prayer, although the messenger describes his meditative stance 'as one who prayed, or some great matter in his mind revolved' (1637–8).[31] Nor does he express a wish to die. Instead he addresses the Philistines in a continuation of the role they have cast him in and promises an 'amazing' version of that role. If there is a prayer, it is silent; Samson's consciousness retreats behind the ironic role he presents to the Philistines. From the perspective of this end, neither the nature of the 'rousing motions' nor the extent of Samson's knowledge at the point of his exit is retrospectively illuminated.

The Tragedy of Deliverance

The principal consequence of Samson's silence is that the significance of the catastrophe is left in obscurity and the play quite deliberately fails to establish the kind of link between inward disposition and outward event that counts as a satisfactory explanation of the event by the standards the play itself has established.[32] Compared with the Old Testament narrative, which displays a perfect harmony of heroic consciousness and action, *Samson Agonistes* is characterized by a disequilibrium of act and intention. The consciousness of the biblical Samson is what Milton's hero has left behind in his repudiation of brute strength and in his search for knowledge. It would therefore be out of character for Milton's Samson to speak the lines of his biblical model. But Milton does not replace the biblical lines with words that more accurately reflect the spiritual state of his hero and establish the catastrophe as its objective correlative; rather he stresses that the catastrophe is at odds with the state of mind that 'produces' it. Although in Samson's inquest the external world had been transformed into a manifestation of a spiritual state, the tragedy returns to a dénouement of physical violence that resists interpretation in spiritual terms. Samson does not become a redeemer, but remains a deliverer. Within his own consciousness, he moves from strength to knowledge, but it is not given to him to bring about a parallel shift in his action. We may call this the tragedy of the *beginning* of deliverance.

Milton emphasizes its tension and suffering by dwelling on the silence and blindness of the protagonist, who attains no clear vision of the goal towards which he has begun to move.[33]

We get an additional view of Milton's strategy of reticence if we compare *Samson Agonistes* with Goethe's *Iphigenie auf Tauris* in which a late Sophoclean play (*Philoctetes*) also provides the model for a drama of deliverance. In both modern plays, the protagonist is condemned to what appears to be a futile period of waiting, but it turns out that this waiting is a form of spiritual activity which results in the decisive action of the play. In both plays, the relationship of waiting to significant action is a transformation of a temporal structure common to the Sophoclean models.

In Greek tragedy time is generally experienced in the contrasting modes of waiting and acting. Only characters who suffer and for some reason are unable to act complain about the slow passage of time. But such characters are frequent, and it is significant that the choruses of Greek tragedy are in the great majority of cases composed of women or old men – characters who are by constitution excluded from the life of action.

If anxious waiting is characteristic of the powerless, impatience often characterizes those qualified to act. Achilles and Oedipus come to mind. The prominence in Greek tragedy of such stock characters as the stage tyrant or the anxiety-ridden woman is not due to a mirroring of social conditions: these literary conventions are concrete manifestations of a particular structure of temporal experience in which a significant action always appears as a dialectic concatenation of time experienced in the modes of waiting and acting.

Depending on the direction of the reversal of fortune, this concatenation takes two principal forms. In a play ending unhappily, the protagonist is plunged into disaster from a state in which he appears to himself and to others to enjoy the full freedom of action. Whether such plays end with the death of the protagonist (*Agamemnon*), his reduction to impotent suffering (*Oedipus Rex*), or both (*Women of Trachis*), it is never the protagonist himself who waits in such drama, since it is essential to the effect of the reversal that until the moment of crisis his time be experienced as active. In such plays, the protagonist's activity is often counterpointed by the waiting of those who depend on him. If, on the other hand, the reversal moves towards a happy end, the crisis will release the protagonist from a period of long suffering. The protagonists of such plays are usually women (Electra, Helen, Iphigenia, Creusa), and the representation of their powerless and painful waiting will form a crucial part of the dramatic structure.

The late plays of Sophocles give a significant twist to this pattern. In *Oedipus at Colonus* and *Philoctetes* the protagonists are men of action whose suffering is a reduction to powerlessness contrary to their essential nature. Therefore the release from suffering in these plays is also a return to a power previously enjoyed. The Sophoclean plays may thus be seen as 'comedies' that in a manner congenial to the Christian universe raise the question of the mysterious concatenation of suffering and action that forms the hero's destiny. Oedipus especially may strike us as a kind of 'holy sinner,' whose holiness consists in a transcendence of his sinfulness.[34] But that would be going too far. It is evident that in these plays the poet considers the totality of suffering and action as a significant and orderly whole. Equally obvious, however, is his refusal to provide a transitional link between the opposites that create destiny: what is asserted is a riddle that manifests itself in the form of contrasting images: the wound and the bow of Philoctetes, the sacredness and filthiness of Oedipus.

In *Samson Agonistes* and *Iphigenie auf Tauris*, the protagonist's consciousness establishes the transition between the extremes of his state. The present becomes the point of intersection at which the past is revealed as preparing the way for and being transcended in the future. Past and future appear as memory and hope in the mind of the hero, whose action in the present is the achievement of that 'translation,' whether or not he is fully aware of his task. From this perspective the similarity between the two protagonists is striking. Like Samson, Iphigenie is condemned to what appears to her as a life of useless waiting, but it turns out that her exile is a form of providential concealment. She too undergoes a development that is contingent on her blindness to its purpose. Both authors seek to establish a link between violence and reconciliation through a psychological development that leads to a spiritual triumph over violence. Just as Samson distances himself from the crude heroism of his former life, Iphigenia, as woman and priestess, moves beyond the world of iron necessity that enslaved her family. But at this point the two plays sharply diverge. In Goethe's play, the transcendence of violence finds its objective correlative in a dénouement that rejects violence. Iphigenia's internal development gathers sufficient force to break the deadlock of the action: her achievement of reconciliation between Thoas and Orest replaces the summary form of divine intervention at the end of *Philoctetes*. She becomes a secular redeemer who in full consciousness brings about a moral revolution.

From the perspective of Goethe's play one sees very clearly what Milton does not do. Whereas Goethe's play enacts the transcendence of tragedy by Christianity, albeit in a form of secular displacement, Milton's Christian tragedy does not take the step of transcendence its classical model invites. Iphigenia is portrayed as a redeemer who in her vision of the unredeemed Tantalus becomes a type of Christ harrowing Hell, but the typological significance of Samson is muted. In Goethe's play, the protagonist's consciousness creates the act that transforms a world of violence and gives full expression to the ethos underlying this act; in Milton's play, the protagonist's consciousness is opaque to us and probably to himself as well, and the final action returns us to a world of destruction that we thought we had left behind.

In *Phèdre* and *Penthesilea*, to which Goethe's play also stands in a systematic opposition, the tragic actions consist of a relapse into a world of monstrous passion or Dionysiac frenzy and lead to chaotic violence in the form of the dismemberment of Hippolytus and Achilles. The silences and discontinuities of *Samson Agonistes*, however terrifying, do not quite return us to such a world. Some resolution of violence is suggested in its interpretation as sacrifice. In the biblical narrative, the angel who announces the birth of Samson ascends to the sky in the flames of a burnt offering. Samson refers to this incident early in the play:

> O wherefore was my birth from Heaven foretold
> Twice by an angel, who at last in sight
> Of both my Parents all in flames ascended
> From off the Altar, where an Off'ring burn'd,
> As in a fiery column charioting
> His Godlike presence, and from some great act
> Or benefit revealed to *Abraham's* race? (23–9)

After the catastrophe the Chorus give some kind of answer to this anguished question by seeing Samson's death as a repetition of the first holocaust:

> So virtue, giv'n for lost,
> Deprest, and overthrown, as seem'd,
> Like that self-begotten bird

In the *Arabian* woods embost,
That no second knows nor third,
And lay erewhile a Holocaust,
From out her ashy womb now teem'd,
Revives, reflourishes, then vigorous most
When most unactive deem'd,
And though her body die, her fame survives,
A secular bird, ages of lives. (1697–1706)

The use of the biblical motif of sacrifice as a controlling metaphor leads us back to Buchanan's *Jephtha* and narrows the gap between Milton and Buchanan that had been the point of departure for this essay. Considered as Iphigenia dramas, Buchanan's and Goethe's versions offer radically different interpretations of the underlying myth. Buchanan asserts the inevitability of sacrificial violence and stresses its indifference to reason and justice. From the perspective of his play, *Iphigenie auf Tauris* is a secularized version of the Abraham and Isaac story, anti-tragic and progressive in its belief in the power of human reason and love. Like Buchanan, Milton insists on the inevitability of sacrificial violence, but his exploration of the theme of sacrifice is much subtler than Buchanan's and rests on the insight that Christianity and Tragedy, which seem mutually exclusive when viewed in terms of the extremes of Abraham and Jephtha, have a common ground in the mystery of sacrifice. *Samson Agonistes* neither dwells on an act of violence as abhorrent as the sacrifice of Jephtha's daughter, nor does it look forward to a transcendence of violence in which the very meaning of sacrifice becomes questionable, as in *Iphigenie auf Tauris*. Is not its enigma of a violent sacrifice most Christian in its foreshadowing of the sacrificial violence of the Crucifixion?

It is very tempting to see in Milton's interpretation of Samson's death as sacrificial both an acknowledgement of and progression beyond Buchanan's *Jephtha*. In the Book of Judges, the story of Samson immediately follows that of Jephtha, which is without any doubt the Old Testament story most remote from the divine promise to Abraham and its fulfilment in Christ. Milton's strategies of pointed reticence and mitigation may well be a way of dramatizing that sequence. The tragedy of Samson stays close to that of Jephtha in time and in spirit, but it is closer, by however little, to the Incarnation. Hence the events begin to resonate with a significance that remains opaque to the participants and is very far from abolishing the darkness of tragedy in a blaze of revelation. Milton was a poet of beginnings, from the *Nativity Ode* on, which celebrates not only the birth of Christ but also the poet's majority and turns on the phrase 'but now begins.' The swain in Lycidas and Adam and Eve at the close of *Paradise Lost* look forward to a new world, and at the end of *Paradise Regained* the angels sing

> Hail, Son of the Most High, heir of both worlds
> Queller of Satan, on thy glorious work
> Now enter and begin to save mankind.

Is it the ultimate irony of *Samson Agonistes* that this final work, written in a genre shaped by catastrophic endings, is a silent meditation on a beginning?

> For, lo, thou shalt conceive, and bear a son; and no razor shall come on his head: for the child shall be a Nazarite unto God from the womb, and he shall begin to deliver Israel out of the hand of the Philistines.

6

EPIC AND TRAGEDY

THE TRAGIC EPIC: *PARADISE LOST* AND *THE ILIAD*

There has been remarkably little disagreement about the place of *Paradise Lost* in the epic tradition ever since Patrick Hume first published his collection of Milton's classical allusions.[1] Scholars and critics have focused almost exclusively on the relationship of Milton's epic to the *Aeneid*, which they considered to have been his dominant model. There are a number of reasons for this consensus. First, there is the frequency and brilliance of Vergilian allusion in *Paradise Lost*. Second, the *Aeneid* holds the central position in the epic tradition and at least until the middle of the eighteenth century dominated all theories of the epic. It was therefore natural to assume that as a *poeta doctus* who observed the laws of decorum, Milton would acknowledge the central position of the *Aeneid* by making it the chief model of a work that was to realize the deepest ambition of every Renaissance poet, the creation of a heroic poem. Third, there can be little doubt that most scholars who have studied the classical antecedents of *Paradise Lost* have known the *Aeneid* more intimately than any other epic and were thus predisposed to seeing Vergilian influences. This is especially true of the eighteenth-century annotators, who collected much of the material on which modern investigators of Milton's allusions have based their work. Without disputing the fact that the Vergilian perspective has greatly contributed to our understanding of Milton's work, I should like to argue that its uncritical acceptance has obscured important structural and thematic affinities between *Paradise Lost* and the *Iliad* – affinities which not only illuminate the principles of organization of *Paradise Lost* but also invite us to reconsider the nature of Milton's attitude towards the epic tradition.

Milton himself drew attention to the thematic affinities between the central actions of *Paradise Lost* and the *Iliad*, for in his poem he followed the *Iliad* more closely than any other epic. The poet of the *Iliad* opens his epic with the announcement of his subject: he will sing of the wrath of Achilles. Unlike Vergil or the author of the *Odyssey*, he takes an action, not a man, as the subject of his epic. Milton follows the Iliadic proem in its general outline. Like the poet of the *Iliad*, he invokes the Muse to sing, and to sing about man's first disobedience. 'Disobedience' here means an act of disobedience, just as *mênis* means an action caused by wrath; in both cases the abstract noun is used in the concrete sense, a parallel that extends to syntactic similarity:'Man's first disobedience' corresponds precisely to *mênis ... Pêlêiadeô* ('the wrath of Achilles'). Milton follows the *Iliad* in describing the consequences of disobedience: whereas the deaths of many Achaeans resulted from Achilles' wrath, disobedience and 'the fruit of that forbidden tree' 'brought death into the world and all our woe.'

The structural debt points to a thematic resemblance. Like Achilles' wrath, man's disobedience causes death, and in both poems the factual statements of the opening lines lead to the central theme of the work. The *Iliad* is an epic of death. At its centre stands a destructive action, the wrath of Achilles, which results in the death of many Achaeans – particularly Patroclus, the friend of Achilles. Beyond that, it leads to the deaths of Hector and of Achilles himself. Ultimately the fall of Troy looms behind the deaths of the major and minor characters.

Death is also the subject of Milton's epic, and like death in the *Iliad*, it is the result of a destructive action. In choosing such a subject, Milton ignored the precedent established by the *Aeneid*. G.N. Knauer has suggested that Vergil's interpretation of Homer was based on a typological view of the Homeric epics.[2] The events in the *Aeneid* repeat, reverse, and fulfil Homeric history, and in retrospect the events of the *Iliad* are shown to have been pregnant with future history. On one level the *Aeneid* is a poem of Trojan revenge. It tells the story of the Trojan victory over the Achaeans as realized by the Romans and symbolically anticipated in the defeat of Turnus, whose Mycenaean connections are deliberately emphasized by the poet. But this repetition and reversal of events does not merely mean that the same events are now happening with changed roles. The *Iliad* was an epic about the destruction of the Trojans by the Achaeans; but the *Aeneid* is not an epic about the destruction of the Achaeans by the Trojans, either in the present or in the distant future. It is a poem about building.[3] The action of the *Aeneid* is constructive, and by an act of deliberate challenge, it is set against the destructive action of the *Iliad*: the fall of Troy, foreshadowed at the end of the *Iliad*, is the beginning of Aeneas' story. Thus Vergil reverses not only the roles of Trojans and Achaeans but also the direction and character of the action. 'Constructive versus destructive,' however, only sums up part of the difference that separates the *Aeneid* from the *Iliad* and from *Paradise Lost*. Death and disobedience are indeed announced as the main themes of the two epics, but in both works the tragic theme of destruction is counterpointed by a theme of reconciliation that mitigates the tragic effect. The wrath of Achilles culminates in the maltreatment of Hector, but the epic concludes with the ceremonious meeting of Achilles and Priam. Their reconciliation and the ransom of Hector balance the theme of wrath which had been announced in the proem. Just as the first programmatic lines of the *Iliad* do not exhaust its full range, so the title of *Paradise Lost* does only partial justice to its content. Milton invokes the Muse to sing of disobedience, but a crucial part of the poem deals with the slow process by which Adam and Eve become obedient again: the story of 'Paradise Lost' includes that of 'Paradise Regained.' In Milton's epic the reconciliation even leads to a resolution of the tragic situation. The reconciliation of Achilles and Priam changes nothing; that of Adam and Eve, everything. But in both poems, the reconciliation of two characters gives at least a sense of 'calm of mind, all passion spent.' Both poets aim at distancing the reader from the horror of events before dismissing him.

Once again, a comparison with the *Aeneid* is instructive. The last book of the *Aeneid* has baffled many critics, not only because it ends so abruptly, but because the cruel death of Turnus seems to conflict with the spirit of Aeneas' mission. Vergil sanctions the Trojan invasion of Latium by the reconciliation of Juno and Jupiter (12.791–840). But this divine concord finds no counterpart on the human level; the scene of reconciliation between Juno and Jupiter is followed by one of the cruellest actions in the entire work, Aeneas' execution of the helpless and wounded Turnus as he implicitly asks for his life. The poem ends on a jarring discord, and no interpretation of the last book can explain away the curious paradox that Vergil was able to formulate the theme of reconciliation but, for whatever reason, did not want to or failed to represent it in an action on the human level. The abrupt and discordant end of the *Aeneid* contrasts significantly with the quiet conclusions of the *Iliad* and of *Paradise Lost*.

The action of the *Aeneid* determined later notions of a proper heroic poem. Its subject had to be some great enterprise of prosperous design. So

Camoens chose the circumnavigation of Africa, and Tasso the liberation of Jerusalem. Milton chose differently. In his epic the event that corresponds to the destruction of Troy is the eventual defeat of Satan by Christ. But this final victory is no more the subject of *Paradise Lost* than the Achaean triumph over the Trojans is the subject of the *Iliad*. The wrath of Achilles and the disobedience of Adam are both apparent setbacks in the larger struggle, but paradoxically they make the final victory all the more certain. The main concern of both poets was not with the splendour of that triumph but with the bitterness of the disastrous event that impeded, and by impeding, necessitated, the final success.

According to Aristotle, the author of the *Iliad* deserved praise for his choice of subject matter. Instead of giving an account of the entire Trojan War, which would have resulted in a work either too long or too condensed to be aesthetically pleasing, he chose one part of the story for his central plot and told the remaining events in 'episodes.' The total structure of the *Iliad* that results from this technique has its only parallel in the structure of *Paradise Lost*. In the linear narrative of the *Odyssey*, plot and story are very nearly co-extensive. The same is true of the narrative structure of the *Aeneid*, even though in that epic the events of Vergil's founding myth point beyond themselves to future history in an almost allegorical fashion. In both these epics, there are many digressions, but their subordinate nature is never in doubt, and even the mechanical device of interrupting chronological sequence by means of flashback narrative does not disturb the linear progress of the story, which comes to its end with the final event. In the *Iliad*, on the other hand, we can distinguish very clearly between two narrative strands: the story of Achilles and the story of the Trojan War. The critic who is not content with the primitive explanation that the poet turned an Achilleid into an Iliad by adding background episodes must ask himself why the Achilleid was chosen as a representative action, how the story of the war is related to it, and what constitutes the aesthetic unity of the resultant whole.

Watson Kirkconnell gave his collection of sources and analogues of *Paradise Lost* the serendipitous title *The Celestial Cycle*.[4] The choice points to the structural problem that Milton had in common with the author of the *Iliad*. He too drew on a tradition that was loosely organized as a sequence of stories. He had the encyclopedic ambitions of the author of the *Iliad*: *Paradise Lost* was to be as comprehensive a treatment of the total Christian myth as the *Iliad* was of the Trojan War, but the size and complexity of the material precluded a chronological approach. Milton, too, chose a part of the story and told the remaining events in 'episodes.' Thus, both in *Paradise Lost* and in the *Iliad*, the critic's task consists in extracting the skeletal action, assessing its significance, and discovering the principles that relate it to the total action.

The central action of *Paradise Lost* is in Aristotle's words a *muthos dramatikos*. The term *dramatic*, as Aristotle uses it, does not primarily refer to drama, nor has it anything to do with direct representation, vividness, excitement, and similar qualities that are usually designated by the term. It is derived from a Greek word for action and, equally embracing epic and tragedy, it refers solely to the 'composition of the action,' which is the first and greatest requirement for tragedy and for epic as well (*Poetics* 7.50b22–3). In Aristotle's theory of plot, the emotional effect is not merely due to the impact of the story's raw material – the physical violence which he calls *pathos* – but to the audience's realization of the logic and coherence of the action.[5] The most 'dramatic' plot is the plot in which the proper pleasure of tragedy is achieved by the arousal of pity and fear by intellectual means, in particular the devices of peripety and anagnorisis, which crystallize the horror of the deed in one moment of awareness, as in *The Women of Trachis* or in *Oedipus Rex*. Aristotle's theory gives meaning to the rigidly observed stage convention of excluding physical violence from the scene. It is not a mere rule of decorum but is rooted in the conviction that physical suffering has limits. Not death, but the death-in-life of tragic survival, is the ultimate degree of suffering in Greek tragedy.

Paradise Lost is dramatic not only in this Aristotelian sense but in a more conventional sense as well. The Fall had been a tragic subject in the literary tradition, and Milton originally conceived of his work on the Fall as a tragedy. Dryden complained, and from his point of view quite rightly, that Milton's epic was a tragedy in disguise: *Paradise Lost* is far more effective in terms of dramatic organization than any of the plays on the Fall that preceded it, and the tragic potential inherent in the story is far more fully realized in its plot than even the most imaginative critic would have guessed from the surviving outlines for a tragedy on the Fall that the young Milton had planned to write.[6]

As told in Genesis, the Fall is a story with two peaks: the fall of Eve is followed by the fall of Adam. The account of Eve's temptation presented the dramatist with at least the outlines of the debate between her and the serpent, but the Bible says nothing about Adam's fall beyond the bare statement that he ate the apple which Eve gave him. Most writers of plays on the Fall merely invented a second scene of persuasion which was modeled on Eve's temptation. We find, therefore, scenes in which Eve alternately pleads seductively or violently, threatens suicide or weeps helplessly, and finally prevails over a reluctant Adam.[7]

This additive solution, in which Adam's fall more or less repeats Eve's, may be theatrically effective, but it is undramatic because it fails to establish a cogent logic of events. Such a logic was established by Augustine, who distinguished between the motives of Adam and Eve and gave a reason why the fall of Eve determined that of Adam. Eve was deceived by the serpent, 'but we cannot believe that Adam was deceived, and supposed the devil's word to be truth and therefore transgressed God's law, but that he by the drawings of kindred yielded to the woman, the husband to the wife, the one human being to the only other human being. ... He was not on this account less culpable, but sinned with his eyes open.'[8] Milton not only chose to express this distinction in his plot, but his choice enabled him to keep close to Genesis, which does not include an account of Adam's persuasion by Eve. His Adam falls as soon as he knows of Eve's fall, which he considers irrevocable from the very first. Its consequence is equally irrevocable: '... for with thee/Certain my resolution is to die' (9.906–7). For Adam, the sight of the fallen Eve is the moment of tragic recognition and peripety. Milton uses a powerful Homeric allusion to show the instantaneous reversal: The duel of Hector and Achilles takes place while Andromache, ignorant of the real situation, prepares a bath in anticipation of Hector's return. When she hears the shrieks of Hecuba, she rushes to the tower only to see her husband dragged in the dust:

> The darkness of night misted over the eyes of Andromache.
> She fell backward, and gasped the life breath from her, and far off
> threw from her head the shining gear that ordered her headdress,
> and diadem and the cap, and the holding-band woven together,
> and the circlet, which Aphrodite the golden once had given her
> on that day when Hektor of the shining helmet led her forth
> from the house of Eëtion, and gave numberless gifts to win her. (22.466–72)

The apparent digression vividly recalls the beginning of the happiness of which Hector's death is the tragic end. When Andromache regains consciousness, she makes a speech in which she expresses what the incident of the fallen circlet had suggested symbolically. Adam's first reaction to Eve's fall is likewise speechless. He had been wearing a wreath of flowers in anticipation of Eve's return:

> On th' other side, Adam, soon as he heard
> The fatal trespass done by Eve, amazed,
> Astonied stood and blank, while horror chill
> Ran through his veins, and all his joints relaxed;
> From his slack hand the garland wreathed for Eve
> Down dropped, and all the faded roses shed. (9.888–93)

The dropping of the wreath fulfils the same symbolic function as Andromache's loss of her circlet, for Eve had been consistently identified with flowers from her first appearance in the poem:[9]

> Not that fair field
> Of Enna, where Proserpin gath'ring flowers
> Herself a fairer flower by gloomy Dis
> Was gather'd, which cost Ceres all that pain
> To seek her through the world... (4.268–72)

Adam's speech, like that of Andromache, only expresses what we have already seen. The implicit use of flower imagery in Adam's speech (9.901) firmly connects the speech with the speechless reaction.

Although Adam's situation does not bear any resemblance to a particular Greek play, he is quite recognizably the tragic survivor so common in the plays of Sophocles and Euripides. But the structure of the Fall in Milton's epic also has striking analogues to the plot of the *Iliad*, if one abstracts the tragic mechanism of that plot from its concrete embodiment in the story of Achilles, Hector, and Patroclus.

The *pathos* of the *Iliad* is the killing of Hector by Achilles. In Aristotelian terms it is a specifically untragic act: a man kills his enemy. A tragic element is introduced by the fact that the death of Hector entails that of Achilles. By deciding to kill Hector, Achilles chooses the glory of a short life, and he is fully aware of the consequences of his deed (18.114–26). But since this resolution is Achilles' own choice, the complication is hardly tragic. Here, the next complication helps: Achilles must kill Hector because the death of Patroclus forces him to revenge. He has no choice; but he wants no choice because the death of Patroclus has robbed him of everything that gave meaning to his life. Even this concatenation of events, however, lacks tragic quality because Achilles appears as the victim of events that have their origin outside himself. The author raised the story above the level of determinism by tracing the chain of events back to an action for which Achilles was responsible. Achilles' actions are motivated by his desire to earn the glory that will recompense his short life. When he calls the assembly that leads to the quarrel with Agamemnon, he for the first time takes his fate into his own hands, and the story of the *Iliad* from that point on may be described as a series of disastrous blunders by Achilles – steps which he takes to speed up the acquisition of the glory he considers his birthright, but which seem to lead further away from that goal. In a disastrous final reversal, however, the events reveal that they have led towards that goal all the time, but with a tragic difference. The reversal that reveals the coherence and necessity of the tragedy is the death of Patroclus, in which Achilles experiences his own imminent death. But the action that ultimately determines this necessity is Achilles' request from Zeus to support the enemy (1.407–12).[10] The poet emphasizes its disastrous consequences by having Achilles allude to this request in the prayer in which he asks for the safe return of Patroclus (16.236–7).

The immediate cause of Patroclus' death, however, is Achilles' decision to allow Patroclus to borrow his own armour and fight Hector. The decision is that of a tragically blinded man, as the poet reveals to us in Achilles' motives for resigning to his friend the responsibility that is so patently his own. Achilles imagines that the victorious return of Patroclus will reflect honourably on himself and that the Achaeans will bring him gifts, the same gifts that he had so violently refused earlier. Achilles indulges in a wish fulfilment that contrasts point by point with the reality that awaits him. He concludes his speech with the outburst:

Father Zeus, Athene and Apollo, if only
not one of all the Trojans could escape destruction, not one
of the Argives, but you and I could emerge from the slaughter
so that we two alone could break Troy's hallowed caronal (16.97–100)

In reality, neither of them will be alive when Troy is taken.

Patroclus not only dies in the armour of Achilles, but the circumstances of his death quite deliberately foreshadow that of Achilles. When Thetis comes to comfort the mourning Achilles, she cradles his head in her lap in a gesture that recalls ritual mourning: she treats her son as if he were dead.[11] And Achilles himself, once the death of Patroclus has awakened him from his delusions, acts in full consciousness of his imminent death.[12] Aeschylus later was to use as a symbol of tragic recognition the fable of the eagle who recognizes as his own the feathers on the arrow that fatally wounded him.[13] Homeric characters are less self-conscious than the characters of Attic tragedies, but even so, the tragic reversal of Achilles' fate is less the result of a changed situation than of Achilles' insight into the nature of his own actions, an insight that is not expressed by reflection but by the instantaneous and wholehearted acceptance of their consequences.

The relationship of the fall of Eve to that of Adam strangely resembles that of the Patrocleia to the Achilleid. Adam's fall hinges on Eve's in such a manner that it becomes a mere consequence of and reaction, to it. That is to say, the fall of Eve determines the fall of Adam in much the same manner that the death of Patroclus determines that of Achilles. The parallels can be pushed further. Although Adam's fall is sudden, it is not unexpected: in the scene in which Eve persuades Adam to let her work by herself, Milton had shown that Adam could not resist his wife. No source is known for this scene, and it is apparently Milton's own invention. But the position and function of the scene in the drama of the Fall bear an astonishing resemblance to the scene in which Patroclus persuades Achilles to let him fight the Trojans. It is the duty of Adam and Achilles to protect Eve and Patroclus, but at the request of the weaker character they both resign a duty that they should have kept. It was Achilles' responsibility to fight Hector; in letting Patroclus do it, he becomes responsible for his death. In letting Eve face Satan by herself, Adam repeats Achilles' disastrous error. Achilles and Adam are both full of warnings that are duly disregarded: Eve and Patroclus suffer precisely those things that Adam and Achilles had feared most. In both epics the hero's abdication of his responsibility also has fatal consequences for himself. The death of Patroclus causes that of Achilles, as Achilles himself is the first to realize. So Eve's fall causes the fall of Adam, as Adam likewise realizes immediately. The manner in which it causes the hero's death is also similar. Eve's fall and the death of Patroclus lead Adam and Achilles to choose actions that will involve their own deaths. For both of them, shame and the horror of living without the person dearest to them far exceed the fear of death. But in both epics, the disaster that befalls the hero, the loss of his dearest friend, is something he himself has caused.

In Aristotle's terms the tragic quality of a *pathos* depends on the bond of *philia* between agent and sufferer which it disrupts. In *Paradise Lost* and the *Iliad* this bond consists of the relationships of Adam and Eve and of Achilles and Patroclus respectively. Hence these relationships are comparable with regard to their function in the tragic mechanism of each work. These relationships provide the charge for the emotional intensity of the tragic climaxes, and without them the heroes' reactions to their tragedies cease to be credible. The crucial significance of these relationships for the credibility of the heroes' tragic reactions is demonstrated by the failure of the *Aeneid* in this respect. Although Vergil imitated the circumstances of the Patrocleia in the story of Pallas, Turnus, and Aeneas, the effect of Pallas' death on Aeneas is unconvincing because Vergil never succeeded in establishing a close relationship between Pallas and Aeneas that would explain or justify the furious revenge that Aeneas takes on Turnus. [14]

In *Paradise Lost* as well as in the *Iliad*, the emotional effectiveness and credibility of the tragic crisis are achieved by a partial identification of hero and reader. The fates of Eve and Patroclus, which 'polarize' those of Adam and Achilles, are witnessed by a reader who has been forced by the author to assume the hero's perspective. Milton apostrophizes Eve, but he never apostrophizes Adam. [15] This special expression of sympathy by the author, an expression also apparent in the pervasive flower imagery, guides the reader's reaction. Adam does not observe the fall of Eve, but the reader takes his place and the vicarious experience of Adam's feelings convinces him that the crystallization of these feelings in Adam's sudden reaction to the fall of Eve is emotionally credible.

Precisely the same handling of the reader's emotions occurs in the *Iliad*. Patroclus is very much like Eve in serving as a contrast figure to the masculine world of the Achaean camp. Although he is a great warrior, his true nature lies in the domestic sphere. He is repeatedly called gentle, and he is compassionate, an example of which is his attention to the wounded Eurypylos (11.828–48). We see him as he entertains the Achaean envoys, prepares a meal, and later makes the bed for Phoenix (9.201–20, 658–9). As in *Paradise Lost*, the sympathy that the author shows for him is an expression of the hero's love. The poet several times addresses him in the second person; he marks the beginning of his tragedy by a rare editorial aside (11.604), and again he comments on the *atê* that Zeus sent to Patroclus when he had decided on his death (16.684–91). [16] The emotional identification of the author, listener, and Achilles is apparent above all in the account of Patroclus' death, which is not heroic, like that of Hector, but is deliberately pathetic in order to give poignancy to the self-accusations of Achilles (18.102–3). The listener replaces Achilles as the observer of the pitiful death of Patroclus, and this experience gives truth to the overwhelming reaction of Achilles when he learns the news of his friend's death.

The comparison with Achilles reveals the formal elements of tragedy in Adam's situation, but in a Christian context the experience of tragic recognition undergoes a radical transformation. The pathos of *Paradise Lost* not only disrupts the relationship of Adam and Eve; above all, it disrupts the relationship of man and God, in which the former is grounded and of which it is a symbol. But for Adam the sense of his loss of Eve is so overwhelming that he takes the symbol for the truth and turns it into an idol. Hence we must distinguish between the false tragic dilemma in which he imagines himself and the actual tragedy of his betrayal of God. Milton puts Adam in the role of a hero confronted with a tragic reversal, but the situation is only apparent. Out of his sense of loss, Adam acts to prevent that loss and in doing so falls into his real tragedy. The death of Patroclus turns the blind Achilles into a seeing Achilles, who recognizes his fate and the connection between death and honour. For Adam, on the other hand, things come apart in the Fall. In choosing to fall, he becomes rapidly and increasingly blind. Adam's consciousness of Eve's fall is a false consciousness. In the *Iliad*, as in many Greek tragedies, the critical situations turn on the contrast of truth and delusion, knowledge and ignorance, rather than on good and evil. Knowledge brings disaster, as in the case of Oedipus, but the insight into the tragic coherence of things is the greatest source of human self-assertion, and thus the moment of tragic recognition is in a paradoxical sense a moment of intense pride, or at least a moment of supreme consciousness of the self. The plot conventions which Aristotle analyzed in the *Poetics* are designed to throw into fullest relief this existential situation of disaster and triumph, of knowledge in defeat. Milton took over the formal pattern of the tragic plot but rejected its metaphysical implications. The situation of tragic recognition becomes the scene in which man wilfully isolates himself from divine grace. The self-consciousness of the tragic hero becomes the source of evil in the Augustinian psychology of sin that governs Milton's epic.

But Adam's tragedy is not irrevocable. The Fall cannot be undone, but its consequences are overcome in the Redemption. The reconciliation of Achilles and Priam leads both to a dignified acceptance of the events. The ritual of the ransom and of the shared meal mitigates the starkness of the disaster. But the meeting changes nothing: Hector and Patroclus are dead, Achilles will die, and Troy will fall. The relationship of Adam and Eve, on the other hand, develops beyond the tragic and towards their reconciliation with each other and with God. Thus, the real crisis of the work is not the illusion of tragic necessity but the gradual resolution of what appeared to be an irrevocable tragic situation. In Milton's universe, conscience replaces tragic consciousness. Adam, blinded by the illusion of tragic isolation, awakens to a new truth:

> since our eyes
> Opened we find indeed, and find we know
> Both good and evil, good lost and evil got ... (9.1070–2)

His conscience drives him into despair, but the mysterious interaction of his repentance and prevenient grace leads towards salvation.

The stories of Adam and Achilles are both episodes in larger struggles, but in the epics themselves these episodes become the central plots, and the 'rest' of the narrative is turned into 'episodes.' The critical problem raised by this curious subordination of the whole to one of its parts is one which Aristotle diagnosed but solved somewhat superficially by stating that the plot of an epic contains a dramatic skeleton fleshed out by episodes. In Aristotle's theory, an epic is basically a drama which compensates for its lack of structural compactness by the pleasure of variety. He did not ask whether the integration of episodes into the central plot might create a kind of unity different from the compact unity of drama, but valid in its own right.

The presence of such a unity can indeed be demonstrated in both the *Iliad* and *Paradise Lost* by examining the organizing principles of the episodes and their relationship to the central plot. In both works the plot obviously deals with an important part of the story: the story of Achilles culminates in the event that seals the fate of Troy, and the Fall is one of the crucial stages in the 'Celestial Cycle.' But in both works, the central plot is chosen not only for its pivotal position in the story but also because the event it deals with crystallizes the total range of experience of the poem's world. The death of the young man and the grief of the survivor, the inexorable logic of the revenge triangle in which the killer is killed – these themes, which run through the epic in innumerable variations, find their fullest expression in the story of Achilles, Patroclus, and Hector.[17] Achilles' experience of the death of Patroclus reveals the truth about the hell of the Iliadic world. It is symptomatic of the human condition as the poet sees it.

Such a thematic approach to the significance of the central plot explains why Milton chose the Fall as the pivot of his epic on the Celestial Cycle. As J.H. Steadman has recently emphasized, *Paradise Lost* is based on the polarity of human depravity and divine mercy.[18] Other Renaissance poets and critics might attempt a fusion of Christian and classical ethics, but for Milton, as well as for the creator of the Red Crosse Knight, a Christian epic had to deal with the central experience of sinful man. Tasso's crusading knights were not serious enough; a Christian epic that wanted to rival the great works of the Greek poets in moral and intellectual penetration had to reveal with ruthless honesty how lost a Christian was without Christ. A historical subject, which would necessarily have involved some compromise of this radical position, was therefore excluded. But the great events of the Celestial Cycle were likewise excluded, because they either did not deal with human experience at all or dealt with it from a divine perspective, as in the Incarnation. The Fall is the one event in the Cycle that is human; at the same time, it was the event which destroyed the original immediate relationship of God and man and created the need for Christ as Mediator. The Fall thus established the typological pattern of Christ and Adam, and showed man's need of Christ in the one man who needed him most: Adam.

In both works the truth about the human condition as the poet sees it is demonstrated in the test case of an individual crisis, and this crisis expresses and crystallizes the experience that informs the work as a whole. In both works the 'story' is organized in such a manner as to frame the central plot and throw into fuller relief its representative and universal nature. In the *Iliad* this frame consists of two gigantic montages that set the beginning of the war against its end.[19] This technique arises from a fundamental habit of the poet's mind: he always expresses a whole by juxtaposing its extremes. Thus Hector, when he is forced to face Achilles, strays back to a past that is no more:

> There is no
> way any more from a tree or a rock to talk to him gently
> whispering like a young man and a young girl, in the way
> a young man and a young maiden whisper together. (22.126–8)

When Achilles chases Hector from the city walls to the two springs and back, the poet takes the time to describe the springs and adds that 'in the old days/when there was peace, before the coming of the sons of the Achaians,' the Trojan women used to wash their clothes in those springs (22.152–6). The end looks back to the beginning so that we may know what it is an end of. Beginning and end, in these examples, are not primarily separated by time. They are polar opposites, and the passage of time is important only in so far as it marks the progression from happiness to unhappiness. Each of these contrasts suggests the totality of experience; each of them is a little war and peace, or rather peace and war, for the contrasts are dynamic and progress towards the tragic.[20]

This tragic dynamic is most powerfully expressed by the relationship of the montages to one another. The montage of the beginning is conceived as an ironic and distinctly ominous foreshadowing of the end, in which the tragic events of the future are rehearsed with as yet untragic consequences. Priam, who refuses to watch the untragic duel of Paris and Menelaus (3.304–9), must be the spectator of the tragic duel of Achilles and Hector. The foolish Pandarus is replaced by the heroic Hector as the victim of Athena's deceit, and Andromache, who rushes to the tower fearing that Diomedes' attack on Troy may be fatal (6.370–439), is in her house when Hector is killed, ignorant of the tragedy and preparing a bath for his return. These and many more ironic correspondences between beginning and end are supported by the geometric pattern of formal symmetry. The events of the last book, for instance, repeat those of the first but reverse their order. The resultant balanced pattern, which Whitman attributed to the poet's innate formalism, is dramatically justified by its relevance to the central action.[21] The correspondences between beginning and end point to the profound differences that underlie the apparent resemblances of the situations, differences that were wrought by the tragic reversal of the central action. By thus appearing as the pivot on which the correspondent montages hinge, the central action receives universal validity.

The framing of the central action in *Paradise Lost* bears obvious formal resemblances to the *Iliad*. The first and last two books clearly are montages (or tableaux) of the fallen world. Hell is an anatomy of the fallen world, and Michael's prophecy describes the fallen world as movement in history. They point inward towards the Fall and show its universal consequences. As in the *Iliad*, the central action occupies only a fraction of the narrative. In the *Iliad* the scenes of general fighting separate the scenes of the Achilleid; in *Paradise Lost* the story of Adam and Eve is divided into two groups of scenes by the narrative of the War in Heaven and the Creation, which occupies the physical middle of the poem. In both works the total structure that results from the interlacing of the central story with episodes and from the framework of corresponding montages maintains a chronological semblance, but it is not based on sequential narrative as the organizing principle. The poet's intention was to achieve patterns that would develop the central theme in multiple variations.

The formal resemblances in the corresponding patterns of the two epics – resemblances which could be developed in considerable detail – must not, however, obscure the great differences in the relationship of the episodes to the central action. Homer's transformation of his story involved a change in the relative importance of events. The choice of the Achilleid as the master plot involved the abandonment of a separate focus for the story of Troy. Its agents – Agamemnon, Menelaus, Paris, and Helen – either become minor characters or exist chiefly in relation to Achilles, Patroclus, and Hector. Such a solution was impossible in *Paradise Lost* because it would have destroyed the typological pattern of Christ and Adam. Milton's subject demanded a bipolar structure: he could not tell the story of Adam at the expense of Christ in the same manner that the poet of the *Iliad* had told the story of Achilles at the expense of Agamemnon.[22]

Milton's problem, then, was to find a principle of organization that would keep the tragedy of Adam in the centre of the work but maintain the typological pattern of Adam and Christ without prejudicing the unity of the whole. His solution was brilliant and literary. He used the contrast of the epic and tragic hero, a commonplace in Renaissance literary criticism, to express the polar opposition of Adam and Christ. Far from compromising his theology to the demands of literary theory, he used literary conventions in the service of his theology.

The central plot, which focuses on Adam, is based on the conventions of classical tragedy. Whatever is not part of this plot – the 'episodes,' which have as their theme the struggle of Satan and the Son – is organized on epic principles. From a merely structural point of view, the epic constituted by these episodes is subordinate to the story of the Fall just as the story of the Trojan War is subordinate to the story of Achilles. But Adam's human tragedy is resolved when it is regarded as an episode in the divine epic. We may speak of a balance of structural subordination and thematic 'superordination.'

Milton made very sophisticated use of one particular epic convention to provide the double focus which the typological contract of Christ and Adam demanded. The flashback narrative is an essential feature of every post-Odyssean epic, and Milton employs it in very prominent fashion. But whereas in the *Odyssey* and in the *Aeneid* the hero tells his own adventures, the hero of *Paradise Lost* hears the adventures of someone else: Adam listens to an epic about Christ. The War in Heaven is the only part of *Paradise Lost* in which the plot conventions of the classical epic are consistently observed. The three days of fighting mirror the fighting in the *Iliad* from the initial encounter of Paris and Menelaus through the nocturnal council of the Achaeans to the final confrontation of Achilles and Hector. Milton's heavy use of epic conventions, which amounts to the creation of an epic within the epic, is more than a concession to the decorum of the genre: it is justified by his theme in two ways. In Milton's radical theology, Christ was the only figure to whom the perfection of the epic hero could be attributed, and the polarization of Christ and Adam as perfect epic hero and flawed tragic hero was a striking device for expressing the central theme. Moreover, the epic hero arouses in the listener that great urge to imitate virtue and valorous exploits of which Don Quixote is at once the parody and the immortal example. Sidney gave eloquent expression to this effect of epic literature: 'Only let Aeneas be worn in the tablet of your memory, how he governeth himself in the ruin of his country, in the preserving his old father, and carrying away his religious ceremonies, in obeying the god's commandment to leave Dido, though not only all passionate kindnesse but even the humane consideration of vertuous gratefulness would have craved other of him ... and I think in a mind most prejudiced with a prejudicating humour, he will be found in excellency fruitful.'[23] Adam is the listener to whom Raphael presents, in the form of a heroic poem and as a warning, the great model of willing obedience which he should follow. The imitation of the epic hero becomes the fitting literary symbol of the laconic biblical 'Follow me.'

One of the most persistent epic conventions is the use of divine machinery. In the epics of Homer, Vergil, and their successors, there is a divine action that runs parallel to the human action. In *Paradise Lost* this literary convention is preserved, but it is radically transformed to fit the needs of the typological pattern. Whereas in the traditional epic the conventions of the genre govern the actions in both spheres, in *Paradise Lost* the conventions of the epic apply only to the divine sphere and the human sphere is governed by the conventions of tragedy. Because Satan is the 'idol,' or hideous double of Christ, he necessarily acts within the conventions of the epic tradition. Christ and Satan do indeed re-enact the divine conflict of the epic tradition which is most clearly represented by the antagonism of Juno and Jupiter, but their conflict is cast in terms of that of Turnus and Aeneas. The patterns of Juno and Jupiter and of Turnus and Aeneas are merged in the conflict of Satan and the Son.

This deliberate restriction of epic conventions in *Paradise Lost* raises important questions about Milton's attitude towards the genre in which he wrote. Critics have, on the whole, been very naïve in their assumptions about his attitude. They have assumed quite unself-consciously that Milton's relationship to the tradition was like that of Vergil to Homer. Vergil counterpointed his radical revaluation of the heroic values with a scrupulous imitation of the formal conventions and plot patterns of the Homeric epic: it is in the likeness of Homeric actions that Vergilian characters reveal their utter difference from the world of Achilles of Odysseus. The post-Homeric literary genres, particularly tragedy, had a great influence on the manner in which Vergil adapted the Homeric pattern, but however un-Homeric the *Aeneid* may be in spirit, there can be no doubt of the supremacy of the *Iliad* and the *Odyssey* as formal models: other literary genres only modified the inherited pattern. The resultant balance of formal sameness and thematic difference not only created the epic which became the great model for the theory and practice of the heroic poem; it also canonized the peculiar process of imitation by which Vergil proceeded. Hence the assumption, implicit in most studies of *Paradise Lost* and the epic tradition, that Milton did to Vergil and Homer what Vergil had done to Homer. But the truth is that Milton departed very radically from the kind of imitation that the epic genre prescribed. He did not, like Vergil, use epic conventions in the spirit of the faithful imitator, but he used them with the ironic consciousness of their conventionality. They are used deliberately wherever the action moves away from the immediacy of human experience; they are, in fact, a device by which the author raises the reader's skepticism about the literal truth of the story: the author faces the problem of Raphael and solves it by using the conventions of the classical epic for the purpose of 'likening spiritual to corporal forms.'

Because the epic parts of *Paradise Lost* are not to be taken literally, Milton escaped the problems posed by the discrepancy between Christian and epic ideals, the discrepancy of which he was so keenly aware. The attribution of the perfection of the epic hero to the Son in the epic within the epic does not commit Milton to any positive judgement about its intrinsic value, because it is merely a literary image of the Son's transcendent perfection. In fact, the very use of the convention of the epic hero demonstrates its limits. As in the *Iliad* and in the *Aeneid*, the war moves towards a decisive confrontation of the two leaders. Milton even makes use of the scenes in the *Iliad* and the *Aeneid* in which the hero expressly forbids his followers to attack the enemy who is reserved for him (*Il.* 22.205–7, *Aen.* 12.760–2), and he fuses this allusion with the biblical 'vengeance is mine' (Rom. 12:19, *P.L.* 6.812–21). But there is no duel, which would have done Satan the honour of elevating him to the level of the Son by making him his legitimate adversary; the Son by his mere appearance routs all the devils. This deliberate anticlimax not only saves Milton from a duel with embarrassing theological implications about dualistic patterns of good and evil, but it also reveals the inadequacy of epic perfection to serve even as the image of a higher perfection, and this inadequacy is further underscored in the quite unepic account of the Creation, which is explicitly called a greater deed than the War:

> Great are thy works, Jehovah, infinite
> Thy power; what thought can measure thee or tongue
> Relate thee; greater now in thy return
> Than from the Giant Angels; thee that day
> Thy thunders magnified; but to create
> Is greater than created to destroy. (7.602–7)

It is the use of epic conventions in the characterization of Satan which expresses Milton's judgement of secular heroism. Satan is circumscribed by these conventions, whereas for the Son they amount only to a role which he plays when he deals with Satan, partly because Satan understands nothing else.

J. Steadman has called Milton's theological revaluation of the ethical norms of the epic a Copernican revolution of the heroic poem.[24] But from a literary point of view, the formal consequences of such a revaluation are perhaps even more significant than the redefinition of the heroic ideal. Milton not only saw that the values of the epic had to be transformed; he also saw that the forms of the epic by themselves could not express the typological pattern which was the theological basis of his revaluation. Christian orthodoxy led to literary heresy, and the result was a unique fusion of the forms of epic and tragedy in such a manner that the new structure boldly transcends the limits of both. That the product of this act of heresy should bear an astonishing resemblance to the structure of the *Iliad* and constitute in a sense a return to the origin of the epic tradition is one of the ironies of literary history.

DIDO AND BÉRÉNICE

Dido tragedies figure prominently in the early development of modern European tragedy. As early as 1524, Alessandro Pazzi wrote a Dido tragedy, and in 1541, Giraldi Cinthio was commissioned by the Duke of

Ferrara to provide a dramatic entertainment, to last for no less than six hours, on the subject of Dido. Some time before 1560, Jodelle wrote a tragedy called *Didon se sacrifiant*, and it hardly needs pointing out that *Dido Queen of Carthage* was Marlowe's dramatic firstling. [25]

In addition to the considerable number of Dido plays, of which these are only four prominent examples, we must add those daughters of the Vergilian Dido that do not go by the mother's name. Garnier's Cleopatra, for instance, is only one of several literary Cleopatras who die like Dido. And when at the beginning of Trissino's *Sofonisba* the heroine puts her suffering into perspective by seeing herself as a descendant of the great and unhappy queen of Carthage, the genealogy points to a literary relationship. Trissino would hardly have chosen this possibly legendary sister of Hannibal as the protagonist of his play if he had not perceived the structural resemblance of her story to that of her more famous 'ancestor.' [26]

Bérénice differs from these famous eastern queens, whose literary careers form an important part of European drama, by virtue both of her obscurity and of the absence of any obvious relationship with Dido. She merited a sentence or so in Suetonious' life of Titus and eked out a meagre existence in the undergrowth of French seventeenth-century literature until, for reasons that have been much debated but which remain obscure to this day, Corneille and Racine simultaneously made her the heroine of competing plays. Racine was the first to associate her with Dido, and he did so emphatically in the first paragraph of his preface to the play:

Cette action est très fameuse dans l'histoire; et je l'ai trouvée très propre pour le théâtre, par la violence des passions qu'elle y pouvait exciter. En effet, nous n'avons rien de plus touchant dans tous les poètes, que la séparation d'Enée et de Didon, dans Virgile. Et qui doute que ce qui a pu fournir assez de matière pour tout un chant d'un poème héroïque où l'action dure plusieurs jours, ne puisse suffire pour le sujet d'une tragédie, dont la durée ne doit être que de quelques heures? Il est vrai que je n'ai point poussé Bérénice jusqu'à se tuer, comme Didon, parce que Bérénice, n'ayant pas ici avec Titus les derniers engagements que Didon avait avec Enée, elle n'est pas obligée, comme elle de renoncer à la vie.

At first sight, Racine's comparison of the two heroines may appear to be no more than a piece of prefatory rhetoric, but as I shall argue below, *Bérénice* is the truest daughter of the Vergilian Dido. The distinctive features of this tragedy – in particular its 'tristesse majestueuse,' which we may alternately translate as 'majestic sadness' or 'sadness of majesty' – appear in their proper light if we consider the play as the most successful response to the peculiar ambivalence that surrounds Vergil's tragedy of Dido – a response to which the many European Dido tragedies bear witness, but which they fail to articulate fully. My interpretation of *Bérénice* as a subtle and profound reponse to the paradigm of tragic love that Vergil created in the drama of Dido and Aeneas will involve a detour of some length, because the nature both of that paradigm and of the response to it by 'modern' writers requires some exposition if *Bérénice* is to be seen as the product of Racine's elective affinity with Vergil.

In analyzing the paradigmatic status that the Dido tragedy acquired for the European consciousness, we may conveniently begin by drawing out the implications of the fact that Trissino's *Sofonisba*, the first European tragedy to aim self-consciously at a restoration of Attic tragedy, is a displaced Dido tragedy. Trissino's choice of subject reveals a sophisticated degree of reflection on the problematical nature of imitation. Whereas with regard to form he aimed at a faithful reproduction of the dramatic conventions of Attic tragedy, with regard to subject matter he was intent on reproducing the relationship between audience and stage characters that obtained in his models. He saw the 'equivalent' of Greek myth in Roman history. What Medea and Phaedra had signified in the drama of fifth-century Athens, Sofonisba was to signify for the new tragedy of sixteenth-century Italy.

Did Trissino realize that this controlled and highly conscious transformation of ancient models into a modern equivalent was most innovative where it unconsciously betrayed its self-avowed intention of restoring the drama of Aeschylus, Sophocles, and Euripides in a modern setting? In the drama of Sofonisba and Massinissa we recognize instantly what has become, for us, one of the oldest dramatic clichés, the conflict between love and honour. But we should also recognize, as Trissino almost certainly did not, that this conflict, while fully prefigured in the tragedy of Dido, is quite alien to Attic tragedy, and we must analyze the significance of his unwitting substitution of a situation like that of Dido and Aeneas for the sexual conflicts characteristic of Greek tragedy.

Until German Romantic critics placed the opposition of ancient and modern tragedy in the philosophical context of the subject-object dichotomy, the treatment of love was generally considered the most important differentiating factor between ancient and modern tragedy. For Renaissance and neoclassical criticism, it was a matter of conventional wisdom that, in modern tragedy, love played a more dominant role, and that its treatment emphasized new sentimental and spiritual values.[27] An Ovidian passage allows us to refine this crude distinction by formulating a typology of ancient and modern love conflicts. In the second book of the *Tristia*, Ovid asks why he should have been banished for writing love poetry when everybody else did it. Even the exalted genre of tragedy, he complains, is full of sexual references:

> omne genus scripti gravitate tragoedia vincit:
>
> > haec quoque materiam semper amoris habet.[28] (2. 381–2)

> Every kind of writing is surpassed in seriousness by tragedy, but this also constantly deals with the theme of love.

Ovid adds a catalogue of some twenty-five love tragedies – mostly Euripidean – to demonstrate the truth of his assertion (2.383–409).

For our purpose, the most striking feature of Ovid's catalogue is that it contains no relationship resembling the case of Dido and Aeneas, although he refers to it a little later in the same book:

> et tamen ille tuae felix Aeneidos auctor
>
> > contulit in Tyrios arma virumque toros,
>
> nec legitur pars ulla magis de corpore toto,
>
> > quam non legitimo foedere iunctus amor. (2.533–6)

> And yet the blessed author of thy *Aeneid* brought his 'arms and the man' to a Tyrian couch.

The instant appeal of the Dido tragedy, to which these lines testify, has its roots not only in the aesthetic excellence of *Aeneid* IV, but in a new conception of tragic love to which Augustan Rome and later ages were able to respond with particular intensity and immediacy. This conception is no longer 'ancient'; indeed, the transitional status of Vergil, which the Church Fathers recognized when they assimilated him into their tradition as an 'anima naturaliter christiana,' is nowhere so apparent as in the relative modernity with which Vergil explores the relationship between Dido and Aeneas.

The tragedy of Dido is based on a separation of public and private values that is unknown in Greek tragedy. In Ovid's catalogue we find tragedies of marital infidelity, such as *Medea* and *Trachiniae*, as well as plays that turn on different forms of generational conflict, such as Pelops or Meleager plays. But the most interesting class is formed by those plays in which the crisis is brought about by the actual or potential violation of a sexual taboo that is both the source of desire and, in its violation, the cause of the tragedy. Ovid's examples include Phaedra's 'incestuous' passion for her step-son, the incest between brother and sister in the story of Canace and Macareus, and adultery with the wife's sister (as in Tereus' rape of Philomela) or with the brother's wife (as in the case of Thyestes and Aerope).[29] By contrast, the relationship of Dido and Aeneas does not violate any family-based sexual taboos; it conflicts instead with the fulfilment of the lovers' public roles.

Vergil did not invent the conflict on which the tragedy of Dido and Aeneas is based. On the contrary, it had a venerable history in popular moral thought, where it usually appeared in the simple version of the destructive impact of invalid private desire on the fulfilment of valid public obligations. Didactic fables about the choice between virtue and pleasure are its earliest literary version. If one chooses wisely, as Hercules did at the crossroads, one will gain glory for one's deeds on behalf of mankind. But disaster ensues if one chooses foolishly, as Paris did when he chose Aphrodite over Hera and Athene. Nor did Hercules always choose wisely: the consequences of his submission to Omphale were humiliating, 'as we see,' to quote from North's Plutarch, 'in the painted tables, where Omphale secretly stealeth away Hercules' club and takes his Lyons skinne from Him.'[30] Mark Antony, finally, the self-avowed descendant of Hercules, became the most famous historical exemplum of the fatal choice of pleasure.

But if Vergil did not invent the conflict, he was the first poet to make it the subject of a dramatic exploration in which the clear premises of the moral fable were suspended. On one level, Vergil clearly intended to demonstrate the rightness of Aeneas' decision to leave Dido. Why else would he have emphasized Mark Antony's folly in the description of Aeneas' shield? Dido is indeed a Calypso or Circe whose sexual charms threaten the hero with the loss of his identity. But nothing illustrates more strikingly the suspension of moral certainty in the Dido tragedy than a comparison of Aeneas' final choice with the clear-cut moral triumph of the choice of virtue in the fable of Hercules at the crossroads. To begin with, sexual pleasure is not the initial cause of the mutual attraction of Dido and Aeneas. In the *Argonautica* of Apollonius Rhodius, a very young Medea loves Jason at first sight, although she knows nothing about him. The onset of sexual passion is described from the detached and almost clinical perspective of Hellenistic erotic psychology, which nowhere transcends the physical sphere. By contrast, the process of Dido's falling in love with Aeneas is governed by hearing rather than by sight, and what she responds to in Aeneas' narrative is not the exotic but the all-too-familiar. Like Aeneas, she has been exiled and like him, she has lost her family. Dryden pointed out that the pathos of Aeneas' separation from Creusa was not lost on her.

There is no other work of ancient literature in which the origin of a sexual relationship is based so exclusively on mature compassion, which recognizes and interprets the sufferings of the other in the light of its own experience. Through the biographies of Dido and Aeneas, Vergil conveys the sense that these are human beings destined for each other, who would integrate sexual passion into a mature human relationship and build upon that basis a life of successful public activity. One need only look at the paleness of Aeneas' eventual dynastic marriage with Lavinia to recognize that such an implication is just and that only a blind and self-righteous puritanism could blame Aeneas for responding to Dido's love. And yet, the vision of integration turns out to be a mirage; the gods themselves condemn Aeneas' response and order his departure. On the other hand, nothing reveals so clearly the genuine values on which the love of Dido and Aeneas is based as the act of departure in which these values are trampled underfoot. Sidney saw this, even though he praised Aeneas for 'obeying Gods commaundement, to leave Dido though not only all passionate kindnesse, but even the humane consideration of vertuous gratefulness, would have craved other of him.'[31]

In many stories of sexual temptation the fate of the rejected temptress leaves us cold. If the Sirens plunge despairingly into the sea after Odysseus resists their song, we do not greatly care. As for Circe and Calypso, they are immortal goddesses who can look after themselves. It is different with Dido. Her fate is so much the focus of Vergil's attention that most critics see the episode as primarily her tragedy, the tragedy of a noble character destroyed by passion. Such a view is correct as far as it goes, but it does not go far enough. The tragedy of Dido is also that of Aeneas, and the meaning of the tragic linking of these figures emerges only from a view of the *Aeneid* as a whole.

The *Aeneid* firmly subscribes to the orthodox view, held by Roman historians and moralists alike, that the original strength of Rome resided in the identity of family, state, and religion. Aeneas carrying the aged Anchises from the ruins of Troy is the most moving symbol of this identity. The constitution of Rome on this triple basis is the goal of Aeneas, but his career involves a progressive severance of the values of the state from those of the family. In the end, even his relationship to his son is more formal and dynastic than his genuinely filial relationship to Anchises. The Dido tragedy is the crucial event in this process of disintegration. Aeneas must leave Dido, but he cannot make the right choice without incurring the responsibility of her destruction, and this constitutes a punishment for himself as well. In losing Dido, Aeneas is forever excluded from a life in the realm of common humanity which their first meeting appeared to have so firmly established. The poignancy of the *Aeneid* derives in large measure from the fundamental contradiction, not always under the poet's control, that on the one hand, the epic celebrates the founding of an empire on the simplest and most basic human values, but that on the other hand, its protagonist faces an irreparable division of the world into private and public spheres.

This contradiction is the most important source of tragic effect in the Dido episode, which locates the cause of tragic destruction precisely in the divorce of public and private values and establishes the fortunes of Aeneas and Dido as complementary aspects of the destructive consequences that ensue. *Furor* is not the cause of Dido's destruction, but the symptom of a tragic division that exacts a human sacrifice: her exclusion from the satisfaction of the most fundamental human needs, long borne in a spirit of noble and melancholy resignation, leaves her vulnerabie to the onslaught of the sacrificed values transformed into 'furor.' The puzzling setting of the cave in which Aeneas and Dido consummate their love may be offered in support of such an interpretation. The world of the temptress usually presents a specious appearance to the unwary hero who, lured by the melodious voice of Circe, does not discover the reality of the pigsty until it is too late. The world of Carthage with its wealth and splendour is in part a false surface, a House of Pride that contrasts with the simple cottage of Evander. But it would be quite wrong to argue that the truth about Dido's world is exposed in the cave into which Dido and Aeneas are driven by the storm. What leads from the first appearance of the Queen who, seated in front of the temple, administers justice, to the creature seeking refuge in the cave, is not a process of disclosure but of regression. Both settings are equally real. But if Dido's regression is a measure of her tragedy, the threat of similar regression hangs permanently over the world of Aeneas, in which necessity has ruled out the possibility of mediating between the public and private poles of existence.

From the perspective of Dido's fate, we begin to understand the instability and vulnerability of Aeneas' life of denial and may account for the uncontrolled rage that characterizes the slaughter of Turnus as well as for the discrepancy between the nobility of his intention and the cruelty of his deeds that has bewildered many critics of the past two decades.[32] The poverty, misery, and instability of a world denied integration are the deepest lesson of the tragedy.

'Why, Sir, [the Romans] would never have borne Virgil's description of Aeneas' treatment of Dido, if she had not been a Carthaginian.[33] Johnson's well-known quip points to the fact that the response to the suspension of moral certainty has been the ground of the great fame of Vergil's tragedy of Dido throughout the ages of European literature. But the articulation of that response in conscious interpretation has taken strange forms. Medieval writers, inspired by the traditions of chivalry, were ardent partisans of Dido and turned Aeneas into a faithless villain. On the other hand, Sidney's brief comment on Dido is the expression of his deeply felt response to the Vergilian ambivalence. And from the status of the Dido episode as a paradigm of tragic love, we may assume that other Renaissance writers also responded strongly to this ambivalence. But their articulation of this response was hampered by a didactic perception of tragedy that assimilated the genre to the categories of rhetoric and moral philosophy.

Trissino's *Sofonisba*, which I have already described as a kind of Dido tragedy, provides a good illustration of the limitations of this perspective. In Trissino's play, the dramatic conflict is thematized in terms of the simple and didactic opposition of virtue and pleasure that Vergil had suspended. For Massinissa, a rash and inexperienced young man and the very embodiment of the audience to which the moral lesson of the tragedy was addressed, Sofonisba is no more than an object of sexual desire. Youthful infatuation describes his feelings well enough; a sense of shared experience or the admiration of a noble and generous mind is in no way the ground of sexual love as it was in the *Aeneid*. Trissino's drama nowhere questions the opposition of virtue and pleasure on which it is founded and remains a rhetorical demonstration of moral commonplaces. And what is true of Sofonisba is true of the Dido tragedies of the later sixteenth century. Despite differences in emphasis and valuation, all of them dramatize the conflict in terms of the simple opposition of virtue and pleasure; none of them follows Vergil in complicating and finally suspending that opposition by exploring the interdependence of public and private values as well as the tragic consequences of their separation. That Racine did so, and succeeded magnificently in the undertaking, will be my contention below.

As in his earlier *Andromaque*, Racine's response to Vergil in *Bérénice* does not manifest itself at the level of plot construction.[34] But the paradigm of Dido and Aeneas is the context within which the tragic consequences of the right choice in this play most fully disclose their meaning.

The action of Racine's play is easily summarized. It begins eight days after the death of the emperor Vespasian. Bérénice, who has lived happily at court for five years, expects that Titus, who has not seen her since his father's death, will propose marriage as soon as he recovers from his grief. But what Bérénice interprets as filial grief is in reality Titus' despair at his recognition that he must part from Bérénice forever, since the laws of Rome do not permit an emperor to marry a foreign princess, let alone an eastern one. The play consists, on the one hand, of Titus' attempts to break this news to Bérénice through intermediaries, and, on the other hand, of Bérénice's growing recognition of the truth. It culminates in a confrontation between Titus and Bérénice in the fourth act and is resolved by their acceptance of their fate and their self-stylization as exempla of faithful but unhappy love. I have left out of this summary the misfortunes of Antiochus, an unrewarded suitor of Bérénice, who keeps the wheels of this most exiguous of plots spinning in slow but steady motion.

Unlike Dido, who is initially an active monarch, Bérénice is a queen only by status. She is a radically private creature: her life is devoted to Titus; she lives 'étrangère dans Rome, inconnue à la cour' (2.2). The line epitomizes the double opposition that characterizes her being. If the Roman people resent her as another eastern queen, like Cleopatra an embodiment of licentious pleasure, that resentment is both unfounded and hypocritical. For the privacy of Bérénice not only turns away from the public duties of the state; it also opposes her to the pursuit of pleasure that characterizes the court. In fleeing it, she seeks to live only according to the values of the heart, which are equally threatened by the court and by Rome.

The two oppositions differ structurally. Whereas Rome and the heart both denote genuine values, the court is an image of the world as the setting that forever opposes the realization of both values by inviting them to unrestrained gratification of power and pleasure respectively. Titus and Bérénice are at one in their opposition to the court. We hear this in the first lines of the play, in which Antiochus describes the setting as the place where Titus 'se cache à sa cour' in order to meet Bérénice. And the first words of Bérénice describe her as escaping from the world of the court to find a setting for her 'heart':

Enfin je me dérobe à la joie importune
De tant d'amis nouveaux que me fait la fortune;
Je fuis de leurs respects l'inutile longueur,
Pour chercher un ami qui me parle du cœur. (1.4)

But the place at which she arrives has already been shown as inhospitable to such a desire. Antiochus has referred to 'la pompe de ces lieux,' and even the room in which Titus and Bérénice hide from the world is 'superbe et solitaire' (1.1).

If their joint opposition to the court is the basis of their love, it is the cause of their tragedy as well. The same moral sensibility that causes Titus to recoil from the world of the court also makes him perceive that demands of Rome in the purity and grandeur of its idea. 'Une cour idolâtre' would see in his marriage to Bérénice an act of sensual indulgence and would approve it just as it had approved the crimes of Nero. But Titus seeks justification before 'un plus noble théâtre.' Thus the play enacts the conflict of Rome and the heart on a stage opposed to the court, but our admiration for that exalted struggle is tempered by our melancholy awareness that outside the noble consciousness of Titus the idea of Rome has often succumbed and will again succumb to the temptations of the court.

The word 'Rome' resounds through the play with implacable hostility to human fulfilment, but the peculiar corruptibility of the idea also surrounds its abstract austerity with an aura of ambivalence. From Racine's careful orchestration of the Rome theme, which adds an increasingly hollow and ominous undertone to the play's 'tristesse majestueuse,' one might single out the climactic moment when Bérénice, in the confrontation with Titus, opposes the rights of the heart to the rights of Rome, and Titus answers with a catalogue of paradigms showing that 'toujours la patrie et la gloire/Ont parmi les Romains remporté la victoire' (4.5). A similar catalogue appeared earlier when Titus' confident, Paulin, warned him of the unalterable opposition of Rome to marriages with foreign princesses. Paulin argued that not even the wicked emperors had dared to break that rule, and cited Antony as an exemplum of the relentless hostility with which Rome pursued transgressors in this regard:

Antoine, qui l'aima jusqu'à l'idolâtrie,
Oublia dans son sein sa gloire et sa patrie,
Sans oser toutefois se nommer son époux:

> Rome l'alla chercher jusques à ses genoux,
> Et ne désarma point sa fureur vengeresse,
> Qu'elle n'eût accablé l'amant et la maîtresse. (2.2)

Titus' catalogue lists paradigms in which loyalty to Rome overrode not only all concern for self-preservation but even led to the destruction of the closest family ties – as with Brutus and Manlius Torquatus, who did not shrink from executing their own sons (4.5). Whatever moral consolation Titus finds in thinking of himself as joining that exalted gallery, Bérénice sees only 'barbarisme' in his professed virtue. And indeed, Titus shares her view, and anticipated it when in the soliloquy preceding the confrontation he tried to steel himself for his task:

> Car enfin au combat qui pour toi se prépare
> C'est peu d'être constant, il faut être barbare. (4.4)

After the confrontation, his confidant Paulin attempts to cheer him up in language reminiscent of Corneille:

> songez, en ce malheur,
> Quelle gloire va suivre un moment de douleur,
> Quels applaudissements l'univers vous prépare,
> Quel rang dans l'avenir ...

But Titus cuts him short and compares his own cruelty with that of Nero:

> Non, je suis un barbare;
> Moi-même, je me hais. Néron, tant détesté,
> N'a point à cet excès sa cruauté. (4.6)

At the highly theatrical conclusion to the fourth act, the polarization of values finds its most emblematic expression. Bérénice, like Dido, has fled from her lover's sight, and Titus receives the news that she has collapsed and may be dying.[35] He is about to rush to her side when Rome imperiously demands his presence. In a messenger's report, the expectations of the Roman Senate and people reveal the true power relationship between Rome and her emperor:

> Seigneur, tous les tribuns, les consuls, le sénat,
> Viennent vous demander au nom de tout l'Etat.
> Un grand peuple les suit, qui plein d'impatience,
> Dans votre appartement attend votre présence. (4.8)

In the *Aeneid*, the consequences of choosing Rome are metaphorically expressed in the curse of Dido, which is the only reference in the poem to the death of Aeneas:

at bello audacis populi vexatus et armis,
finibus extorris, complexu avulsus Iuli
auxilium imploret videatque indigna suorum
funera; nec, cum se sub leges pacis iniquae
tradiderit, regno aut optata luce fruatur,
sed cadat ante diem mediaque inhumatus harena. (4.615–20)

But let brave people harass him with war.
Driven from home, torn from Iulus' arms,
let him beg for help, and see his people die
disgraced. Make him surrender under terms
unjust, and know no happy years of rule,
but die untimely, untombed, in miles of sand.

The prophecy locates the curse of empire in the destruction of the most intimate human ties ('complexu avulsus Iuli ... videatque indigna suorum/funera') and culminates in the most powerful negative metaphor of human fellowship in ancient literature, the image of denied burial. The reader of the second half of the *Aeneid* comes to verify the truth of Dido's clairvoyance when he sees in the career of Aeneas a progress towards, and anticipation of, this death, and if he knows Homer well, he may wonder whether it is not a happier fate to die and be mourned like Hektor than to live like Aeneas.

Racine's play similarly foreshadows the human consequences of the choice of Rome, and in this foreshadowing a muted version of Dido's curse plays an important role. The spectator is bound to recall the convention of the dying curse when Bérénice protests that she does not seek vengeance. In particular, her 'quelque vengeur' alludes to the 'aliquis ... ultor' of Dido's famous allusion to Hannibal, which follows immediately on the prophecy of the death of Aeneas (4.625). The Vergilian allusion lends to the words of Bérénice the status of a dying curse as clairvoyant prophecy, although the substance of Bérénice's curse is 'modern' in its emphasis on subjectivity:

Si je forme des vœux contre votre injustice,
Si, devant que mourir, la triste Bérénice
Vous veut de son trépas laisser quelque vengeur,
Je ne le cherche, ingrat, qu'au fond de votre cœur.

Je sais que tant d'amour n'en peut être effacée;
Que ma douleur présente, et ma bonté passée,
Mon sang, qu'en ce palais je veux même verser,
Sont autant d'ennemis que je vais vous laisser:
Et, sans me repentir de ma persévérance,
Je me remets sur eux de toute ma vengeance.
Adieu (4.5)

The final act of Racine's play reveals the truth of Bérénice's prophecy. If the end of the fourth act showed Titus as choosing Rome, the final act shows his inability to survive the consequences of this decision. We saw that in the *Aeneid* the tragic conflict of the love of Dido and Aeneas is complicated by the fact that the perception of virtue is the ground of sexual attraction. When Mercury seeks out Aeneas to deliver the command of the gods, he finds him 'fundantem arces et tecta novantem' (4.260), for Aeneas, even when in love, is always building or trying to build something. Vergil uses one line to describe Aeneas as engaged in a manly task – leaving aside for the moment the problem that he is building the wrong city – but a full four lines (261–5) are given over to the description of his rich attire, and the weighting of the description alone is sufficient to damn the oblivious hero by putting him in a context suggestive of luxury, indolence, and a future in which love would destroy the virtue from which it had been born.

In Racine's play, this dilemma is even more finely shaped and explicitly envisaged in the consciousness of the protagonist. Here love is in part the cause of virtue, because the desire to please Bérénice and merit her love has been the motive that has diverted Titus' youth, 'nourrie à la cour de Néron,' from the pursuit of thoughtless pleasure and directed it towards virtue and glory (2.2). Titus sees clearly that for him there is no honourable way of choosing the values of the heart, since by choosing them he would destroy the identity of love and virtue that has characterized his relationship with Bérénice. He is acutely aware of the irony of this situation:

Je lui dois tout, Paulin. Récompense cruelle!
Tout ce que je lui dois va retomber sur elle.
Pour prix de tant de gloire et de tant de vertus,
Je lui dirai: Partez, et ne me voyez plus. (2.2)

But he is equally aware of the impossibility of a life with Bérénice in defiance of his duty to the empire. In his vision of such a life, we may recall Mercury's sight of the oblivious Aeneas – and also, on the low mimetic plane of the bourgeois novel, the futility of Anna Karenina's relationship with Vronsky.

> Oui, madame; et je dois moins encore vous dire
> Que je suis prêt pour vous d'abandonner l'empire,
> De vous suivre, et d'aller, trop content de mes fers,
> Soupirer avec vous au bout de l'univers.
> Vous-même rougiriez de ma lâche conduite:
> Vous verriez à regret marcher à votre suite
> Un indigne empereur sans empire, sans cour,
> Vil spectacle aux humains des faiblesses d'amour. (5.6)

Since Titus can neither live with Bérénice nor endure the thought of a life which counts as virtue the denial of the heart, he resolves to commit suicide, and is joined in this resolution by Antiochus, who is in his minor way equally unhappy. But Bérénice prevents both from executing this desperate resolution and urges them to follow her in stylizing their lives into memorials of their faithful but unrewarded loves.

This ending must, I think, be read against the knowledge of the historical Titus that the audience was bound to possess and which it could not easily forget. Titus was the best-loved but one of the most short-lived of Roman emperors. He died within two years of ascending the throne. His death was surrounded by mystery: according to Suetonius, he confessed on his deathbed that his conscience was troubled by only one action, but he would not reveal what that action was.[36] Ausonius' epigrammatic obituary reads:

> Felix imperio, felix brevitate regendi,
>   Expers civilis sanguinis, orbis amor.
> Unum dixisti moriens te crimen habere;
>   Set nulli de te, nec tibi credidimus.[37]

Happy in thy sway, happy in the shortness of thy reign, guiltless of thy country's blood, the world's darling, thou! Dying, thou saidst only one fault was thine; but we believe none speaking thus of thee – not even thee thyself.

It is tempting, though perhaps too speculative, to interpret *Bérénice* as Racine's answer to the mystery of Titus' death-bed confession and to argue that the 'crime' of Titus was his necessary betrayal of Bérénice. But there can be little doubt that Racine makes use of his audience's knowledge by foreshadowing Titus' early death and by interpreting it as the consequence of his decision to part with Bérénice. No other Racinian character speaks so explicitly about the possibility of imminent death as Titus does, or displays so much uncertainty about the time of life left to him. When Titus asks Antiochus to break the news of his decision to Bérénice, he also asks him to convey to her that his own future will be, like hers, a life of exile:

> Mon règne ne sera qu'un long bannissement,
> Si le ciel, non content de me l'avoir ravie,
> Veut encor m'affliger par une longue vie. (3.1)

In Suetonius we find the brief statement that whenever Titus had gone through a day without doing some good deed for a subject, he would say, 'diem perdidi.'[38] This motif appears in Act 4, where Titus reproaches himself for having neglected his empire during the first eight days of his reign, when he did nothing for honour and everything for love:

> Sais-je combien le ciel m'a compté de journées?
> Et de ce peu de jours si longtemps attendus,
> Ah! malheureux! combien j'en ai déjà perdus! (4.4)

Titus himself raises the possibility that he will die from his decision:

> Je sens bien que sans vous je ne saurais plus vivre,
> Que mon cœur de moi-même est prêt à s'éloigner;
> Mais il ne s'agit plus de vivre, il faut régner. (4.5)

In these passages, as in several others, the text yields its full irony only if the audience brings into play the external fact of Titus' early death. This is also true of another peculiar feature of this tragedy. Like *Britannicus*, *Bérénice* is full of references to past processes of specific duration that come to a head on the day of the crisis. The three years of Nero's virtuous reign correspond to the five years of the love of Titus and Bérénice. But in addition, *Bérénice* contains very prominent speculations about a future of indefinite extension. The confidant of Antiochus argues on two occasions that the passage of time will lessen the love of Bérénice for Titus and make her susceptible to the love of Antiochus. But this complacent view of the healing power of time is confuted in the most famous lines of the play, in which Bérénice envisages the ocean of the future:

Dans un mois, dans un an, comment souffrirons-nous,
Seigneur, que tant de mers me séparent de vous;
Que le jour recommence, et que le jour finisse,
Sans que jamais Titus puisse voir Bérénice,
Sans que, de tout le jour, je puisse voir Titus? (4.5)

To this uncertain future, the audience again opposes its knowledge of the two years that separate Titus from his death, and it is meant to see in the intended suicide of Titus a superfluous gesture, not only because Titus' death is imminent, but because in a sense it has already been enacted on the stage.

Racine's use of the audience's knowledge serves the purpose of surrounding the decision of Titus with an aura of futility. Whether we think of Titus dying of his decision or as dying shortly after it, our knowledge of the little time that Titus has left to him, activated by a whole network of ironic allusions, threatens to deprive his sacrific of meaning and raises the quintessentially Vergilian question: what possibility of achievement does Rome, with its abstract and cruel disregard of human happiness, offer in return for the private sacrifices it so relentlessly exacts?

One is likely to hear this question even more insistently if one remembers *Britannicus*, with which *Bérénice* shares many thematic and technical features. Both plays turn on the theme of restraint that the idea of Rome imposes on the passions of individual emperors. In *Britannicus*, we are shown how after three years the criminal disposition of Nero emancipates itself from the restraints of Rome and ruins the lives of Britannicus and of Junie, whose purity, seclusion, and pastoral upbringing mark her as another private victim of the public world. In *Bérénice*, the idea of Rome prevails over the happiness of Titus and Bérénice. To see the two plays together is to gain yet another perspective from which a heavy shadow falls on Rome as an idea strong enough to defeat the values of the heart, but powerless to restrain man's criminal passions.

The paucity of tangible connections between Bérénice and Dido is an instance of the difficulty that the critic faces whenever he pursues 'Longinian' affinities, that are no less significant for being elusive and even resistant to commentary and critical elucidation. *Bérénice* is not a transformation of the Dido tragedy in the same manner in which Buchanan's *Jephtha* or Racine's *Iphigénie* are transformations of the Euripidean *Iphigenia*. On the contrary, Racine purposely refrained from elaborating the relationship of his heroine to her ancient paradigm by an extensive network of explicit allusions, because here the model is more powerfully evoked by being dimly seen – almost in the manner in which in *Aeneid* IV the hero dimly sees and recognizes Dido,

> per umbras
> obscuram, qualem primo qui surgere mense
> aut videt aut vidisse putat per nubila lunam. (6.452–4)

> through dark shadows, as when someone sees, or thinks he sees, the new moon through a cloud.

Such a technique of transformation, in which the significance of allusions is measured by their very scarcity and obscurity, is appropriate to this most muted of tragedies, in which the plot is 'quelque chose de rien,' the violence of open death is eschewed, and the tragic emotions of pity and fear give way to a pervasive sense of 'tristesse majestueuse.'*

This procedure on the poet's part requires tact on the part of the critic: how is he to illuminate, without dispelling, the shadow of Dido so

---

* Bérénice is not Racine's only Dido. The turning point of Phèdre's moral struggle ('Que fais-je? Où ma raison se va-t-elle égarer?') alludes to the following lines of Dido's last speech:

quid loquor? aut ubi sum? quae mentem insania mutat?
infelix Dido, nunc te facta impia tangunt? (4.595–6)

What am I saying? Where am I? What madness changes my mind? Unhappy Dido, do your godless deeds come home to you now?

This is more direct and more immediately powerful than the Dido allusions in *Bérénice*, as is appropriate to the style and tone of this play. Despite its brevity the allusion has a strategic function and establishes Dido as the governing model for precisely that aspect of Phèdre that has no precedent in the dramatic models of Euripides and Seneca. Only Dido has something that approaches conscience in the modern sense, and it is highly significant that the triumph of Phèdre's conscience should, on the literary level, be another instance of a response to the modernity of Vergil's heroine. But although as this supreme moment of Racine's tragedy Dido intervenes to govern the richly allusive context of Phèdre's analysis of her conscience, that context itself is filled in by non-Vergilian detail. In *Phèdre*, as in *Bérénice*, the powerful image of Dido is invoked from a distance: the very depth of Racine's response to this paradigm of tragic love ruled out the procedure of adaptation that he adopted in his Greek plays.

hauntingly evoked by the figure of Bérénice? In the end he can only say that it is there, and trust that the reader will see it with him in the infinite suggestiveness of its half light.

In any case, comparison remains an effective critical tool, and perhaps one's sense of the Vergilian aura of *Bérénice* is enriched by a brief glance at a very different daughter of Dido – Shakespeare's Cleopatra. She is also a true descendant, in the sense that Shakespeare's dramatization suspends the traditional solutions of the moral oppositions on which it is based. But this suspension occurs in a most un-Vergilian manner, as Shakespeare indicates through Antony's astonishing vision of an Elysium in which Dido and Aeneas are forever united:

> Eros! – I come, my Queen. Eros! – stay for me.
> Where souls do couch on flowers, we'll hand in hand,
> And with our sprightly port make the ghosts gaze.
> Dido and her Aeneas shall want troops,
> And all the haunt be ours. Come, Eros, Eros! (4.14.50–4)

Garnier's *Marc-Antoine* provides the genetic link that identifies Antony's vision as an allusion by contrast to the 'most telling snub in all poetry,' the encounter of Dido and Aeneas in the underworld.[39] In Garnier's play, which I quote in the translation by Mary Sidney, the dying Cleopatra is cast in the role of the dying Dido, as she contemplates her image:

> And now of me an Image great shall goe
> Under the earth to bury there my woe.

Her resolution to die is enhanced by her desire to rejoin Antony, whom she sees in a doleful setting strongly reminiscent of Vergil's 'lugentes campi,' the posthumous haunts of unhappy lovers:

> Die will I straight now, now streight will I die,
> And streight with thee a wandring shade will be,
> Under the Cypres trees thou haunt'st alone,
> Where brookes of hell do falling seeme to mone.[40]

This crude assimilation of the posthumous life of Antony and Cleopatra to the Dido scene of *Aeneid* 4 was in all likelihood the stimulus for Shakespeare to define the theme of imaginary fulfilment, which is so crucial to *Antony and Cleopatra*, by a deliberate transformation of the image of ultimate separation in *Aeneid* 4 into the apotheosis of Antony's vision. The allusion measures the immense distance that separates Shakespeare's play from the *Aeneid*, but in so doing it also measures Racine's affinity to Vergil in *Bérénice*.

NOTES

1 The *Iephthe* of Gieronimo Giustiniano (Parma 1583) is identified in the dedication as a work of the author's youth, composed before he took up the
practice of law. Similarly, Del Carretto's *Sofonisba* (Vinegia 1546) is called a
youthful work in the dedication addressed to the author's grandson (Beatrice
Corrigan, *Catalogue of Italian Plays, 1500–1700, in the Library of the University
of Toronto* [Toronto 1961], 46–7, 34). The tragedies of de La Taille and
Montchrestien were also the works of young men who left literature behind
for more active pursuits.

2 *Essais* I, 26: 'Mettray-je en compte cette faculté de mon enfance: une à asseu-
rance de visage, et souplesse de voix et de geste, à m'appliquer aux rolles que
j'entreprenois? Car, avant l'aage, *Alter ab undecimo tum me vix ceperat annus*,
j'ai soustenu les premiers personnages és tragedies latines de Bucanan, de
Guerente, et de Muret, qui se representerent en nostre college de Guienne
avec dignité' (Pléiade edition 176).

3 *Œuvres complètes de Pierre de Bourdeille Seigneur de Brantôme*, ed. L. Lalanne
(Paris 1873) VII, 346.

4 The most magnificent of these special occasions was no doubt the special
performance of *Oedipus Rex* at Vicenza in 1585, which has been the subject of
a monograph by Leo Schrade, *La représentation d'Edipo tiranno au Teatro
Olimpico* (Paris 1960). I mention with regret the loss of the translation or
adaptation of the Sophoclean *Ajax* that was intended to be performed before
Queen Elizabeth on the final day of her visit to Cambridge, but the performance of which was cancelled because 'Tyred with going about to see the
Colledges, & hearyng of Disputacōns, and oū watched ... with the former
Playes [she] could not ... heare the sayed Tragedie, to the great Sorowe not

onlye of the Players, but of all the whole Univsitie,' F. Boas, *University Drama in the Tudor Age* (Oxford 1914) 97.

5 Ed. Henri Chamard (Paris 1948) 125–6 (Bk II, ch. 4).

6 *Opera omnia*, ed. Thomas Ruddiman (Lugduni Batavorum 1725) I, g⁴.

7 'Imitatio vitae, speculum consuetudinis, imago veritatis,' a definition attributed to Cicero in the essay 'de fabula,' by Evanthius, which was included in the Donatus commentary on Terence.

8 *Tristia* 2.381. Quoted as a commonplace by Dryden in 'Of Dramatic Poesy,' *Of Dramatic Poesy and Other Critical Essays*, ed. George Watson (London 1962) I, 41.

9 The Sophoclean cothurnus makes its first and most famous appearance in Vergil, *Ec.* 8.10. In his gloss on the passage, De la Cerda quotes instances of the phrase in other writers and adds a comment that throws a revealing light on the perception of Greek tragedy by Humanists: 'Sed illud in confessione omnium est, Sophoclem praestare gravitate & maiestate; a quibus virtutibus optat Poeta cothurnum Sophoclis ...' ('But all agree that Sophocles excels in gravity and majesty, and it is these virtues that make the poet wish for the Sophoclean cothurnus.') *P. Virgilii Maronis Bucolica et Georgica Argumentis, Explicationibus, Notis illustratae Auctore Io. Ludovico De La Cerda* (Lugduni 1619) 135.

10 Scholion to *Ajax* 1123.

11 *La Sofonisba di Giangiorgio Trissino con note di Torquato Tasso*, ed. F. Paglierani (Bologna 1884) 10, 11, and passim.

12 In a letter dated 3 September 1601, Grotius praises Buchanan as a restorer of tragedy but argues that even he 'a Cothurni gravitate degenerasse videtur' ('seems to have strayed from the gravity of the cothurnus'), *Epistolae ad Gallos* (Lugduni Batavorum 1648). For a discussion of sub-tragic diction in *Jephtha*, see R. Lebègue, *La tragédie religieuse en France* (Paris 1929) 241–2.

13 *Aesthetics*, tr. T.M. Knox (Oxford 1975) II, 1175.

14 'Of Modern Poetry,' *Collected Poems of Wallace Stevens* (New York 1965) 240.

15 Brantôme, *Œuvres*, III, 288.

16 Letter 57.5. Saint Jérôme, *Lettres*, ed. J. Labourt (Paris 1949–61) III, 61. Du Bellay, *Deffence*, ed. Charmard, p. 36 (I, 5).

17 A convenient list of the known titles of Roman tragedies is found in Otto Ribbeck, *Die römische Tragödie im Zeitalter der Republik* (Leipzig 1875) 684–6. Classical scholars still debate whether Terence regressed from the Plautine experiment to domesticate New Comedy in Rome, or whether his avoidance of a 'local habitation' has other reasons. From the perspective of Shakespeare and Molière, however, it is difficult not to feel that the apparent failure of post-Terentian comedy as a literary form is due to the prestige of the Greek models, which frustrated the evolution of a fully vernacular genre.

18 The sneer at Mlle de Scudéry occurs in the 'Epitre à la Duchesse du Maine,' *Œuvres*, ed. Moland, v, 85. But it is in Voltaire's *Oreste* that a repentant Clytaemnestra says to her daughter: 'Je voudrais dans le sein de ma famille entière/Finir un jour en paix ma fatale carrière' (1, 3).

19 Marvin T. Herrick, *Italian Tragedy in the Renaissance* (Urbana, Ill. 1965) 57–62.

20 Emrys Jones, *The Origins of Shakespeare* (Oxford 1977) 127–41, has advanced the very attractive hypothesis that the three parts of *Henry VI* are an 'intentional trilogy' in the manner of Greek tragedy, mediated through the example of Legge's trilogy *Richardus Tertius*. The resort to such a structural device presupposes a conception of history as tragic. See the following section for the role of this conception in sixteenth-century tragedy.

21 Erasmus does not, however, say so in his preface. For the parallel of Iphigenia and Isaac see Alexander Ross, *Mystagogus Poeticus* (London 1648) 208; cf. A. Henkel and S. Schöne, *Emblemata: Handbuch der Sinnbildkunst des XVI. und XVII. Jahrhunderts* (Stuttgart 1957) 1678.

22 See below, pp 25–8, for a discussion of the themes of tragic times.

23 *Les Juifves. Bradamente. Poésies diverses*, ed. R. Lebègue (Paris 1949) 10.

24 The occasional performance of tragedies on biblical subjects by the Comédie française does not refute this argument. *Athalie* itself, however, did gain a firm position in the eighteenth-century repertoire of the Comédie française: between the date of its première on a public stage in 1716 and 1750 it was performed 94 times. See A. Joannides, *La Comédie française de 1680 à 1920: Tableau de représentations par auteurs et par pièces* (Paris 1921) 86, and Georges Mongrédien, *Athalie* (Paris 1929) 90.

25 For a discussion of the relationship of Shakespeare's play to that of Legge, see G. Bullough, *Narrative and Dramatic Sources of Shakespeare*, III (London 1960) 233–7.

26 'Iam vero quod Latinae tragoediae grandiloquentiam, *ampullas et sesquipedalia* (vt Flaccus ait) *verba* hic nusquam audient, mihi non debent imputare, si interpretis officio fungens eius quem verti pressam sanitatem elegantiamque referre malui quam alienum tumorem, qui me nec alias magnopere delectat.' ('If the grandiloquence of Latin tragedy – its bombast and yard-long words as Horace calls it – is not heard here, do not blame me if in the office of translator I have preferred to stick to my author's succinctness and elegance rather than resort to a fustian that is foreign to him and in any event gives me no pleasure.') *Opera omnia Desiderii Erasmi Rotterodami*, 1.1 (Amsterdam 1969) 218.

27 For a discussion of these commentaries see Bernard Weinberg, *A History of Literary Criticism in the Italian Renaissance* (Chicago 1961) I, 388–423, 461–6.

28 The best account of these editions and of the techniques of commentary and annotation employed in them is found in T.W. Baldwin, *Shakespeare's Five-*

Act Structure (Urbana, Ill. 1947). A late and famous example of school editions of Terence is the translation and commentary by Mme Dacier, first published in 1688 and reprinted with revisions and additions throughout the eighteenth century.

29 Headnote on *Andria* I, 1.

30 *Sophoclis tragoediae septem. Una cum omnibus Graecis scholiis et cum Latinis J. Camerarii* (Geneva 1568) 209. A marginal gloss on *Oedipus at Colonus*, 270 in the translation of T. Naogeorgos marks the arrival of Creon as the 'epitasis fabulae.' (*Sophoclis tragoediae septem, Latino carmine redditae* [Basel, 1558] 288). C. Stiblinus, author of a very undistinguished edition of Euripides' plays, which included a translation and commentary, also divided each play of Euripides into five acts, according to the rules of Donatus. In the *Hippolytus*, for instance, the revelation of Phaedra's love to Hippolytus is marked as the first epitasis and Act III. His description of Act IV is as follows: 'actus quartus habet secundam partem epitaseos, suspendium videlicet Phaedrae, adventum Thesei et lamentationes eiusdem cum Choro, super miserabili funere uxoris' (*Euripides ... in Latinum sermonem conversus ... autore Gasparo Stiblino* [Basel, 1562] 213.) ('The fourth act includes the second part of the epitasis, that is, the hanging of Phaedra, the arrival of Theseus, and his joint lamentations with the chorus over the death of his wife.')

31 Friedrich Solmsen, 'Zur Gestaltung des Intrigenmotivs in den Tragödien des Sophokles und Euripides,' *Philologus*, 87 (1932) 1–17; and 'Euripides' Ion im Vergleich mit anderen Tragödien,' *Hermes*, 69 (1934) 390–419. Both essays are reprinted in *Euripides*, ed. E.-R. Schwinge, Wege der Forschung, 89 (Darmstadt 1968).

32 Garnier's play is quoted from *La Troade. Antigone*, ed. R. Lebègue (Paris 1952). In the discussion of *Antigone* I have benefited much from Gillian Jondorf, *Robert Garnier and the Themes of Political Tragedy in the Sixteenth Century* (Cambridge 1969).

33 *Antigone*, ed. Lebègue, p. 269.

34 *Œuvres complètes de Robert Garnier*, ed. Louis Pinvert (Paris 1923) I, 17.

35 *Julii Caesaris Scaligeri Poetices libri septem* (Lyons 1561) 144 (Book 3, ch. 97).

36 In the dedication of *La Troade* to the Archbishop of Bourges. *La Troade*, ed. Lebègue, p. 9.

37 *Ursprung des deutschen Trauerspiels* (Frankfurt 1963) 247.

38 Objections to the form of the play go back to antiquity, but it also appears from the frequency of quotations preserved on papyrus fragments that *Phoenissae* was the most popular tragedy in later antiquity; see J. Geffcken, 'Der Begriff des Tragischen in der Antike,' *Vorträge der Bibliothek Warburg*, 1927–8, p. 150 n7. For a recent defence of the *Phoenissae* as a political tragedy

see Elizabeth Rawson, 'Family and Fatherland in Euripides' *Phoenissae,'*
Greek Roman and Byzantine Studies, 11 (1970) 109–27.

39 'Breviter haec erit muneris nostri commendatio, quod in omni dicendi opere
poëma excellit, in poëmatis haud dubie tragoedia, in tragoediis etiam
philosophorum consensu Euripides, in Euripideis Phoenissae, quod et veterum grammaticorum judicium fuit, adeo hic artis plena structura est, casus
varii, densae sententiae, in quibus ille, qui justitiae descriptionem ac laudem
continet locus, tanta sapientia tractatus est, ut, qui cum cura legerit quintum
Nicomachiorum Aristotelis ... is praeclarissime hujus libri cogitata hinc
fluxisse dicturus sit.' ('Briefly this will be the justification of our enterprise
[sc. the translation of the *Phoenissae*] that poetry excels among rhetoric
tragedy among poetry, Euripides, according to the consensus of the
philosophers, among the tragedians, and the *Phoenissae* among the works of
Euripides. That was the judgement of the ancient grammarians, for the play is
so well structured and full of events and commonplaces. In particular the
description and praise of justice are handled with such wisdom that a careful
reader of the fifth book of Aristotle's *Nicomachean Ethics* will declare the
thought of that work to have derived from this passage.') *Briefwisseling van
Hugo Grotius*, ed. B.B. Meulenbroek ('S-Gravenhage 1964) IV, 216. Grotius'
translation was published in 1630.

40 *Ursprung des deutschen Trauerspiels* 51.

41 The phrase, which occurs in a letter to Hermann Bahr (8–22 May 1904?), refers
specifically to his vague plans for an adaptation of Calderón's *Life is a Dream*,
realized two decades later in *Der Turm*, but it applies more forcefully to his
Greek plays of this period, in which womb-cave images recur with compulsive frequency. *Briefe, 1900–1909* (Wien 1937) 155.

42 *Dramen, II* (Frankfurt 1954) 294–5.

43 It is, however, true that in Shakespearean tragedy 'tragic reversal' is sometimes seen as 'metamorphosis.' *Titus Andronicus* and *King Lear*, but also
Othello ('He is much changed' IV.1.260) and even *Hamlet* come to mind.

44 For a judicious appraisal of this much discussed topic, see F.W. Walbank,
'History and Tragedy,' *Historia*, 9 (1960) 216–34.

45 *Q. Sept. Florentis Christiani Andromacha Euripidea tragedia. Cum notatis ad
ipsam Graecam fabulam* (Lugduni Batavorum 1594) 4.

46 *Sophoclis Antigone: tragoedia a Gentiano Herveto Aurelio traducta e Graeco in
Latinum.* (Lugduni 1541) 4–5.

47 Quoted from Richard Griffiths, *The Dramatic Technique of Antoine de
Montchrestien* (Oxford 1970) 89.

48 Preface to *Cornélie, Œuvres complètes* I, 90.

49 'A M. le Cisse,' *Les Juifves. Bradamante. Poésies diverses*, ed. Lebègue 243.

50 *Œuvres complètes* I, 165.
51 *Œuvres complètes* I, vii.
52 *Interpretatio tragoediarum Sophoclis ad utiliatem juventutis, quae studiosa est Graecae linguae*, edita a V. Winshemio (Frankfurt 1549) 181.
53 *Ibid.* 181.
54 *Ibid.* 182.
55 *Evvres en rime*, ed. Ch. Marty-Laveaux (Paris 1881–90) III, 117.

CHAPTER TWO: TOWARDS *PHEDRE*

1 *De fabula* 3.9. Translated from *Comicorum graecorum fragmenta*, ed. G. Kaibel, vol. I.1 (Berlin 1958²) 66. A later age was to see in Terence's practice a kind of original sin. In the preface to *Bérénice* Racine wondered aloud what the pristine simplicity of Menander must have been like if it took two of his plots to make one plot of Terence.
2 *Aesthetics* II, 1224.
᾽3 *Reason of Church Government, Complete Poems and Major Prose*, ed. M.Y. Hughes (New York 1957) 670.
4 *Hercule Mourant* and *Médée* certainly illustrate this tendency, of which an extreme example is found in Genest's *Pénélope*, a thoroughly undistinguished play which was first performed in 1684 and frequently revived until its last performance in 1764. Genest succeeded in remaining blind to the magnificent crescendo of recognitions and reunions that culminate in the reunion of Odysseus and Penelope. The dénouement of his play primarily answers the momentous question (in the affirmative) whether young Telemaque will get the Princess Iphis, whose father Eurymache, king of Samos and Penelope's chief suitor, regrettably lost his life during the tumults attending the return of Odysseus. In his *Laokoon* Lessing poked merciless fun at the *Philoctetes* of Chateaubrun, in which the hero shares his solitude with a daughter who naturally falls in love with Neoptolemos.
5 Rotrou's version opens with a report on the death of Creon's son Menoecus, which is an important incident in *The Phoenician Women*. He also restored the Sophoclean scene between Creon and Tiresias, which Garnier had omitted out of religious scruples.
6 See *Griechische Dramen in deutschen Bearbeitungen von Wolfhart Spangenberg und Isaac Fröreisen*, ed. Oskar Dähnhardt, 2 vols, Bibliothek des literarischen Vereins in Stuttgart, 211–12 (Stuttgart 1896–7) I, 25ff., II, 3ff.
7 Quoted from *Œuvres de Jean Rotrou*, ed. Viollet-le-Duc (Paris 1820) IV, 30.
8 The most useful discussions of Racine's use of classical and other versions of the Hippolytus myth are by R.C. Knight in *Racine et la Grèce* (Paris 1951)

334–67 and by Paul Bénichou in his broadly based survey of the myth in 'Hippolyte requis d'amour et calomnié,' *L'écrivain et ses travaux* (Paris 1967) 237–326.

9 *Théâtre des Grecs* (Paris 1730) I, 390.

10 In his comparison of his father's play with its ancient models, Louis Racine comments acutely on this line: 'Il semble que par ce détour elle ait voulu s'excuser d'avoir nommé celuy qu'elle aime,' 'Comparaison de l'Hippolyte d'Euripide avec la Tragédie de Racine sur le même sujet,' *Academie des Inscriptions et Belles Lettres. Memoires de Litterature* 8.303. But he does not pursue the seminal importance the line had for his father's version.

11 This was clearly perceived by Batteux, who in general favours ancient simplicity and unity but who, after complaining of the distorting effects of the sub-plot in *Phèdre*, remarks: 'Quant à l'action épisodique, elle se réunit dans le quatrième Acte, à l'action principale & y produit une scène sublime, dont le mérite fait oublier la duplicité d'action & la rachète.' 'Observations sur l'Hippolyte d'Euripide et la Phèdre de Racine,' *Académie des Inscriptions et Belles Lettres. Mémoires de Littérature*, 42, 462. The essay dates from 1776.

12 It could be argued that Thésée's hasty exit at the end of 4.4 prevents Phèdre from speaking out and gives her no chance to recover from the shock of the news. But when in the soliloquy of 4.5 she articulates the meaning of the 'Quoi, seigneur!' with which she responded to the news, her mind is full of hatred and revenge.

13 Racine's recovery of the mythical dimension of tragedy has a distant analogue in the evolution of Shakespearean tragedy. The origin of Shakespearean tragedy in historical and political drama is obvious: the historical tragedies of *Henry VI, Richard III, Richard II,* and *King John* are followed by the political tragedy *Julius Caesar*. Shakespeare's later 'Northern' tragedies can be seen as a movement away from the clear light of history and ascertainable fact into a twilight realm of myth: *Hamlet,* and to a much larger extent, *King Lear* and *Macbeth* (which even includes vernacular deities!) abandon the historical for a world that is in important respects mythical. But Shakespeare's appropriation of the mythical dimension of tragedy does not occur through the encounter with Greek myth.

14 Bernard Weinberg, *The Art of Jean Racine* (Chicago 1963) 271–9, has a detailed discussion of Racine's strategy of reconciling the données of the myth with the demands of vraisemblance, but unlike George Steiner in *The Death of Tragedy* (New York 1961) 84–97, he pays little attention to the thematic significance of their clash. For a recent and sceptical survey of discussions of myth in Racine, see R.C. Knight, 'Myth in Racine: A Myth?' *L'Esprit créateur* 16, 1976, 95–104.

15 The association of Phèdre with the sun derives from Seneca's *Phaedra*, where the heroine cites as the causes of her persecution by Venus the disclosure by the sun of the affair between Venus and Mars (124–8). Racine suppressed this piece of motivation, not simply because of its frivolity, but because it involved an application to the mythical world of canons of plausibility appropriate to the historical world and thus would have destroyed the systematic opposition of myth and history in his play.

CHAPTER THREE: THE NEOCLASSICAL VISION OF GREECE: *IPHIGENIE AUF TAURIS* AND *PENTHESILEA*

1 *Gedenkausgabe der Werke, Briefe und Gespräche* (Zurich 1949) 10, 700.
2 19 January 1802. *Gedenkausgabe* 20, 872.
3 *Œuvres*, ed. Moland II, 318.
4 The boundary character of these two myths is implicitly recognized in André Dacier's choice of Sophocles' *Oedipus* and *Electra* as the first plays to receive a vernacular commentary addressed to a literary rather than a scholarly audience. Dacier's edition was first published in 1692, but the title of the 1693 edition is a more accurate description of its purpose: *Tragédies Greques de Sophocle, Traduites en François, avec des notes critiques, et un Examen de chaque pièce selon les regles du Theatre. Par Dacier* (Paris 1693).
5 This is clearly demonstrated by the *Tragedy of Orestes*, a play performed by students of Christ Church, Oxford, about 1616, and whose author, Thomas Goffe, opted for the representation of deliberate matricide. His Orestes is a mad avenger in the tradition of Elizabethan revenge tragedy. Orestes' revenge is portrayed in the most barbarous terms possible: Orestes and Pylades persuade Aegisthus and Clytaemnestra that they are physicians who can give them permanent health and vigour. They succeed in trapping them in an isolated room, where Orestes kills the infant child of Aegisthus and Clytaemnestra before their eyes (and those of the spectators), squirts the blood in their faces, and offers it to them in a cup before he kills them both. To this Senecan delight in horrors corresponds a harsh ending: after being punished by Tyndareus, Orestes, Pylades, and Electra commit suicide.
6 *Writings on the Theatre*, ed. H.T. Barnwell (Oxford 1965) 48–9.
7 In the second *Discours* Corneille wrote: 'Je ne puis même pardonner à Electre, qui passe pour une vertueuse opprimé dans le reste de la pièce, l'inhumanité dont elle encourage son frère à ce parricide,' *Writings on the Theatre* 48. Cf. Racine's marginal comment in his copy of Sophocles: 'Ce vers est un peu cruel pour une fille; mais c'est une fille depuis longtemps enragée contre sa mère' (Pléiade edition, II, 853).

8 Crébillon's play is quoted from *Théâtre complet* (Paris 1923).
9 *Writings on the Theatre* 49.
10 *Sémiramis* and *Oreste* are quoted from the Moland edition, vols. IV and V respectively.
11 Voltaire's conflation of Athalie and Clytaemnestra reflects his recognition of the 'identity' of these two figures; it also reflects his boundless admiration of Racine's play, which in the *Dictionnaire Philosophique*, s.v. Art Dramatique, he called 'le chef-d'œuvre de l'esprit humain,' arguing that 'la pièce est ce que nous avons de plus parfaitement conduit, de plus simple et de plus sublime' (Moland XVII, 415). Cf. the 'Epitre à la Duchesse du Maine,' where the absence of erotic intrigue and the simplicity of action are among the reasons given for the extravagant assertion that Athalie is 'l'ouvrage le plus approchant de la perfection qui soit jamais sorti de la main des hommes' (Moland III, 84).
12 Voltaire, too, changes Electra's 'strike again.' In his version Electra, hearing her mother off-stage trying to stop Orestes from killing Aegisthus, urges him to take his revenge on him:

> Il frappe Egisthe. Achève, et sois inexorable;
> Venge nous, venge-la; tranche un nœud si coupable:
> Immole entres ses bras cet infâme assassin;
> Frappe, dis-je. (5.8)

13 *Académie des Inscriptions et Belles Lettres. Mémoires de Littérature* 8, 293, 307.
14 In the preface to *Sémiramis* Voltaire called the *Théâtre des Grecs* one of the best and most useful books of the age (Moland, IV, 497).
15 *Théâtre des Grecs* (Paris 1730) I, cxliii–iv.
16 *Ibid.* II, 416–7.
17 Moland II, 321 n2.
18 In a letter reprinted in Moland IV, 177.
19 Robert R. Heitner, 'The Iphigenia in Tauris Theme in Drama of the Eighteenth Century,' *Comparative Literature*, 16 (1964) 289–309, gives a convenient survey of these plays.
20 *Œuvres de La Harpe* (Geneva: Slatkine Reprints 1968) II, 377.
21 *Ibid.* 378.
22 This discussion of *Iphigenie auf Tauris* draws in part on my earlier essay, 'Time and Redemption in *Samson Agonistes* and *Iphigenie auf Tauris*,' *UTQ* 41 (1972) 227–45.
23 *The Disinherited Mind* (London 1971[3]) 42, 41–2.
24 *Ibid.* 40.
25 Goethe may well have been familiar with Voltaire's play in the original, but he certainly knew it through the German adaptation by Gotter, as was shown by

Hans Morsch, 'Aus der Vorgeschichte von Goethes Iphigenie,' *Viertel-jahresschrift für Literaturgeschichte*, 4 (1891) 80–115; cf. Rudolf Schlösser, *Friedrich Wilhelm Gotter: Sein Leben und seine Werke*, Theatergeschichtliche Forschungen, vol. 10 (Leipzig 1894) 200–3.

26 *Théâtre des Grecs* II, 207. The *Eumenides* strained even Brumoy's patient commitment to historical understanding: 'On sent assés que les traits rudes & un peu grossiers de cette Piece sont fort opposées à notre goût, & au vrai goût du Théatre ... Le ronflement des Furies, & ce spectacle de monstres difformes ne vaut du tout rien,' *ibid.* 215. For La Harpe, writing two generations later, all the plays of Aeschylus 'se ressentent de l'enfance de l'art,' and he goes through them with an air of condescension bordering on contempt. Of the acquittal of Orestes at the end of the *Eumenides* he has this to say: 'Voilà Oreste hors d'affaire, et le poëte aussi: mais il faut convenir que voilà une étrange pièce,' *Cours de littérature ancienne et moderne* (Paris 1880) I, 83, 86.

27 On this point see Arthur Henkel, 'Die verteufelt humane Iphigenie,' *Euphorion*, 59 (1965) 7–9.

28 The decision to cast Iphigenie in the 'role' of Neoptolemus was probably influenced by the structural resemblance between the dilemmas of Neoptolemus and of Iphigenia in *Iphigenia in Aulis*: in both plays the machinations of a corrupt adult world lead to a deadlock that is broken by the uncompromising and idealistic decision of a young person.

29 Iphigenia's hope to purify the house of Atreus 'mit reiner Hand und reinem Herzen' (1700) may recall the powerful hand/heart contrast in *Phèdre*, but the echo, though precise and suggestive, should not be forced.

30 *Goethe: His Life and Times* (London 1965) 27–8.

31 'Dem Schauspieler Krüger mit einem Exemplar der Iphigenie,' *Gedenkausgabe* II, 295.

32 In his adaptation of Euripides' *Ion*, produced in Weimar in 1802, A.W. Schlegel tried to turn the charlatan god of Euripides' Delphi into the patron god of an 'Apollinian' vision of sweetness and light. In the middle of the nineteenth century, F. Halm, like Hauptmann after him, was stimulated by Goethe's discussion in *The Italian Journey* of his plans to dramatize Hyginus' account of Iphigenia's return to Delphi and of her narrowly averted assassination by Electra. In the play the healing power of Iphigenia is manifested in the encounter with the sister as it was with the brother in Goethe's play.

33 *Briefe 1900–1909* (Vienna 1937) 383–4.

34 This is a deliberately crude and one-sided summary to emphasize the contrast with Goethe's play, but the womb-cave-palace image complex is a recurrent feature in Hofmannsthal's plays of this period; its most obvious appearance is in the Pentheus sketches: 'Pentheus schlummert. Die Mutter erscheint durch einen geheimen, stets verschloßnen Gang' ('Pentheus is asleep. The mother

appears through a secret and always locked hallway.'), and 'Ein symbolisches Motiv: daß Pentheus seinen eigenen Palast nicht kennt: nicht die Grotte, nicht die unterirdischen Teiche, nicht den Schacht, der in den Berg führt durch eine Falltür (an dieser steht er dann und schreit hinab: Mutter, Mutter!)' ('A symbolic motif: that Pentheus does not know his own palace, not the grotto, not the subterranean ponds, not the shaft that leads into the mountain through a secret trap door (where he stands and shouts down; Mother, Mother.)') *Dramen* II, 523, 526.

35 Brumoy noted that the play dealt with the god of tragedy himself but commented: 'On verra assés que ce Poeme n'en est pas meilleur, que la Tragedie ne devint bonne, qu'à mesure qu'elle sçut s'éloigner de l'objet qui lui avait donné la naissance, pour y substituer de plus nobles sujets' (*Théâtre des Grecs* II, 612). La Harpe lists the play among the first of those plays 'qui ne sont pas dignes de la représentation de l'auteur, et qui semblent se rapprocher de l'enfance de l'art.' He calls it 'une espèce de monstre dramatique en l'honneur de Bacchus,' and while conceding that the story might have a place in Ovid's *Metamorphoses*, 'elle est dégoûtante dans un drame, et Euripide a mêlé à ces horreurs absurdes le délire des orgies et le ridicule de la farce,' *Cours de littérature ancienne et moderne* (Paris 1880) I, 113.

36 Kleist's letter (24 January 1808) and Goethe's reply (1 February 1808) may be found in Kleist, *Sämtliche Werke* (Munich 1964) II, 805–6.

37 The first version of the play was written in a rhythmic and enthusiastic prose. The change to verse, undertaken during Goethe's stay in Italy, gave to the play its classical form and distanced it even further from its biographical matrix.

38 Benjamin Hederich, *Gründliches Mythologisches Lexikon* (Leipzig 1770; rptd Darmstadt 1967).

39 Moland V, 82.

40 The rescue of the brother by the sexless sister is a motif that is almost certainly influenced by the fact that in Racine's *Andromaque* the instability and madness of Oreste are primarily motivated by his unrequited passion for Hermione.

41 'Über das Studium der griechischen Poesie,' *Kritische Schriften*, ed. Wolfdietrich Rasch (Munich 1964) 169.

42 'Die Geburt der Tragödie,' *Werke in drei Bänden*, ed. K. Schlechta (Munich 1966) I, 23.

CHAPTER FOUR: CHILDREN OF OEDIPUS

1 For a discussion of this performance see Leo Schrade, *La representation d'Edipo tiranno au Teatro Olimpico* (Paris 1960).

2 The phrase is that of an anonymous critic who complained that Giraldo Cinthio's *Didone* was not patterned on *Oedipus Rex*. B. Weinberg, *History of Literary Criticism in the Italian Renaissance* (Chicago 1961) II, 913.

3 See above, p 21, for a more detailed discussion of this point.

4 Johann Wolfgang von Goethe, *Gedenkausgabe der Werke, Briefe und Gespräche*, II (Zurich 1950) 435.

5 *Poetics* 1460a29–30.

6 The most spectacular instance of 'Sophocles verbessert' occurs in Houdar de la Motte's version, where the servant of Laius, in order to ward off a charge of cowardice, makes up the story that Laius had been devoured by a lion, thus removing the need for any criminal investigation on the part of Oedipus. 'Exit Laius pursued by a lion. ...'

7 'la faute d'Edipe, c'est la faute d'un homme, qui emporté de colère pour l'insolence d'un cocher ... tuë quatre hommes deux jours apres l'oracles l'a averti qu'il tuéroit son propre père,' *La Poetique d'Aristote. Traduite en Francois. Avec Des Remarques Critiques sur tout l'Ouvrage* (Amsterdam 1692) 192.

8 *Oedipus Rex* is quoted from the translation by David Grene in *The Complete Greek Tragedies* (Chicago 1959). Line references are to the Oxford Classical Text edition, as in the Chicago translation.

9 These remarks follow Heidegger's interpretation of the etymology of *alêtheia* in *Sein und Zeit*.

10 *Freud and Philosophy* (New Haven 1970) 516.

11 *Ibid.* 519.

12 *Ibid.*

13 *The Works of Nathaniel Lee*, ed. Thomas B. Stroup and Arthur L. Cooke (New Brunswick 1954) I, 413.

14 Voltaire's critique of *Oedipus Rex* occurs in the third of a sequence of letters that were intended as a critical introduction to his own *Oedipe* and included remarks on the Oedipus plays by Sophocles, Corneille, and himself. The letter as well as the play are quoted here from the Moland edition, vol. II.

15 'Ce n'est proprement, ny son inceste, ny son parricide qui le rendent malheureux, cette punition auroit été en quelque maniere injuste, puisque ces crimes étoient entierement involontaire, & qu'il les avoit commis sans le sçavoir; il ne tombe dans ces affreuses calamitez que par sa curiosité, par sa temerité, & par ses violences,' *La Poetique d'Aristote* (Amsterdam 1692) 192.

16 After having criticized Corneille's treatment of the twenty-year lapse in the fourth of his letters, Voltaire goes on, in the fifth letter, to criticize himself for having endowed his Oedipus with 'trop de discrétion et trop peu de curiosité' (II, 36).

17 Hegel, in the *Phenomenology of Spirit* (Oxford 1977) 446–7, casually but sug-

gestively linked Macbeth and Oedipus through the relationship of oracle to consciousness.

18 Page references in the text are to *Writings on the Theatre*, ed. H.T. Barnwell (Oxford 1965).

19 Kleist could not of course have known Schiller's letter, which was first published by Goethe in *Kunst und Alterthum* about a decade after Kleist's death.

20 Kleist's play is quoted from *Sämtliche Werke und Briefe*, ed. H. Sembdner (Munich 1961) Vol. I.

21 This translation of the German 'Gerichtsrat Walter' keeps and indeed makes more explicit the pun on the name 'Walter.'

22 Licht's description of Marthe's suit as 'Lärm um nichts' (504) clearly echoes the German title *Viel Lärm um Nichts*.

23 Wolfgang Schadewaldt, '"Der zerbrochene Krug" von Heinrich von Kleist und Sophokles' "König Ödipus",' *Hellas und Hesperien* (Zurich 1970) II, 333–40, emphasizes Sophoclean truth as the theme to which Kleist's comedy provides a counterpoint with its elaboration of lying and evasion but he does not analyze Kleist's conflation of the myth of Oedipus with that of Adam.

24 See below, pp 222–4, for my discussion of Milton's derivation of the tragedy of Adam from the plot patterns of the Greek tragedy of knowledge.

25 By allusion the phrase distances the drama of Adam from the genuine comedy of forgiveness, of which one may find a contemporary example in the 'Contessa perdono' in the finale of *The Marriage of Figaro*.

26 The following paragraphs are indebted to the excellent essay by Ilse Appelbaum-Graham, 'The Broken Pitcher: Hero of Kleist's Comedy,' *MLQ* 16, 1955, 99–113.

27 So in the original version, which in the final scene included a detailed account by Eve of what really happened on the previous night (2209–12, 2230–7). In the final version, from which that account was deleted, the detail disappeared, and with it the explicit thematic correlation of jug and wig.

28 See above, p 98, for the discussion of this strategy in *Penthesilea*.

29 Wilamowitz commented sarcastically on the conventional wisdom that Sophocles and Müllner wrote tragedies of fate *Euripides Herakles* (rptd Darmstadt 1959) I, 116. But no less a man than Freud was a victim of popular theories about the centrality of fate when he assumed that Sophocles had concealed the true meaning of his Oedipal drama by means of an 'uncomprehending secondary elaboration of the material, which sought to make it serve a theological intention,' *Basic Writings of Sigmund Freud* (New York 1938) 309.

30 *Julius Caesar* 1.2.140–1. The same thought appears in *Sejanus*, where the 'times,' like Shakespeare's 'stars,' are considered an illegitimate excuse. To

Sabinus' argument that 'these our times are not the same,' Arruntius replies:

> Times! the men
> The men are not the same! 'tis we are base,
> Poor and degenerate from the exalted strain
> Of our great fathers. (1.1)

31 The protagonist of this play, which was written in 1722 in response to Voltaire's *Oedipe*, reflects on his crimes in the following manner:

> Seul et libre artisan de mon sort déplorable,
> Ma main seule a tramé le malheur qui m'accable.
> Le Ciel, pour m'éloigner de l'abîme où je cours,
> A prodigué pour moi ses plus rares secours,
> Ses Augures divins, ses Songes, ses Oracles
> Mille secret remords, mille éclatants miracles,
> Tout m'a dit: Romps le fer qui brille à ton côté,
> Au seul nom de l'Hymen recule épouvanté.
> Et je tire l'épée! et j'allume la flamme
> D'un monstrueux Hymen ...

The passage is quoted from Aloys de Marignac, *Les Imitations françaises de l'Oedipe Roi de Sophocle* (Cairo, nd) 70.

32 In *L'Héroisme cornélien* (Paris 1968) II, 358, André Stegman argues that Oedipe is 'authentique coupable, et d'abord par son caractère d'usurpateur et son comportement tyrannique.' This 'fault' of Oedipe is an aspect of the political tragedy that Stegman sees in the play and is to that extent part of the strategy of evasion that characterizes Corneille's response to the myth.

33 *Writings on the Theatre* 31.

34 Stegman sees in Corneille's adaptation a contribution to the Jansenist controversy (*L'Héroisme cornélien* I, 149, II, 618). This specific biographical context does not invalidate the wider perspective adopted here.

35 Opinion about *Die Braut von Messina* was divided from a very early date, and dissent focused on the role of fate and on the question of whether the play should be rescued from or be condemned by its implication with the spurious genre of 'Schicksalstragödie,' which in the plays of Zacharias Werner and Adolf Müllner celebrated a noisy though ephemeral triumph on German stages during the teens of the nineteenth century. For a discussion of the early

reception of *Die Braut von Messina* see Ludwig Bellermann, *Schillers Dramen. Beiträge zu ihrem Verständnis* (Berlin 1905) III, 1–4.

36 'Gallerie zu Schillers Gedichten ... Szenen aus der Braut von Messina,' *Minerva*, 6 (1814) 50.

37 Don Cesar characterizes himself as an open person on two occasions: 572–4, 1458–60.

38 *The Theatre of Revolt* (Boston 1964) 67.

39 *Ibsen: A Biography* (New York 1971) 149.

40 In a letter to Bjørnson (28 January 1865) Ibsen described his reaction to the sculpture of the 'Tragic Muse' in the Vatican and argued that 'the indescribably calm, noble and exalted joy in the expression of the face' made him understand Greek tragedy, Meayer, *Ibsen* 235.

41 Quoted from Halvdan Koht, *Life of Ibsen* (New York 1971) 333.

42 *Henrik Ibsen: A Critical Study* (London 1899) 80.

43 Francis Ferguson, *The Idea of a Theatre* (Princeton 1949) 151.

44 *The Oford Ibsen*, v (London 1961) 378.

45 *Ibid.* 384.

46 *Ibid.* 381.

47 *Ibid.* 385.

48 *Ibid.* 382.

CHAPTER FIVE: SCRIPTURAL TRAGEDY À L'ANTIQUE

1 *Ursprung des deutschen Trauerspiels* (Frankfurt 1969) 75.

2 *Sophoclis tragoediae septem, Latino carmine redditae, et annotationibus illustratae per T. Naogeorgum* (Basel 1558).

3 *Comoediae ac tragoediae aliquot ex Novo et Vetere Testamento desumptae* (Basel 1540); *Dramata Sacra. Comoediae atque Tragoediae aliquot e Veteri Testamento desumptae* (Basel 1547).

4 The criticism occurs in his preface to *Saul le Furieux*, ed. E. Forsyth (Paris 1968) 4–5.

5 See above, pp 35–6.

6 *Jephtha* was first published in 1544, but it was written about a decade earlier during Buchanan's stay at Bordeaux as a schoolmaster. The play is quoted here from *Opera omnia*, ed. Thomas Ruddiman (Leyden 1725).

7 *Elizabethan Critical Essays* I, 24.

8 St Jerome, *Adversus Jovinianum*, Migne. 23.252; St Ambrose, *De officiis ministrorum*, Migne. 16.167–8.

9 *La tragédie religieuse en France* (Paris 1929) 237.

10 The following paragraphs owe much to Lebègue's discussion of Buchanan's intentions in *La tragédie religieuse* 229–34.

11 Quoted from *La tragédie religieuse* 231 n4.

12 *Ibid.* 233–4.

13 *De officiis ministrorum*, 3.12, Migne. 16.169.

14 De La Taille's plays are quoted from *Saul le Furieux. La Famine ou Les Gabéonites. Tragédies*, ed. Elliott Forsyth (Paris 1968). The edition includes valuable biographical and critical information about the plays and their author.

15 The title-page of *Les Gabéonites* calls the play a 'Tragedie prise de la Bible, & suivant celle de Saül.'

16 Garnier's tragedy is quoted from *Les Juifves. Bradamante. Poésies diverses*, ed. Raymond Lebègue (Paris 1949).

17 'Aequalis astris gradior et cunctos super/altum superbo vertice attingens polum.' Jonson's Sejanus varies the words shortly before his fall: 'My roof receives me not; 'tis air I tread;/And, at each step, I feel my advanced head/Knock out a star in heaven!' (*Sejanus* 5.1).

18 The biblical sources are 2 Kings 11, 2 Chronicles 22–4.

19 See above, pp 65–75.

20 See below, pp. 238–47.

21 Taking a sociological perspective, Lucien Goldman speaks of the 'realism' of Racine's portrayal of Athalie as an illustration of the ideological and intellectual crisis that overcomes a ruling class on the eve of a revolution. *Le Dieu caché* (Paris 1955) 445.

22 The motif of the vain embrace does not appear in the apparition of Hector, but in that of Creusa (*Aen.* 2.790–5) and in that of Anchises (*Aen.* 6.700–2).

23 *Writings on the Theatre* 49.

24 Preface to *Samson Agonistes*.

25 January 1830. *Gedenkausgabe*, XXIV, 390. John Payne Collier reports a similar statement by Coleridge, which rests probably on a firmer knowledge of both Greek tragedy and Milton: 'Milton's "Samson Agonistes" being introduced as a topic, Coleridge said, with becoming emphasis, that it was the finest imitation of the ancient Greek drama that ever had been, or ever would be written.' *The Romantics on Milton*, ed. Joseph Anthony Wittreich (Cleveland 1970) 195–6.

26 From the preface to the second book of *The Reason of Church Government*, quoted from *Complete Poems and Major Prose of John Milton*, ed. M.Y. Hughes (New York 1957) 670.

27 Carol Kessner, 'Milton's Hebraic Herculean Hero,' *Milton Studies* 6 (1974)

243–58, makes an unpersuasive effort to see Euripides' *Heracles* as a model for *Samson Agonistes*. The traditional link between Samson and Heracles is discussed by F. Michael Krouse, *Milton's Samson and the Christian Tradition* (Princeton 1949) 44–5 and passim. Cf. Raymond Waddington, 'Melancholy against Melancholy,' *Calm of Mind*, ed. J.A. Wittreich (Cleveland 1971) 260–1.

28 The 'substitution' of Prometheus/Oedipus for Heracles may have an analogue in *Paradise Regained* 4.560–80, where Christ's triumph over Satan is elaborated in a complex classical simile that moves from Heracles to Oedipus and sees the literal 'falls' of Satan and the Sphinx brought about by the words of Christ and Oedipus. Here Christ is more closely foreshadowed by the word of Oedipus than the strength of Heracles. See Kathleen Swaim, 'Hercules, Antaeus, and Prometheus: A Study of the Climactic Epic Similes in *Paradise Regained*,' SEL 18 (1978) 137–53. Swaim points out that in Bacon and other allegorizers the liberation of Prometheus by Heracles after the defeat of Antaeus is seen as a type of the redemption of man by Christ. Her argument corroborates my point about Milton's shift of models: the identification of Samson with Prometheus rather than Heracles sees him as standing in need of knowledge and in need of redemption.

29 *Œuvres complètes (théâtre et poésies) de Robert Garnier*, ed. Lucien Pinvert (Paris 1923) I, 186, 209.

30 *Aesthetics*, transl. T.M. Knox (Oxford 1975) II, 1219.

31 For Albert Cirillo, 'the messenger's description suggests [that] Samson achieves his closest communion with God, as the actual intense light of noon becomes the inner light which displaces the darkness of his despair,' 'Time Light, and the Phoenix: The Design of *Samson Agonistes*,' *Calm of Mind*, ed. J.A. Wittreich (Cleveland 1971) 225. Perhaps he is right, but should the critic make explicit what the text leaves unsaid? And since Milton often 'said' the things Cirillo attributes to the messenger's report – eg, in the opening of *Paradise Lost* III – should one not respect what he leaves unsaid? The unsaid, by the way, is a very different category from the 'unsayable,' which is often invoked by Milton to suggest the limits of human rhetoric. The explicitly 'unsayable' invites further elaboration; the 'unsaid' asks for its silence to be honoured.

32 Stanley Fish, 'Question and Answer in *Samson Agonistes*,' *Critical Quarterly*, 9 (1969) 237–64, bases his reading of the play on the absence of a necessary connection between Samson's regeneration and the pulling down of the temple.

33 Irene Samuel, 'Samson Agonistes as Tragedy,' *Calm of Mind*, ed. J.A. Wittreich (Cleveland 1971) 239, knows for sure that because 'Milton called *Samson*

Agonistes a tragedy, not a martyr play [,] its subject cannot be Samson restored to divine favor.' This seems to me to misread Milton's silence in another way. Had it been Milton's intention to portray a hero whose final act of destruction was fully in character, why not attribute the words of the biblical Samson to him?

34 On this point see Günther Zuntz's charming essay on the 'medieval Oedipus,' 'Ödipus und Gregorius: Tragödie und Legende,' *Antike und Abendland*, 4 (1954) 191–203. (Rptd in *Sophokles. Wege der Forschung*, 95. Darmstadt 1967.)

CHAPTER SIX: EPIC AND TRAGEDY

1 Patrick Hume, *Annotations on Paradise Lost* ... (London 1695).
2 G.N. Knauer, *Die Aeneis und Homer: Studien zur poetischen Technik Vergils mit Listen der Homerzitate in der Aeneis* (Göttingen 1964) 354–9.
3 Aeneas is frequently shown either himself building or watching others build. When he first sees Carthage, he exclaims: 'O fortunati quorum iam moenia surgunt' (1.437). Mercury surprises him as he assists Dido in the building of Cathage (4.260). During his wanderings he twice tries to build towns, in Thrace and in Crete, and he visits Helenus (3.293–505), who in Buthrotum has realized Aeneas' sentimental dream of building a monument to the past (4.340–4). In Sicily he leaves behind many of his weary followers and measures out the city limits of their new settlement (5.755–7), and once he arrives in Italy he builds again, not yet a city but a Roman camp on Latin soil (7.157–9).
4 Watson Kirkconnell, *The Celestial Cycle: The Theme of Paradise Lost in World Literature with Translations of the Major Analogues* (Toronto 1952).
5 Aristotle *Poetics* XI, XIV.
6 *Of Dramatic Poesy and Other Critical Essays*. Ed. George Watson (London 1962) II, 84, 233.
7 This pattern, with minor variations from play to play, is found in Hugo Grotius, *Adamus Exul* (Kirkconnell, *Celestial Cycle* 176–85), Giambattista Andreini, *L'Adamo (ibid.* 253–7), Serafino della Salandra, *Adamo Caduto (ibid.* 326–33), and Joost van den Vondel, *Adam in Ballingschap (ibid.* 467–70).
8 Augustine, *City of God*, 14.11; trans. Marcus Dods (New York 1950) 459.
9 E. Le Comte in his Mentor edition of *Paradise Lost* (New York 1961) was the first to point out the allusion to Andromache, but he did not grasp its full significance. He traces Adam's wreath back to the flowers Andromache embroiders on a mantle, but the embroidery is merely an associative link in the genesis of the parallel. Its point is the ironic portrayal of the tragic survivor engaged in activities that contrast with the tragic reality. Thus the wreath

corresponds not to Andromache's embroidery but to the bath she is preparing for Hector, who is being dragged in the dust. The parallels between the two scenes can be pushed further: both depend on the cumulative effect of an image pattern. In *Paradise Lost* this pattern is the flower motif, which constantly accompanies the appearance of Eve: 4.268–72, 304–7, 708–10; 5.377–8; 7.40–7; 9.217–19, 395–6, 425, 430–3; 11.273–9. In the *Iliad* it is the motif of Thebe, Andromache's home town, whose tragic fate mirrors and foreshadows that of Troy. Achilles sacked Thebe and killed her father and brothers (6.414–28), and the quarrel over Briseis, which leads to the death of Hector – the only person left to Andromache (6.429–30) – has its ultimate origin in the fall of Thebe (1.366–7). Patroclus, another victim of the tragedy, listens to Achilles as he accompanies himself on a lyre got at the sack of Thebe.

10 G.E. Duckworth in a review (*AJP*, LXXI, 1950, 442) argued rightly that this request rather than his intransigence in Bk. IX is the tragic mistake of Achilles. See also Karl Reinhardt, *Die Ilias und ihr Dichter* (Göttingen 1961) 370.

11 Johannes Th. Kakridis, *Homeric Researches* (Lund 1949) 65–75.

12 Passages which express this consciousness of imminent death are 18.98–126; 14.420; 23.43–53, 144–51, 243–8; and, above all, Achilles' speech to Lycaon, 21.106–13.

13 *Die Fragmente des Aischylos*, ed. H.J. Mette (Berlin 1959), Fr. 231: τὰδ οὐχ ὑπ ἀλλων, ἀλλὰ τοῖς αὐτῶν πτεροῖς ἀλισκόμεσθα.

14 Brooks Otis, *Virgil: A Study in Civilized Poetry* (Oxford 1963) 361.

15 Milton does, however, apostrophize Adam and Eve together (4.773–5). Adam and Eve as a couple are much closer to Eve than they are to Adam; Adam's feelings for Eve crystallize our feelings for Adam and Eve.

16 Unlike in the *Odyssey*, the poet addresses his characters very rarely in the *Iliad*; Patroclus is the only character consistently singled out by this device: 16.584, 692, 754, 787, 812, 843. Similes about him are unusually emotional: Achilles compares him to a crying little girl wanting to be taken up by her mother (16.7–10), and after his death Menelaus bestrides his body like a cow that protects her first-born calf (17.4–5).

17 The fallen warrior in the *Iliad* is frequently given a necrologue either by the poet himself or by one of his characters. The grief of the surviving young wife or old father is a standard theme of these necrologues: no death without a mourner (5.151–8, 684–8; 11.241–5, 391–5, 450–5, 374–82; 13.427–44; 14.501–5). The first victim of the war, Protesilaus, leaves a young wife behind (2.698–702). The theme of the death of the young warrior cuts across the 'national' bias of the poem: the death of Achilles is seen in terms of the mourning father; the death of Hector mainly in terms of the mourning wife. Homer's impartiality culminates in the meeting of Achilles and Priam, the

only meeting of father and son in the *Iliad*. A fine but minor instance is the sympathy that the poet extends to Euphorbus, the youth who gave Patroclus his first wound. His death is compared to the sudden uprooting of a young olive tree, which a man had raised 'in a lonely place and drenched with generous water' (17.50–60). Cf. Seth Benardete, 'Achilles and the *Iliad*,' *Hermes*, XCI (1963) 1–16.

18 J. Steadman, *Milton and the Renaissance Hero* (Oxford 1967) vii.

19 See C.H. Whitman, *Homer and the Heroic Tradition* (Cambridge 1958) 259–74, for a detailed analysis of the montages.

20 Whitman, *Homer and the Heroic Tradition* 256. A particularly touching example of the opposition of beginning and end occurs when the ghost of Patroclus asks Achilles to be buried in the same urn with him. He makes the request in the name of their friendship, as we might say, but Patroclus much more concretely evokes the occasion of their first meeting (23.83–8).

21 Whitman, *Homer and the Heroic Tradition* 255–6.

22 A similar bipolar structure was demanded by the story of the Red Crosse Knight, and it could be argued that Spenser's solution of opposing Arthur to the Red Crosse Knight is a less successful way of expressing the absolute difference between Christ and Adam in the typological pattern.

23 Sir Philip Sidney, *The Defense of Poesy*, in *Elizabethan Critical Essays*, ed. G. Smith (Oxford 1904) I, 180.

24 Steadman, *Milton and the Renaissance Hero* vii.

25 For a good discussion of sixteenth-century Dido tragedies in France, Italy, and Spain see Eberhard Leube, *Fortuna in Karthago* (Heidelberg 1969) 86–112, 194–216, 294–303. D.C. Allen takes a broader view of the Dido tradition in his urbane and learned essay, 'Marlowe's Dido and the Tradition,' *Essays on Shakespeare and Elizabethan Drama in Honour of Hardin Craig* (Columbia 1962) 55–68.

26 It cannot be ruled out that Livy's dramatic episode was in fact inspired by the Dido episode, and in particular, by the curse in which Dido invokes Hannibal as her avenger. Moreover, Sofonisba's fear of being surrendered to the Romans and her suicide by poison are suspiciously close to the famous circumstances of Cleopatra's death and may have been derived from them by Livy. It is evident, at any rate, that the life of the historical Sofonisba, if she existed at all, was less dramatic than that of Livy's romantic figure.

27 Dryden's Eugenius, expressing the conventional wisdom of the modern position, argues that ancient tragedies have few love scenes because the ancient tragedians 'dealt not with that soft passion, but with lust, cruelty, revenge.' Dryden's Crites concedes the point but states it differently when he speaks of

Homeric heroes as 'men of great appetites, lovers of beef broiled on the coals, and good fellows,' and continues: 'So in their love-scenes ... the Ancients were more hearty, we more talkative: they writ of love as it was then the mode to make it.' *Of Dramatic Poesy and Other Critical Essays*, ed. George Watson (London 1962) I, 41–3.

28 This and the subsequent passages and translations are quoted from the Loeb edition of the *Tristia*.

29 This contrast is highlighted by the respective sources and distinctive qualities of tragic effect. In Greek sexual tragedies the emotion aroused is horror, which increases with the strength of the taboo violated: in the ultimate example of the Oedipus myth the sexual taboo is so absolute that it was never dramatized in antiquity as a consciously desired or consummated relationship. In the Dido tragedy tragic effect arises from the depth and integrity of the human relationship that causes and validates, but is finally destroyed by, sexual passion. Here the distinctive emotions are pathos and regret rather than horror.

30 Plutarch, *The Lives of the Noble Grecians and Romans*, tr. Thomas North (London 1929–30) IV, 362.

31 *Elizabethan Critical Essays*, ed. G. Smith (Oxford 1904) I, 180.

32 See my 'Turnus and Hotspur: The Political Adversary in the *Aeneid* and *Henry IV*,' *Phoenix* 23 (1969) 278–90.

33 Boswell, *Life of Johnson*, ed. G.B. Hill and L.F. Powell (Oxford 1934) IV, 196.

34 Bérénice's 'curse' and her physical collapse reported in 4.7 are two details of plot that are most easily referred to the *Aeneid*.

35 Antiochus' description of Bérénice's collapse (4.7) after her expression of her peculiar kind of vengeance is reminiscent of Vergil's description of Dido's collapse after the last words she addresses to Aeneas (4.388–92).

36 Suetonius, *Lives of the Caesars* 8. 10.1–2.

37 Text and translation are quoted from the Loeb edition of Ausonius, I, 341.

38 Suetonius, *Lives of the Caesars* 8.8.1.

39 T.S. Eliot, *On Poetry and Poets* (London 1957) 64.

40 Quoted from *Narrative and Dramatic Sources of Shakespeare*, ed. G. Bullough (London 1966) v.

BIBLIOGRAPHY

Adam, Antoine *Histoire de la littérature française au XVIIe siècle* 2nd ed. Paris 1962.
5 vols

Aeschylus *Die Fragmente des Aischyles* Ed. H.J. Mette. Berlin 1959

Allen, Don C. 'Marlowe's Dido and the Tradition,' *Essays on Shakespeare and Elizabethan Drama in Honour of Hardin Craig* New York 1962

Ambrosius *De officiis ministrorum* Patrologiae Latinae Tomus XVI

anon. 'Gallerie zu Schillers Gedichten. Sechste Schaustellung. Szenen aus der Braut von Messina.' *Minerva* 6 (1814) 1–60

Appelbaum-Graham, Ilse 'The Broken Pitcher: Hero of Kleist's Comedy' *Modern Language Quarterly* 16 (1955) 99–113

Augustine *City of God*. Tr. Marcus Dods. New York 1950

Ausonius Ed. Hugh G. White. London 1919 (Loeb Library)

Baïf, Ian Antoine de *Evvres en rime; avec une notice biographique et des notes* Ed. Charles Marty-Laveaux. Paris 1881–90. 5 vols

Baldwin, Thomas W. *Shakespeare's Five-Act Structure: Shakespeare's Early Plays on the Background of Renaissance Theories of Five-Act Structure from 1470* Urbana 1947

Barthes, Roland *Sur Racine* Paris 1963

Batteux, Charles 'Observations sur l'Hippolyte d'Euripide et la Phèdre de Racine' *Academie des Inscriptions et Belles Lettres. Memoires de litterature* 42, 452–77 [1776]

Bellermann, Ludwig *Schillers Dramen: Beiträge zu ihrem Verständnis* Berlin 1905. 3 vols

Bénichou, Paul 'Hippolyte Requis d'amour et calomnié' *L'écrivain et ses travaux* Paris 1967, 237–326.

Benjamin, Walter *Ursprung des deutschen Trauerspiels* Ed. Rolf Tiedemann. Frankfurt 1969

Bèze, Thédore de *Abraham sacrifiant* Edition critique avec introduction et notes par Keith Cameron, Kathleen Hall, Francis Higman. Geneva 1967

Bloom, Harold *The Anxiety of Influence* New York 1973

Boas, Frederick S. *University Drama in the Tudor Age* Oxford 1914

Boswell James *Life of Johnson* Ed. G.B. Hill and L.F. Powell. Oxford 1934

Brandes, Georg *Henrik Ibsen: A Critical Study* London 1899. Rptd New York 1964

Brantôme. *Œuvres complètes de Pierre de Bourdeille Seigneur de Brantôme* Ed. Ludovic Lalanne. Paris 1873. 11 vols

Brumoy, P. *Théâtre des Grecs* Paris 1730. 3 vols

Brustein, Robert *The Theatre of Revolt* Boston 1964

Buchanan, George *Sacred Dramas* Translated into English Verse by Archibald Brown. Edinburgh 1906

– *Opera omnia* ... Ed. Thomas Ruddimann. Lugduni Batovorum 1725

Bullough, Geoffrey *Narrative and Dramatic Sources of Shakespeare* Vol. 3. London 1960

Charlton, H.B. *The Senecan Tradition in Renaissance Tragedy* Manchester 1946

Cloetta, Wilhelm *Beiträge zur Litteraturgeschichte des Mittelalters und der Renaissance* Halle 1890–2. 2 vols. Vol. I: *Komödie und Tragödie im Mittelalter*. Vol. II: *Die Anfänge der Renaissancetragödie*

Comoediae ac tragoediae aliquot ex Novo et Vetere Testamento desumptae ...

Corneille, Pierre *Théâtre complet* Ed. Maurice Rat. Paris, nd

– *Writings on the Theatre* Ed. H.T. Barnwell. Oxford 1965

Corrigan, Beatrice *Catalogue of Italian Plays, 1500–1700, in the Library of the University of Toronto* Toronto 1961

Crébillon, Prosper Jolyot de *Théâtre complet* Paris 1923

Dacier, André *La Poetique d'Aristote ... traduite en François. Avec des Remarques Critiques sur tout l'Ouvrage* Amsterdam 1692

– *Tragédies Grecques de Sophocle. Traduites en François, avec des notes critiques, et un Examen de chaque pièce selon les regles du Theatre* Paris 1693

Dähnhardt, Oskar *Griechische Dramen in deutschen Bearbeitungen von Wolfhart Spangenberg und Isaac Fröreisen*. Bibliothek des literarischen Vereins in Stuttgart, vols 211–12. Stuttgart 1896–7

Delcroix, Maurice *Le sacré dans les tragédies profanes de Racine: Essai sur la signification du dieu mythologique et de la fatalité dans la Thébaide, Andromaque, Iphigénie, et Phèdre*. Paris 1970

Donatus *Commentum Terenti* Ed. P. Wessner. Stuttgart 1962. 3 vols

Dramata Sacra Comoediae atque Tragoediae aliquot e Veteri Testamento desumptae Basel 1547

Driver, Thomas *The Sense of History in Greek and Shakespearean Drama* New York 1960

Du Bellay, Joachim *La deffence et illustration de la langue francoyse* Ed. Henri Chamard. Paris 1948

Eliot, T.S. *On Poetry and Poets* London 1957

Elliott, Revel *Mythe et légende dans le théâtre de Racine* Paris 1969

Erasmus, Desiderius *Opera omnia Desiderii Erasmi Rotterdami* Vol. 1.1 North Holland Publishing Company 1969

Euripides in Latinum sermonem conversus, adjecto e regione textu Graeco cum annotationibus et praefationibus in omnes ejus tragoedias ... Ed. G. Stiblinus. Basel 1562

Euripides *Q. Sept. Florentis Christiami Andromacha Euripidea tragoedia. Cum notatis ad ipsam Graecam fabulam* Leyden 1594

Ferguson, Francis *The Idea of a Theatre* Princeton 1949

Fish, Stanley 'Question and Answer in Samson Agonistes' *Critical Quarterly* 9 (1969) 237–64

Forsyth, Elliott *La tragédie française de Jodelle à Corneille (1553–1640): Le thème de la vengeance* Paris 1962

Freud, Sigmund *Basic Writings of Sigmund Freud* New York 1938

Freytag, Gustav *Die Technik des Dramas* Rptd Darmstadt 1969

Friedenthal, Richard *Goethe: His Life and Times* London 1965

Friedrich, Wolf-Hartmut *Vorbild und Neugestaltung Sechs Kapitel zur Geschichte der Tragödie.* Göttingen 1967

Fritz, Kurt von *Antike und Moderne Tragödie: Neun Abhandlungen* Berlin 1962

Garnier, Robert *Les Juifves. Bradamante. Poésie Diverses* Ed. Raymond Lebègue. Paris 1949

Garnier, Robert *La Troade. Antigone.* Ed. Raymond Lebègue. Paris 1952

– *Œuvres complètes (théâtre et poésies) de Robert Garnier.* Ed. Lucien Pinvert. Paris 1923. 2 vols

Geffcken, Johannes 'Der Begriff des Tragischen in der Antike' *Vorträge der Bibliothek Warburg* (1927–8) 89–166

Goethe, Johann Wolfgang von *Gedenkausgabe der Werke, Briefe und Gespräche* Ed. Ernst Beutler. Zurich 1949

– *Iphigenia in Tauris.* Tr. John Prudhoe. Manchester 1966

Goffe, Thomas *The Tragedy of Orestes* London 1633

Goldmann, Lucien, *Le dieu caché: étude sur la vision tragique dans les Pensées de Pascal et dans le théâtre de Racine* Paris 1955

Grene, David and Richmond Lattimore *The Complete Greek Tragedies* Chicago 1958. 4 vols

Griffiths, Richard *The Dramatic Technique of Antoine de Montchrestien: Rhetoric and Style in French Renaissance Tragedy* Oxford 1970

Grotius, Hugo *Epistolae ad Gallos* Leyden 1648
– *Briefwisseling* Ed. B.L. Meulenbroek. 'S Gravenhage 1964
Hamburger, Käthe *Von Sophokles zu Sartre: Griechische Dramenfiguren antik und modern* Stuttgart 1962
Hederich, Benjamin *Gründliches Mythologisches Lexikon* Leipzig 1770. Rptd Darmstadt 1967
Heller, Erich *The Disinherited Mind: Essays in Modern German Literature and Thought* 3rd ed. London 1971
Hegel, Georg W.F. *Aesthetics* Tr. T.M. Knox. Oxford 1975
– *Phenomenology of Spirit* Tr. A.V. Miller. Oxford 1977
Heitner, Robert R. 'The Iphigenia in Tauris Theme in Drama of the Eighteenth Century' *Comparative Literature* 16 (1964) 289–309
Henkel, Arthur 'Die verteufelt humane Iphigenie' *Euphorion* 59 (1965) 1–17
Henkel, Arthur and Albert Schöne *Emblemata: Handbuch der Sinnbildkunst des XVI. und XVII. Jahrhunderts* Stuttgart 1957
Herrick, Marvin Theodore *Italian Tragedy in the Renaissance* Urbana 1965
Hieronymus *Lettres* Texte établi et traduit par Jérôme Labourt. Paris 1949–61. 7 vols
– *Adversus Jovinianum* Patrologiae Latinae Tomus XXIII
Hofmannsthal, Hugo von *Briefe 1900–9* Wien 1937
– *Dramen II* Ed. Herbert Steiner *Gesammelte Werke in Einzelausgaben* Vol. IX. Frankfurt 1954
Horn-Monval, Madeleine *Repertoire bibliographique des traductions et adaptations françaises du XVe siècle à nos jours* Paris 1958–64. 3 vols
Horne, Philip Russell *The Tragedies of Giambattista Cinthio Giraldi* Oxford 1962
Hume, Patrick *Annotations on Paradise Lost ...* London 1695
Ibsen, Henrik *The Oxford Ibsen* Translated and edited by James Walter McFarlane. London 1961. Vol. V
Jacquot, Jean *Les Tragédies de Sénèque et le théâtre de la Renaissance* Paris 1964
Joannides, A. *La Comédie-Française de 1680 à 1920: Tableau de représentations par auteurs et par pièces* Paris 1921
Johnson, Charles *The Tragedy of Medaea ... With a Preface Containing Some Reflections on the New Way of Criticism* London 1731
Jondorf, Gillian *Robert Garnier and the Themes of Political Tragedy in the Sixteenth Century* London 1969
Kaibel, Georg, ed. *Comicorum graecorum fragmenta* Berlin 1958 Vol. I, 1
Kaufmann, Walter *Tragedy and Philosophy* Garden City 1968
Kirkconnell, Watson *The Celestial Cycle: The Theme of Paradise Lost in World*

Literature with Translations of the Major Analogues Toronto 1952
Kleist, Heinrich von *Sämtliche Werke und Briefe* Ed. Helmut Sembdner. Munich 1961. 2 vols
– *The Broken Jug.* Tr. John T. Krumpelmann. New York 1962
– *Penthesilea* Tr. Humphrey Trevelyan, in *The Classic Theatre* Ed. Eric Bentley. Vol II Garden City 1959
Knauer, G.N. *Die Aeneis und Homer: Studien zur poetischen Technik Vergils mit Listen der Homerzitate in der Aeneis* Göttingen 1964
Knight, Roy Clement 'Myth in Racine: A Myth?' *L'esprit créateur* 16 (1976) 95–104
– *Racine et la Grèce* Paris 1951. Rptd 1974
Koht, Halvdan *Life of Ibsen* Translated and edited by Einar Haugen and A.E. Santaniello. New York 1971
Kommerell, Max *Lessing und Aristoteles; Untersuchungen über die Theorie der Tragödie* Frankfurt 1960
Krouse, F. Michael *Milton's Samson and the Christian Tradition* Princeton 1949
La Harpe, Jean François de *Œuvres de La Harpe* Geneva 1968.
– *Cours de littérature ancienne et moderne* Paris 1880. 3 vols
Lapp, John C. *Aspects of Racinian Tragedy* Toronto 1956
La Taille, Jean de *Saul le Furieux. La Famine, ou Les Gabeonites Tragedies* Ed. Elliott Forsyth. Paris 1968
Lancaster, Henry Carrington *A History of French Dramatic Literature in the Seventeenth Century* Baltimore 1929–42. 9 vols
– *French Tragedy in the Time of Louis XV and Voltaire, 1715–1774* Baltimore, 1950. 2 vols
Lebègue, Raymond 'Les représentations dramatiques à la cour des Valois' *Les Fêtes de la Renaissance* Ed. J. Jacquot. Paris 1956, 84–91
– *La tragédie française de la Renaissance* Brussels 1954
– *La tragédie religieuse en France: Les débuts (1514–1573)* Paris 1929
Lee, Nathaniel *The Works of Nathaniel Lee.* Ed. Thomas B. Stroup and Arthur L. Cooke. New Brunswick 1954
Lesky, Albin *Die tragische Dichtung der Hellenen* Göttingen 1964
Leube, Eberhard *Fortuna in Karthago* Heidelberg 1969
Low, Anthony *The Blaze of Noon: A Reading of 'Samson Agonistes'* New York 1974
Marignac, Aloys de *Les imitations françaises de l'Oedipe Roi de Sophocle* Publications de la faculté des lettres de l'Université Farouk Ier. Cairo, nd [1937–9?]
Maurer, K. 'Racine und die Antike' *Archiv* 193 (1956) 15–32
Mauron, Charles *L'inconscient dans l'œuvre et la vie de Racine* Gap 1957
Meyer, Michael *Ibsen: A Biography* New York 1971
Milton, John *Complete Poems and Major Prose* Ed. M.Y. Hughes. New York 1957

Mongrédien, Georges *Athalie* Paris 1929

Montaigne, Michel de *Essais*. Ed. A. Thibaudet. Paris 1950

Morel, Jacques '"Hercules sur l'Oeta" de Sénèque et les dramaturges français de l'époque de Louis XIII' *Les Tragédies de Sénèque et le théâtre de la Renaissance* Ed. Jean Jacquot. Paris 1964, 95–111

– *Jean Rotrou, dramaturge de l'ambiguité* Paris 1968

Morsch, Hans 'Aus der Vorgeschichte von Goethes Iphigenie' *Vierteljahresschrift für Litteraturgeschichte* 4 (1891) 80–115

Mourgues, Odette de *Racine or the Triumph of Relevance* London 1967

Mueller, Martin 'Turnus and Hotspur: The Political Adversary in the *Aeneid* and Henry IV,' *Phoenix* 23 (1969) 278–90

Nelson, Robert J. *Corneille and Racine: Parallels and Contrasts* Englewood Cliffs 1966

Otis, Brooks *Virgil: A Study in Civilized Poetry* Oxford 1963

Parker, William R. *Milton's Debt to Greek Tragedy in Samson Agonistes* Baltimore 1937

Pommier, Jean Joseph *Aspects de Racine, suivie de l'histoire littéraire d'un couple tragique* Paris 1954

Plutarch *The Lives of the Noble Grecians and Romans* Tr. Thomas North. London 1929–30

Racine, Jean. *Œuvres Complètes* Ed. Raymond Picard. Paris 1950. 2 vols

– *Athalie* Ed. Peter France. Oxford 1966

Racine, Louis 'Comparaison de l'Hippolyte d'Euripide avec la tragédie de Racine sur le même sujet' *Academie des Inscriptions et Belles Lettres: Memoires de littera-ture* 8 (Dec. 1728) 300–14

Rawson, Elizabeth 'Family and Fatherland in Euripides' *Phoenissae*' *Greek, Roman, and Byzantine Studies* 11 (1970) 109–27

Reinhardt, Karl *Sophokles* Frankfurt 1947

– 'Die Sinneskrise bei Euripides' *Tradition und Geist* Göttingen 1960, 227–56

– *Die Ilias und ihr Dichter* Göttingen 1961

Ribbeck, Otto *Die römische Tragödie im Zeitalter der Republik* Leipzig 1875

Ricoeur, Paul *Freud and Philosophy* New Haven 1970

Roston, Murray *Biblical Drama in England: From the Middle Ages to the Present Day* Evanston 1968

Ross, Alexander *Mystagogus Poeticus* London 1648

Rotrou, Jean *Œuvres de Jean Rotrou* Ed. Viollet-Le-Duc. Paris 1820 Rptd. Geneva 1967. 5 vols

– *Hercule Mourant* Ed. Derek Watts. Exeter 1971

Schadewaldt, Wolfgang. '"Die zerbrochene Krug" von Heinrich von Kleist und Sophokles' "König Ödipus"' *Hellas und Hesperien* Zurich 1970, II, 333–40

Scherer, Jacques *La dramaturgie classique en France* Paris 1950

Schiller, Friedrich von *Sämtliche Werke* Ed. Gerhard Fricke and Herbert G. Göpfert Munich 1965. 5 vols

– *The Bride of Messina. William Tell. Demetrius* Tr. Charles E. Passage. New York 1962

Schlegel, August Wilhelm *Kritische Schriften und Briefe* Ed. Edgar Lohner. Stuttgart 1962–6. 6 vols

Schlegel, Friedrich *Kritische Schriften* Ed. Wolfdietrich Rasch. Munich 1964

Schlösser, Rudolf *Friedrich Wilhelm Gotter: Sein Leben und seine Werke* Theatergeschichtliche Forschungen, vol. 10. Leipzig 1894

Schrade, Leo *La représentation d'Edipo tiranno au Teatro Olimpico (Vicence, 1585): Etude suivie d'une edition critique de la tragédie de Sophocle par Orsatto Giustiniani et de la musique des choeurs par Andrea Gabrieli* Paris 1960

Seneca *Tragedies* Ed. F.J. Miller. London 1917 (Loeb Library) 2 vols

Smith, Gregory *Elizabethan Critical Essays* Oxford 1904. 2 vols

Smith, W.A.P. and P. Brachin *Vondel (1587–1679): Contributions à l'histoire de la tragédie au XVIIe siècle* Paris 1964

Solmsen, Friedrich 'Zur Gestaltung des Intrigenmotivs in den Tragödien des Sophokles und Euripides' *Philologus* 87 (1932) 1–17. Rptd in *Euripides: Wege der Forschung* Darmstadt 1968

– 'Euripides' Ion im Vergleich mit anderen Tragödien' *Hermes* 69 (1934) 390–419. Rptd in *Euripides: Wege der Forschung*

Sophoclis tragoediae septem, Latino carmine redditae, et annotationibus illustratae per T. Naogeorgum Basel 1558

Interpretatio tragoediarum Sophoclis ad utilitatem juventutis, quae studiosa est Graecae linguae, edita a V. Winshemio Frankfurt 1549

Sophoclis tragoediae septem. Una cum omnibus Graecis scholiis et cum Latinis J. Camerarii Geneva 1567

Sophoclis Antigone: tragoedia a G. Herveto traducta e Graeco in Latinum. In *Gentiani Herveti ... quaedam opuscula* Leyden 1541

Scholia graeca in Sophoclem; ex editione Brunckiana Oxford 1810

Steadman, John M. *Milton and the Renaissance Hero* Oxford 1967

Stegmann, André 'La Médée de Corneille' *Les tragédies de Sénèque et le théâtre de la Renaissance* Ed. Jean Jacquot. Paris 1964, 113–26

– *L'héroisme cornélien: genèse et signification* Paris 1968. 2 vols

Steiner, George *The Death of Tragedy* New York 1961

Suetonius *The Lives of the Twelve Caesars* New York 1931

Swaim, Kathleen 'Hercules, Antaeus, and Prometheus: A Study of the Climactic Epic Similes in *Paradise Regained*' SEL 18 (1978) 137–53

Tasso, Torquato *Opere*. Ed. Bortolo Tommaso Sozzi. Turin 1956. 2 vols

Thomson, James *Works* London 1750. 4 vols

Trissino, Giangiorgio *La Sofonisba di Giangiorgio Trissino con note di Torquato Tasso* Bologna 1884

Vergil P. *Virgilii Maronis Bucolica et Georgica argumentis, explicationibus, notis illustratae a Ioanne Ludovico de la Cerda Toletano e societate Iesu* Frankfurt 1608

Voltaire *Œuvres complètes* Ed. Louis Moland. Paris 1883. 52 vols

Walbank, F.W. 'History and Tragedy' *Historia* 9 (1960) 216–34

Watson, Thomas *A Humanist's 'trew imitation': Thomas Watson's Absalom: A Critical Edition and Translation* [by] John Hazel Smith. Illinois Studies in Language and Literature. Vol. 52. Urbana 1964

Weigand, Hermann '*Œdipus Tyrannus* und *Die Braut von Messina*' Schiller 1759/1959: *Commemorative American Studies*. Ed. J.R. Frey. Illinois Studies in Language and Literature. Vol. 46. Urbana 1959

Weinberg, Bernard *A History of Literary Criticism in the Italian Renaissance* Chicago 1961. 2 vols.

Weinberg, Bernard *The Art of Jean Racine* Chicago 1963

Wells, G.A. 'Fate, Tragedy, and Schiller's Die Braut von Messina' *JEGP* 64 (1965) 191–212

Whitman, Cedric H. *Homer and the Heroic Tradition* Cambridge 1958

Wilamowitz-Moellendorf, Ulrich von *Euripides Herakles* Rptd Darmstadt 1959

Wittreich, Joseph Anthony, Jr, ed. *Calm of Mind: Tercentenary Essays on Paradise Regained and Samson Agonistes* Cleveland 1971

Wittreich, Joseph Anthony, Jr, ed. *The Romantics on Milton* Cleveland 1970

Woodhouse, A.S.P. *The Heavenly Muse: A Preface to Milton* Toronto 1972

Zuntz, Günther 'Ödipus und Gregorius: Tragödie und Legende' *Antike und Abendland* 4 (1954) 191–203. Rptd in *Sophokles: Wege der Forschung* Darmstadt 1967

INDEX